SOUTH-WESTERN PROGRAMMING LANGUAGE SERIES

PRACTICAL PASCAL

GILBERT LARKY

PRACTICAL PASCAL

Harry M. Gilbert
Gilbert Consulting Group
San Jose, California

Arthur I. Larky
Professor, Electrical and Computer Engineering
Lehigh University
Bethlehem, Pennsylvania

Published by

J40 **SOUTH-WESTERN PUBLISHING CO.**

CINCINNATI WEST CHICAGO, ILL. DALLAS PELHAM MANOR, N.Y. PALO ALTO, CALIF.

UCSD PASCAL is a trademark of The Regents of the University of California. Use thereof, in conjunction with any goods or services, is authorized by specific license only. Any unauthorized use is contrary to U.S. Trademark Law.

ISBN: 0-538-10400-7

Library of Congress Catalog Card Number: 82-62633

1 2 3 4 5 6 7 8 K 7 6 5 4

Printed in the United States of America

CONTENTS

Preface **viii**

1. Language and Computers **1**

Objectives 1

Talking to Computers 1

Computer Languages: Easier Than People Languages 2

Processing Is Not Thinking 6

Processing Logic 10

Binary Code 11

Programming Languages for People 13

Compiling Programs 14

The Pascal Language 15

A Note on Style 16

2. Speaking Pascal **21**

Objectives 21

Getting Started: Defining the Problem 21

Developing a Solution 23

Developing a Program 24

Program *Adder* 25

Coding *Adder* 31

Pascal—A Strongly Typed Language 36

Entering A Pascal Program 37

Compiling a Pascal Program 42

Executing a Pascal Program 44

Debugging a Pascal Program 44

3. Designing for Quality **50**

Objectives 50

Defining Results 51

Set Your Standards 52

Problem Analysis 53

Program Design 60

Top-Down Design 63

Defining Program Steps 65

Pseudocoding 67

Planning for Quality: Verification of Results 70

Program *Adder* Becomes *AddingMachine* 71

4. Organizing Your Programs **83**

Objectives 83

Procedures and Block Structure 84

Functions 94

Scope of Variables in Procedure Calls 98

Further Characteristics of Procedures and Functions 99

Coding Mathematical Expressions 104

Pascal Structure Expanded 106

Naming Variables, Procedures, and Functions 108

Program *BalanceCheckbook* 109

5. Designing the User Interface **121**

Objectives 121

The User's 'Window' 121

Design Options for User Input 123

Formats for Data Input 128

Input Editing 130

User Messages 132

The Display Screen 133

Design of Program *BalancePlus* 136

6. Implementing Program Controls **143**

Objectives 143

Program Control Structures 143

Logical Comparisons and the Boolean Data Type 145

Looping and Repetition Control 149

Arrays 153

Entering and Debugging *BalancePlus* 158

Program *BalancePlus* 159

7. Designing Useful Outputs **170**

Objectives 170

Value and Permanence of Output 170

Physical Design for Convenience and Clarity 173

Physical Constraints of Display Devices 173

Other Hard Copy Devices 178

Design for Device Independence 180

Designing *BasicAccounting* 182

8. Coding Program Output **192**

Objectives 192

Coding Techniques for Formatting Output 193

Coding *BasicAccounting* 205

9. Saving and Using Information **225**

Objectives 225

Data Structures: Records and Files 226

Records 227

Fields 229

Files 233

SEEK 245

CLOSE 246

File Management 248

10. Testing and Debugging **258**

Objectives 258
Anticipating Errors 259
The Goal of Testing 259
Program Entry and Test Techniques 261
Incremental Testing 262
Commonly Encountered Errors 263
Devising Test Data 265
Debugging Techniques 266
Program *AccountManagement* 269

11. Rearranging and Maintaining Information **289**

Objectives 289
File Processing 290
File Organization and Structure 291
Sorting 292
Merging 303
Lists 304
Trees 318
Design Trade-offs 324
Extracting Useful Information From Lists 327
Search Techniques 328
Search Technique Trade-offs 332

12. Applying List Management **339**

Objectives 339
Program Design for List Management 339
The ORDinal Function 344
Program *AccountsReceivable* 346

13. Tricks of the Trade: Compiler Options **362**

Objectives 362

Building Proficiency in Pascal 362

Compiler Options 363

14. Tricks of the Trade: Memory Management **381**

Objectives 381

Data Representation 381

Conversion of Data Types 385

Packed Structures 388

Memory Efficiency 390

Block I/O and Dynamic Memory 393

Additional UCSD Extensions for Memory Management 404

Variant Records 408

Multi-Dimensional Arrays 411

Recursion 415

A. Pascal Library **421**

B. Syntax Diagrams **427**

Reading Syntax Diagrams 427

Use of Syntax Diagrams 428

C. Record Representations in Memory **438**

The Importance of Consistent Data Definition 438

Packed Data Structures 440

Glossary **444**

Index **459**

PREFACE

A BUSINESS APPROACH

Pascal's usefulness as a teaching language is well known, both for its reinforcement of structured programming principles and for the way its orderly presentation mirrors the actions of the compiler and the general architecture of computer systems. Although Pascal is designed for use by novices after minimal training, the language is powerful enough to provide a tool for more sophisticated users, particularly those who must maintain applications libraries based on modular programming.

The Pascal language has emerged from the classroom and is moving rapidly into more widespread application. The size of the Pascal compiler is well-suited to today's microcomputers, and it may be that this powerful language will be credited with bringing structured program development methodologies to the personal computing field.

Beyond its availability for microcomputers, Pascal has an even more fundamental advantage—its exceptional program clarity. The features of Pascal program text that make it easy to learn for novices also make it relatively easy for programmers to read and understand one another's work. Programming shops in business data processing facilities are taxed heavily by the sheer effort of maintaining systems of programs and program libraries. Programmers must be able to work in teams and must be able to grasp quickly the tasks at hand. The inherent modularity of Pascal's block structure further enhances its usefulness in this fast-paced business environment. With modular programming, updates and modifications to individual program modules are straightforward and have a minimum impact on other portions of the program or system.

In view of these trends, this text attempts to place the Pascal language in an applications perspective. Students are introduced to the language as a tool that extends their work in the classroom into realistic business data processing and computer information systems tasks. In keeping with this objective, the program examples given in the text form a continuity. Examples begin with a simple adding machine problem and build up in stages to result in a fully developed accounts receivable application.

SYSTEMS THINKING AND GOOD PROGRAMMING PRACTICES

A philosophy carried through the text is that program coding is a relatively mechanical aspect of the overall program development process. Good programs stem from sound logical designs that are essentially independent of computer languages and hardware. Thus, there is a strong reliance on the top-down design approach and on the visualization and documentation of program modules in structure charts and pseudocode. Pascal is presented as a language that reinforces this kind of systematic thinking.

Where appropriate, the design choices that bear on good programming practices and clarity of program style are presented. Attention to user requirements is a key concern. Students can come to an understanding that, in a business environment, their work may be an integral part of a team development effort aimed at solving a real information need. In such an environment, there are few programmers who write code solely for their personal use.

In general, the scheme of this text is to present systems concepts first, followed closely by the corresponding coding skills. For example, a chapter on designing the user interface presents systems concepts relating to good functional design. Then, this chapter is followed by presentation of the specific coding skills needed to implement program controls.

To complete work in this text, students should have access to a microcomputer system or timesharing terminal for purposes of entering and testing the example programs and for carrying out the programming practice exercises. All programs are designed around a minimum hardware configuration. A 40-column console display is assumed and a printer is optional. Many program examples incorporate Pascal language extensions as developed at the University of California, San Diego (UCSD), and this version of the language is referenced most often in the discussions.

The first nine chapters of the text deal with basic systems and programming concepts and their counterparts in coding Pascal. Because longer programs are evolving, Chapter 10 is devoted to testing and debugging. Since the longer programs build upon each other with certain common modules, students are introduced to incremental program entry and testing, first briefly in Chapter 6, and then in depth in Chapter 10.

Chapters 11 and 12 deal with file processing and list maintenance. This treatment reflects an information management orientation, again from the business point of view. In effect, a business organization is composed of the information and relationships contained in its files. This discussion should provide an excellent background for later work in file and database design.

The last two chapters present advanced programming methods. Emphasis is placed on the kinds of technical problems encountered in realistic programming situations. Students are reminded that, although some of these advanced techniques amount to temporary suspension of Pascal's rules, such methods should be applied with caution and a healthy respect for the safeguards afforded by those rules.

Three appendixes are provided for the programmer's ongoing reference. Appendix A lists all Pascal terms presented in this book. Appendix B explains the use of syntax diagrams for the programmer's reference in determining the correctness of program structures and statements. Appendix C gives the impact on memory allocation of certain RECORD definitions. These concepts are especially important to the successful use of a file by multiple programs, as in building master files within a data processing system.

ACKNOWLEDGMENTS

A special note of thanks is extended to Dr. Brian L. Crissey of Illinois State University, Normal, for his thoughtful review of the manuscript.

The cooperation of Van Jahnes-Smith at the University of California, San Diego, is appreciated for his help in securing permission to reference the UCSD trademark.

Recognition is given to Gerald E. Jones, i/e inc., for editorial services in bringing this book to finished manuscript.

Designs for the cover and interior pages of this book were executed by Gary Palmatier.

1 LANGUAGE AND COMPUTERS

OBJECTIVES

On completing the reading and other learning assignments for this chapter, you should be able to:

- ☐ Explain the key similarities and differences between human languages and computer languages.
- ☐ Describe the logical functions involved in processing data to yield information.
- ☐ Tell how logical functions differ from physical functions.
- ☐ Use properly the key computer terms listed at the end of this chapter and discuss the data processing concepts presented in the text.
- ☐ Describe the role of Pascal as a structured programming language.

TALKING TO COMPUTERS

Language is a natural tool for communicating. People have used languages to communicate with each other for thousands of years. During this time, many languages have evolved. By using each language, people have expanded its vocabulary, added subtler meanings, and added variety.

Languages have also served to create boundaries, or barriers, between people. People communicate well as long as they are using their own language. However, a person who knows and uses only English has very limited communication abilities in a group of people or in a society that speaks French, Spanish, Italian, Russian, German, Chinese, Japanese, Swahili, or Hebrew.

Learning a language that is foreign to you can be difficult because of the vocabulary to be memorized. For example, a typical six-year old entering first grade may already have a vocabulary of some 4,000 words. An adult may be able to understand and use as many as 10,000 words. A standard English dictionary may have more than 100,000 words. Even if you, personally, don't know the meaning of all these words, you do have enough of a vocabulary to use the dictionary to look them up, learn what they mean, and use them if necessary.

COMPUTER LANGUAGES: EASIER THAN PEOPLE LANGUAGES

The great writer and humorist, Mark Twain, once observed that the French must be a lot smarter than the Americans because in France even the little children can speak French.

The real problem in learning languages, of course, is not intelligence. Rather, it's a question of discipline and memorization. Most people who take the time and trouble can learn any language. There are people who speak a half-dozen or more languages. To do so, they have had to remember and master the use of thousands of words in each of the languages. Yet, these same people who can master vocabularies running into thousands of words often tend to think of computer languages as complicated or especially difficult. Computer languages, however, are neither complicated nor difficult.

You can learn to use the language of computers in the same way native speakers of a human language learned their first words and phrases. Everyone has learned at least one language as a child, without any prior experience, and without any understanding of the technicalities of grammar and syntax. You learned to speak in this way. You started by imitating a few words and phrases that worked for you in fulfilling some need. You built on your vocabulary and communication skills by adding more words and phrases that also worked to fulfill your needs. In fact, at this point there was probably no difference in your mind between words and phrases.

A series of instructions that cause a computer to do a specific task is called a *program.* The vocabularies and rules that govern the preparation of computer programs form *programming languages.* These languages are tools for people, tools for communicating with and directing the *operations* performed by computers.

You can learn the rules for the Pascal programming language in much the same way you learned your own native language—in a series of small steps—each one building on those you have completed. By familiarizing yourself with the programming examples presented in this book, and by imitating them through exercises that you complete, you can master gradually the Pascal programming language. You will develop increasingly sophisticated Pascal programs by using combinations of these simple steps. Mastery of the Pascal language will result as you learn the meaning and use of a few dozen relatively simple English-like terms.

Computer languages are not especially complex because computers are simple—so extremely simple that you have to think in terms of steps or explanations that you would never bother with if a person were involved.

People have the ability to think about statements you make—because of the fairly large and generalized body of knowledge that human beings share. By contrast, a computer always must be given very precise directions. The number of operations it can perform is very limited, and its environment is restricted to the devices that are connected to it. When speaking of computers, an operation is a logical or mathematical step that causes the transformation of *data* according to a specific rule. For example, adding two numbers together is an operation.

To illustrate the difference between communication with people and programming computers, consider the following example:

```
A := A + 1;
```

At first glance, this expression resembles an equation in elementary algebra. However, the expression is nonsensical as a valid algebraic equation. How can something equal itself plus one? For example, if A were to stand for the number 9, the above equation would tell us that 9 equals 9 plus 1, or 9 = 10.

The expression above is actually a *program statement,* or instruction, in Pascal. The (:=) sign stands for *assignment of value,* meaning to replace the value on the left with the value on the right. The semicolon (;) is used to separate this statement from other statements that might follow it.

The computer will interpret the program statement very differently from the way a human would interpret an algebraic equation. To describe the action of the computer, it is first necessary to describe what meaning the computer will give the symbol A.

A computer has an electronic *memory.* Memory is an electronic device that records and holds data for use by the computer. A computer's memory is divided into discrete *memory locations.* Each memory location is known within the computer by its number, or *address.* Within a program, areas of memory may be given names by the programmer. In the program statement above, the programmer has used A to refer to an area of memory.

The computer, then, translates the program statement something like this:

> "The memory location named A will receive the results of the operations following the assignment of value sign: Take the value currently held in the memory location named A, add 1 to it, and put the result back in memory location A."

Notice that the computer deals with the statement one element at a time, beginning at the left and proceeding in sequence to the right. The computer does not "grasp a concept" as humans do. It cannot "understand" the program statement; rather, it can perform only the operations contained within the statement, one step at a time, as a series of *processing,* or data transformation, steps.

This example illustrates that the level of detail the computer requires leaves nothing out. Every step is discrete and exactly defined.

Here's another example that contrasts human communication with languages used to control computers. You might say to another person:

> "Find out who that person is and say hello."

A Pascal program that will direct a computer to do the same thing is presented in Figure 1-1.

Figure 1-2 shows the console as it might appear after *SayHi* has been *executed,* or run by the computer. This brief example of an actual Pascal program helps demonstrate that computers have no understanding in the human sense. A computer is dependent upon your program to provide all requirements for successful problem solving.

```
PROGRAM SayHi;
 VAR
  PersonsName: STRING;
BEGIN
 WRITELN('WHAT IS YOUR NAME?');
 READLN(PersonsName);
 WRITELN('HI ',PersonsName);
END.
```

Figure 1-1. Program *SayHi.*

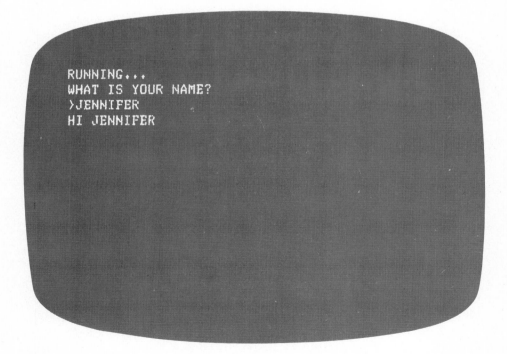

Figure 1-2. *SayHi* produces a question to which the user replies. Using the information provided, *SayHi* displays a greeting message.

PROCESSING IS NOT THINKING

A computer does not think. It processes data through a series of very small, orderly, steps. That is, it receives data that are entered into it, and may process, or transform, the data in some way. This transformation adds to or organizes the given data in a way that will be more meaningful, and useful, to people.

Data are any basic pieces of *information* that have meaning. Examples of data items could include your name, social security number, height, weight, etc. Data that have been organized for added meaning become information. A computer program, then, is a series of processing steps that cause data to be acted upon by the computer to produce information. The processing operations that computers perform on data include:

- Arithmetic operations
- Logical operations.

Arithmetic operations include the mathematical functions of addition, subtraction, multiplication, division, and exponentiation.

Logical operations performed by computers are simple and limited. A computer can compare a given value with another value that is presented. Based on instructions within programs, the computer then can determine whether the presented value is *greater than, equal to, less than, less than or equal to, not equal to,* or *greater than or equal to* the given value. The computer then can follow processing instructions based on the results of these basic logical operations. The result of any such comparison is either *true* or *false.* This type of logic is known as *Boolean logic,* named after the nineteenth century mathematician George Boole.

Boolean logic can be used to perform comparisons that segregate, or *sort,* groups of data. Suppose a company wanted a list of all employees who are high school graduates. The data items stored by the company's computer include numeric entries for the level of education completed by each employee. Each entry is a number indicating the grade level completed. An entry of 12 or higher, then, would indicate high school completion. A computer program could compare grade-level data items for all employees with the value 11. Logical tests would identify and cause a listing for all persons whose records contain grade level values greater than 11, that is, all persons who had completed high school.

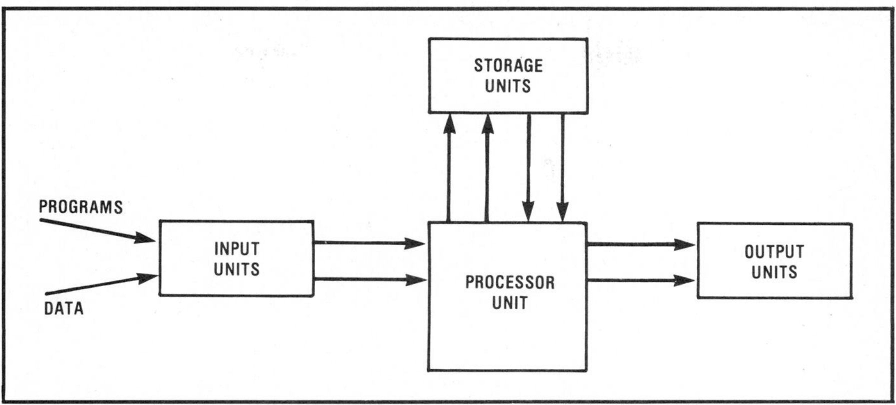

Figure 1-3. The basic data processing functions are input, storage, processing, and output.

Processing Functions

As illustrated in Figure 1-3, data and programs are introduced into a computer system as *input.* This input undergoes processing, a series of logical and/or mathematical steps that cause the input data to be transformed in some way. The result is *output,* which should be some form of useful information. While processing occurs, the computer may be called upon to bring in data that have been placed in *storage* previously, or to place intermediate results in storage. A computer goes through this functional cycle in the course of each operation contained within a program instruction.

The functions of input, output, and storage involve data *manipulation operations,* or the movement of data from one place in the computer to another. An important task for computers is the storage and retrieval of information, which may involve the manipulation of large volumes of data.

Computer Equipment

Computer equipment, a collection of various *physical devices* that perform specific tasks, is referred to as *hardware.* The actions of a computer's physical devices are known as its *physical functions.*

The physical function of input involves presentation of data to a computer. One method of input is simply to type data items or program statements on a keyboard. Data also can be recorded on special storage devices for input. The input function is limited to the physical act of presenting data to a computer.

The processing function applies arithmetic and/or logical operations as directed by a program. This work is done by a device known as a *processor.* The processor, as shown in Figure 1-4, consists of a *control unit,* and an *arithmetic logic unit,* or *ALU.* The control unit directs the flow of processing. It accepts inputs to the processor and guides the handling of outputs. The ALU performs the arithmetic and logic operations described previously.

Associated with the processor is a *main memory,* or *primary storage device.* This device holds the data and programs that are under active processing. To support processing, the main memory must operate at speeds

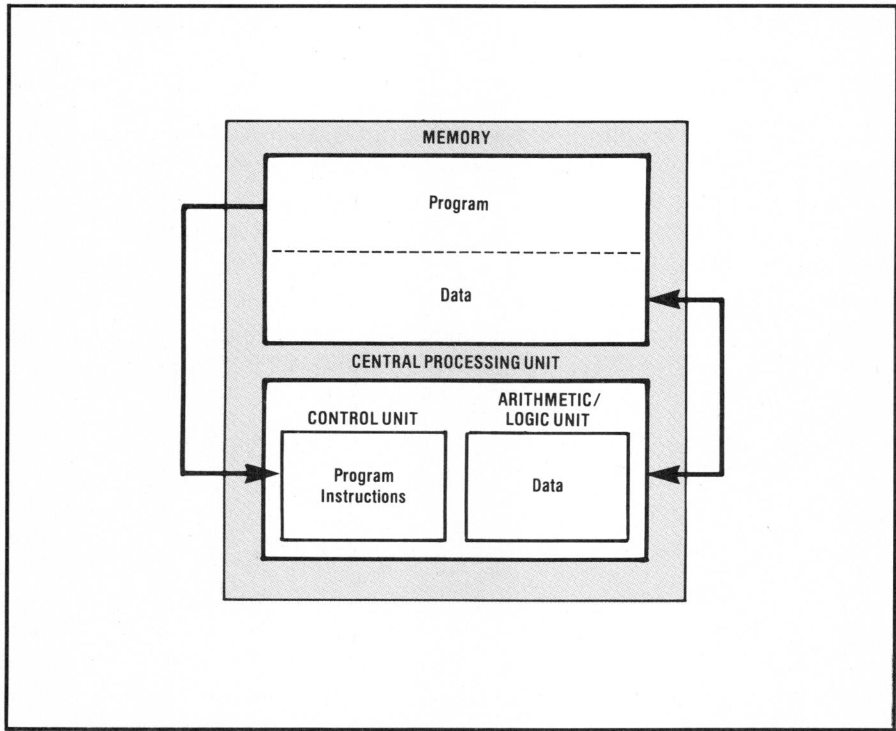

Figure 1-4. The processor of a computer includes a memory that holds data and programs during processing, and a central processing unit in which arithmetic and logic functions are performed.

comparable to that of the processor itself. On the largest and fastest computers (known as *mainframes*), processing cycles are executed in a matter of billionths of a second. Typically, most microcomputers operate at speeds a thousand times slower—millionths of a second for a single cycle.

In mainframe computer systems, the processor and main memory are sometimes housed together in a single device or cabinet. The combined equipment unit may be called a *central processing unit,* or *CPU.* Microcomputers typically have a processor contained in a single *integrated circuit,* referred to as a *microprocessor chip,* with main memory located in a separate chip, or chips.

Support of processing is the primary function of main memory. This unit does not retain, or store, data for long-term use. As a matter of fact, for most types of memory, the information in main memory is lost each time power is turned off to the computer.

Yet, the processing of data into useful information often requires the long-term storage and reuse of data. This function is handled by *secondary storage devices.* Most storage devices record data magnetically. The signals that represent data are recorded on, and read from, magnetically coated surfaces such as those on tapes and disks. In effect, storage devices provide a pool, or reservoir, to hold the collections of data and the programs required for continuing computer operations. Among the items held in storage, for example, is the master program that enables you to use the Pascal language. This program, or collection of programs, is transferred to main memory as needed to process the instructions you write.

Storage devices can be among the output destinations for processed data. However, for outputs to be used by people, data are either displayed or documented. On microcomputers, *displayed outputs* are shown on the video screen of your *console,* which often is referred to as a *CRT* (for *cathode ray tube*). The term *console* usually refers to whatever device is used to control the computer. The combination of a video monitor and keyboard is a typical console device for a microcomputer and is referred to commonly as a *VDT,* or *video display terminal.* Alternatively, a printing terminal with a keyboard may be used as the console device. *Documented output,* or *hard copy,* usually is created by printers attached to the computer. Figure 1-5 shows a typical microcomputer installation with a console and printer.

Figure 1-5. A typical microcomputer installation includes a console (CRT and keyboard input unit), microcomputer processing unit, and a printer to create documented output (hard copy).

PROCESSING LOGIC

Before a program can be written, there must be a clear understanding of its purpose and the results to be delivered. Each program solves a specific problem or meets a definite need. The understanding of this underlying problem or need establishes the *logical processing* for a program. There is an important distinction here. *Logical functions* are those that describe the flow and transformation of data within a system. Physical functions describe the actions of physical devices.

Programs must be designed to achieve the desired logical processing and *physical processing*. The design for logical processing provides the basis for developing physical processing methods. Thus, before programs can be written, there must be a logical design. One of the most common and costly errors committed by inexperienced programmers is to begin writing instructions for physical processing before the underlying logic is understood fully. When this happens, the programmer's efforts may be wasted totally.

The underlying need from which this logic is derived is stated without regard to computer devices or functions. For example, the purpose of a program may be to meet a business need. Suppose you were asked to develop a payroll system for a company. First, you would try to develop an understanding of the basic business need and its logical requirements. For a payroll system, you would begin by identifying all needed results, or outputs. Included would be descriptions of the content of paychecks, stubs listing deductions, reports to company management, reports to government agencies, information provided to unions, and other requirements.

With outputs defined, your next step is to identify where the data needed to produce these results can be found. Then, a logical design must be produced to specify the steps necessary to transform the raw, or source, data into the needed outputs. For example, one payroll input will be the number of hours worked by each employee. Another is employee pay rates.

It doesn't matter, logically, that these two data items may be collected separately and may require computer processing to bring them together. Before computer programming can begin, the basic information structures and needs—the logic of the system—must be understood. The physical processing instructions developed to meet logical needs are provided by computer programs. Pascal is a tool for bridging the gap between the logical design of a solution and the specific instructions required for physical handling and processing of data to produce defined results.

BINARY CODE

Computers do not use languages such as Pascal directly; rather, computers respond to very elementary instructions that represent operations to be performed. These instructions are based on the principle that electronic switches (known in computers as *gates*) can be in one of two states: *on* or *off*. Thus, a gate is said to be a *two-state device*. Two-state devices also are called *binary*. Binary, in turn, means sets of two.

Binary devices operate based on a system of counting in which only the numeric values of 0 and 1 are used. A 0 means off. A 1 means on. Sets of 0 and 1 *codes*, in the form of electrical signals, represent values for numbers, letters, and symbols. Most computers have binary-level operations that respond to combinations of 0 and 1 signals.

Therefore, the vocabulary of a typical computer rests on combinations of entries of 0 and 1. A single 0 or 1 is known as a *binary digit,* or *bit.* A set of bits that forms a symbolic unit for the computer processor is referred to as a *byte.* Microcomputers typically use bytes composed of eight bits. Since a bit can represent two values, namely 0 and 1, a byte consisting of eight bits can represent 2^8, or 256, different values. The order of bits within a given byte forms a code that may be interpreted by the computer to represent a letter, number, or symbol. Formats for bytes represent the lowest level of standardized communication between people and computers. An *American Standard Code for Information Interchange (ASCII)* has been devised to assign codes to values from 0 to 127. A table of ASCII codes is given in Figure 1-6.

In the version of the Pascal language you will be using, two bytes make up a grouping of information known as a *word.* The significance of words in Pascal will be discussed later in this book.

Character	ASCII-7	Character	ASCII-7	Character	ASCII-7
0	011 0000	D	100 0100	Q	101 0001
1	011 0001	E	100 0101	R	101 0010
2	011 0010	F	100 0110	S	101 0011
3	011 0011	G	100 0111	T	101 0100
4	011 0100	H	100 1000	U	101 0101
5	011 0101	I	100 1001	V	101 0110
6	011 0110	J	100 1010	W	101 0111
7	011 0111	K	100 1011	X	101 1000
8	011 1000	L	100 1100	Y	101 1001
9	011 1001	M	100 1101	Z	101 1010
A	100 0001	N	100 1110		
B	100 0010	O	100 1111		
C	100 0011	P	101 0000		

Figure 1-6. Binary representations of ASCII codes for numerals and letters. Note that this format uses seven bits to encode characters.

At one time, it was necessary for people to communicate at the computer's language level, that is, in *machine language.* Machine language consists of binary signals that can be executed directly by a computer. Such programs had to be written as strings of 0 and 1 entries. Programming at this level of detail is extremely time-consuming. Programs took a long time to write. Changing programs was a major job. It was extremely difficult to translate the needs of people into machine language. Thus, the use of computers was limited by the tremendous amount of detail that had to be completed before a job could be processed.

At length, systems evolved that made it possible to communicate instructions to computers in languages more natural to people. This development of programming languages went through several stages. First developed were programs called *assemblers,* or *assembly language* programs, which allow the programmer to use letters and numbers instead of binary coding when writing a program. An assembler, in effect, is a program that converts alphabetic and numeric instructions into machine language. (Although sometimes mistakenly referred to as machine language, assembly language cannot be executed directly by a computer.) Programming in assembly language is simpler than coding in machine language but is still a fairly complex task.

PROGRAMMING LANGUAGES FOR PEOPLE

Through the years, computers have gotten bigger and more powerful, and the costs of computer processing and computer devices have come down. In these circumstances, it has become possible to reduce the demands made upon people and to increase the services actually performed by computers. Two important things happened, gradually, to programming languages:

- Programming commands, or instructions written by programmers, became more powerful. Instead of generating just a single machine operation for each programming instruction, it became possible for single programming commands to represent entire sets of machine-level instructions, even complete processing procedures.

- Programming instruction formats could take on more people-oriented formats. People could use words or other expressions that they understood more readily. The languages then could translate each instruction into a series of machine language instructions.

The implementation of programming languages that generate multiple computer commands is made possible by specialized sets of programs known as *compilers.* These programs serve as language translators between the instructions written by people, known as *source code,* and the instructions required by the computer, known as *object code.*

Closely related to compilers are programs called *interpreters.* Interpreters translate English-like language instructions given by the programmer and act directly to cause the computer to perform the tasks described.

The distinction between compilers and interpreters is an important one. Compilers translate source code into object, or machine, code and then, in a separate step, the machine code program is run to perform the desired task. If the task is to be done again, the machine code is reused, without the need to translate the source code again. Interpreters, on the other hand, work from the source code and must retranslate it each time a task must be performed. For this reason, interpreters are comparatively slow in performing tasks. An interpreter must reside in main memory alongside the program being run, while a compiler needs to be present only while the source program is being compiled into machine language.

The Pascal language system is supported by a Pascal compiler. The Pascal programmer is able to describe complex machine tasks in concise, structured terms. Because of the logical constraints and order it imposes on a program, Pascal is referred to as a *structured programming language.* This property of Pascal makes it a powerful tool for problem solving.

COMPILING PROGRAMS

Programming languages that use compilers or interpreters are known as *high-level languages.* The more closely a computer programming language resembles the *syntax,* or rules of structure, of human language, the higher level it is considered to be.

Developing programs through use of a compiler is a two-step process. First you write the source code for a program in a language such as Pascal. Then, the program is processed by the compiler to produce object code that can be used by the computer. If changes have to be made in a program, the changes are done at the source code level. In Pascal, the source code is kept in a **TEXT** file. Then, an entirely new set of object code has to be produced by compiling the text file. In Pascal, the resulting object code is placed in a **CODE** file.

THE PASCAL LANGUAGE

Pascal was developed specifically as a tool for teaching beginners to program. It is known widely as a teaching language and has achieved an impressive record of success at numerous schools, colleges, and universities.

As programming languages go, Pascal is relatively young. The acceptance of Pascal has grown since the early 1970s with the popularity of minicomputers at first and then personal-sized computers, or microcomputers. Although Pascal is widely used on large, central computers, particularly on university campuses, its major attraction has been that the structure and size of the Pascal compiler lend themselves well to smaller computer systems. As microcomputers have become more commonplace in classrooms and school computing laboratories, Pascal has become an increasingly attractive and popular method for introducing students to programming skills.

Unlike the names of many earlier programming languages, the name Pascal is not an acronym. For example, *FORTRAN* is a composite of FORmula *TRAN*slator. *COBOL* stands for *CO*mmon *B*usiness-*O*riented *L*anguage. Instead, Pascal is named after the French mathematician-scientist Blaise Pascal (1623-1662), who created one of the forerunners of modern computers. In 1641, Pascal, then 19, invented a calculating machine to ease the workload of his father, a tax collector in southern France. Pascal's mechanical calculator greatly reduced the work involved in computing taxes. Any history of the development of computers should mention Blaise Pascal.

Pascal, then, was used as the namesake for a computer language developed during 1970 and 1971 by Niklaus Wirth of the Eidgenossische Technische Hochschule (ETH), a technical institute in Zurich, Switzerland.

Use of Pascal spread rapidly through universities in Europe and the United States. In 1977, a version of a Pascal compiler now widely accepted for use on microcomputers was developed at the University of California, San Diego (UCSD). The *UCSD Pascal* system includes standard terms, standard programs, and a structured methodology for program development. Programming examples in this book are based upon UCSD Pascal.

Program exercises in this book are designed to be used with the UCSD Pascal operating system. An *operating system* is a collection of programs residing in the computer that directs the use of computing equipment and serves to support programming languages. This operating system usually is provided on a diskette that can be read into a microcomputer. The Pascal operating system includes the compiler, an editing program, a file maintenance program, and a number of other tools that, together, form a complete base of support for writing programs in Pascal.

A NOTE ON STYLE

Certain conventions are used throughout this book in an effort to clarify the differences among terms in general usage, specific Pascal terms used for writing programs, and terms that the programmer may invent or "coin" in the writing of program text.

When a general term is introduced for the first time, it appears in *italics* and is listed under "Key Terms" at the end of each chapter. When a specific term in the Pascal language is introduced, it appears in **BOLDFACE** capital letters and is listed under "Pascal Library." Thereafter, both in the book references and in program text, these terms are shown in CAPITALS. Terms that have been coined as examples appear as UpperLower text. Note that coined words sometimes will be run together, since Pascal does not allow spaces to appear within a single term.

Remember that, in the case of program text, these typographical distinctions exist only for clarity. The Pascal language does not make any distinction between upper- and lowercase letters.

A complete list of Pascal terms is presented in Appendix A. A summary of key terms is given in the Glossary.

Summary

Computer languages are simpler and more straightforward than human languages. Computers do not think; rather, computers process data by a series of discrete steps that are specified in a program.

Developing a computerized solution to solve a problem or meet a need first requires a correct description of the logical functions to be performed. Logical functions deal with identification, processing, and transformation of data into information without regard to the physical devices or functions to be used. By contrast, descriptions of the tasks performed, methods followed, and controls applied represent physical, rather than logical, descriptions of computer systems.

Pascal is a structured programming language that assists the programmer in bridging the gap between the logical functions required to solve problems and the physical functions of computer systems.

Computers do not use languages like Pascal directly; computer hardware is controlled by binary electrical signals. Programs called assemblers have been written to simplify the task of writing instructions at the level of machine operations. However, most application programs now are written in high-level languages. These languages are made up of sets of instructions using English-like terms. In high-level languages, individual instructions written by the programmer may generate several instructions, or even whole processes, in machine language. Programs called compilers are used to translate high-level languages such as Pascal into code that the computer can process.

The collection of programs residing in the computer that directs the use of computing equipment and supports programming languages is known as the operating system.

Review Questions

1. Why are the steps described in computer programming languages so specific?
2. Are computer languages more complex than human languages? Why or why not?
3. What is the relationship between data and information, and what is meant by processing data?
4. What is the function of memory within a computer system?
5. What operations do computers perform?
6. What is Boolean logic, and what does it have to do with computers?
7. What are logical functions?
8. How do logical functions differ from physical functions?
9. What is the role of the compiler?
10. How is Pascal related to compilers?
11. What is meant by a structured programming language?
12. Typically, how many bits form a byte, and what is the relationship of bytes to words?

Pascal Practice

1. Examine the USER'S GUIDE that accompanies the version of Pascal that you will use. How are mathematical equations described in program text? What symbols are used to represent the operations of addition, subtraction, multiplication, division, and exponentiation?
2. Familiarize yourself with the computer hardware you will be using to run the Pascal operating system.

Key Terms

1. program
2. programming language
3. operation
4. data
5. program statement
6. assignment of value
7. memory
8. memory location
9. address
10. processing
11. execute
12. information
13. arithmetic operation
14. logical operation
15. greater than
16. equal to
17. less than
18. less than or equal to
19. not equal to
20. greater than or equal to
21. true
22. false
23. Boolean logic
24. sort
25. input
26. output
27. storage
28. manipulation operation
29. physical device
30. hardware
31. physical function
32. processor
33. control unit
34. arithmetic logic unit (ALU)
35. main memory
36. primary storage device
37. mainframe
38. central processing unit (CPU)
39. integrated circuit
40. microprocessor chip
41. secondary storage device
42. displayed output
43. console
44. cathode ray tube (CRT)
45. video display terminal (VDT)
46. documented output
47. hard copy
48. logical processing
49. logical function
50. physical processing
51. gate
52. on
53. off

54. two-state device
55. binary
56. code
57. bit
58. byte
59. American Standard Code for Information Interchange (ASCII)
60. word
61. machine language
62. assembler
63. assembly language
64. compiler
65. source code
66. object code
67. interpreter
68. structured programming language
69. high-level language
70. syntax
71. FORTRAN
72. COBOL
73. UCSD Pascal
74. operating system

Pascal Library

1. TEXT
2. CODE

2
SPEAKING PASCAL

OBJECTIVES

On completing the reading and other learning assignments in this chapter, you should be able to:

- ☐ Explain why a problem must be understood and defined fully before any computerized solution can be formulated.
- ☐ State the definition of an algorithm and explain its role in programming.
- ☐ Explain what is meant by block structure and strong typing.
- ☐ Write a simple program in Pascal.
- ☐ Edit, compile, save, and execute a Pascal program.
- ☐ Explain the process of debugging.

GETTING STARTED: DEFINING THE PROBLEM

Computer programs are instructions that tell a computer how to solve a problem or to meet an identified need. Before you can write a computer program, therefore, you must know—and understand—the problem you are solving or the need you are meeting.

There can be a great temptation to begin working on the solution before you understand the problem. This is one of the classic difficulties encountered in developing effective programs. Programmers sometimes give in to the temptation of writing the program text, or the processing instructions, before they have a clear idea of what the program is supposed to accomplish. It is as though, knowing that you want to build a house, you started by laying bricks instead of by drawing plans.

In business, for example, an overall problem or need might lie in managing money. Managing money may involve controlling deposits and withdrawals from a checking account. If you consider the problem to be one of managing money rather than merely maintaining a checkbook, you must be concerned about all sources of deposits into the bank account as well as all recipients of money. You also must think about whether you need to report checks separately for certain kinds of expenses—such as payroll, purchases of material, and so on. Maintaining the checkbook becomes a method; the real need is to manage money by controlling cash flow. A cash flow system, for example, would involve making sure there is money in the account before you write checks. This broader approach is part of the logical design of a program to maintain the checkbook rather than the physical design of computing balances.

Identifying problems and needs is the starting point from which computerized solutions are developed. When programming difficulties arise, one of the most common problems is that there has been a lack of understanding about what the program is to do—about the problem to be solved.

For example, a large chain-store organization developed a management plan in which merchandise was shipped to its stores on the basis of a relationship between goods in stock and sales revenues. Management decided that whenever the value of a store's goods in stock was at or less than eight times that store's current sales revenues, the store would be restocked with a standard selection of inventory items. As long as this restocking was done, management expected that each store would turn its entire inventory at least six times a year.

When the company failed and went into bankruptcy, the flaw in management's statement of the problem became apparent. This flaw arose out of a mistaken assumption that was part of the logical design of the restocking plan. Because the stores had been restocked continually with the same kinds of inventory items, in some cases duplicating items in stock that had not been sold, the company gradually filled its stores with slow-moving goods that the public didn't want to buy. Eventually, there was no way for the stores to meet management's total turnover goals when only a small portion of the total goods in stock were selling. The stores' turnover quota had been mistakenly defined by management in terms of a relationship between sales revenue and inventories. In reality, the problem should have been defined as a relationship between public demands and inventories.

The chain store management's plan produced unexpected results. The results were vastly different from those predicted by what seemed a clearly defined formula. Similarly, it is possible to have a sophisticated computer program that produces completely worthless information. No computer solution, whether it be a personal task you want to do for yourself or a major job for a large business organization, can be any better than your definition of the problem to be solved.

The example points up another relationship in the development of computer systems. There is a distinct difference between the statement of a problem and the method used in solving it. Problems and solutions are different entities.

DEVELOPING A SOLUTION

The job of solving a problem shouldn't begin until the problem itself is clearly understood and stated. In computer systems, the description of the method for solving a defined problem is called an *algorithm.* An algorithm, typically, is a listing of a series of steps that, when followed in order, delivers a predictable result.

Suppose you had to paint a wall. Your end result, or need, would be to end up with a uniform coat of color on the wall with no mess left over. An algorithm for painting the wall is presented in Figure 2-1.

ALGORITHM FOR PAINTING A WALL

1. Choose a color for the wall.
2. Estimate how many gallons of paint will be required to cover the wall.
3. Purchase paint in the selected color and quantity.
4. Assemble all needed tools, including roller, pan, and cleaning supplies.
5. Mix paint thoroughly.
6. Pour enough paint into the pan to fill the bottom.
7. Wet the roller with the paint.
8. Apply paint from the top of the wall downward, in narrow strips, covering any drips as paint is applied.
9. Repeat steps 6, 7, and 8 until the entire wall is covered.
10. Clean roller and pan.
11. Put away the tools and any remaining paint.

Figure 2-1. The steps involved in painting a wall form an algorithm.

Referring to Figure 2-1, notice some characteristics of this algorithm:

- Some of the steps in the algorithm involve preparation, or *initialization*, of a process. These are steps 1, 2, 3, 4, and 5.
- There is a basic procedure, or process, to be followed. This *processing* includes repeating several steps until the job is done and is demonstrated in steps 6, 7, 8, and 9.
- There is a concluding, or *termination*, portion of the algorithm, as shown in steps 10 and 11.

Thus, the basic, minimal portions of a complete algorithm involve three clear-cut activities: initialization, processing, and termination.

DEVELOPING A PROGRAM

In developing a computer program, the first step in problem definition involves creation of the design, or specifications, for the *outputs* to be delivered. The product of the program will be a specific collection of information, in a certain output format. The person or organization to use the output of computer processing should review the information content and output format carefully.

Once the output has been defined and that definition accepted by the user of that output, the system designer or programmer must identify the *input* data that are needed to produce the desired output. Sources of input data also are identified as a basis for planning the development of a workable program.

Once both outputs and inputs are understood, specifications can be developed for the processing that must be applied to the inputs to deliver the required outputs. In the design phases of program development, processing is specified in an algorithm, or description of the processing to be carried out.

The idea of a high-level programming language like Pascal is to make it easy to implement your algorithms as computer programs that deliver defined output. To illustrate the relative ease in building skills with Pascal, you can begin by developing a simple program. This same program is expanded in later chapters. Each modification of the program involves new skills in writing Pascal.

PROGRAM *Adder*

Your friend just bought a home computer and has asked you to help him solve a problem. He tells you that, periodically, he must add two numbers together and show a total. His stated need, then, is to develop a total when figures are entered into the computer on the keyboard.

In general, the best way to start development of any program is to define the outputs you want to deliver. You decide to call the program you write for your friend *Adder.* Your output should consist of a total amount displayed after two inputs have been entered. This display is to appear on the computer console as shown in Figure 2-2.

To produce the output shown in Figure 2-2, the program user must provide two numeric inputs. Remember, in communicating with people, the computer receives information through the keyboard and displays it on the console (usually the CRT screen, or video monitor) or on the printer. The computer reads the information from the keyboard associated with the console device. Thus, the input needed to develop the output for this program can be illustrated as shown in Figure 2-3.

To process the data values the user enters when the program is run, the values must be placed in memory locations that have names. These names allow the programmer to refer to the values that are to be input, without knowing what the actual values are or where those values are

Figure 2-2. The desired output of a program to add numbers is a display of the correct total.

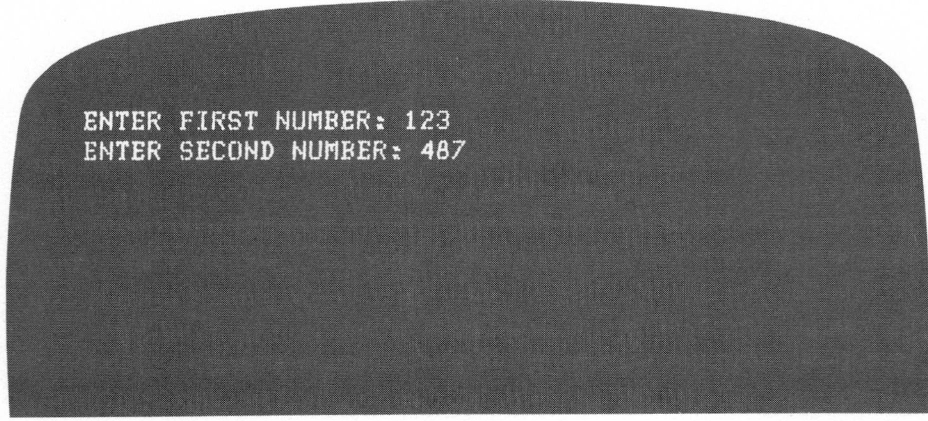
ENTER FIRST NUMBER: 123
ENTER SECOND NUMBER: 487

Figure 2-3. Once the desired output is known, the necessary inputs can be determined.

---

located physically in memory. Since the contents of these memory locations may vary, the names of such memory locations in Pascal are called *variables.* The term variable is used in Pascal programs in much the same way that it is used in mathematics—to refer to a name or symbol that can have any one of a wide range of values.

Figure 2-3 shows that the program is to display a message instructing the user to enter a number. The number 123 is entered, for example. Then the user hits the <RETURN> key. This tells the program that the first numeric entry is complete. These actions are repeated for entry of the second number. Once the second number has been entered, followed by <RETURN>, processing can begin.

The processing to be done by this program is shown graphically in Figure 2-4. A box is used to indicate the memory of the computer. The diagram shows three named locations in that memory area. Two of these memory locations are to contain the numbers the user enters. The third is to hold the total.

To review, the program you intend to write must use the computer's processing capabilities as well as its memory. Memory supports the processing of data. Information received for processing resides in memory until it is used. Results of processing are also held in memory until they can be output.

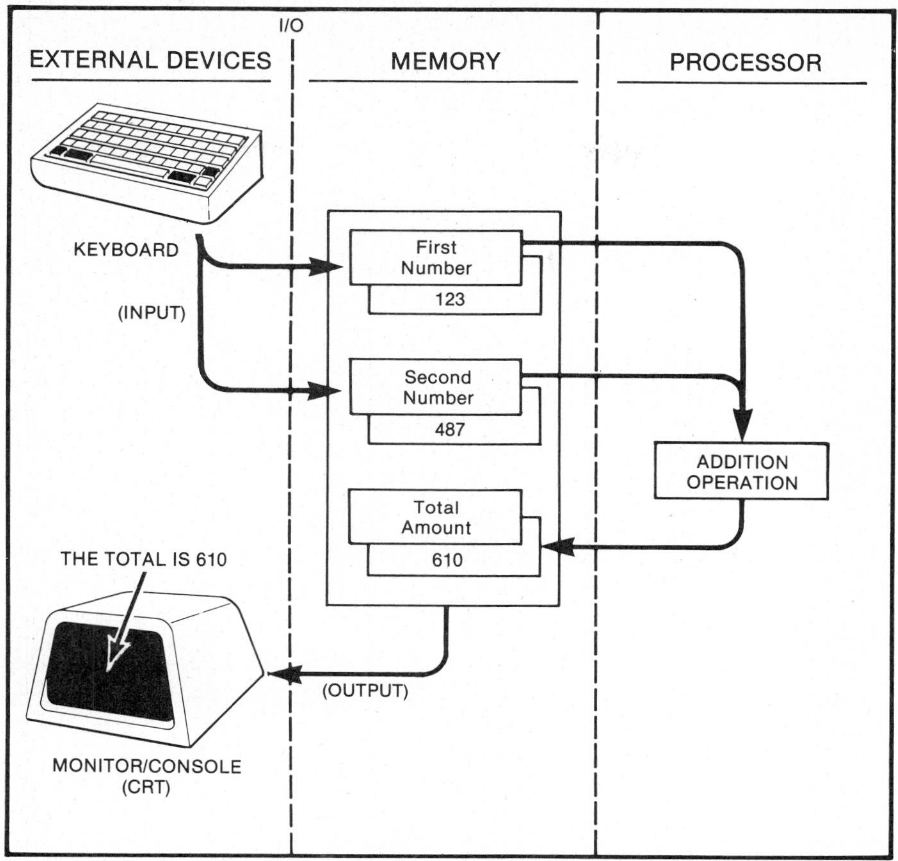

Figure 2-4. Two numeric accumulators in memory hold input numbers, and a third holds the total.

For the purposes of visualizing the entire program, the three elements can be combined in sequence, showing input, processing, and output. These are the three basic physical functions performed by a program. Each step in Figure 2-4 is labeled for the function being implemented. This diagram is, in effect, the basic design of the program you are going to develop. In developing programs, you may find it valuable to prepare diagrams of this type yourself. Even if you don't actually prepare the diagrams, it may help to visualize what is happening within your program by organizing input, processing, and output steps, as well as content, in your own mind. This image of the program steps, in turn, can be described to produce the algorithm from which the program is to be written.

Developing the Algorithm

Figure 2-5 shows only one possible algorithm for the *Adder* program. There is no single way to solve a specific problem, nor is there only one way to organize a program to deliver a computerized solution. Any program that works can be considered satisfactory and correct, depending upon the standards, or criteria, used to evaluate the work.

To develop an algorithm, simply list all the major steps that must be performed, logically, to initialize the program, process data, and produce outputs. In doing this, remember that the computer can't think for you in defining the problem and designing the program. It is up to you to anticipate not only the user's output requirements but also all steps required to perform the physical processing that produces those outputs.

Notice that all of the statements in the processing steps of the algorithm start with verbs, or action words. Processing is an action. By starting with a verb, the instruction clarifies what action is to be taken.

Note the last line of the algorithm. Since the initialization and processing steps of the program are complete, this last line calls for program termination.

```
                    ALGORITHM FOR PROGRAM Adder

INITIALIZE:
    Start with variables named TotalAmount, FirstNumber, and SecondNumber.
    Ask the user to enter a new value for FirstNumber.
    Get the new value for FirstNumber.
    Ask the user to enter a new value for SecondNumber.
    Get the new value for SecondNumber.
PROCESS:
    Add FirstNumber to SecondNumber and put the result in TotalAmount.
TERMINATE:
    Display the new value for TotalAmount.
    End of program.
```

Figure 2-5. Listing possible steps for initializing, processing, and producing outputs can help in formulating an algorithm.

The statements in Figure 2-5 are not program text. They are English directions that describe the instructions to be carried out when the actual program is *executed,* or run. In fact, these instructions have the general format of a Pascal program. Because of this close correspondence between the form of such algorithms and the actual instructions of the program itself, a set of statements of this type is called *pseudocode.* This use of pseudocode in program design should not be confused with the pseudocoding of object code, otherwise known as *p-code,* which is a special feature of UCSD Pascal. Pseudocoding, when speaking of program design, means that English statements are used where actual program text eventually is to be written.

The algorithm in Figure 2-5 can now be used as a basis for developing a Pascal program, following the structured procedures implied by use of that language. In effect, the algorithm describes a solution of a problem in terms of logical requirements, independent of programming languages. The actual Pascal program instructions then restate the algorithm in terms of physical processing. That is, the instructions are in a form suitable for translation by the compiler into code for physical processing by the computer.

Writing Pascal

The Pascal language follows a structure that helps assure that all programs are complete and written in a format that can deliver the needed information to the compiler. The structure of a minimum Pascal program is shown graphically in Figure 2-6. The program is structured as a series of sections containing needed information and also providing a place for optional statements or explanations.

The top box in Figure 2-6 contains the word **PROGRAM**. PROGRAM is one of the *reserved words,* or standard terms, of the Pascal language. This means that the term has a *predefined* meaning that is applied each time it is presented to the compiler. The programmer has no control over words on the reserved list and may use them in a program only with their predefined meanings.

The three words in boldface in Figure 2-6 (PROGRAM, BEGIN, and END) are all reserved words. Further, these three words are the minimum terms that must appear in each Pascal program.

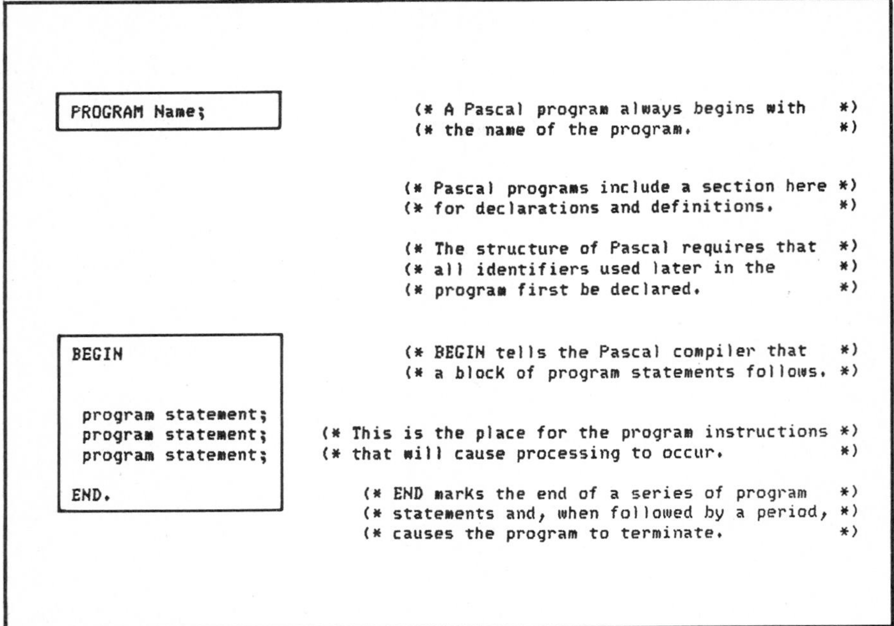

PROGRAM Name;
(* A Pascal program always begins with *)
(* the name of the program. *)
(* Pascal programs include a section here *)
(* for declarations and definitions. *)
(* The structure of Pascal requires that *)
(* all identifiers used later in the *)
(* program first be declared. *)
BEGIN
(* BEGIN tells the Pascal compiler that *)
(* a block of program statements follows. *)
program statement;
program statement;
program statement;
(* This is the place for the program instructions *)
(* that will cause processing to occur. *)
END.
(* END marks the end of a series of program *)
(* statements and, when followed by a period, *)
(* causes the program to terminate. *)

Figure 2-6. The structure of Pascal assures program completeness and information in the correct format needed by the compiler.

The term PROGRAM begins a *header,* or *block delimiter.* This reserved word precedes the name of the program. In Pascal, a program may be considered a single *block* of processing instructions.

Following the PROGRAM header, Pascal structure requires certain data *declarations* and *definitions.* Key terms, or *identifiers,* are introduced here to the compiler before being used in the later processing sections. A declaration defines a name for a given data item and declares a *data type,* or restriction, on the data. Data typing is discussed later in this chapter. Declarations and definitions are of several kinds and are discussed further in Chapter 3.

The term **BEGIN** indicates the start of actual program text—instructions to be executed.

The term **END** marks the end of a block of instructions.

The term *block* has a special meaning in Pascal. A program block is a group of source code statements that includes:

- A header
- Definitions and/or declarations
- Program statements.

Program statements define processing actions. A group of program statements included within the same program block is referred to as a *compound statement* and must be set off from the rest of the program by the delimiters BEGIN and END. Thus, a short Pascal program of the form given above that has one BEGIN statement and one END statement can be thought of as one block. However, a single Pascal program may consist of many blocks. Blocks contained within a larger program are sometimes referred to as *subprograms,* or *subroutines.* Program statements that may use subprograms and that define the main processing tasks of a program are referred to as the *main block* or *main program.*

When the END statement ends with a period, it indicates to the compiler that the program text is complete. Any statements after **END.** are ignored by the compiler. If the word END is used without a period, it concludes a block of instructions but does not conclude the program itself. If other program blocks follow, the form **END;**, with the semicolon included, is used.

The terms BEGIN and END contribute to Pascal's structured form. That is, Pascal programs are formed of a series of blocks of instructions that are executed as processing units. For this reason, Pascal is sometimes referred to as a *block-structured* language.

CODING *Adder*

In Figure 2-7, the header and main body of the *Adder* program have been put in place. There are some additional terms and symbols in the *Adder* program that have specific meanings and help to implement Pascal's structure.

The semicolon (;) is used at several points. This punctuation mark identifies the end of a statement or declaration. The use of the semicolon is optional before an END statement and usually is required after it. The semicolon is not used after such delimiters as BEGIN and other terms that

```
(***********************************************************************)
(*    This program called Adder will ask the person who is running the   *)
(*    program to enter two integers (whole numbers). These two numbers   *)
(*    will then be added together and displayed.                         *)
(***********************************************************************)

PROGRAM Adder;                                   (* program name is Adder *)



(* Program declarations and definitions go here *)



BEGIN                                    (* begin programming instructions *)
  WRITE('ENTER FIRST NUMBER: ');          (* tell user to enter first number *)
  READLN(FirstNumber);                   (* get value from user, await RETURN *)
  WRITE('ENTER SECOND NUMBER: ');                (* ask for second number *)
  READLN(SecondNumber);                  (* get value from user, await RETURN *)
  TotalAmount := FirstNumber + SecondNumber;           (* add two numbers *)
  WRITELN('THE TOTAL IS: ',TotalAmount);       (* display answer, start new
                                                          display line *)
  WRITELN('END OF PROGRAM');                     (* display ending message *)
END.                                                    (* end of program *)
```

Figure 2-7. Program *Adder*. Note the order of terms and symbols.

serve primarily as block delimiters rather than as statements to be executed. A frequent programming error occurs when the semicolon is omitted between program statements or when it is included incorrectly after block delimiters. The compiler will flag these errors for you and will complete a successful compilation only when the errors have been corrected.

The use of parentheses and asterisks (* *) identifies optional comments included by the programmer for use by people. Any text set off by (* *) is ignored by the Pascal compiler. Note that commands and reserved words within comments lose their special meaning and are ignored. As an alternative, comments may be enclosed in braces { }, if your computer keyboard has these keys. The braces have the same meaning as the parentheses and the asterisks. Adding comments to certain lines of your program text is a way to document your program objectives for future reference by you or by other programmers. Such comments make your program text more understandable to other people.

The equal sign (=) is used within the sample program in a special way. Notice that the = follows a colon. The symbol := has a particular meaning in Pascal. The meaning is *assignment of value.* The results of computing the expression to the right of := are assigned to the variable that appears to the left of this sign. Thus, in the fifth line of the main body of the *Adder* program, the variable TotalAmount is assigned a value. The assignment is made with the := symbol. If the = were used alone, without the colon, it would indicate a *comparison* to be performed. (The = has other uses in Pascal, but this is the principal one.) A test is made to see if the expression on the left of the = sign is equal to the expression on the right. This is an important and fundamental concept in Pascal. There is a considerable difference between the processing caused by := (assignment of value) and that caused by = (comparison or test of equality).

The plus sign (+) has its traditional mathematical meaning within the Pascal language. The data represented by the two expressions separated by the + sign are added to each other.

WRITE is an instruction that causes information to be output. This output often takes the form of a display on the console. Within the *Adder* program, the WRITE instruction is used to display *prompts* to the user (on the CRT or console device): 'ENTER FIRST NUMBER:' and 'ENTER SECOND NUMBER:'.

Notice that, within the WRITE statement, the message to be displayed is enclosed in single quotation marks (' '). Character strings within single quotation marks are *character string constants,* just as a number such as 1, 2, 3 (when used in an expression like x + 1) is a *constant,* or value that remains unchanged throughout program execution. **WRITELN**, the term that begins the last program statement, is actually a special case of WRITE. WRITELN causes the same processing as just described for WRITE, except that WRITELN causes the display device to advance to the next writing line after it has displayed the specified message. By contrast with the action caused by WRITELN, if several WRITE statements are executed in sequence, the data presented is displayed all on the same line, or in a continuity over a series of lines. Note also that the variable name TotalAmount is not enclosed in quotation marks when it is included in the WRITELN statement. Variable names are not enclosed in quotation marks in WRITE or WRITELN statements. This is because whatever is included in quotation marks is output literally—just as it appears in the program text. On the other hand, a variable name, when included in one of these statements, indicates that the *value* that resides in memory under that variable name is output.

Two other kinds of program statements in *Adder* have features similar to WRITE and WRITELN. These are **READ** and **READLN**. Both of these commands allow the program to accept input from the keyboard or other input device. These commands provide the most common way to enter data for processing by a Pascal program from the keyboard. The main difference between the two is that READLN is used when you want the user to press the <RETURN> key (labeled RET, ENTER, or CR—Carriage Return—on some keyboards) after entering the requested data.

The program text in Figure 2-7, then, is a Pascal language version of the algorithm in Figure 2-5. The computer is instructed to add the two input values and to place the result in the memory location named TotalAmount. The program then displays the value in TotalAmount on the console. Once the total is displayed, the program displays an END OF PROGRAM message and terminates.

Note that the program includes three terms that are picked up from the original algorithm. These are: FirstNumber, SecondNumber, and TotalAmount. These terms now are used formally in the program text to name variables. To use variables within a Pascal program, you first must identify them in a section of the program known as the *declaration section.* The declaration section of the *Adder* program has been left blank so far. This section follows the PROGRAM header and precedes the BEGIN statement.

Figure 2-8 shows the *Adder* program completed to include a series of variable declarations. The new Pascal term used here is **VAR**.

VAR is an abbreviation of VARiable. The VAR portion of a Pascal program is part of the declaration section. The variable declaration section is used to name and define all of the data items to be introduced into the main program for processing. In the *Adder* program, the variables are FirstNumber, SecondNumber, and TotalAmount. Again, the variables must be declared in the declaration section before reference can be made to those variables in the program. This is because Pascal requires that all terms be defined or declared before they can be used in processing.

To restate the definition: Variables hold data items to be used in the program. For each variable declared, a memory area is set aside

```
(****************************************************************************)
(*    This program called Adder will ask the person who is running the     *)
(*     program to enter two integers (whole numbers). These two numbers    *)
(*     will then be added together and displayed.                          *)
(****************************************************************************)

PROGRAM Adder;                                (* program name is Adder *)

VAR
 FirstNumber:INTEGER;                 (* declare VARiables for the program *)
 SecondNumber:INTEGER;
 TotalAmount:INTEGER;

BEGIN                                      (* begin programming instructions *)
 WRITE('ENTER FIRST NUMBER: ');            (* tell user to enter first number *)
 READLN(FirstNumber);                    (* get value from user, await RETURN *)
 WRITE('ENTER SECOND NUMBER: ');                  (* ask for second number *)
 READLN(SecondNumber);                   (* get value from user, await RETURN *)
 TotalAmount := FirstNumber + SecondNumber;               (* add two numbers *)
 WRITELN('THE TOTAL IS: ',TotalAmount);       (* display answer, start new
                                                              display line *)
 WRITELN('END OF PROGRAM');                      (* display ending message *)
END.                                                      (* end of program *)
```

Figure 2-8. Variable declarations for the program *Adder* name and define all of the data items to be introduced for processing.

automatically. The programmer can assign almost any meaningful description to indicate a variable name. Each name must start with an alphabetic letter. After that, any combination of letters or numbers may be used. The first eight characters in a variable name must be unique, since only these characters are used by the compiler to distinguish among identifiers, or names, in the program. In naming variables, it is a good practice to choose a description that indicates the use of the data. (Just as using appropriate comment lines can help to make your program self-documenting, choosing particularly descriptive variable names can be a help to you or any other programmer who must read and understand your program.) The variable names used in the *Adder* program describe clearly that the variables represent numeric totals and new numbers to be input.

For each variable introduced, a declaration of the type of data the variable is to contain also must be given in the declaration section. In the

Adder program, the variables FirstNumber, SecondNumber and Total-Amount are typed as *integers.*

INTEGER is a predefined Pascal data type. Recall that, in the declaration section, a data item must be named and typed. Typing a variable as INTEGER means that data items having the given name must be whole numbers. Whole numbers are those that have no fractional parts. In UCSD Pascal, the numbers defined as integers can have any value from −32,768 to +32,767. These are the processing limits for numbers typed by the term INTEGER within the compiler. Examples of integer values are: 1, −35, 3456, and 0.

PASCAL—A STRONGLY TYPED LANGUAGE

The Pascal language employs strong typing. Strong typing means that rigorous distinctions are enforced in the Pascal compiler between certain data types. For example, operations on integers may not be performed on characters. That is, numbers can't be added to letters.

All operations imply some data type. The operations involved in counting imply the use of numbers of type INTEGER, for example. Because operations imply certain variable types, and because of the strong typing constraints of Pascal, the programmer must restrict the use of a variable to the operations that are valid for that variable's declared type. For example, it would be invalid to try to perform the operation of addition on a variable whose type indicates that its values are letters.

One of the powerful features of Pascal is that it allows the programmer to "coin" data types by defining those types within the **TYPE** definition section of the program. One predefined data type is already familiar to you, INTEGER. Pascal predefines several other commonly used data types. Besides the INTEGER type in the *Adder* example, some other predefined data types in Pascal are **REAL** (a number containing a decimal point), **CHAR** (for CHARacter, an individual alphanumeric symbol), **long INTEGER** (whole numbers with up to 36 digits), and **STRING** (a sequence of characters). These data types are discussed further as each is incorporated into actual programming examples in later chapters. Remember that the Pascal language is strongly typed; the Pascal compiler does not let you specify operations on a variable that are invalid for its declared type.

ENTERING A PASCAL PROGRAM

Once you have written a program on paper, you are ready to go through a series of steps that make your program operational on the computer. These steps include:

- Enter the program text into the computer through use of the *editor* that is part of the UCSD Pascal operating system.
- Store the program, once it has been entered, to form a text file. This also is done under the editor.
- Compile the text file to create a code file. This is done by the compiler within the operating system. At this point, any errors in *syntax* (incorrect use of terms, codes, or format) cause the compiler to generate error messages. Each error must be corrected by returning to the editor before the program can be compiled successfully. Once all of the errors have been eliminated, the compiler produces a code file.
- The code file is the version of the program that can be run by the computer. A program is run with the R (for Run) or X (for eXecute) option offered by the operating system.

To enter your program, start by loading the UCSD Pascal operating system—or by verifying that it has already been loaded. If you are working with a microcomputer, the operating system probably is supplied on a diskette. This diskette should be inserted into the disk drive and the computer should be turned on following standard instructions for your own computer. This process is called *booting* the operating system. (The actual techniques for using the compiler and entering programs will vary with the number of disk drives on your system and other factors. Therefore, specific instructions are not provided in this text. Rather, you should refer to the manual that accompanies the diskette for the UCSD Pascal operating system.)

Booting, the process of starting an operating system, is depicted in Figure 2-9. Booting is done differently for different types of computers. On some computers, a diskette must be loaded before the computer can be turned on. Then, turning on the computer also loads the program automatically. In other systems, the computer must be turned on first, then the diskette inserted in a drive before a booting action is taken.

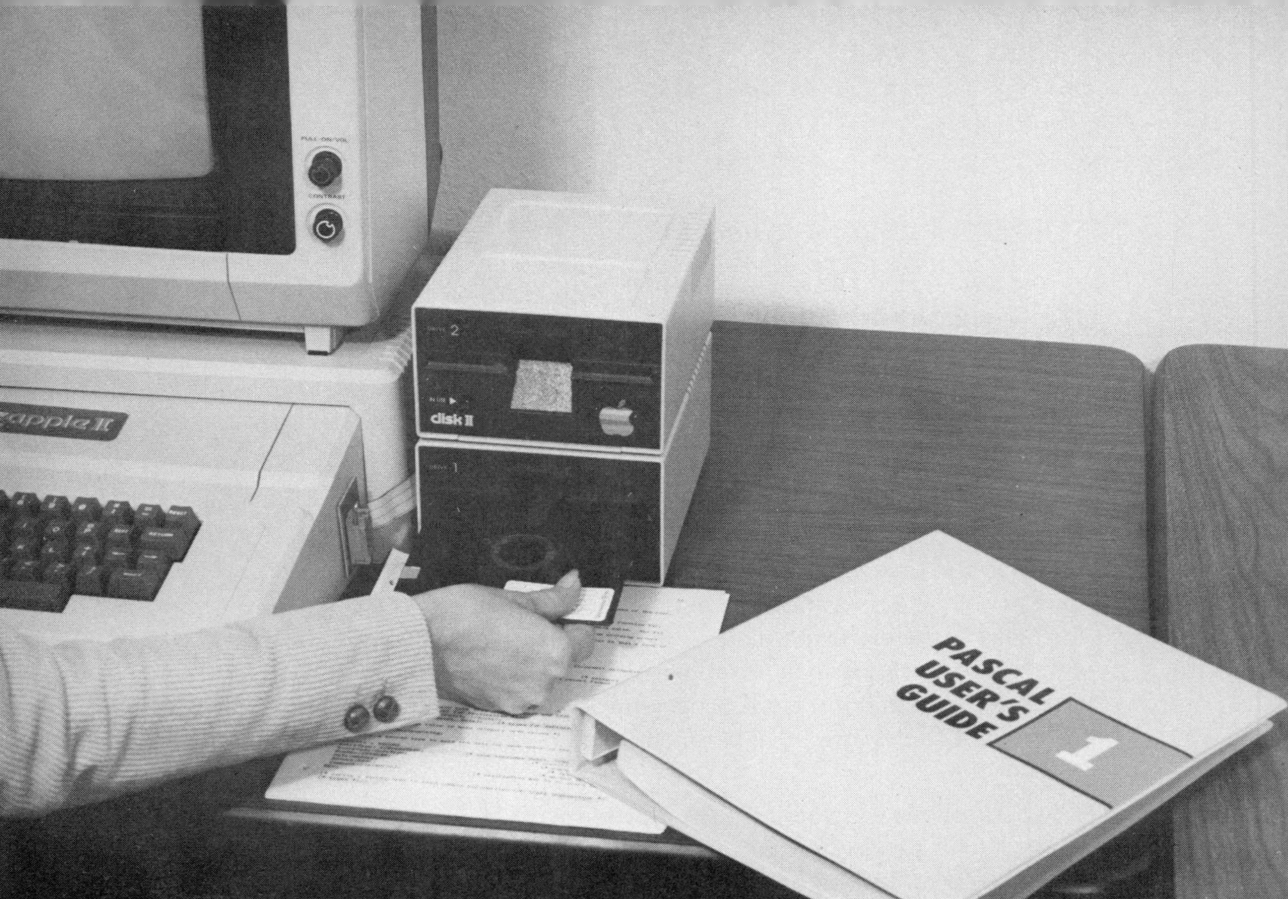

Figure 2-9. Booting is the first step in using the UCSD Pascal operating system.

Another term for boot is *cold start*. Both terms describe what happens. Boot is derived from the term bootstrap, or bootstrap loader. Booting means that the computer is caused to build up, one by one or in small groups, the programs needed to support its operations. In effect, the system is caused to lift itself by its own bootstraps, by a series of small steps, then groups of steps, until the operating system has been loaded.

When you have booted the UCSD Pascal system, a *command line* is displayed. This is illustrated in Figure 2-10. A command line is a *menu*, or list of selections, from which you make a choice of functions you want to use. For your purposes in getting started, you need to use three of the command functions that are offered—E (Edit), C (Compile), and X (eXecute). Each of these commands calls up a separate program module within the operating system. Note that these key commands and the functions they stand for are not reserved words within the Pascal

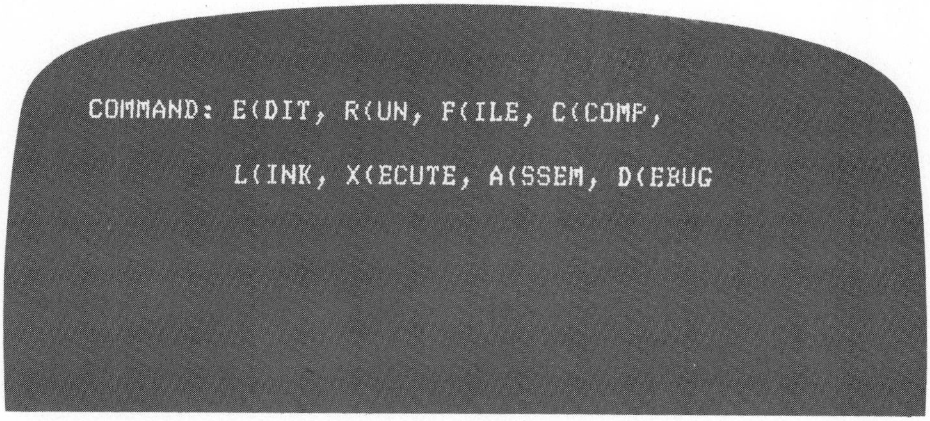

```
COMMAND: E(DIT, R(UN, F(ILE, C(COMP,
         L(INK, X(ECUTE, A(SSEM, D(EBUG
```

Figure 2-10. The command line displayed on the console is a menu, or list of selections, from which a choice of processing functions can be made.

---

language. Such commands are not used in program statements but are entered at the keyboard in response to options presented by the operating system.

To use your own Pascal program, the Edit, Compile, and eXecute modules are applied in sequence.

The Edit module is used first. It can be called up on UCSD Pascal language systems by entering the letter E at the keyboard. At this point, a display like the one shown in Figure 2-11 appears. On entering the Edit module, you have a choice to make. You can choose to work on an existing file by entering the name of that file, or you can begin creating a new file by pressing the <RETURN> key.

At this point, a new command line is displayed. This menu gives you a choice of functions offered by the Edit module. To enter the text of your program into the computer, you must use the Insert mode. So, you press the letter I on the keyboard. As you enter the Insert mode, a new command line appears. You don't need any further commands to start entering your program. Begin keying in the text of the program you have written.

As you key in entries, notice that the *cursor,* usually a small rectangular shape, moves across the screen. The cursor marks your place on the console. If you backspace while in the Insert mode, the cursor

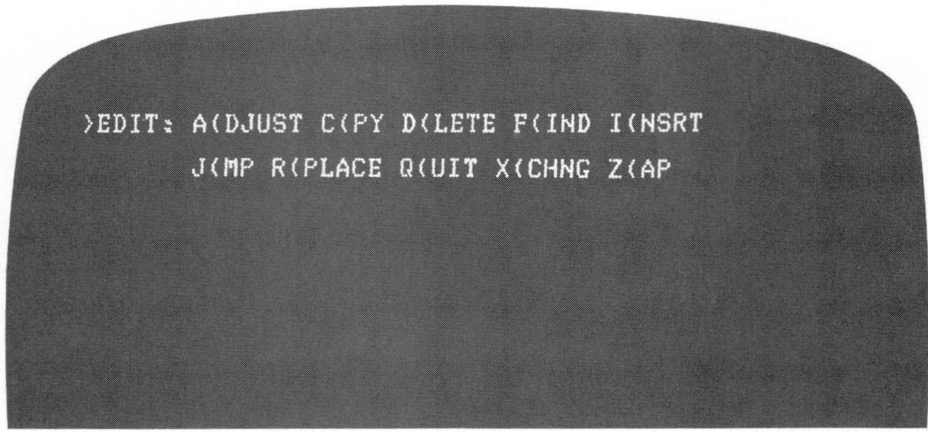

Figure 2-11. The E(dit menu has its own menu of further options.

moves back over the text you have entered, erasing your entry one space at a time. This is often the easiest way to make simple corrections—as long as you discover errors as you make them.

While in the Insert mode, key in the entire text of your program. All text you enter in this mode is held in an area of memory allocated for temporary storage. After you have reviewed the text you've entered, the Insert mode gives you two alternatives: You can cause the text to be retained in memory, or you can discard the material you have entered in the Insert mode. To retain your text, you use the ETX command. On most microcomputers, this is done by depressing the <CTRL> key, then pressing the C while you are holding the <CTRL> key down. (CONTROL C is sometimes written ^C, <CTRL>–C, or [C]. Even though the notations vary, the required action is the same in all cases.) When you do this, the computer returns to the Edit mode, keeping your text in memory for further work.

The other alternative is to depress the <ESC> (for ESCape) key. This command causes everything you have entered in the Insert mode to be discarded from its temporary location in memory and to disappear from the console screen.

Assume that you have keyed in the program, retained it in memory, and returned to the Edit mode. Now you want to proofread the work

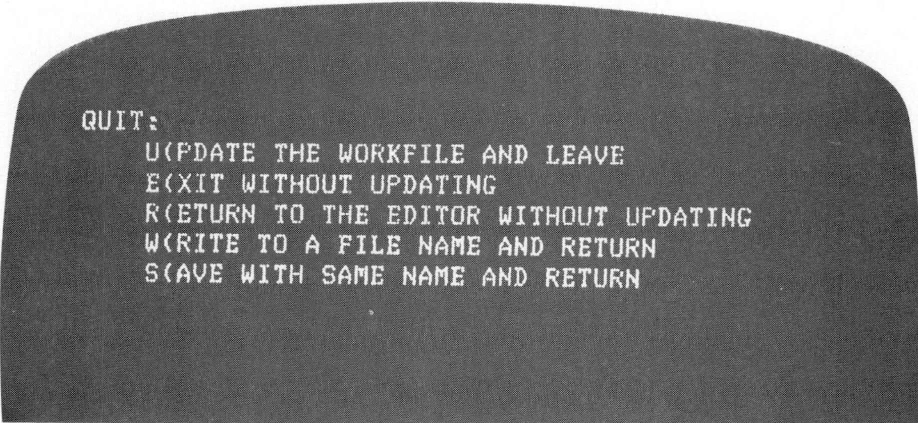

QUIT:
U(PDATE THE WORKFILE AND LEAVE
E(XIT WITHOUT UPDATING
R(ETURN TO THE EDITOR WITHOUT UPDATING
W(RITE TO A FILE NAME AND RETURN
S(AVE WITH SAME NAME AND RETURN

Figure 2-12. The Q(uit option allows you to create a file to store the program text you have created.

you have done. If you find any errors, you can use Edit commands to correct them. You can insert letters or larger text portions by using the Insert mode. You can delete portions of text with the D (for Delete) command.

Both insertions and deletions of text are made at the point where the cursor is located on the screen. There are special keys, which vary from one computer to the next, designated for moving the cursor up, down, left, or right. Once you position the cursor, you go into another mode, such as Insert or Delete, to make changes to the text. After each correction or change to the text, you come back into Edit mode, saving the new version of the text as you do.

When you are satisfied that you have an accurate text of your program, you can leave the Edit mode and save your text permanently on diskette. To do this, type the letter Q (for Quit). At this point, a number of options are displayed. One example of these options is shown in Figure 2-12. If you have just entered this program text for the first time (or if you wish to save this program under a new file name), you can choose the W command (for Write), which causes the system to create a new disk file containing your program text. You are then asked for the name of the file that is to contain your text. The text file name can contain up to 10 letters or numbers and must begin with an alphabetic character.

The name you provide will have the suffix **.TEXT** appended to it by the editor unless you have done so yourself. This suffix is necessary because the compiler cannot act on the file unless it has a file name of the form:

```
FileName.TEXT
```

Also, throughout the UCSD Pascal system, all source code files have the .TEXT suffix. When you enter the file name of your program text and depress the <RETURN> key, the editor writes your file onto a disk for permanent storage.

If you already have a working file, you use the S option to indicate a Save command. This command causes the editor to save the text under the file name already established. Be aware that when you use a Save command, the previous version of the text of the same name on the diskette is overwritten and wiped out. So, be sure that the present version is the one you want to save.

At this point, you have entered your source program into the computer. You have a text file ready for compilation.

COMPILING A PASCAL PROGRAM

After you have created and saved the text of a program in a file, you have a choice. Within the options for the Quit command, you can go back to the editor (by entering R for Return), or you can Exit back to the main operating system by pressing E. To compile, you go back to the main operating system. Remember that the text that was in memory during editing is erased once you have exited from the edit module. If you have followed the above instructions, however, your text has been saved to a diskette.

Having returned to the main operating system, you choose the Compile function by pressing the letter C. The compiler then asks the name of the text file that you want to compile. You enter the name of the file you have just saved and press <RETURN>. The compiler asks you the name to be given to the code file that will result from the compilation of your source code file. When you have entered the name and pressed the <RETURN> key, the compiler begins to translate the statements in your text (source) file into a code (object) file. The compiler displays its progress as it does this translation, printing a dot (period) for each line of text scanned. The display indicates the length of each portion of the code file, as well as the total length of the file, as shown in Figure 2-13.

If there are no errors of syntax in your program text, you now have a compiled program that is ready to run. If, on the other hand, an error is encountered by the compiler, it stops upon encountering the error and offers you the following options:

<SPACE BAR> This option tells the compiler to continue compilation. Since an error has been found, the compiler will not produce a code file if you choose this option. However, continuing may help you find any further errors in your program and thus save you another aborted compilation.

E (Editor) This option returns you to the editor to modify the source code file at the point where the compiler encountered the error.

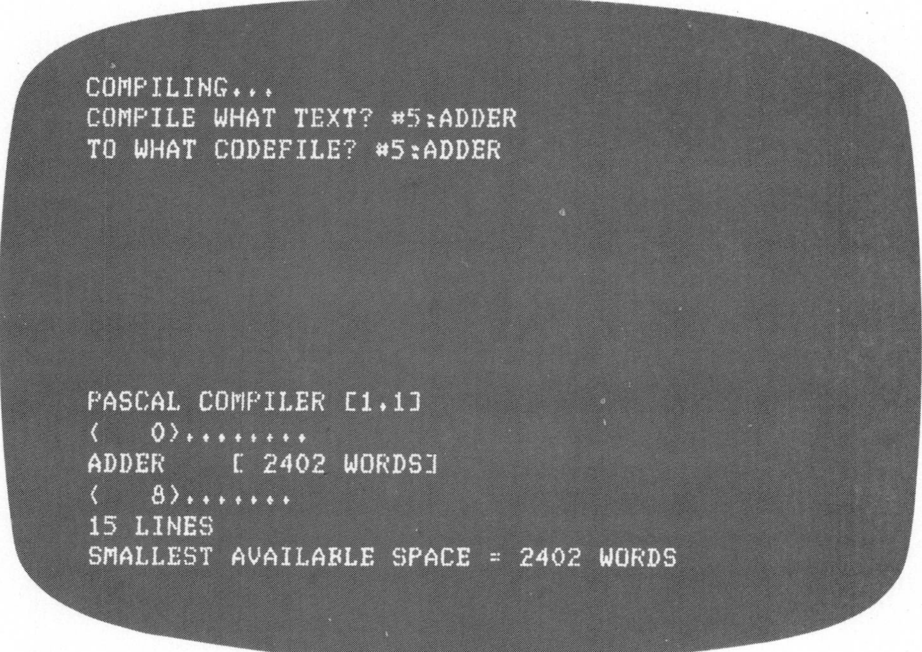

COMPILING...
COMPILE WHAT TEXT? #5:ADDER
TO WHAT CODEFILE? #5:ADDER
PASCAL COMPILER [1.1]
(0)........
ADDER [2402 WORDS]
(8).......
15 LINES
SMALLEST AVAILABLE SPACE = 2402 WORDS

Figure 2-13. Console display as it might appear during the compilation of *Adder*.

<ESC> (ESCape) This option causes the system to quit compilation with no further action.

EXECUTING A PASCAL PROGRAM

After the program is compiled, you see the command line of the operating system displayed. To run the program just compiled, you may enter R (for Run) and the operating system will load the file and execute it. To execute any program, you press the letter X and specify the name of a code file. This file name is of the form:

```
FileName.CODE
```

The compiler assumes the **.CODE** suffix if you enter only FileName. If no code file exists, of course, an error message is displayed. When you enter the file name and press <RETURN>, the program is read into memory from the disk file and executed. The *Adder* program now asks you to enter the first number. After entering the number, you press the <RETURN> key. The program then asks you for the next number. When you have made that entry and pressed <RETURN>, the program shows you the total, displays an END OF PROGRAM message, and terminates. Figure 2-14 shows the console as it might appear after executing the *Adder* program.

DEBUGGING A PASCAL PROGRAM

A *bug* is any error encountered either in compiling or executing a program. There are two general types of programming errors, or bugs. One is a *syntactical error.* Syntactical errors are those errors identified by the compiler during compilation. The other type of error is a *logical error.* Logical errors, or bugs, appear as inappropriate processing results.

If you have committed a syntactical error, the compiler presents a message that identifies the point within the program at which the error has occurred. You also get a coded message, usually in the form of a number code, that identifies the type of error made. (More information on these error codes may be found in the manual that accompanies your particular version of the Pascal operating system.) If you go back to the Edit mode, the compiler can give you a more complete description of

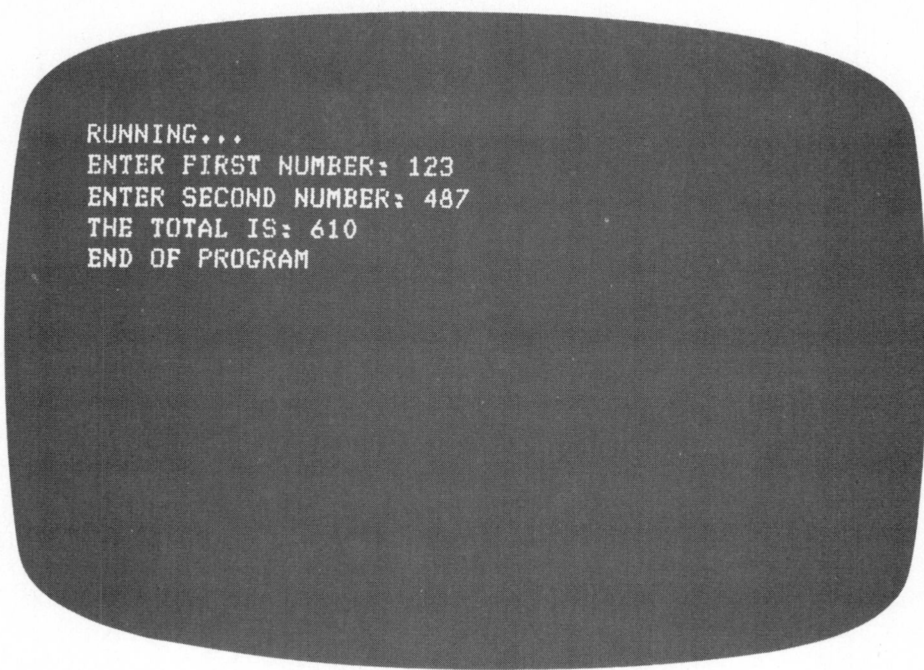

RUNNING...
ENTER FIRST NUMBER: 123
ENTER SECOND NUMBER: 487
THE TOTAL IS: 610
END OF PROGRAM

Figure 2-14. Console display after execution of *Adder*.

your syntactical error. As you gain experience, it becomes relatively easy to look at errors that have been identified for you and to enter correct program text.

Logical errors are far more difficult to track down. In some cases, you get an error message when the program is executed because you have prepared program text that cannot process the data, even though the syntax of the text is correct. More often, a logical error can be discovered only through the outputs of programs. Logical errors may be diagnosed by doing test runs of the program. As part of the specifications for the design of a program, test data should be developed. Such a group of data includes sample inputs along with corresponding output, or answers the computer is expected to return. In testing, you enter the test inputs and compare the output of your program with the sample output, the expected result. If the two don't match, something is wrong in the processing logic. Logical errors can be difficult to identify and correct and always require some degree of programming experience to diagnose. Ways to diagnose commonly encountered logical errors are pointed out at appropriate points in this book.

Summary

Before you can write a computer program, you must understand the underlying problem, or need. The problem to be solved must be defined. Problems and solutions are different entities.

A description of the method for solving a defined problem is an algorithm. Most algorithms involve these activities: initialization, processing, and termination. To develop an algorithm, list all the major steps that must be performed, logically, to initialize the program, process data, and produce outputs. A further refinement of the steps of an algorithm into English-like statements is referred to as pseudocoding. Writing a Pascal program can involve translating pseudocoded statements into Pascal program text.

A Pascal program must start with a PROGRAM header, and its processing instructions must be set off by the block identifiers BEGIN and END. Because of this structure, Pascal is referred to as a block-structured language. A Pascal program may consist of many blocks, or subprograms.

In Pascal program statements, the symbol := refers to an assignment of value, whereas the symbol = indicates a comparison, or test of equality, to be performed. Console displays are accomplished by the WRITE and WRITELN statements. Keyboard inputs are accomplished by the READ and READLN statements. Variables used in the program must be declared in the variable declaration section before these variables can be referred to elsewhere. Variables contain data to be used in the program. A type must be given for each variable declared.

Pascal is said to employ strong typing because rigorous distinctions are enforced in the compiler between types of data. Some predefined types in Pascal are: INTEGER, long INTEGER, REAL, CHARacter, and STRING. Data types may also be coined by the programmer.

Once a Pascal program has been written, it must be keyed into the computer using the Edit module. Within the Edit module, the Insert and Delete functions may be used. The resulting text file may be retained in memory through the use of the ETX (^C) command and saved to a disk file with the Save or Write commands. The text file is then compiled by entering the Compile module, which either displays syntactical errors that have been encountered or creates a code file ready to run. Running a program is accomplished through use of the Run command or the eXecute command used with the code file name. Errors found in the execution of a program in the form of unexpected results are known as logical errors. Correcting errors found in the program is known as debugging.

Review Questions

1. Why is the task of problem definition so critical to writing good programs?
2. What is the form of a block in Pascal?
3. What specific Pascal program statements are used to describe the actions of input and output?
4. What is meant by a variable in Pascal?
5. Where are variables declared in a Pascal program, and why is it necessary for this declaration to be made?
6. What are some predefined data types in Pascal, and how is each used?
7. What two similar symbols are used in Pascal to denote assignment of value and comparison, and what circumstances could cause each to be used?
8. What is the form for the file name of a Pascal text file, and why is it important that these files be distinguished from code files?
9. What commands are used to enter a text file into memory and to save it to the disk, and how do the results of these actions differ?
10. Why doesn't the compiler produce a code file once it has encountered a syntactical error?
11. What is the difference between a syntactical error and a logical error?
12. Why are logical errors apt to be more difficult to find and correct than syntactical errors?

Pascal Practice

1. Enter the text file for *SayHi* given in Chapter 1, but omit all semicolons. Describe what happens when you try a compilation on this file.
2. Modify the text file for *Adder* so that the program first displays a statement welcoming the user to the program, asks for that person's name (refer to the program text of *SayHi*), and uses the person's name when the final total is displayed.

Key Terms

1. algorithm
2. initialization
3. processing
4. termination
5. output
6. input
7. variable
8. execute
9. pseudocode
10. p-code
11. reserved word
12. predefined
13. header
14. block delimiter
15. block
16. declaration
17. definition
18. identifier
19. data type
20. program statement
21. compound statement
22. subprogram
23. subroutine
24. main block
25. main program
26. block structure
27. assignment of value
28. comparison
29. prompt
30. character string constant
31. constant
32. value
33. declaration section
34. integer
35. editor
36. syntax

37. boot
38. cold start
39. command line
40. menu
41. cursor
42. bug
43. syntactical error
44. logical error

Pascal Library

1. PROGRAM
2. BEGIN
3. END
4. WRITE
5. WRITELN
6. READ
7. READLN
8. VAR
9. INTEGER
10. TYPE
11. REAL
12. CHAR
13. long INTEGER
14. STRING
15. .TEXT
16. .CODE

3 DESIGNING FOR QUALITY

OBJECTIVES

On completing the reading and other learning assignments in this chapter, you should be able to:

- ☐ Explain how a problem is defined in terms of meeting an underlying need and why problem definition is a critical program design step.
- ☐ Describe the importance of setting standards of quality for program results and what these standards mean in terms of accuracy, completeness, and reliability.
- ☐ Describe examples of the steps followed and techniques used in problem analysis, including data flow diagrams and flowcharts.
- ☐ Define logical design and discuss the differences between logical and physical characteristics of an information system.
- ☐ Define top-down design and explain how structure charts help to implement this method of problem definition.
- ☐ Explain how pseudocode is derived from structure charts and logical design.
- ☐ Describe verification procedures used to test logical designs.
- ☐ Define control functions and explain how they are used to assure accuracy, completeness, and reliability in program results.
- ☐ Use the Pascal REPEAT and UNTIL statements to construct program loops and explain the importance of a termination condition in controlling the execution of this type of loop.

DEFINING RESULTS

In organizations that use large computers, design specifications for programs generally are developed by specialists other than programmers, such as systems analysts. However, the situation is quite different in small organizations that use minicomputers or microcomputers. In these situations, as well as in some of the learning exercises in this book, you must do your own definition and design before beginning to write program instructions. This need for planning also exists even if you are writing programs for your own personal computer. In any case, *program specifications* must be prepared before a quality program can be written.

Preparation of program specifications involves a series of steps. The programmer must:

- Identify the real, or underlying, problem. Don't confuse the problem with either a symptom of the problem or with methods used in its solution. A symptom may be expressed as a perceived need. A perceived need is one that has been identified by the user but may not describe fully or accurately the essential problem. For example, the real need in a payroll system might be to produce checks each Friday to pay for work done through the previous Friday. The payroll office is working overtime every weekend to process time cards, and management feels a computer payroll program can eliminate that overtime. But the need for the system has nothing directly to do with any perceived need to eliminate overtime. That's an effect, or symptom, of a problem; it is not in itself a basic business need. Neither is the underlying need related to running the job on a specific computer or to writing programs in a given language.

- Determine the scope and depth of the problem. There are limits to the amount of processing that can be done efficiently in any program. Don't overload yourself with work. Also, don't take a chance on writing a program so big that it won't run efficiently on a small computer. For example, in processing a payroll, you probably would specify one program just to capture and list the data on employees, regular hours, and overtime hours for the week. You would prove the accuracy of the data before going on to prepare checks. Then, you would plan still other programs to meet obligations for government reports, etc. Data processing systems are made up of groups of related programs. As a programmer, you first identify the required outputs and inputs. This specification must be done before you design the program. Most of your programs will be designed to deliver individual outputs or, at most, small groups of related outputs.

- Define major program objectives. Remember that you are solving a specific problem you have identified. Each time you receive a suggestion—or originate an idea—for expanding a programming job, measure it against your objectives. You should not make major changes in the design or scope of your program when you are in the midst of program development unless you have considered carefully the impact of altering your design.

Defining results that anticipate user demands involves forming a mental picture of the environment in which the program is to be used. You must, in effect, anticipate and describe human actions before these actions occur. In doing so, you are trying to define important details that, if taken into account in the logical design of your program, will make its output useful and reliable.

SET YOUR STANDARDS

There's a standard response often used by programmers who are pressed to complete jobs under impossible deadlines: "How *bad* do you want it?" When writing programs, compromising program objectives leads in only one direction, to bad programs.

As part of the planning that goes into program design, you have to make certain decisions about the quality of the work to be delivered. This isn't to say that every program must be perfect. The same kinds of tradeoffs are found in the world of computers as in everyday life. There isn't always a need for perfection or the time to achieve perfection. Your task, instead, is to understand the need. How good is good enough? Define appropriate quality standards. Then meet those standards.

For example, one option available for input of data to a system is to key in all entries twice. One person enters the data initially. A second person reenters the same transactions. A comparison is made for all entries that do not agree. Any disagreements are resolved before data are processed. This procedure is highly accurate, but also relatively expensive.

Another approach is to key input once, in relatively small transaction batches. These data are processed by a computer to develop totals for the items entered. These totals then are compared with totals developed manually prior to input. If the two totals balance, the data are assumed to be correct. There is no item-by-item comparison unless the totals are out of balance. Thus, there is a chance that two mistakes in the same batch could cancel each other out. The accuracy of this verification method is not as great as when all entries are keyed twice. But there are many situations in which accuracy requirements are such that the less expensive method is justified.

In each system you develop, therefore, make it a routine practice to set standards for:

- *Accuracy.* Are the results mathematically or computationally correct?
- *Completeness of data and processing.* Have all input data been processed and were all intended results produced?
- *Reliability of results.* Can critical decisions be made or actions taken with confidence based on these results?

As a way of implementing these standards, you also should set a requirement for the degree of user participation in assuring accurate design criteria and input data.

PROBLEM ANALYSIS

Once the problem or need has been defined in terms of desired results, you must:

- Analyze the output requirements of the program. This requirement involves specification of the actual information items that will be produced.
- Identify which data are needed as input to the program and find sources for the data.
- Devise a logical design that specifies the processing steps that must occur to transform the input data into the required outputs.

Identifying Outputs

To make sure that your program develops results that meet the stated need or solve the identified problem, begin by preparing specific layouts of the end products to be delivered. If the result of the program will be a display on a screen, you can use an editor or word processing program to create sample outputs for review. Actually key in sample outputs to be displayed on the screen. Review the display carefully to see if these outputs do the job. If the program is being prepared for use of other persons, consult the users. Try different combinations of data displays until the user is willing to agree that one example represents the information content and format that will meet the stated need.

If the output of a program is to be a printed report, prepare typewritten samples of the proposed outputs or prepare output layout forms like the one in Figure 3-1. Again, make sure that the end product meets your needs or the needs of the program user.

Note that this process is not concerned with any physical considerations of what machines will be used to create the outputs or with the processing and control steps that will deliver the results. The only concern at this point is to identify the result that will do the job.

Identifying Inputs

Once specifications are established for outputs, the next step is to identify the data inputs required to produce those results. The necessary line of reasoning is straightforward: To determine how much money a worker earned, you need to know how many hours were worked, at what pay rate. This method of reasoning will identify needed inputs for any data processing system.

Inputs then are described logically, in terms of data content. One tool for such definition is an input layout form like the one shown in Figure 3-2.

Determining Processing Requirements

The next logical step is to define the processing that must be performed on the inputs to deliver the needed outputs. The resulting series of processing steps is an algorithm. One method for documenting an algorithm, as previously presented, is to prepare a series of stylized English statements, or pseudocode, that describes the sequence of processing steps to be followed.

There are also graphic tools available that can help you visualize the processing that your program will perform. Graphic tools can be especially valuable if you are preparing programs for users who are

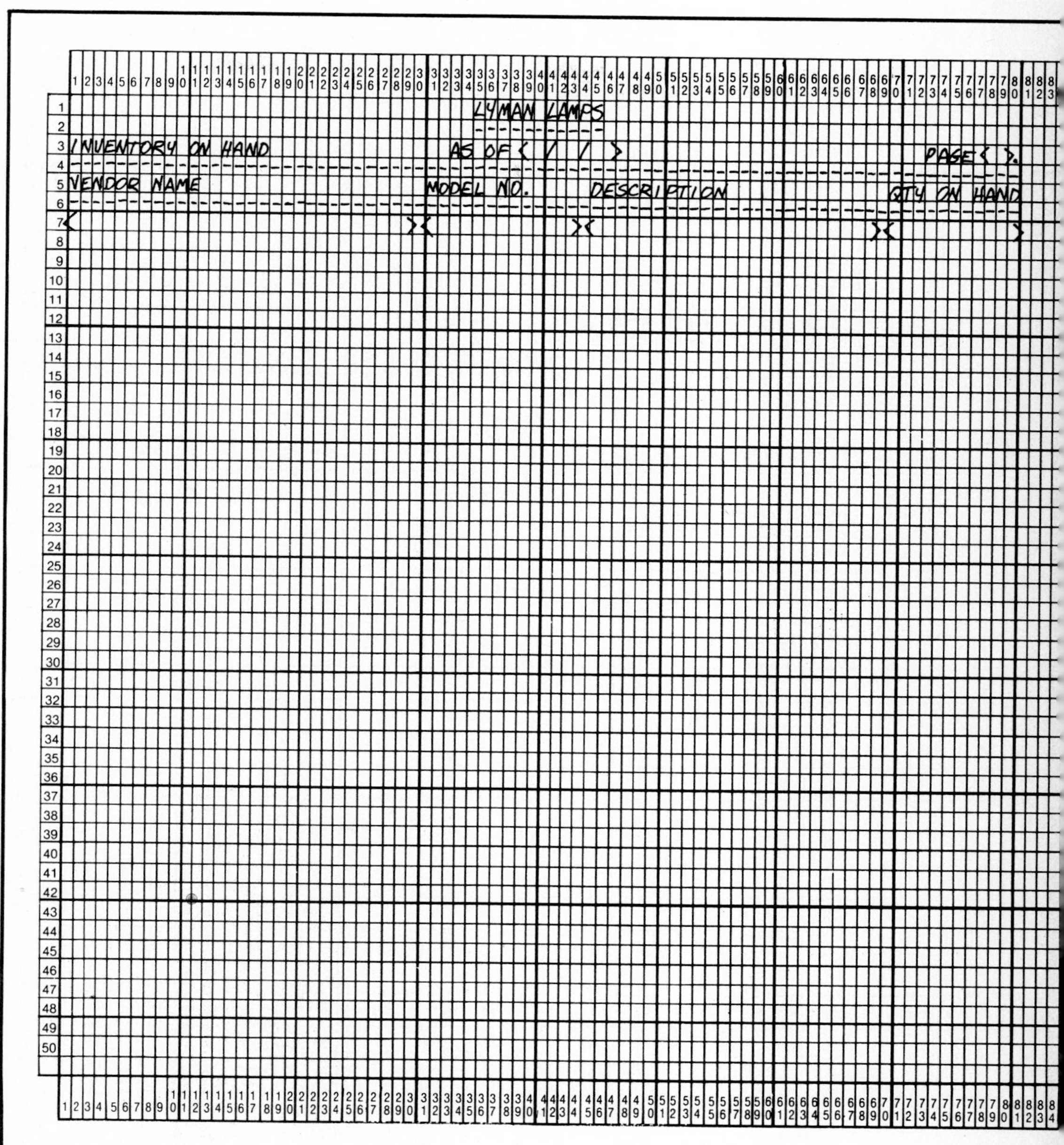

Figure 3-1. The identification and specification of outputs on an output layout form can assist in problem analysis.

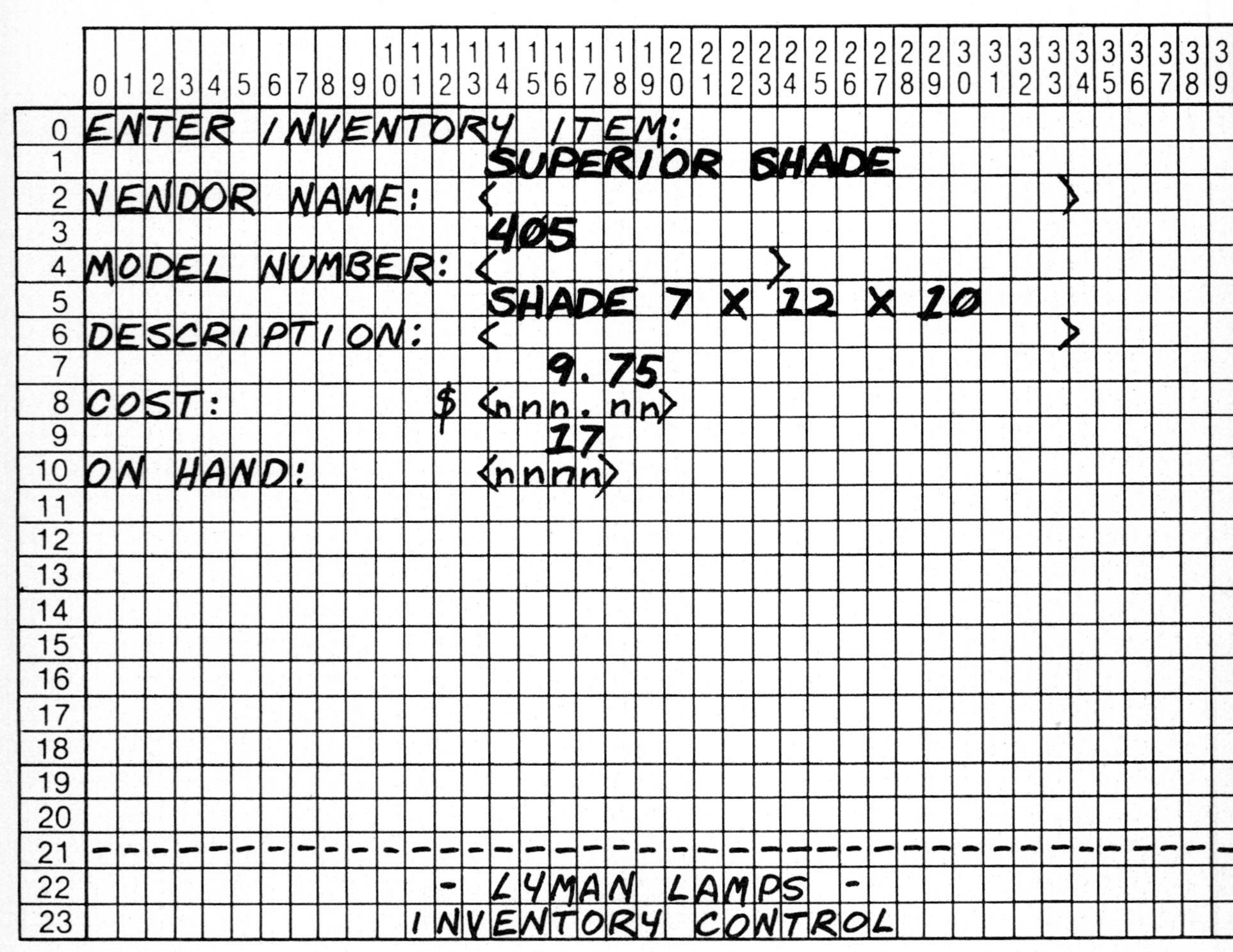

Figure 3-2. A logical description of inputs, in terms of data content, is specified by the entries on an input layout form.

relatively unfamiliar with computers and computer programs. With graphic presentations, it is possible to follow processing diagrams in much the same way as a driver follows a road map in proceeding from starting point to destination. Graphic tools used to describe processing functions and sequences include:

- Data flow diagrams
- Flowcharts.

At this point, remember that you are still designing logical solutions to identified problems. Your work is still independent of the computer hardware to be used or the language in which the actual program instructions will be written.

One method for describing a series of processing steps is a *data flow diagram* like the one shown in Figure 3-3. This diagram depicts the flow and transformation of data for a typical payroll report program. Each circle, or *bubble,* in the diagram stands for one processing step. The arrows that connect the bubbles represent the flow of data passing from one processing step to another. This technique is useful for understanding either existing procedures or proposed designs that modify those procedures.

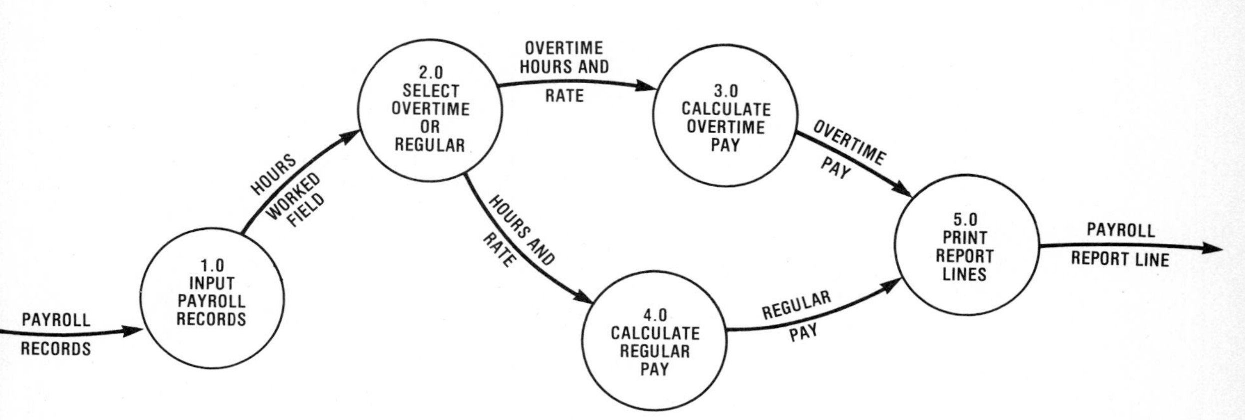

Figure 3-3. An understanding of existing procedures or proposed design changes can be gained from a data flow diagram that depicts the flow and transformation of data.

In the course of analyzing and defining the processing to be done in solving a problem, you can use data flow diagrams as a general-purpose tool. That is, you can represent existing systems using data flow diagrams. Then, you can use the same kind of diagram to represent the solution you propose for a problem. Typically, analysis follows a predictable pattern:

1. Review existing systems and procedures within which the need or problem has been identified. Use a graphic representation of physical processing functions in a data flow diagram to build both an understanding of the business situation and agreement with users on what is actually happening.

2. From the graphic representation of present physical processing, develop a data flow diagram that describes the current picture at a logical level. This second data flow diagram usually will be less complex than the initial representation of the physical system because the details of control can be disregarded. The logical diagram presents only points at which data are transformed, or altered. You are, in effect, deriving the algorithm upon which the existing system is based.

3. The logical diagram of the present system, also called a *model,* is modified as necessary to produce a logical design of data flow and processing in the proposed new system. The *logical design* consists of the program specifications that describe processing in a manner independent of physical processing. This becomes a tool for evaluating how well the new system will meet the business needs or problems it is designed to handle. The logical diagram is also used as a basis for review and ultimate agreement with system users. The diagram is simple enough so that even persons with virtually no computer background can visualize the data gathering and processing that will take place and the results that will be delivered.

4. Once the logical design has been approved, a final data flow diagram is prepared to represent the physical processing that will take place. This diagram becomes the basis for program design.

With these four analysis and design steps, the process of developing an algorithm is complete.

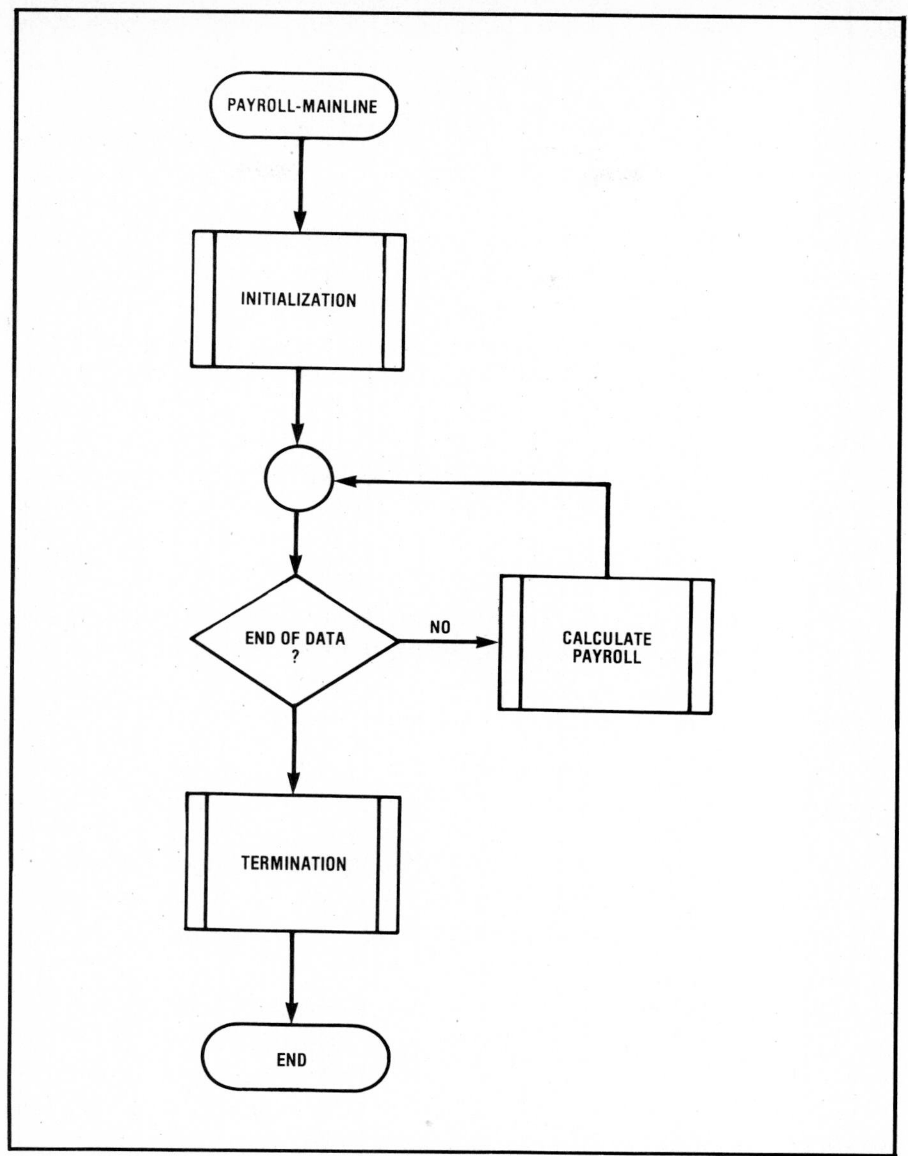

Figure 3-4. A flowchart can be used to help conceptualize the physical processing steps of a program before it is written. Flowcharts also can be used to document or analyze existing programs.

A more traditional method of documenting processing actions within a program is the *flowchart*. An example flowchart for a portion of a payroll report program is shown in Figure 3-4. Flowcharts may be used as tools to help conceptualize the physical processing steps of a program before it is written. Flowcharts also may be used to document or analyze existing systems. Flowcharts use a specialized set of symbols to represent various physical functions performed by computer hardware under program control. Processing controls also are represented in traditional flowcharts.

Standard flowchart symbols and their meanings are given in Figure 3-5. In a flowchart, actions are presented in sequence just as those actions occur in the actual program text. Because a flowchart typically reflects physical functions rather than logical functions, its use as a design tool is being replaced by other techniques such as structure charts, described below. Flowcharting remains useful, however, for documenting a program just before code is written, as a means of identifying the processing and control functions to be coded.

It should be pointed out that different logical design problems often require different analysis techniques. Bear in mind that analysis techniques such as data flow diagrams and flowcharts are not mandatory design practice but tools that may be helpful to you in evolving a workable design.

PROGRAM DESIGN

Once an underlying need or problem has been defined and a processing solution has been devised, you are ready to start design of the program that will implement the new system.

The logical starting point for understanding program design lies in an understanding and appreciation of the underlying *structure*, or logic, that is basic to all computer processing programs. There are certain processing steps that must be performed any time a computer is used to process data and deliver information. These are the steps the program must instruct a computer to follow within every program:

- Initialization
- Main processing
- Termination.

Initialization

The *initialization* portion of a program contains programming steps that must be performed before main processing can begin. In this initialization portion, variables may be cleared or assigned initial values. Files may be

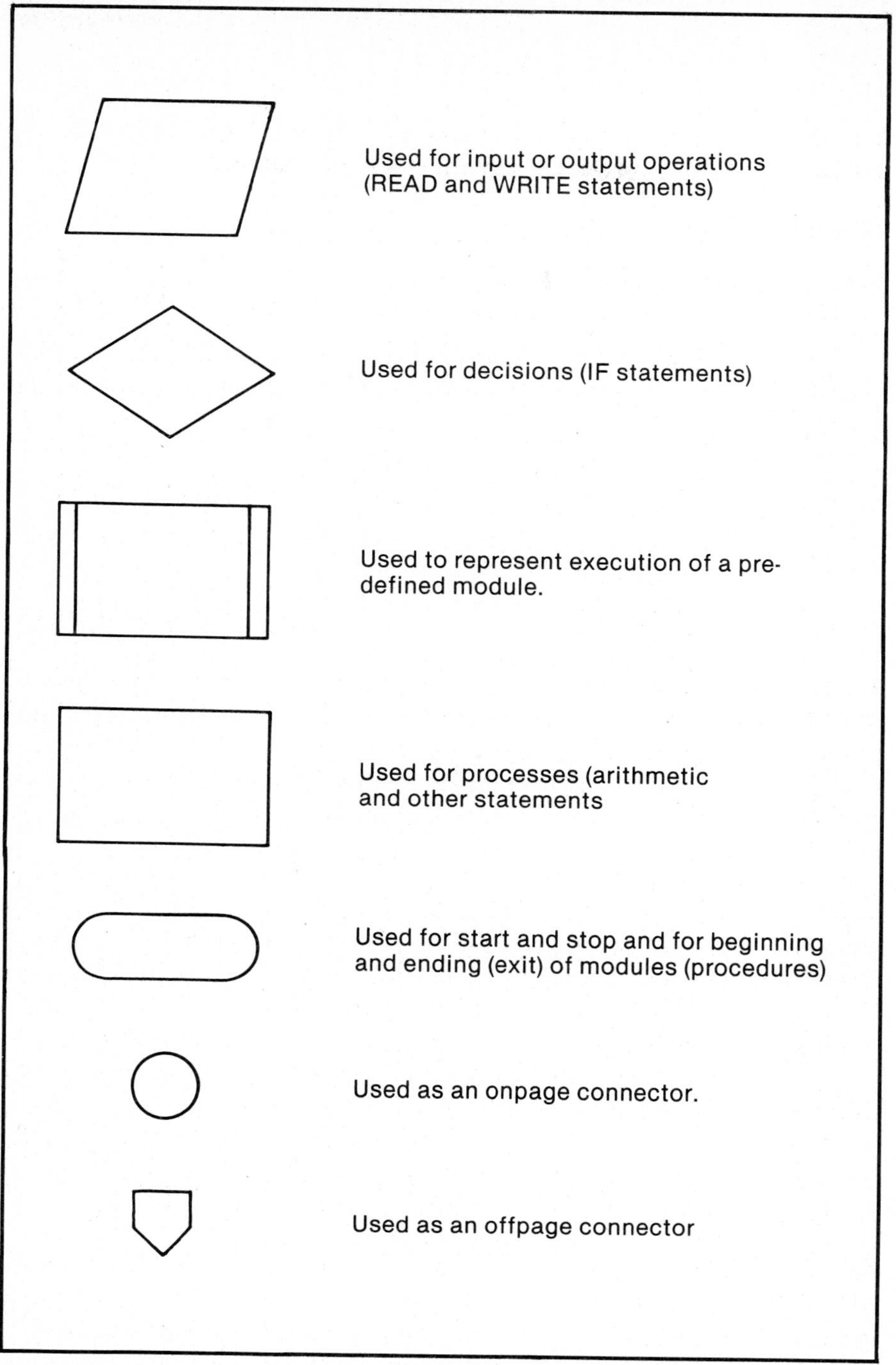

Figure 3-5. Standard symbols are used in flowcharts to document the processing steps and controls.

opened, or prepared for access; and any program-wide values, such as current date, may be solicited from the user.

Main Processing

The *main processing* segment performs most of the work. This processing phase implements the algorithm upon which the program is based.

There are limitations, or constraints, upon the kinds of processing that can be done. Only three basic kinds of processing *control structures* are needed in programs to do any possible job:

- Sequence
- Selection
- Repetition.

All structured programs are based on this set of control structures.

Sequence. A processing *sequence* is a series of steps that are followed from beginning to end. A sequence is run one time with each execution of the program. No variations or choices of direction are introduced. For example, in the *Adder* program, the main processing sequence causes the adding of two numbers and the display of the sum. This sequence, and only this sequence, is followed each time the program is run.

Selection. In *selection,* a program can cause the computer to make a choice, or *decision,* on the basis of the content of data being processed. Depending on some *condition* identified by a comparison, the program can cause the computer to follow alternate courses of processing. Consider a payroll program. The program will have to choose alternate courses, or *branches,* for persons who receive regular pay only and for those who are entitled to overtime pay. The program applies a condition test to the data processed. The overtime processing branch is followed only for those workers whose total hours worked are greater than 40 in any given week.

Repetition. A *repetition,* also known as an *iteration,* causes the computer to repeat a given processing sequence until some condition is reached that causes the program to do otherwise. Because the computer keeps repeating the same sequence of instructions, this is also known as a processing *loop.* The computer ends a processing loop and goes on to other instructions on the basis of condition tests that are contained within the instructions for the loop. That is, each time a loop is run, the computer tests for a given condition. When that condition is met, processing moves to the next identified instruction in the program following the loop. For example, the last data record to be entered in a payroll might have an *end-of-file* indicator (physical identifier). When the end-of-file indicator is encountered by a condition test, the program leaves the main processing loop and proceeds to the termination segment.

Termination

Termination is the segment that closes down the program run. Producing processing summaries and creating system backup files are among the steps that may be performed during termination. The termination portion occurs once for each program run.

TOP-DOWN DESIGN

The arrangement, or ordering, of *modules,* or processing tasks, to be executed is known as *program structure.* A tool for representing the structure of a program graphically is a *structure chart* like the one shown in Figure 3-6. In this structure chart, one rectangle represents each module in a typical payroll program. Note that the chart is organized into a series of horizontal lines, or *levels.* Each level represents a further detailing of the processing to be done as an addition to the end items of the level above.

Tools like structure charts are used to design the relationships among program modules. To restate the definition, a module is an individual processing task. Because problem analysis and design begin at the top, or most general levels on the chart, and proceed to lower, more detailed, levels, such methods are referred to as *top-down design.* Each of the vertical segments of a structure chart—the full sets of modules for initialization, main processing, and termination—is called a *leg* of the structure chart.

To design a structure chart or to follow the sequence of a chart you are reading, work your way from left to right on succeeding levels. The top level always has one rectangle that identifies the program, giving its name. The second level has at least three rectangles for the major sections of the program. (Occasionally, there may be more than one processing leg in a structure chart.) These levels are read from left to right to follow the sequence of module execution. At succeeding levels, the

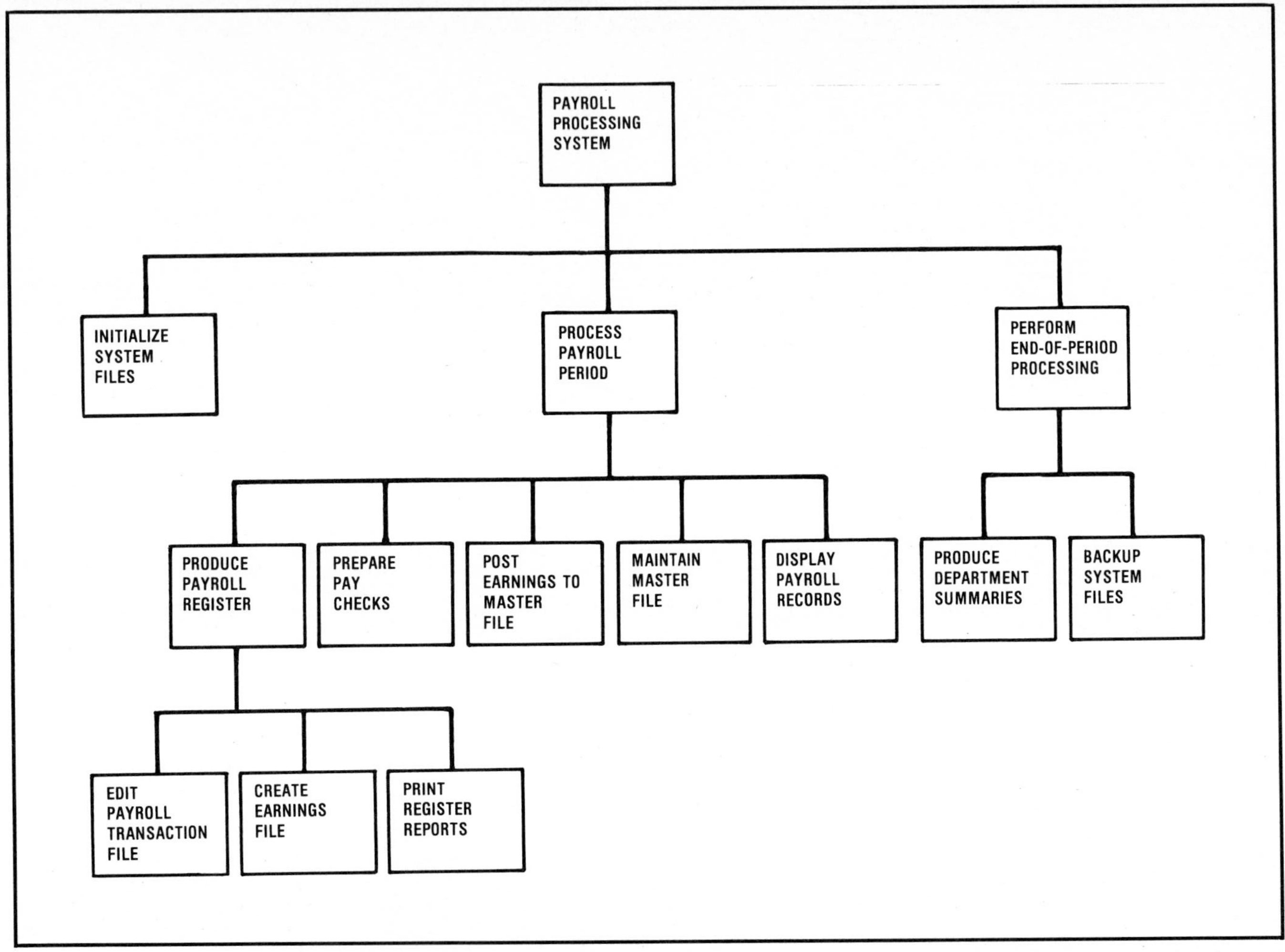

Figure 3-6. A structure chart documents the hierarchical relationships among program tasks, or modules.

three main parts of the program are expanded. Again, the processing sequence is from left to right. Note that the rectangles in the chart are numbered in sequence according to this top-down, left-to-right pattern. Modules of a structure chart should be identified to correspond with the execution sequence.

The structure chart that represents a program also can be called a *hierarchy* chart. This means that a structure is established under which the parts, or *partitions,* of a job are related to each other in a logical sequence. Accordingly, *hierarchical design* is another name for top-down design.

The structured approach can be likened to a series of related work assignments in an organization. The program itself represents an overall job. The succeeding levels of modules, then, are the tasks and subtasks to be performed in completing the overall job. In this respect, the hierarchical organization of a program resembles the organization chart of a company. To illustrate, note the similarity between the structure chart in Figure 3-6 and the organization chart in Figure 3-7. Both graphic diagrams use a top-down approach. Both are organized into levels. At each level, the tasks performed supplement the responsibilities and functions for the level above.

DEFINING PROGRAM STEPS

Think back to the wall-painting example in Chapter 2. If this algorithm were to be represented by a structure chart, following one branch of the problem definition from the top down, more specific descriptions would be needed at each level:

- OVERALL PROGRAM GOAL: Paint a wall.
- EXPECTED RESULTS: Apply a single coat of paint uniformly over a wall.
- TASK: Purchase the paint.
- SUBTASK: Read the label on the paint can in the store and determine whether oil-base or latex paint is required.

In this example, the larger task, "Purchase the paint," requires many other subtasks besides "Read the label." These would include "Drive to the store," "Carry the paint to the counter," "Pay for the paint," etc. The description of tasks and subtasks in top-down design ends when all

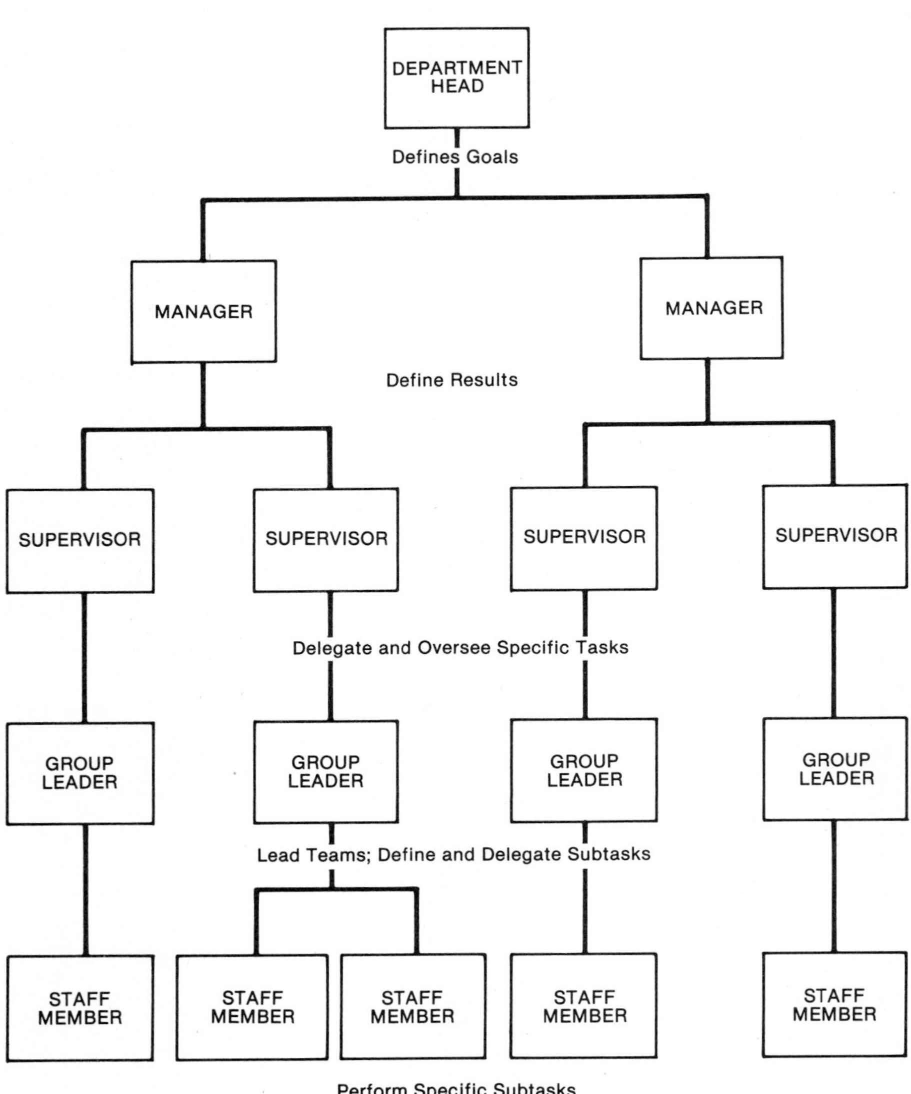

Figure 3-7. The organization chart of a business reflects the hierarchy and delegation of authority and tasks within the business.

actions required to achieve the intended results have been specified. Where, then, does this level of description end where computers are concerned?

Providing rules for the level of description required in a computer program is one of the characteristics of a structured programming language like Pascal. Whereas top-down design is a way of describing the tasks necessary to solve a problem, structured programming languages implement logical designs by providing for the physical implementation of individual tasks. While structured programming is not the same as top-down design, it implements the principles of top-down design by the structures, or the programming rules, that it imposes on the program text.

PSEUDOCODING

The form of the structure chart—which is well suited for use with top-down design—simplifies the programming task by making a particular logical design a special case of a single, generalized model. Individual program modules, or tasks, then may be described in pseudocode. Pseudocoding may be thought of as a series of English statements or phrases that describe a given logical design. Figure 3-8 shows how the structure chart for a payroll report program can be used to form the sequence and structure of pseudocode. Notice now the usefulness of the numeric indexes on the chart, which serve as labels for each pseudocoded statement and, by numerical relationship, preserve the hierarchy of the design.

There are no formal rules for writing pseudocode. Basically, pseudocode may be thought of as a series of statements employing active verbs that resemble commands used in programming. A logical design written in pseudocode should be understandable by any nonprogrammer. As stated earlier, a logical design exists independently of the computer's physical functions or the programming language to be used. Pseudocode serves to develop fully the concepts and structure of the program before it is translated into the instructions of a particular programming language. As described earlier, a programming language serves only to bridge the gap between the logical design of a program and the particular physical functions that are to be performed by a specific computer system.

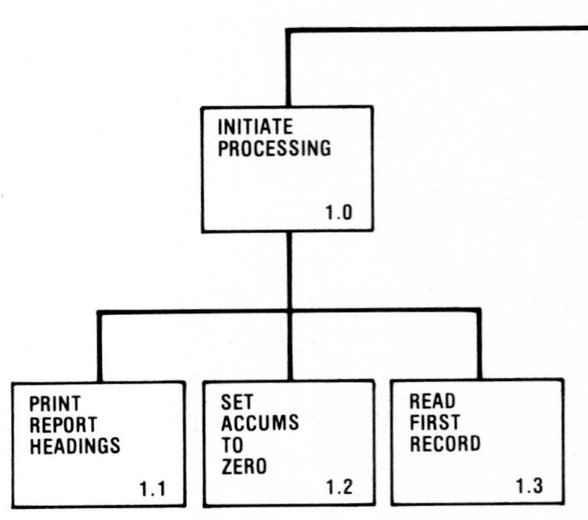

0.0 PRODUCE PAYROLL REPORT

1.0 INITIATE PROCESSING

1.1 PRINT REPORT HEADINGS
Print main heading line
Print blank line
Print column heading line 1
Print column heading line 2
Print blank line

1.2 SET ACCUMS TO ZERO
Set Total Regular Pay = 0
Set Total Overtime Pay = 0
Set Total Gross Pay = 0
Set Total Employees = 0

1.3 READ FIRST RECORD
Read Employee Number, Employee Name,
Pay Rate, Total Hours

2.0 MAIN PROCESSING
REPEAT: until end of payroll file

2.1 DETERMINE HOURS WORKED
SELECT: on Total Hours comp. to 35

2.1.1 DETERMINE HOURS FOR OVERTIME
Set Regular Hours = 35
Set Overtime Hours = Total Hours – 35

2.1.2 DETERMINE HOURS FOR NO OVERTIME
Set Regular Hours = Total Hours
Set Overtime Hours = 0

END SELECT

2.2 COMPUTE PAY AMOUNTS
Compute Regular Pay = Pay Rate * Regular Hours
Compute Overtime Pay = Pay Rate * Overtime
Hours * 1.5
Compute Gross Pay = Regular Pay + Overtime Pay

2.3 ACCUMULATE TOTALS
Add Regular Pay to Total Regular Pay
Add Overtime Pay to Total Overtime Pay
Add Gross Pay to Total Gross Pay
Add 1 to Total Employees

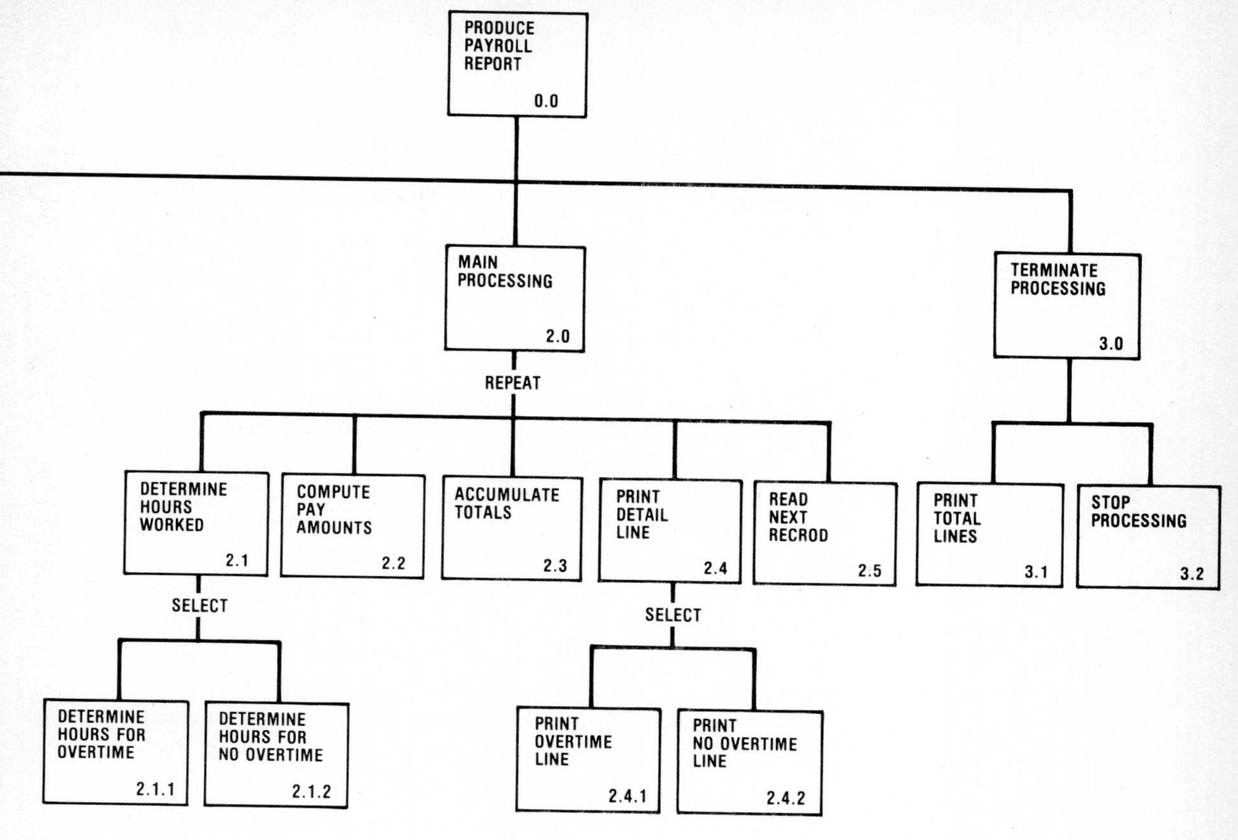

2.4 PRINT DETAIL LINE

SELECT: on Overtime Pay comp. to 0

2.4.1 PRINT OVERTIME LINE

Print Employee Name, Regular Pay, Overtime Pay, Gross Pay

2.4.2 PRINT NO OVERTIME LINE

Print Employee Name, Regular Pay, Gross Pay

END SELECT

2.5 READ NEXT RECORD

Read Employee Number, Employee Name, Pay Rate, Total Hours

END REPEAT

3.0 TERMINATE PROCESSING

3.1 PRINT TOTAL LINES

Print blank line

Print Total Regular Pay, Total Overtime Pay, Total Gross Pay

Print blank line

Print Total Employees

3.2 STOP PROCESSING

Stop

Figure 3-8. The tasks identified by a structure chart may be described in pseudocode.

PLANNING FOR QUALITY: VERIFICATION OF RESULTS

Before you begin to write any program, you should also have a good idea of how its results will be verified. Earlier in this chapter, it is pointed out that you must anticipate ways of assuring the accuracy, the completeness, and the reliability of your program results. Of course, inherent in your statement of the goal of the program is some sense of what will constitute an acceptable result. So, a close examination of your original specifications for the program goal is an obvious starting place. Beyond this, however, you should plan ahead for some more independent means of verifying that your program will do its job.

One way of verifying a logical design is to work your way through the pseudocoded processing steps manually with a sample of the data to be input to the program. You perform each step manually, tracking the data flow on paper. Particular attention should be given to the value of each data item as it is transformed at each processing step. This technique of verifying a logical design is called a *manual stepthrough* or *walkthrough,* or simply "playing computer." A variation of this technique is the *structured walkthrough.* This type of walkthrough is done with two programmers. One of the participants in a structured walkthrough should be uninvolved in development of the program. This person then can review the design objectively, providing constructive challenges and criticisms as necessary to improve quality.

Mechanisms should also be designed in advance to verify the quality and correctness of results produced by the program. Remember, quality of any given program lies in the accuracy, completeness, and reliability of results. One way the programmer assures quality is by developing test data and the corresponding output results to be delivered when the test data are processed. Quality assurance, then, consists of comparing the results produced by the program with the outputs developed in advance for the test data.

The test data for any given program should cause all of the modules to be applied. That is, if there are condition tests within the program, data items should be included that cause the program to follow all selection branches. Also, input procedures should be tested by including incomplete or incorrect data items in the test data. The idea is to make sure that the program recognizes and deals properly with both acceptable and unacceptable inputs.

PROGRAM *Adder* BECOMES *AddingMachine*

Another look at the *Adder* program developed in Chapter 2 will reveal that it was written before its goal had been defined clearly.

The original problem stated for *Adder* seemed simple—to add two numbers together. This was the problem as your friend originally stated it (the perceived need). However, once he has run *Adder,* he phrases his problem differently. He now says, "Although I said that I wanted to be able to add two numbers together, I should also have told you that I want to do this because I'd like to use my home computer as an adding machine." Reexamining the algorithm for *Adder* shown in Figure 2-4, it is obvious that it falls short of performing the way an adding machine does. *Adder* works fine as long as your friend has only two numbers to enter. To perform like an adding machine, however, the program would have to provide for entry of a whole column of numbers. Ideally, it should display a running total after each new entry. A programmer who rushes headlong into writing code at this point might try to replicate the program instructions in *Adder* a large number of times in anticipation of the longest column of numbers the user is likely to have. This solution would be tedious, to say the least. Look again at a simplified version of the algorithm for *Adder* in Figure 3-9.

You must now devise a new algorithm for a program called *AddingMachine* that allows for input of a column of numbers. You would have a working algorithm if you could get the program to *repeat* the *Adder* steps again and again *until* some specified condition is met. The revised algorithm might look something like the one shown in Figure 3-10.

Pascal offers several ways of repeating a block of steps. One of these uses two reserved words named, appropriately enough, **REPEAT** and **UNTIL**. These terms define the boundaries of a program block that will

ALGORITHM FOR PROGRAM *Adder*

Get a number.
Get another number.
Add the two together.
Display the result.

Figure 3-9. An algorithm for *Adder*.

REVISED ALGORITHM FOR PROGRAM *AddingMachine*

Get a number.
Repeat the following steps over and over again.
Get another number.
Add the two together.
Display the result.
Do this *until* the user requests a stop.

Figure 3-10. Revised version of *Adder* algorithm, showing a repetition of steps that will continue until a stop is requested by the user.

be repeated until a specific condition is met. REPEAT and UNTIL are used within the body of a Pascal text file just as you see their English language counterparts used in the above example. REPEAT is used at the beginning of the program block to indicate that what follows are the steps to be repeated. UNTIL appears after the last line of the program block to be repeated and contains within it the condition that must be met before the program can proceed to the next program block. Notice that the REPEAT . . UNTIL structure always causes execution of its programming steps at least once, since the *termination condition* is not encountered until after the program statements. The use of REPEAT and UNTIL is one example of program looping. Looping is a kind of control structure, a repetition, offered by the REPEAT and UNTIL commands. Control structures are another instance of the way Pascal provides a structured language to assist in program design.

Designing *AddingMachine*

A structure chart for the revised program *AddingMachine* is shown in Figure 3-11. Recalling the original algorithm for *Adder,* there are two variable names for program inputs, FirstNumber and SecondNumber. Looking now at the new input requirements for *AddingMachine,* it is apparent that the number of entries on any particular run cannot be determined. Further, repetition of the main processing portion of the program must be done to cause subsequent entries to be added repeatedly to a running total. Accordingly, the variables that represent the required data inputs can be reduced to two: NewNumber, for the new data entry,

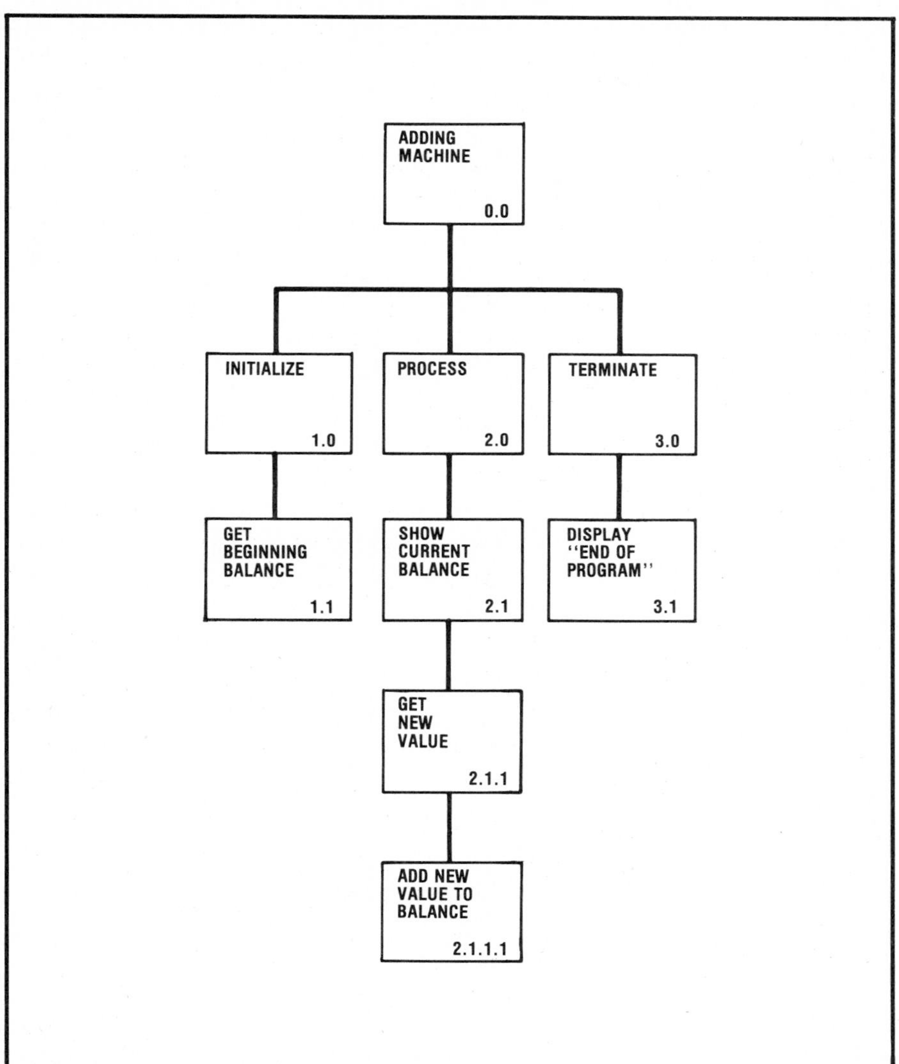

Figure 3-11. Structure chart for *AddingMachine*.

---

and Balance, for the current value of the running total. A value for NewNumber will be added to the existing value for Balance, resulting in an updated value for Balance. There is no need to store previous values for Balance, since a running total is all that is required.

Now, referring to Figure 3-12, pseudocoded statements can be written for *AddingMachine* by referring to the structure chart in Figure 3-11.

Notice that a condition has been set that will terminate the program loop set up by REPEAT and UNTIL. In this case, entering a 0 will cause the program to end. It is very important that some condition be specified to terminate a loop; otherwise the program would be caught in an *infinite*

0.0 ADDING MACHINE
Program name is *AddingMachine*.
Variables will be Balance, and NewNumber, both Integers.

1.0 INITIALIZATION
Begin main body of program.

1.1 GET BEGINNING BALANCE
Ask user to input a beginning value for Balance.
Get the value for Balance.

2.0 MAIN PROCESSING
REPEAT
Repeat the following steps:

2.1 SHOW CURRENT BALANCE
Display the value for Balance.

2.1.1 GET NEW VALUE
Ask user for a value for NewNumber.
Get the value for NewNumber.

2.1.1.1 ADD NEW VALUE TO BALANCE
Add NewNumber to Balance.
Until user inputs a 0 (Test to see if NewNumber=0)
(If not, repeat above steps.)

3.0 TERMINATION

3.1 DISPLAY ''END OF PROGRAM''
Announce the end of the program.

End.

Figure 3-12. Using the structure chart in Figure 3-11, pseudocode can be written to describe the processing steps for *AddingMachine*.

loop that would repeat endlessly. The possibility of an infinite loop seems rather easy to avoid here; however, errors in coding program text sometimes can result in an unwanted infinite loop. This usually happens because whatever condition is set for the termination of the loop is never encountered during processing. This is one example of a potential logical error that cannot be detected by the compiler and may or may not be detected by executing test data.

Coding *AddingMachine*

The above pseudocode now can be translated into formal Pascal program text. Figure 3-13 shows the resulting text, with comment lines that describe processing actions.

Most of the coding terminology used in *AddingMachine* already has been presented. There are, however, some details that are new. A section following the PROGRAM header is designated VAR, referring to the

```
(*************************************************************************)
(*     This program called AddingMachine will first ask the user for a    *)
(*     beginning balance, and will then ask for numbers to be added to    *)
(*     this balance.  After each new number, the balance is displayed.    *)
(*     When the user enters zero as a new number, the program will stop.  *)
(*************************************************************************)


PROGRAM AddingMachine;                        (* program name is AddingMachine *)

VAR
 Balance,                                    (* declare VARiables for the program *)
 NewNumber:INTEGER;                              (* these two are INTEGER types *)

BEGIN                                          (* begin programming instructions *)
 WRITE('ENTER BEGINNING BALANCE ');                 (* tell user to enter balance *)
 READLN(Balance);                            (* get value from user, await RETURN *)
  REPEAT                                       (* repeat the following; see UNTIL *)
   WRITELN('THE BALANCE IS ',Balance);       (* show balance, start new line *)
   WRITE('ENTER NEW NUMBER, OR ZERO TO END ');          (* ask for new number *)
   READLN(NewNumber);                        (* get value from user, await RETURN *)
   Balance := Balance + NewNumber;                  (* add new number to balance *)
  UNTIL NewNumber = 0;                            (* test to see if entry is zero *)
                                                   (* if not, go back to REPEAT *)
 WRITELN('END OF PROGRAM');                         (* announce end of program *)
END.                                                   (* end of program coding *)
```

Figure 3-13. Program *AddingMachine*, derived from pseudocode.

variable declaration section. The format of the variable declarations might be expected to be:

```
VAR
 Balance:INTEGER;
 NewNumber:INTEGER;
```

Instead, the text appears as:

```
VAR
 Balance,
 NewNumber:INTEGER;
```

This second form is simply a "shorthand" that is allowed in Pascal. Whenever two or more variables are of the same type, those variables may be separated by commas, with the type definition following the last variable name. For example:

```
VAR
 AccountNumber, Balance, Charges, Due: INTEGER;
```

For the sake of clarity, the above also may be written as:

```
VAR
 AccountNumber,
 Balance,
 Charges,
 Due: INTEGER;
```

The choice of format may relate to how easily it accommodates later changes. A suggested style for large programs might be to list variable names alphabetically, one per line. Note that using the shorter forms given above does make later insertions and deletions to the source code more difficult. Another technique is to group variables with similar purposes together, such as:

```
VAR
 LinesPerPage,
 PageNumber: INTEGER;
 FirstNumber,
 Balance: INTEGER;
```

AddingMachine asks the user to input a beginning balance before the program will continue. Requiring the user to enter Balance and NewNumber explicitly before any processing occurs has the effect of *initializing* these variables, clearing any prior values that may be stored there and substituting the values given by the user.

Failing to initialize the values of variables in your program before they are used in processing is another example of a common logical error. If a value is not assigned explicitly to a variable by an input statement, for example, it often is necessary to initialize that variable explicitly, usually by assigning it a value of 0, as in:

```
CounterValue := 0;
```

Note that READLN is used in the program rather than READ when requesting the Balance entry from the user. READLN has the effect of accepting all input until a <RETURN> is entered (by pressing the key on the keyboard labeled RET or RETURN).

A *prompt* for the user is included in the second WRITE statement to indicate what action can be used to end the program. Informing the user what options are available at various points in the program is another feature of good program design.

Like the BEGIN statement, the REPEAT statement is not followed by a semicolon (;), because it introduces a program block; only a space or a new line separates it from the statements that follow. However, UNTIL is followed by a condition that is used to terminate the program loop, thus ending the REPEAT .. UNTIL statement:

```
UNTIL Newnumber = 0;
```

Accordingly, a semicolon is required after the line.

Both uses of the equal sign (:= and =) are made in *AddingMachine.* The := symbol is used for assignment of value to perform the addition of NewNumber to Balance. The = by itself is used to perform a test in the UNTIL statement to see if the user has entered a 0 for NewNumber, indicating a desire to terminate the program.

Summary

The logic, or series of processing functions, used to transform data exists independently of any physical means of processing. Program specifications must be prepared before quality programs can be written. Program specifications involve identifying the underlying problem, determining the scope and depth of the problem, and determining major program objectives.

Defining results involves forming a mental picture of the environment in which the program will be used. In designing a program, you must set standards for the quality of the results the program will produce. Make it a routine practice to set standards for accuracy, completeness, and reliability.

Problem analysis involves analyzing output requirements, identifying input needed and its source, and devising a logical design that specifies the processing steps that must occur to transform the input data into the required outputs. Data flow analysis and flowcharting are two techniques used to understand processing steps within a system.

Program design first breaks the overall processing task into three basic phases: initialization, main processing, and termination. This is the basic structure of most programs. Main processing is a collection of structures that can include sequence, selection, and repetition. This set of control structures typifies structured programs.

Program modules may be shown graphically in a structure chart. Each module is given an index number. The structure chart shows the hierarchy of modules. The order of processing is shown by reading the chart from the top downward and from left to right.

Program design may be refined further by top-down design. Top-down design is a hierarchical partitioning of a problem into individually solvable tasks. Structured programming languages enforce the structure inherent in top-down design by providing for the physical implementation of individual tasks.

Pseudocode may be written for each module in the structure chart. Pseudocode may be thought of as a series of English statements that describe a given logical design.

Verification of results from a program design may be accomplished by some form of walkthrough. As part of the design process, test data should be prepared. These data provide for the application of all modules in the design. Expected outputs are developed for the test data and the program results are compared with the expected result. This is a quality assurance step.

A Pascal structure that implements repetition is provided by REPEAT and UNTIL. All such program loops require conditions to be set that cause the eventual termination of the loop.

Variables in the VAR section may be separated by commas if all those variables are of the same data type. A colon separates the last variable name in the list from the type declaration.

Review Questions

1. Why is a clearly stated definition of the problem essential to good program design?
2. What is the difference between an underlying need and a perceived need?
3. What criteria should be used in setting standards for your program results?
4. What processing steps are common to most programs and what does each accomplish?
5. How is the sequence of the main processing portion of a program determined?
6. How do data flow diagrams assist in gaining an understanding of a system?
7. How do data flow diagrams differ from traditional flowcharts, and what are the typical uses of each?
8. Explain how the logical design of a program differs from physical functions or programming languages.
9. How does top-down design resemble the delegation of authority in an organization?
10. How do structure charts relate to a top-down design approach?
11. What is the relationship between the structure of a problem and a structured programming language?
12. What are some verification procedures that may be incorporated into a program design?
13. How does the concept of a program loop relate to program control structures?
14. What is the use of the condition within a REPEAT . . UNTIL loop, and why is it necessary?
15. What variations are allowed in the form of the VAR declaration?

Pascal Practice

1. Write a narrative describing the processing flow depicted in the data flow diagram presented in Figure 3-3.
2. Write a narrative describing the processing controls depicted in the flowchart presented in Figure 3-4.
3. Explain the differences between the above graphic representations as they relate specifically to logical design.
4. Modify *AddingMachine* so that it performs the following processing:

```
Balance := Balance + (Balance DIV 10) - NewNumber;
```

This series of operations implements a classic loan payment problem. Describe the algorithm that is being implemented. What processing action is caused by DIV?

Key Terms

1. program specification
2. accuracy
3. completeness
4. reliability
5. data flow diagram
6. bubble
7. model
8. logical design
9. flowchart
10. structure
11. initialization
12. main processing
13. control structure
14. sequence
15. selection
16. decision
17. condition
18. branch
19. repetition
20. iteration
21. loop
22. end-of-file
23. termination
24. module
25. program structure
26. structure chart
27. level
28. top-down design
29. leg
30. hierarchy
31. partition
32. hierarchical design
33. manual stepthrough
34. walkthrough
35. structured walkthrough
36. termination condition
37. infinite loop
38. initializing the variable
39. prompt

Pascal Library

1. REPEAT
2. UNTIL

4
ORGANIZING YOUR PROGRAMS

OBJECTIVES

On completing the reading and other learning assignments in this chapter, you should be able to:

- ☐ Define and use the Pascal structure PROCEDURE and describe its relationship to block structure and to program tasks, or modules.
- ☐ Describe how the block structure of Pascal helps implement the tasks described by top-down design and tell what advantages block structure offers the programmer.
- ☐ Describe what is meant by nested block structure.
- ☐ Explain how the scope of identifiers is related to block structure, resulting in distinctions between local and global data.
- ☐ Explain the use of parameters by procedures.
- ☐ Define and use the Pascal structure FUNCTION and describe how parameters are used within functions.
- ☐ Apply rules that must be adhered to in passing arguments to procedures or functions.
- ☐ Demonstrate how mathematical equations are translated into Pascal program text.
- ☐ Correctly use the Pascal terms CONST and TYPE and give the form of PROCEDURE/FUNCTION declarations.

PROCEDURES AND BLOCK STRUCTURE

Recall that one of the characteristics of Pascal is its use of block structure. One way to recognize a program block is to look for a group of program statements set off from the rest of the program by BEGIN and END. BEGIN and END are *block delimiters* that define the *logical boundaries* of a program block. A program block also may be referred to as a *compound statement* because it contains a group of program statements that are treated logically as if they were a single statement.

One of the structuring techniques provided within Pascal is that it allows you to assign names to program blocks. One way that a block of program statements may be given a name is through the use of the reserved word **PROCEDURE**. A procedure provides a means for naming and reusing the statements in a program block without having to code those statements all over again. For example, when writing a Pascal program in source code, you may want to make use of a block of program instructions that is identical to one you've written before. To do this, you may refer to the desired procedure by name rather than by rewriting its instructions. (Procedure names are unique names for blocks of instructions, just as variable names are unique names for variables within a program.)

The program *SayHi* in Chapter 1 may be rewritten as a procedure as follows:

```
PROCEDURE SayHi;
VAR
 PersonsName: STRING;
BEGIN
 WRITELN('WHAT IS YOUR NAME?');
 READLN(PersonsName);
 WRITELN('HI ',PersonsName);
END;
```

Variables used within any procedure (in this case, the variable PersonsName) must be declared—that is, defined and typed—before being encountered in program statements in the procedure. The above example is not a program; there is no PROGRAM header and END is not followed by a period.

The procedure SayHi represents a module that may be included within a larger program. Further, a larger Pascal program is really a series of modules, or blocks. Notice that the block in the above illustration has three main sections, just as a program does:

> *Header section.* The block is named by the statement PROCEDURE SayHi;.
>
> *Definition and declaration section.* In this case, a variable is declared to hold a string of characters for the user's name.
>
> *Program statements.* These are processing instructions that are bounded by the delimiters BEGIN and END.

The structure of a procedure block is the same as the structure of the program in general, except that the first line is a PROCEDURE declaration statement. Also, the final END reserved word of a procedure is followed by a semicolon rather than a period.

The basic structure of a procedure is illustrated in Figure 4-1.

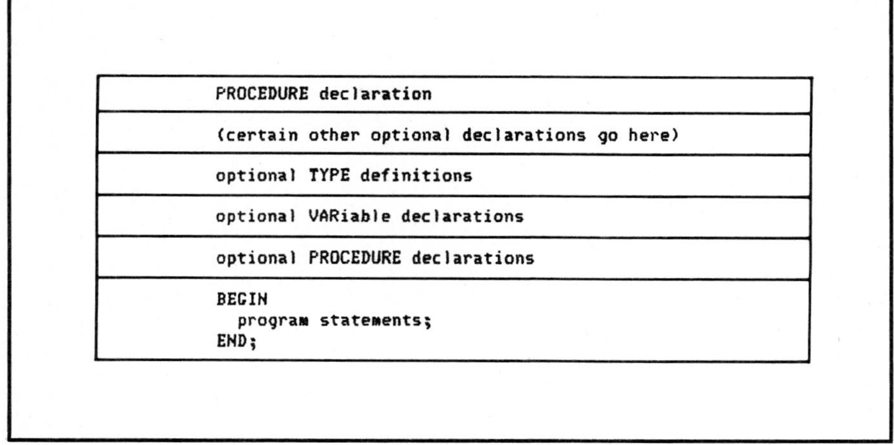

PROCEDURE declaration
(certain other optional declarations go here)
optional TYPE definitions
optional VARiable declarations
optional PROCEDURE declarations
BEGIN
program statements;
END;

Figure 4-1. The structure of a PROCEDURE in Pascal.

Note that the structure of a procedure is identical to that of the larger program with two important differences: The header uses the reserved word PROCEDURE, rather than PROGRAM, and the END delimiter is followed by a semicolon rather than a period. Remember that only the final END in the program is followed by a period.

Should you wish to cause SayHi's program instructions to be executed anywhere within the same program after the procedure has been declared, you need only code:

```
SayHi;
```

The appearance of the above statement causes the program code previously defined for SayHi to be executed. This is referred to as *calling* the procedure. A *procedure declaration* appears before the main program statements. Unless the compiler already has encountered the procedure name and its program statements, it will not have any point of reference when you try to call the procedure. Also, a procedure may, in turn, contain other procedures.

The careful naming of procedures has a practical advantage: Descriptive procedure names help make your program self-documenting and readable. The name of a procedure should describe the task that it performs. Remember, although these names may be of any length, the first eight characters of the name uniquely identify that procedure. For example, the names GetFirstName and GetFirstNumber will be treated as the same name, since the first eight characters, GetFirst, are the same. Further, this rule holds true for all identifiers coined by the programmer in Pascal.

Tasks and Procedures

Returning again to the concept of tasks in top-down design, notice that a procedure, a kind of program structure, is also a way of providing a name for a series of programming steps that accomplish a specific task. This is actually a fundamental way the structured programming language Pascal reinforces the principles of top-down design: For every task defined in the top-down design process, a procedure can be written using Pascal program structure. If you can reduce your problem definition to a series of specific tasks, or modules, you also have outlined the main procedures that must be written within your program. To restate the top-down approach:

- The overall program objective, or desired result, is broken down into specific tasks, or actions.
- Each task is broken down into a series of smaller subtasks.
- Subtasks are broken down further into more detailed subtasks until each action required is described completely.
- Each task and subtask is assigned to an individual program block, or module, to be coded as program text.

Advantages of Coding with Block Structure

A top-down design assists the programmer in writing code of both technical and functional quality. A block-structured program can provide a very effective implementation of a top-down design. The first and most significant advantage of block-structured code is that it reinforces the coherent, orderly development of top-down task descriptions. The actual coding of program text is the final step in proceeding from a general description of the desired outcome to specific instructions for the individual tasks required to perform the desired processing. Other advantages of block-structured code are:

- Coding the program as a series of discrete, self-contained tasks makes changes in design easier to implement. Precisely because each task, or program block, is self-contained, changes within a module have a minimum impact on other blocks in the program.
- Each block, or module, in the program is easier to test and debug—also because each task is self-contained. This is true at every level of program development, from stepping through a proposed algorithm to isolating program bugs in individual blocks of source code. Because the result of each task has been defined explicitly, it is possible to measure, in specific terms, how well each task is performed by its corresponding program block. Debugging can be the most costly and time-consuming phase of program development. By far the most complex aspect of debugging is tracking down logical errors. By the

discipline it imposes on program design, a top-down technique helps to prevent logical errors. Should processing errors occur, a block-structured program makes such errors easier to isolate and correct. For example, Pascal reports run-time errors by identifying the procedure number in which the error is encountered, thus isolating the block that needs attention.

- Focusing on program design at the task level and then coding each task as a program block lessens what might be called "logical myopia"—losing track of the goal of the program. Coding a computer program is a highly detailed activity, and it is all too easy to lose sight of the overall task of the program in working through its technicalities.

As described earlier, use of the reserved term PROCEDURE is one way of naming program blocks in Pascal. Every time the name of a previously defined procedure appears in a Pascal program, the program statements set forth in that procedure will be executed. The program block in which the procedure name reappears is known as the *calling block*, because it calls a procedure, or other subprogram, from another block of the program.

Procedures, because they represent individual program tasks, are inherently modular. That is, they may be reused again and again throughout a program, or they may be incorporated into other programs that require the performance of similar tasks. For example, if you were to develop a procedure for printing data in columnar format, it could have uses in several applications and programs with little reworking of its code.

Nested Blocks

The kinds of program blocks encountered so far are fairly short compound statements, or subprograms, that detail the actions required to do a given task. One quick way to locate program blocks is to look for a pair of delimiters such as BEGIN and END. Remember, though, that a block is not only the compound statement that appears between these delimiters, but also its header and a declaration section. In the case of the simplest program block, a small program, the header is the PROGRAM name.

In more complex programs, program blocks may be contained within other program blocks. This occurs when a new procedure is declared within another procedure. Blocks occurring within larger program blocks that, in turn, are themselves included in even larger program blocks, are said to be *nested.* Figure 4-2 illustrates this concept of nested blocks, or blocks-within-blocks.

Scope of Identifiers

Note in Figure 4-2 that all procedures are contained within the main program block, TrialBalance. One variable, Balance, appears in its declaration section. Such variables are available to, or may be used by, any block in the program and are referred to as *global* variables. The range of program blocks within which a variable, or other program identifier, has meaning is referred to as its *scope.* Therefore, the scope of the variable Balance is global, encompassing the entire program.

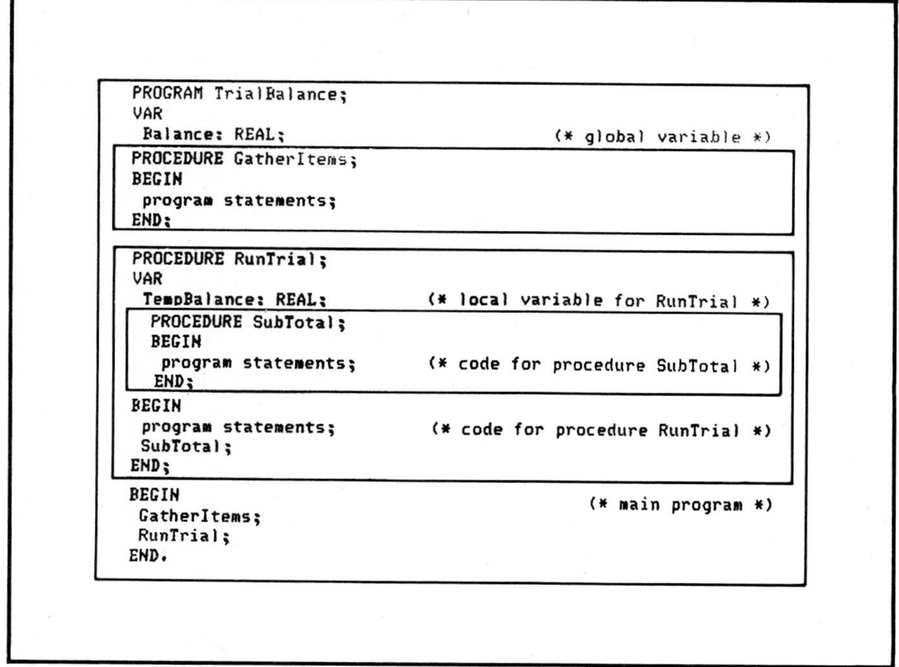

```
PROGRAM TrialBalance;
VAR
 Balance: REAL;                                  (* global variable *)
PROCEDURE GatherItems;
BEGIN
 program statements;
END;

PROCEDURE RunTrial;
VAR
 TempBalance: REAL;                    (* local variable for RunTrial *)
  PROCEDURE SubTotal;
  BEGIN
   program statements;                (* code for procedure SubTotal *)
  END;
BEGIN
 program statements;                  (* code for procedure RunTrial *)
 SubTotal;
END;
BEGIN                                             (* main program *)
 GatherItems;
 RunTrial;
END.
```

Figure 4-2. Program blocks may be nested, or included within other blocks, within a program.

On the other hand, the procedure GatherItems exists outside of the program block containing the procedures RunTrial and SubTotal. Rather than being declared globally, the variable TempBalance is declared within the RunTrial program block. In this case, the scope of TempBalance is *local.* That is, it is available to a restricted portion of the program. From the nesting relationship of the procedures RunTrial and SubTotal, it is apparent that the local variable has meaning within either of those procedures. However, TempBalance has no meaning within GatherItems, since this block is outside the block within which the local variable is declared.

The rules of scope apply to all identifiers in Pascal. An *identifier* is the name of a program, type, constant, variable, procedure, or function. (Functions are discussed later in this chapter.)

In general, global variables are declared for values that must be referenced by many blocks within the program. Typically, local variables are used by a few program blocks to hold intermediate results. Global and local scope also apply to other identifiers, such as procedure names. The scope of a procedure encompasses all succeeding blocks within the immediate block containing the procedure. Thus, in the TrialBalance program, the procedure SubTotal is declared within, and is within the scope of, the RunTrial block. By contrast, the name SubTotal has no meaning within GatherItems, which is outside its scope, nor is it defined in the main block.

Use of Parameters with Procedures

The programmer may give a procedure any data item to work with by passing that item explicitly as a *parameter.* Parameters are placeholders for passing values to, or returning values from, program blocks such as procedures.

For example, it might be necessary in the program TrialBalance to pass the data item TempBalance to the procedure GatherItems. Even though GatherItems is outside the scope of this variable, the value of TempBalance may be passed to the procedure GatherItems by using a specific syntax in the declaration of the GatherItems procedure header:

```
PROCEDURE GatherItems(VAR IncomingValue:REAL);
```

A formal *parameter list* is declared in the procedure header and must specify the data type of the variables expected. Notice also the optional reserved term VAR preceding the parameter variable IncomingValue.

TempBalance then may be passed to GatherItems by:

```
GatherItems(TempBalance);
```

This procedure call causes the location in memory, or memory address, of TempBalance to be passed to the procedure. The VAR syntax in the header enables *passing by reference,* because it is a reference to a memory location that is provided to the procedure rather than a specific value. During execution, when the variable InComingValue is referenced, the memory location of TempBalance (the parameter passed by reference) is accessed, and the value held there is made available to the procedure. Before the procedure terminates, the memory location may be accessed again to place a new value there for TempBalance, perhaps altered by the process that has occurred within the procedure. The effect of passing a parameter by reference, then, is to enable a procedure to use and change the value of a given variable.

An alternative syntax is *passing by value.* The form of the procedure declaration is:

```
PROCEDURE GatherItems(IncomingValue:REAL);
```

The corresponding procedure call, then, would be:

```
GatherItems(TempBalance);
```

Note in the above procedure declaration that the term VAR is omitted. This syntax declares that only a copy of the value stored in TempBalance is to be given to the procedure. The procedure may use the value, but when the procedure terminates, the original value held in memory remains unchanged because the procedure has been given no information as to where that original value is located.

More than one parameter may be passed to a procedure. This is done in the parameter list in the procedure declaration, such as:

```
PROCEDURE GatherItems(X:INTEGER; VAR Y,Z:REAL);
```

The corresponding call might be:

```
GatherItems(Item1,Item2,Item3);
```

Whether passing by reference or by value, the items passed are known as *arguments* of the procedure and their appearance in the call syntax forms the *argument list*. In other words, parameters are placeholders within procedure declarations, and arguments are values or references to values supplied to the parameters in a called procedure.

A strict correspondence must exist between the argument list in a procedure call and the parameter list in the called procedure's declaration. The rules for this correspondence are that the argument list must match the parameter list with respect to having:

- The same number of data items
- Corresponding items in the same order of appearance within their respective lists
- Corresponding items of the same data type.

Restated, the parameter list is a formal device for declaring placeholder positions for data items to be operated upon by the procedure. The term VAR may be used to allow data to be passed by reference to memory location rather than by value. In effect, the use of VAR extends the scope of the argument passed to include the called procedure.

Names given in the parameter list cannot be the same as variable names used within the procedure. Outside the procedure, the parameters are referenced by their declared names. Within the procedure, they are referenced by the corresponding variable names in the parameter list.

The parameter list in the procedure declaration header is referred to as the *formal declaration* of parameters. Names appearing in the formal declaration are local to the procedure. If it happens that a parameter name is identical to a variable of greater scope, such as a global variable, the more global variable cannot be accessed within the scope of the procedure. Further, the variable names in the argument list of a procedure call need only be valid names within the calling block.

The following example illustrates how parameter names are disregarded within procedures:

```
PROCEDURE Crash(Sam, Fred : REAL);
VAR
 Gosh : REAL;
BEGIN
 Sam := Sam + 3 * Fred;
 Gosh := Sam / 2.76;
 WRITELN(Gosh);
END;

PROCEDURE Bang;
VAR
 Fred, Sam : REAL;
BEGIN
 Fred := 5.5;
 Sam := 3.14159;
 Crash(Fred, Sam);
END;
```

Note that procedure Bang calls the procedure Crash and passes the arguments Fred and Sam in that order. The variable names of the parameters are not the same as the variable names of the arguments. Crash receives the values 5.5 and 3.14159 and uses those values without regard to any names used to refer to them in other program blocks. The fact that Bang uses duplicate names in the apparent wrong order is irrelevant. The names in Bang are local identifiers only.

The above example illustrates how local variables, in this case parameters passed by value, have names that are meaningful only within the scope of the procedure in which they are declared. However, a distinction must be made here between what is possible and what is practical. From the viewpoint of anyone who must read and understand your program, its clarity suffers when duplicate variable names may have different meanings. It is good programming practice to use variable names that are obviously different. For example, it is permissible to use variable names TimeZero and Time0, but better programming practice would be FirstTime and NextTime.

FUNCTIONS

Pascal has another way of naming and calling program blocks, or subprograms. This method uses the reserved word **FUNCTION**. Just as a procedure may be called from within a program block, a function is said to be *invoked* by the appearance of the function name. A function is a Pascal program block that usually has one purpose—to calculate a single value and return it to the program block in which it is invoked. Functions, like procedures, are compound statements that, once declared, may be called, or invoked, by other program blocks.

Functions are program blocks that have many characteristics in common with procedures. The principal difference is that functions are treated in Pascal syntax as variables. A function is the syntactic equivalent of a noun, since its name stands for a single value. A procedure, on the other hand, is syntactically equivalent to a verb because its name calls a set of actions. Unlike procedures, the name of a function is assigned a value within the body of the function itself, and that value is passed to the calling block. Accordingly, functions are declared as having a specific data type, which may be any non-structured data type. (Non-structured types include scalar and REAL. Scalar types are covered in Chapter 6.)

Calling a procedure within a program causes its program statements to be executed; several values may be returned to the calling block, depending on how many parameters are given in the parameter list. Invoking a function causes its program statements to be executed. However, functions differ from procedures in that the function returns to the calling block not only new values for parameters called by reference but also the single value identified by the function name.

To summarize, a variable name stands for any one of a range of data values; a function name stands for the single value that results from executing the program steps set forth when the function was declared.

A FUNCTION in Pascal performs in much the same way as a *mathematical function.* Mathematical functions determine single values that are the result of a series of mathematical operations. Examples of mathematical functions would be *absolute value, square root,* and *logarithm,* to name a few. Functions in Pascal often are used to represent mathematical functions, although a Pascal function can be used for any program block that returns a single value.

Suppose, in the course of writing a Pascal program, you had to compute the area of a circle several times for circles of different radii. The mathematical calculation for the area of a circle is derived from the formula:

$$A = \pi r^2$$

(Note that the = symbol here has its traditional mathematical meaning of equality and is not the same as the symbol used in Pascal to indicate a comparison.)

Rather than rewriting the program statements for computing this value each time you need it for a different circle, it would be more convenient to write FUNCTION AreaCircle:

```
FUNCTION AreaCircle (Radius: REAL): REAL;
 CONST
  Pi = 3.1416;
 BEGIN
  AreaCircle := Pi * Radius * Radius;
 END;
```

The first line, the *function header,* names the function AreaCircle and then gives a parameter list. (Arguments are used by, and may be passed to, functions as well as procedures.)

In AreaCircle, the parameter given is Radius. The colon immediately after Radius indicates that a definition of data type follows. The definition of the parameter Radius is that it is a REAL number. That is, it may have a fractional part represented as a decimal. As is the case with procedures, more than one parameter may be given within the parentheses as part of the function's parameter list. Data type must be specified for each parameter defined in the parameter list.

Notice that there is a colon outside the second parenthesis that encloses the parameter list. This colon precedes a declaration of the data type of the function itself, the single value to be returned to the calling block. This single value must be established at some point by the program statements within the function. In this example, the value returned to any program block that calls the function AreaCircle will be a REAL number. Since the function name serves as a placeholder for the value to be returned by executing the function, the name of the REAL value returned by FUNCTION AreaCircle is AreaCircle. Each time AreaCircle is invoked, the function is executed and a new value is calculated for AreaCircle.

The second line of the example function begins with the reserved term **CONST**, which is an abbreviation of *constant*. This line is a *constant declaration*. A constant declaration serves to attach a name to a value. (Notice that this usage of the = symbol in constant declarations differs from usages previously presented.) All subsequent references to the constant name yield the original value. Unlike a variable, a declared constant cannot have any other values assigned to it after its initial declaration. In the case of AreaCircle, the programmer has chosen to use a constant declaration to assign a value to Pi (π).

Note that the programmer also chose to have this constant declaration appear within the function itself, rather than in a global constant declaration earlier in the program. Constants, variables, and parameters that are declared within a function or procedure are local data. Recall that local data are values restricted to a specific program block. Hence, Pi has no meaning outside the scope of AreaCircle.

The next line of AreaCircle, following the block delimiter BEGIN, describes the operations that are to be performed to compute the value of the function. Alternatively, many lines of program statements might have appeared here if the function required a series of computations to find its value.

END; marks the conclusion of FUNCTION AreaCircle. Remember that a semicolon always follows the END of a procedure or function, indicating that other program statements follow.

Of course, the calculation for the area of a circle also could be written as a procedure using a variable that is called by reference in the parameter list. The differences in the declaration illustrate the basic differences between procedures and functions:

```
PROCEDURE Area(Radius:REAL; VAR Result:REAL);
 CONST
  Pi = 3.1416;
 BEGIN
  Result := Pi * Radius * Radius;
 END;
```

Passing Arguments to Function Parameters

When the function AreaCircle is invoked, a value for Radius must be passed to it, as in:

```
BEGIN
Answer := AreaCircle(5.0);     (* function call *)
 program statement;
 program statement;
END;
```

In this example, the value 5.0 is passed to AreaCircle, which returns a value to the calling block of 78.54.

The above example shows an argument passed to a function parameter as an explicit value. As stated earlier in this chapter, an argument also may be passed to a procedure or function parameter as the name of some other value within the program. For example, suppose the same program that contains the function AreaCircle also contains the variable Width. The current value of this variable may be passed to AreaCircle with the statement:

```
SomeValue := AreaCircle(Width);
```

Outside of the block (function) AreaCircle, the name of the passed argument is Width. Within AreaCircle its name is Radius, until the processing defined in the function is complete. Radius may not be referenced globally by the program: It remains a placeholder within the AreaCircle program statements, awaiting some value to be passed to it. The scope of Width must include any block that uses it in invoking AreaCircle, of course. Thus, Width can be either local or global, but in neither case will its value be changed by the execution of AreaCircle.

Any combination of explicit values and variable names, or even function calls, may be passed as arguments to a procedure or function, provided that the following rules are observed:

- The number of arguments must match the number of parameters.
- The order of the arguments must match the order of the parameters.
- The argument passed must be of the same data type as the parameter in the corresponding position in the parameter list of the procedure or function.
- If a parameter in the parameter list is to be called by reference (i.e., is preceded by VAR), the argument passed to the procedure or function must be a variable. It may not be a constant or a function call, since it must receive a new value from the called block.

To summarize, a function returns a single value to the calling block, and the name of that value is the name of the function itself.

SCOPE OF VARIABLES IN PROCEDURE CALLS

The program example, *Scope*, in Figure 4-3 illustrates several of the points covered above regarding the scope of variables and rules for passing parameters to procedures.

The program style in this case is somewhat different from previously encountered examples. Styles of capitalization and indentation are matters of convention rather than strict programming rules. Indentation is really a tool the programmer has for keeping track of the nesting relationships among program blocks. The actual nesting relationships are derived by the compiler from the program logic rather than from explicit indentations. Similarly, the compiler ignores capitalization, whether the text is in upper- or lowercase letters. This does not mean that a consistent style has no purpose. To the contrary, a consistent style in your program text enhances clarity for you and for anyone else who must work with your program in source code form.

The program Scope presented in Figure 4-3 demonstrates the scope of variables in procedure calls.

FURTHER CHARACTERISTICS OF PROCEDURES AND FUNCTIONS

An interesting, and powerful, property of both procedures and functions is that they may, in turn, call other procedures or functions from within the same program. In fact, procedures and functions (subprograms) may even call themselves, an action that at first resembles a snake eating its own tail. Subprograms that call themselves are known as *recursive.* Recursive subprograms are quite permissible in Pascal as long as the format of their statements is correct. Recursive subprograms are especially useful in solving certain kinds of mathematical problems. Recursion is discussed in greater depth in Chapter 14.

Another property of procedures and functions in Pascal can prove extremely useful for writing more involved programs. This is your ability to coin your own extended version of the Pascal language within a program. By naming new procedures and functions carefully within a program, you may create the equivalent of your own verbs, nouns, and conditionals.

Once you have defined these subprograms, you may use their names throughout the program to call their actions and results into the program. By doing so, your coding of program text becomes more like writing a simplified form of English. Because of this clarity, other programmers who may study your program may pick up its flow very quickly without having to examine the program statements of each procedure or function in depth. For example, it is possible to make some general statements

```
Program Scope;        (* Demonstrate scope of variables in procedure calls. *)

CONST
        three = 3.0;

VAR
        globe,
        everywhere : REAL;              (* These are global variables common to
                                           all parts of the entire program.  *)

Procedure Example(VAR param1 : REAL; param2 : REAL);
                (* The scope of param1 and param2 is this procedure only.
                   Values for both param1 and param2 are supplied to this
                     block by the calling block.  However, a new value of
                                param1 can be passed to the calling routine. *)

VAR
        tempo : REAL;                         (* The scope of the variable temp
                                                 is this procedure only. *)

BEGIN
        tempo := 5.0;
        writeln('Parameters passed to Example are: ',param1,param2);
                                                (* Print original values. *)
        param2 := tempo * param2;
                        (* This changes the local value of param2 but not the
                           calling block value from which param2 is derived. *)
        param1 := three + param2 / param1;
                            (* The value of param1 in the calling block is
                               changed by this assignment because param1 is
                                      prefixed by VAR in the parameter list. *)

END;                                            (* end of procedure Example *)

Procedure User(thing : REAL);
                            (* This procedure uses the procedure 'Example.' *)

BEGIN
        everywhere := thing / 6.0;
                        (* globe is declared in the main program block, so it is
                           global to all other blocks.  This statement assigns a
                                                 new value to 'everywhere.' *)

END;                                              (* end of procedure User *)

BEGIN                                             (* start of main program *)

        globe := 4.5;
        everywhere := three;

        writeln('Original Values are ',globe,everywhere);

        User(globe);
            (* Call the procedure 'User.' User changes the value of
               'everywhere' but does not affect the value of 'globe' even
               though the value of 'globe' is passed to it as a parameter. *)

        Example(globe, everywhere);
                        (* Call the procedure 'Example.'  Example changes
                               the value of 'globe' but not of 'everywhere.' *)
        writeln('Final Values are ',globe,everywhere);

END.                                                    (* end of program *)
```

Figure 4-3. The scope of variables in procedure calls can be seen in this example program *Scope.*

about the following main program without knowing the programming statements contained within the procedures and functions called:

```
BEGIN
  GetStartBalance;
  SumDebits;
  SumCredits;
  CalculateCurrentBalance;
END.
```

All of the program statements above are procedure calls with coined names. Each name stands for a previously declared subprogram. The processing actions caused by each procedure are described clearly by the coined names. The above block is actually the main program block from the example program presented at the end of this chapter.

FORWARD Declaration of Procedures and Functions

There are times when a procedure or function must be referenced before it is defined. That is, the name of the procedure or function is used in the program text before the body of code for it has been defined.

Consider the example of two procedures A and B, each of which refers to the other, such as:

```
PROCEDURE A;
BEGIN
 B;
END;

PROCEDURE B;
BEGIN
 A;
END;
```

If this program text were compiled, the reference to B in procedure A would cause an error—undefined identifiers. The means provided in Pascal to solve this dilemma is the **FORWARD** declaration to "predeclare" the name and parameter list (and data type, for functions) at an earlier point in the text. In the above example, procedure B would have to have a FORWARD declaration for it placed somewhere before the declaration of procedure A. The syntax for this is:

```
PROCEDURE B; FORWARD;
```

When the actual procedure B is coded, only the name of the procedure is repeated, not any parameter list or function type. The second declaration would be:

```
PROCEDURE B;  (* followed by the body of the procedure *)
```

Where would this situation arise? Actually, it is fairly common. Consider the program *Report* presented in Figure 4-4.

Referring to Figure 4-4, notice (1) the FORWARD declaration of the procedure SkipLines. The parameter list also must be given, and the type clause (: TYPE) if a function is involved.

The FORWARD declaration is required because the procedure PrintTitle calls SkipLines (2) and the procedure SkipLines calls PrintTitle (3).

Notice the comment line (4), indicating that the parameter list cannot be duplicated after it has been provided in the FORWARD declaration. It is good practice to repeat the parameter list within comments, for the sake of documentation. For example:

```
PROCEDURE SkipLines; (* N:INTEGER *)
```

For a function, an example of the FORWARD declaration might be:

```
FUNCTION Percent(Amount : REAL) : INTEGER; FORWARD;
```

Then, the following would begin the function coding:

```
FUNCTION Percent; (*(Amount : REAL) : INTEGER*)
```

```
PROGRAM Report;

CONST
 LinesPerPage = 50;

VAR
 LineCounter,
 PageCounter : INTEGER;

PROCEDURE SkipLines (N:INTEGER); FORWARD;                    (*** (1) ***)

PROCEDURE PrintTitle;
BEGIN
 PAGE(OUTPUT);      (* this statement causes start of new page of printing *)
 PageCounter := PageCounter + 1;
 LineCounter := 0;
 WRITELN('PAGE ',PageCounter);
 SkipLines(3);              (* skip three lines *)             (*** (2) ***)
END;

PROCEDURE SkipLines; (* notice parameter list not duplicated *) (*** (4) ***)
BEGIN
 LineCounter := LineCounter + N;                      (* add to line count *)
 IF LineCounter > LinesPerPage THEN
  PrintTitle              (* page full; start new page *)      (*** (3) ***)
 ELSE
  REPEAT                                        (* until all lines skipped *)
   WRITELN;                                        (* print a blank line *)
   N := N - 1;                                 (* decrement line skip count *)
  UNTIL N = 0;                                  (* until skip counter is 0 *)
END;

BEGIN                                              (* main program block *)
 program statements;
END.                                                  (* end of program *)
```

Figure 4-4. Program *Report.*

Note also that SkipLines contains an IF . . THEN . . ELSE statement that implements a comparison and a program loop. Such statements are discussed in depth in Chapter 6.

CODING MATHEMATICAL EXPRESSIONS

Implementing a particular algorithm often requires that a mathematical equation be translated into program text. This is the case with the AreaCircle example. As a general rule in translating mathematical equations into program text, remember that equations must be coded in the following form:

```
VariableName := expressions;
```

For example:

```
NetIncome := Earnings - Expenses;
```

An equation must be put in the form of an assignment statement with a single variable on the left of the := sign and any expressions and operations to be performed on the right. Program processing *evaluates* all expressions on the right side of the statement and assigns the resulting value to the variable on the left. An expression is said to be evaluated when all operations given in the expression have been performed. The result is usually a single value, in which case the expression has been reduced to its simplest form.

Mathematical equations sometimes contain parentheses and brackets to indicate the order in which operations must be performed. Consider this mathematical expression:

$$2[(a + b) \div c]$$

To evaluate this expression, the operation within the parentheses (a + b) should be performed first, followed by the operation within the brackets (divide by c), and then the operation outside the brackets (multiply the result by 2).

Pascal program text uses pairs of parentheses to indicate the sequence of operations, or evaluation. In Pascal, you could cause the result of the above expression to be placed in the variable m by writing the following statement:

```
m := 2 * ((a + b) / c);
```

In Pascal program text, the slash symbol (/) calls for a division operation that yields a real number, while **DIV** calls for integral division, or division of whole numbers that yields a whole number.

The compiler evaluates expressions that appear within the innermost pair of parentheses first, before evaluating any other expressions, then proceeds outward as indicated by pairs of parentheses. Remember, parentheses are always evaluated in pairs. A common syntactical error results from having an odd number of, or "un-paired," parentheses in an expression. (A good way to check parenthesis syntax is to start counting at the left of the expression, adding 1 for each left parenthesis and subtracting 1 for each right parenthesis. The result must be 0, or a syntax error exists.)

The order of operations within an expression often is critical to achieving a valid result. For example, if the values of 12, 3, and 3 were assigned to a, b, and c, respectively, the above program statement would return a result to m of 10. Accordingly, a different result would be obtained from:

```
m := 2 * (a + (b / c));
```

With the same values for a, b, and c, this program statement would return a value to m of 26. If, in fact, 26 were the desired result, this order of evaluation, or parenthesizing, would be correct and the previous form incorrect. Another result is obtained when no parentheses are used:

```
m := 2 * a + b / c;
```

The result in this case is 25. Thus, parentheses may be used to control the order of evaluation and the meaning of expressions. The default precedence of operations assumed by the compiler in the absence of parentheses is multiplication and division first (*, /, and DIV) and addition and subtraction second (+ and −). However, parentheses should be used when in doubt and for program clarity in general.

PASCAL STRUCTURE EXPANDED

Figure 4-5 expands upon Pascal program structure. Note the similarity between this form and the form of a procedure block, illustrated in Figure 4-1. Some structural elements not yet encountered are covered below.

CONSTant Declarations

Constants whose scope is global are declared in the main declaration section of the program. An example would be:

```
CONST
 ExchangeRate = 1.235;
```

A constant declaration need not be restricted to traditional mathematical constants like π, but also may be used to assign strings or characters to any name that is not to be subject to change during program execution. In the above example, a constant is used to set the rate of exchange between the currencies of two different countries. The value of this exchange rate is not subject to change by the action of the program. Notice that no data type is given for constants. None is necessary, since the compiler merely will use the declared value whenever the declared name occurs in the program. The data type of the constant is implied by the value assigned to it.

Constant definitions are useful when a common, or fixed, value must appear in several places in a program. By defining a constant with a name, you can avoid the error of mis-typing it, avoiding the possibility that its data type might not match from one use to another.

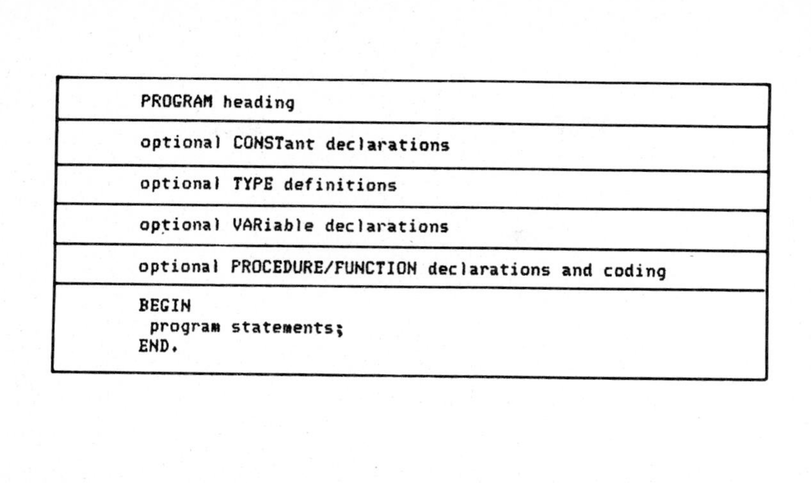

```
PROGRAM heading
optional CONSTant declarations
optional TYPE definitions
optional VARiable declarations
optional PROCEDURE/FUNCTION declarations and coding
BEGIN
 program statements;
END.
```

Figure 4-5. Pascal program structure.

TYPE Definitions

Predefined data types (INTEGER, REAL) that need not be defined by the programmer already have been described. Additionally, the programmer may define, or coin, specific data types in the **TYPE** definition section of the program. The type definition provides a way for the programmer to structure, or restrict, the data that are used within the program.

For example, you might wish to use any one of the names of the days of the week as a specific data type. Coining a type Weekday (whose possible values are given as Monday, Tuesday, Wednesday, Thursday, and Friday) causes the program to allow only the names of weekdays as values for any variable of that coined type. The type definition in the declaration section of your program would look like this:

```
TYPE
 Weekday = (Monday, Tuesday, Wednesday, Thursday, Friday);
```

The above statement is a form of coining types referred to as an *enumeration type.* Enumeration types are discussed in depth in Chapter 8.

A later variable declaration that makes use of this type might be:

```
VAR
 Payday : Weekday;
```

Pascal provides a powerful structuring ability in the TYPE definition without requiring the programmer to write much code. In this case, the program will not allow the input of Sunday into the contents of the variable Payday. This is one instance of a program control, or reasonableness test, that has been implemented in a concise way through a carefully devised TYPE definition.

PROCEDURE/FUNCTION Declarations

Procedures and functions are coded at this point in the program. Also, procedures and functions may be coded locally within other procedures in the corresponding section of the procedure or function block.

NAMING VARIABLES, PROCEDURES, AND FUNCTIONS

Here are some general rules for naming variables, procedures, and functions:

- Any number of letters or numbers may be used, as long as the first character is a letter and the first eight characters are unique.
- Names may not contain spaces or other special characters such as punctuation marks (with the exception of the underscore character).

These same rules also apply to the names given to other identifiers, such as constants and parameters. It is good practice to be as descriptive as possible in naming, since this helps to document programs. Variable names, such as PERSONSNAME, all run together in capital letters, are certainly permissible but are not necessarily good programming form. Sometimes clarity requires that entire phrases stand for a procedure or variable. There are several ways to do this and still present valid names to the Pascal compiler.

If your computer supports upper- and lower-case characters, you can use a form like PersonsName instead. Another technique involves the use of the underscore character to take the place of a blank, or space. The underscore character is an exception to the prohibition against special characters in names and is ignored by the Pascal compiler. Using the underscore character, names might look like this:

```
PERSONS_NAME
```

One of these techniques should be useful in entering the following programming example that uses procedure names such as CalculateCurrentBalance.

PROGRAM *BalanceCheckbook*

You discover that your friend with the home computer has been using the *AddingMachine* program to help in balancing his checkbook. You point out that a program specifically designed to balance his checkbook would save him time and effort. You've determined, then, that the goal of a new program, *BalanceCheckbook*, is to combine the monthly statement the bank sends your friend with the more recent manual entries he has made in his check register. The program's main output will be a current checkbook balance.

In applying the principles of top-down design, you ask your friend to describe the steps, or tasks, that he must go through each month to balance the checkbook manually. When you have completed your interview, the list of tasks looks like this:

- Get the statement balance from the bank statement.
- Sum all checks and other debits shown in the check register as outstanding (those not appearing on the bank statement).
- Sum all deposits and other credits shown in the check register as outstanding (those not appearing on the bank statement).
- Deduct the subtotal for debits and add the subtotal for credits to the balance shown on the bank statement to compute the current balance.

Having satisfied yourself that these tasks describe completely the actions required to balance the checkbook, you then can develop a structure chart that identifies these steps as separate modules. Pseudocode may be written for each module. Such a structure chart is shown in Figure 4-6. Pseudocode has been written in the margin of this chart and

0.0 BALANCE CHECKBOOK

1.0 INITIALIZATION

1.1 GET START BALANCE
PROCEDURE GetStartBalance

1.1.1 ASK FOR VALUE
Tell user to enter a starting balance

1.1.2 READ VALUE
Get a value for starting balance

2.0 MAIN PROCESSING

2.1 SUM DEBITS
PROCEDURE SumDebits

2.1.1 INITIALIZE DEBIT TOTAL TO ZERO
Start with the sum of all debits equal to zero
(initialize the debit sum variable)

2.1.2 GET DEBIT VALUES
Repeat the following steps:

2.1.2.1 ASK FOR DEBIT VALUE
Tell the user to enter a debit amount entry

2.1.2.2 READ DEBIT VALUE
Get a value for the debit amount

2.1.2.3 ADD TO DEBIT TOTAL
Add the debit amount entered
to the sum of all debits
Until the user enters a zero
for the debit amount

2.2 SUM CREDITS
PROCEDURE SumCredits

2.2.1 INITIALIZE CREDIT TOTAL TO ZERO
Start with the sum of all credits equal to zero
(initialize the credit sum variable)

2.2.2 GET CREDIT VALUES
REPEAT
Repeat the following steps:

2.2.2.1 ASK FOR CREDIT VALUE
Tell the user to enter a credit amount entry

2.2.2.2 READ CREDIT VALUE
Get a value for the credit amount

2.2.2.3 ADD TO CREDIT TOTAL
Add the credit amount entered
to the sum of all credits
Until the user enters zero
for the credit amount

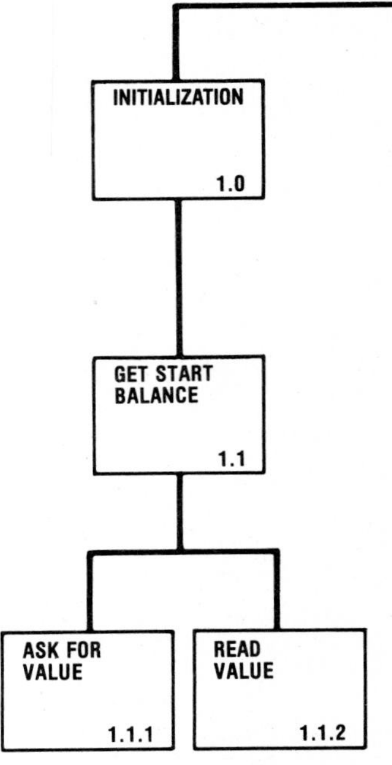

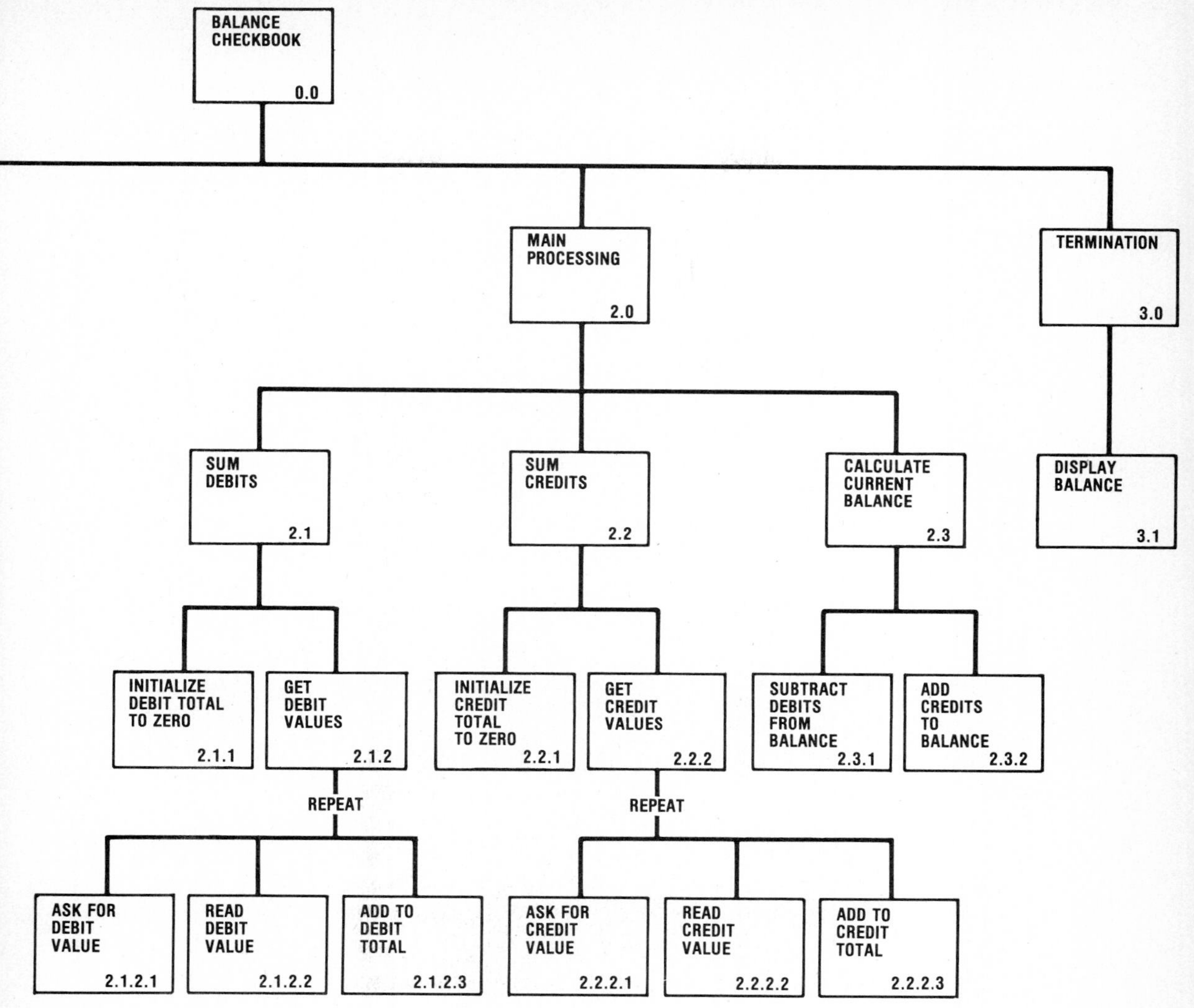

2.3 CALCULATE CURRENT BALANCE

PROCEDURE CalculateCurrentBalance

2.3.1 SUBTRACT DEBITS FROM BALANCE

Subtract the sum of all debits
from the starting balance

2.3.2 ADD CREDITS TO BALANCE

Add the sum of all credits

3.0 TERMINATION

3.1 DISPLAY BALANCE

Display the result as the current balance

End.

Figure 4-6. Structure chart and pseudocode for *BalanceCheckbook*.

indexed to the module numbers shown on the chart. Note that each task, as described in pseudocode, becomes a PROCEDURE in the program. Procedure names for each task described in pseudocode for the main processing module are:

```
GetStartBalance
SumDebits
SumCredits
CalculateCurrentBalance
```

Accordingly, these steps, taken together, form the main task level of the program to be written. In general, the program will have the form:

```
PROGRAM BalanceCheckbook;

VAR declarations;

BEGIN
  GetStartBalance;
  SumDebits;
  SumCredits;
  CalculateCurrentBalance;
END.
```

The pseudocode shown in Figure 4-6 can form a basis for writing the programming statements within each procedure. Looking back over the pseudocode for the procedures, you can assemble a list of variables that must be used within the program. Then, names are given to the variables:

```
StartBalance
DebitSum
Debit
CreditSum
Credit
CurrentBalance
```

The data type of these variables is REAL, since these variables will contain whole dollars and fractional dollars shown as decimals.

Now the program text for *BalanceCheckbook* can be written by taking the following steps:

- Supply the program header.
- Define and type variables in the variable declaration section.
- Code program statements for each procedure from the pseudocode and include these program statements with appropriate headers in a procedure declaration section of the program immediately following the variable declaration section.
- Include calls in the main body of the program to each procedure by invoking the names of the procedures as needed in processing.

The resulting program text is shown in Figure 4-7.

Once a text file has been created for this program, it can be compiled and executed. Figure 4-8 shows the console display as it might appear after *BalanceCheckbook* has been compiled and executed with test data.

Figure 4-7. Program *BalanceCheckbook*.

```
PROGRAM BalanceCheckbook;                                  (* program header *)

VAR
 StartBalance,                                     (* variables declaration *)
 DebitSum,
 Debit,
 CreditSum,
 Credit,
 CurrentBalance:REAL;     (* All variables are of predefined data type REAL. *)
PROCEDURE GetStartBalance;                (* procedures definition section *)
BEGIN
 WRITE('ENTER STARTING BALANCE $');
 READLN(StartBalance);
END;

PROCEDURE SumDebits;
BEGIN
 DebitSum := 0;
 REPEAT                                                 (* until Debit is 0 *)
   WRITE('DEBIT SUMMARY IS $',Debitsum:7:2,' ENTER DEBIT AMOUNT $ ');
                               (* For a discussion of the syntax :7:2
                                         in the above, see Chapter 8. *)
   READLN(Debit);
   DebitSum := DebitSum + Debit;
 UNTIL Debit = 0;
```

```
 WRITELN('---END OF DEBITS---');
END;

PROCEDURE SumCredits;
BEGIN
 CreditSum := 0;
 REPEAT                                                (* until Credit is 0 *)
   WRITE('CREDIT SUMMARY IS $',CreditSum:7:2,' ENTER CREDIT AMOUNT $ ');
   READLN(Credit);
   CreditSum := CreditSum + Credit;
 UNTIL Credit = 0;
 WRITELN('---END OF CREDITS---');
END;

PROCEDURE CalculateCurrentBalance;
BEGIN
 CurrentBalance := StartBalance - DebitSum + CreditSum;
 WRITELN('YOUR CURRENT BALANCE IS $',CurrentBalance:8:2);
END;

BEGIN                    (* This BEGIN is for the main program instructions. *)
 GetStartBalance;                (* Calls are made to the above procedures. *)
 SumDebits;
 SumCredits;
 CalculateCurrentBalance;
END.                                                (* end of program coding *)
```

Figure 4-7. (Conclusion)

```
RUNNING...
ENTER STARTING BALANCE $1000
DEBIT SUMMARY IS $      0.0   ENTER DEBIT AMOUNT $ 125.00
DEBIT SUMMARY IS $    125.00  ENTER DEBIT AMOUNT $ 12.00
DEBIT SUMMARY IS $    137.00  ENTER DEBIT AMOUNT $ 40.00
DEBIT SUMMARY IS $    177.00  ENTER DEBIT AMOUNT $ 250.00
DEBIT SUMMARY IS $    427.00  ENTER DEBIT AMOUNT $ 32.00
DEBIT SUMMARY IS $    459.00  ENTER DEBIT AMOUNT $ 0
---END OF DEBITS---
CREDIT SUMMARY IS $      0.0   ENTER CREDIT AMOUNT $ 100.00
CREDIT SUMMARY IS $    100.00  ENTER CREDIT AMOUNT $ 100.00
CREDIT SUMMARY IS $    200.00  ENTER CREDIT AMOUNT $ 150.00
CREDIT SUMMARY IS $    350.00  ENTER CREDIT AMOUNT $ 100.00
CREDIT SUMMARY IS $    450.00  ENTER CREDIT AMOUNT $ 0
---END OF CREDITS---
YOUR CURRENT BALANCE IS $     991.00
```

Figure 4-8. Displayed results of *BalanceCheckbook* after compilation and execution.

Summary

The Pascal structure PROCEDURE is used to name blocks of program statements, or subprograms, and to call them from within other program blocks once they have been defined. Procedures reinforce the tasks described by top-down design. The form of this statement is a PROCEDURE header followed by program statements that are bounded by BEGIN and END. A procedure must have been defined before it is called. All variables used in the procedure must have been declared previously either in the main program block or in declarations within the procedure block.

In general, tasks defined by top-down design correspond with procedures in program text. For each task described in the top-down design process, a procedure can be written. Block-structured code reinforces the orderly application of top-down design. A block structure makes changes in design easier to implement. Program blocks are easier to test and debug, and coding with blocks helps prevent "logical myopia"—losing sight of the goal of the program.

Whenever the name of a previously defined procedure is used as a command in a Pascal program, that procedure's program statements are executed. The program block that uses a procedure is a calling block.

Blocks contained within other program blocks are nested. Identifiers (names of procedures, variables, constants, etc.) used by nested blocks may be either global or local. Local identifiers are valid within the outermost program block in which the identifiers are declared and in any other blocks nested within that block. The outermost block within which an identifier is valid is its scope. It is important to know the scope of identifiers within a called procedure or function and whether those values are valid within the calling block.

Expressions appearing within parentheses in a procedure header are parameters. Parameters are placeholders for passing values to, or returning values from, program blocks such as procedures. Arguments are the values or variables supplied to the parameters by the calling block. The arguments must appear in the call statement syntax in the order in which the parameters appear in the parameter list in the procedure declaration. The number of arguments must match the number of parameters. Each argument's data type must match that of its parameter. Called procedures are the syntactic equivalent of verbs.

Functions are subprograms, or program blocks, that are identical to procedures, except that a function also returns a value to the calling block through its name. A FUNCTION in Pascal may be used to implement a mathematical function. The heading of a function names the function, gives a parameter list, and identifies the data type it returns. Parameter names also may be used as placeholders for passing values to, or returning data values from, functions. A data type is given in the parameter list for each parameter. Program statements contained within a function must be bounded by BEGIN and END. Invoked functions are the syntactic equivalent of nouns.

Identifiers are names for constants, variables, types, procedures, and functions. Declarations immediately following the main program header are for global identifiers, names available to all blocks in the program. Declarations made within a procedure or function are local identifiers, names that have meaning only within the program block in which the declaration is made and in the blocks nested within that block.

A parameter list in a header serves to declare the parameters to the compiler. If VAR precedes a parameter in the parameter list, any value assigned to that parameter within the procedure or function is passed back to the calling block. Such parameters are said to be called by reference.

A parameter not identified by VAR in the procedure's parameter list receives its value from its argument in the call statement, but the procedure cannot change the argument's value in the calling block. In other words, a parameter called by value may be changed within a procedure or function, but any changes will not be applied to the parameter's value in the calling block.

Procedures and functions may call other procedures or invoke other functions. A procedure or function also may call or invoke itself, in which case it is said to be recursive. By effectively naming functions and procedures, the programmer may coin verbs, nouns, and conditionals that are useful in producing clear program text.

A FORWARD declaration serves to declare the name and parameter list of a procedure or function before the body of the procedure or function has been coded.

In coding mathematical equations, the expressions on the right will be evaluated and the resulting value assigned to the variable name on the left of the := sign. Pascal program text uses pairs of parentheses to indicate the sequence of operations. The innermost pair of parentheses contains the expression that is evaluated first. Evaluation proceeds outward as each successive pair of parentheses is replaced by the single value equivalent of the expression contained.

TYPE definitions allow the programmer to coin data types and restrict the types of data that are used in the program. In naming variables, procedures, and functions, as well as constants and parameters, any number of letters or numbers may be used. The first character must be a letter and the first eight characters must be unique. Names may not contain spaces or special characters like punctuation marks. An exception is the underscore character, which may be used for clarity.

The program *BalanceCheckbook* is derived from a structure chart and pseudocode based on a top-down description of the tasks to be performed.

Review Questions

1. How does the difference between a task (as described by top-down design) and a procedure (as coded in Pascal) reflect the difference between logical design and physical processing?
2. How does implementing tasks by block-structured code assist the programmer in coding and debugging a program?
3. What is the correct form for coding a procedure in Pascal?
4. What is the correct form for coding a function in Pascal, and how does this form differ from that used for a procedure?
5. How are parameters used by procedures and functions?
6. When is it desirable to code an algorithm as a function instead of as a procedure?
7. What are the rules for providing arguments for parameters in a procedure or function?
8. What is the effect of the appearance of the term VAR within the parameter list for a procedure or function?
9. Why must procedures and functions be declared before they are called?
10. What circumstances might make use of recursion?
11. When are program blocks said to be nested, and what effect does nesting have on the scope of an identifier?
12. How does the difference between local and global data make it important to know the scope of the variables or parameters used by a called procedure or function?
13. How are mathematical equations translated into Pascal program text?
14. How is the CONST declaration useful?
15. What are the rules for specifying names in Pascal?

Pascal Practice

1. Modify *BalanceCheckbook* to display a prompt to the user so it is clearly understood that the entry of a zero (0) for a Debit or Credit will terminate that portion of the program.
2. Expand the program to include comparison of the calculated current checkbook balance with the balance currently showing in the manually prepared check register. Provide for the display of messages to the user on the console for both the possibilities of correct and incorrect check register balances.
3. Rewrite PROCEDURE CalculateCurrentBalance as FUNCTION CurrentBalance. Be sure to pay attention to any changes this may require in other sections of the program.
4. Referring to the procedures Crash and Bang in the text, modify Bang to call Crash twice. Test it and describe what happens. Modify the header of procedure Crash to:

```
PROCEDURE Crash(VAR Sam,Fred:REAL);
```

Now what would you expect to see if Bang called Crash twice?

Key Terms

1. block delimiter
2. logical boundary
3. compound statement
4. call
5. procedure declaration
6. calling block
7. nested
8. global
9. scope
10. local
11. identifier
12. parameter
13. parameter list
14. pass by reference
15. pass by value
16. argument
17. argument list
18. formal declaration
19. invoke
20. mathematical function
21. absolute value
22. square root
23. logarithm
24. function header
25. constant
26. constant declaration
27. recursive
28. evaluate
29. enumeration type

Pascal Library

1. PROCEDURE
2. FUNCTION
3. CONST
4. TYPE
5. FORWARD
6. DIV

5
DESIGNING THE USER INTERFACE

OBJECTIVES

On completing the reading and other learning assignments in this chapter, you should be able to:

- ☐ Describe how design of the user interface is critical to assuring program quality.
- ☐ Give additional considerations for evaluating how a program is to be used.
- ☐ Explain the advantages and disadvantages of command-driven and prompt-driven user interfaces.
- ☐ Describe the formats for data input and explain their advantages and disadvantages.
- ☐ Explain input editing and its use.
- ☐ Apply a series of techniques to inform the user of a program's progress.
- ☐ Demonstrate how the display screen and cursor may be controlled by use of PAGE and GOTOXY and tell why this control is essential to designing an effective user interface.

THE USER'S 'WINDOW'

Programs that are easy to use, self-explanatory, and tolerant of user errors are said to be *user-friendly.* A set of programs designed for a specific application often is termed a *package.* What users see a program do, including the external actions caused by its execution, forms a "window" on the program. The user's evaluation of what is seen in that window forms a perception of the program's style.

Style, in general, does not affect results. Rather, it is a characteristic of how pleasing or satisfying an experience may be. In technical terms, *programming style* exists apart from a program's accuracy or validity. Once a user has had the opportunity to run a program, he or she will have a definite impression—a good feeling, or one that is not so good—about the experience. This impression may be the only value judgment a user ever makes about the program, regardless of the correctness of its results. That impression, in turn, can determine whether the program is used frequently or whether its diskette carrier gathers dust on a shelf.

The programmer must look through the user's window in designing a program. You should assume that most users have no knowledge of the technical details behind the visible result. Good programming style evolves from careful attention to what the user sees and, sometimes just as important, what the user expects to see. Writing a program that pays attention to these considerations frequently takes more lines of text than the main problem the program was written to solve.

Each programmer evolves a personal programming style based on experience. There are probably as many different ways of presenting programs as there are programmers. There is no single, correct programming style. If your program encourages use and reuse by the people it was designed for, you have a style that works—and you have performed a valuable service.

One of your tasks in program design is to anticipate and describe the human actions that will surround your program. In meeting this challenge, these basic factors should be considered:

- What is the potential user's familiarity with the program's *application area*? How knowledgeable is the user likely to be about the problem the program was written to solve? For example, the operator of the program might be a manager running a decision support program. Such a user is likely to be highly familiar with the application area and will know what specific results are needed. On the other hand, the program may be run in the data processing department by personnel whose job it is to run a wide variety of applications. In this case, less familiarity with the application is likely, and results might have to be more comprehensive.

- What is the potential user's familiarity with the *target computer system?* Will the user be comfortable with the keyboard or other input device that must be used to control the program? For example, the manager in the above example may not use a keyboard routinely. Single keystroke responses might be best. Within the data processing department, however, some staff members are specially trained for key entry of data, and responses involving multiple keystrokes could be employed.

Beyond these basic considerations, some other factors might be weighed:

- Is the program intended for processing volumes of data on a routine basis? An example of this type of application would be a payroll program for a large company.
- Is use likely to be occasional? An example here would be a sales analysis program designed to provide a manager with alternate marketing strategies in response to competitive price changes.
- Will data be input to the program by the same person who will evaluate the results? In the case of the company payroll, it is likely that clerical staff will input new payroll data and a financial manager will review the results of the processing run. The sales analysis program, on the other hand, might be run by a manager on a desk-top computer or terminal whenever news of price changes is received.

Complex programs generally do not lend themselves to simple programming approaches. This is especially true for systems with high volumes of input that are subject to change. The programmer should always strive for the simplest and most direct approach. The portions of the program that enable a user to control—and react to—the running of a program are referred to as the *user interface.*

DESIGN OPTIONS FOR USER INPUT

One basic consideration in design of the user interface is frequency of use for the program. This factor determines how much assistance the program should provide to the user. Even an expert user who runs a program only occasionally is apt to forget particular input steps, especially if some kind of code or command must be keyed in. Infrequent program use or lack of user familiarity with the computer system would require that the program provide a considerable amount of assistance in *prompting* inputs. Prompts are displayed messages that guide the user through the proper entry and execution sequence.

On the other hand, an input operator who runs the same program frequently during the business day may memorize a fairly long series of commands in a short time. Such a user could adapt quickly to efficient, concise commands that could be entered with a minimum number of keystrokes. In this case, the program need not give the user much in the way of assistance; indeed, too much interference from the program might be seen as bothersome.

Instructions on program use are a form of *documentation.* Programs that display explanatory information about the functions of the program are said to be *self-documenting.* The amount of *external documentation* required to support the use of the program is an important consideration. External documentation usually takes the form of a *user's guide* or *user's manual.* The user's guide is a document to be read by people who are learning to run the program for the first time. A user's manual is generally a more comprehensive reference volume that may be consulted by people who have encountered difficulty in running the program. In general, programs that rely on a great deal of external documentation require longer training periods than self-documented, heavily prompted programs that often can be used without any prior training. However, as already pointed out, such programs can be needlessly tedious to people who must use them frequently.

The choice here is between two basic user interface strategies, each with its own strengths and weaknesses. Evaluating these strengths and weaknesses is a question of analyzing *trade-offs* between speed of operation and ease of training and use. This is the fundamental choice between programs that are *command-driven* and those that are *prompt-driven.*

Command-Driven Programs

Command-driven programs assume that the user has prior knowledge of a set of commands, or coded phrases, that can be entered at the keyboard. One requirement in the use of commands is that an exact form and syntax must be used for each entry. Very often, a command-driven approach is used when the complexity of the program requires short, concise inputs. Commands also are used when the number of options is so large that all choices cannot be displayed without making the program hopelessly slow.

Users of a command-driven program must memorize the exact commands, know how those commands are applied, and must be able to use the program frequently to build and maintain a mastery of the application.

Command-driven programs require external documentation that is thorough and clear. Extensive *error-checking* information must be given so that users know how to get back on track when they do enter invalid commands. Errors on entry of commands may reflect either incorrect syntax within the command itself or use of a command in an inappropriate place in the program.

From the programmer's standpoint, using a command-driven approach has these clear advantages:

- A large "universe" of commands may be included, allowing for a wide range of available user inputs. Complex programs with many inputs and outputs frequently use a command-driven approach. A statistical modeling or financial forecasting program might employ commands because the range of input options is typically large in such applications.
- A command-driven program usually consists of fewer program statements than programs using other input techniques.
- Comparatively faster session times can be achieved, especially once users have become familiar with the command vocabulary. Programs that rely heavily on high volume, repetitive, clerical input procedures, such as payroll processing, may be command-driven.
- Commands can be made to resemble everyday language, making them easier to remember. Training expense, especially in a data processing facility, is an important consideration.

Again from the programmer's point of view, disadvantages of a command-driven approach are:

- The program must *scan* and *parse* each command as it is entered. This involves writing program instructions that evaluate each command to verify that its form and syntax are correct and that the command is valid for use at the given point in the program.

- Detailed *error messages* must be provided within the program. These messages must be descriptive enough to provide guidance if processing has been disrupted.
- A comprehensive user document must be prepared to instruct the user on the valid commands and their uses.
- The overwhelming disadvantage of a command-driven approach is that casual users may not apply the effort needed to learn the commands. Even those who have studied the commands may tend to forget them—or confuse the syntax enough to trigger frequent error messages. This type of experience can be frustrating, even to people who are otherwise comfortable with computer systems.

During the early development of computer programming languages, most programs were command-driven. Traditionally, this design approach has a reputation for being the least user-friendly. Partially for this reason, other program control techniques have evolved. Also a factor in the evolution of other techniques is the rapidly expanding use of microcomputers by people whose principal activities and expertise are outside the computer field. As the use of microcomputers and the scope of their applications have expanded, it has become necessary to design programs that can be used on a casual basis and run by users with a minimum of training.

Although command-driven approaches can be cumbersome in many instances, for some applications this technique may be the best choice. The challenge to the programmer is to design programs that minimize the drawbacks.

Prompt-Driven Programs

One kind of prompt-driven approach that is an alternative to commands is the use of *menus*. A menu is a multiple-choice listing of the options available to the user at a given point in the program. Before processing can begin, this type of control structure requires the user to make a choice from a list of functions. Menus almost entirely eliminate the possibility that the user will make an error in the syntax of an entry. From the user's standpoint, menus are excellent for casual use and require very little external documentation. Such an interface might be ideal for a manager's decision support program, for example.

A disadvantage already mentioned is that a menu format can become tedious with frequent use. One other drawback is that the need for frequent prompting breaks the program run into small options and control steps. This series of small steps can fragment a user's thought processes enough to distract from the application itself. The programmer gains these advantages when using a menu format:

- Use of menus is a good match with structured programming techniques. The menu becomes a starting point for top-down design. Each option in the menu can represent a task definition for which a program module may be written.
- The text of the questions within the program itself helps the programmer identify what specific actions must be provided for.
- Because of the correspondence between menu options and programming tasks, menu-driven programs, once designed, are comparatively easy to write.
- Minimal documentation usually is needed to instruct the user.

The programming disadvantages in the use of menus include:

- Menu-driven programs contain a lot of text. Such programs are not compact, since the text of every possible menu option must be included.
- Menus usually are not appropriate for sections of a program in which a large volume of data must be entered, especially if this must be done repetitively. Clearly, a menu is not the approach for high volume clerical applications.

Another form of prompt-driven program control involves the use of prompting questions that have strictly yes or no answers. The advantages of this approach to the user are simplicity and speed. Responses are easily anticipated, almost no training time is required, and the program progresses rapidly. A program that implements a market survey questionnaire might employ this technique. Advantages of *yes/no prompting* to the programmer are:

- The choices given to the user are clearly defined and predictable.
- Prompting questions can be phrased so that, during user sessions and in the most commonly encountered instances, the answers are mostly yes (or mostly no). In such cases, the frequently encountered re-

sponse can be set in the program as a *default condition* so that only exceptions must be keyed in. This approach greatly reduces session time.

- Program coding is straightforward. Some similarity exists with the structured approach to coding menus.
- Yes/no options are easy to code. The range of inputs is so narrow that it is easy to be sure that the input possibilities have been anticipated.

A disadvantage of yes/no prompting, of course, is the fact that it is so simplistic. Not all problems or tasks can be reduced easily to two options.

The ideal user interface for a particular programming problem actually may be a mixture of these techniques. Further, there are many variations on each approach. The design decision ultimately comes down to a question of programming style. Experience can show which technique will be the most useful for a specific situation.

Example displays of commands and prompts for these techniques are presented in Figure 5-1.

FORMATS FOR DATA INPUT

User entries may be used to control the sequence of processing. Three basic programming strategies for formatting user inputs are discussed below. However, the possibilities and variations for input data formats are limited only by the creativity of the programmer. Three basic formats are:

- Free-form
- Ask-and-answer
- Fill-in-a-form.

Free-form. A *free-form* data entry format usually requires the user to input all data on a single line, with entries separated by some kind of *delimiter,* typically a comma. Although this technique is relatively easy to program, it has several drawbacks. Because there is no *feedback* to prompt the user, a high incidence of data entry mistakes is likely. It is all too easy for the user to lose track of the meaning and exact form of each data entry, especially when long strings must be entered. This technique, like the purely command-driven technique, is not used often and is not considered a user-friendly programming practice.

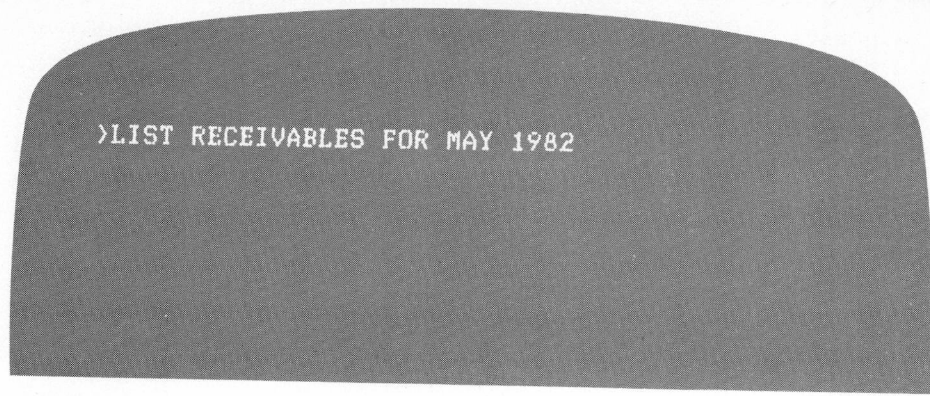

COMMAND

```
OPTIONS: L(IST, P(OST, S(TOP?
>L
LIST:  P(AYABLES R(ECEIVABLES, T(IMESHEETS S(TOP
>R
FOR WHAT MONTH?
>MAY
FOR WHAT YEAR?
>1983
```

MENU / PROMPT

```
LIST (Y/N)?
>Y
PAYABLES (Y/N)?
>N
RECEIVABLES (Y/N)?
>Y
```

YES / NO PROMPTING

Figure 5-1. Sample commands and prompts. Note that for this example yes/no prompting is inappropriate.

Ask-and-answer. An *ask-and-answer* format requires display of a specific prompt for each user entry. This technique is easy to program and does not confuse the user. Program text for ask-and-answer is fairly concise and can be self-documenting. This technique is useful primarily for shorter programs for which only a few data items must be entered. For longer programs and data input requirements, objectionably long session times can result because of the need to display each prompt and wait for a response.

Fill-in-a-form. *Fill-in-a-form* is similar to ask-and-answer except that, as its name implies, all prompts are displayed simultaneously as a kind of form to be completed. Input typically is done at a VDT. The cursor moves from one input item on the form to another as the user responds by entering data. This method is ideal for large input requirements, especially for those tasks that are highly repetitive and for which the input formats remain the same from one job run to the next. This technique becomes particularly user-friendly if the form displayed is similar to a manual form already familiar to the user. Another clear advantage is that all input requirements are displayed and may be anticipated easily by the user so that the required data are readily available at the console. One drawback, from the programmer's standpoint, is that the program text may have to implement techniques such as *highlighting.* This involves use of arrows and other graphic display techniques to lead the user through a complex form. These techniques require program text that can be lengthy and fairly sophisticated.

INPUT EDITING

Data inputs should be *validated* before use in processing. The objective here is to screen out data that have been entered in error, perhaps accidentally, and to prevent the entry of inappropriate commands that may interfere with the intended processing. Any of these circumstances, if uncorrected, might cause the program to return invalid results or even terminate in error. The user then would have to restart the program from the beginning, after taking time to determine what was wrong with the input. Potentially worse, a wrong answer might be produced without the user detecting that it is wrong.

In general, the user should be given the option of recovering from an input error as soon as possible after the error has been made and with a minimum of disruption to the processing flow.

The program code required to provide this protection is referred to as *input editing,* which constitutes program *overhead* that can be quite extensive. Like other aspects of the user interface, this process of input editing can consume more lines of program text than the processing steps that produce the actual program results. There is no hard and fast rule here; rather, the choice of how much input editing is enough is a matter of style and programming preference. Consider instead the range of options, which extend from doing no input editing at all to a user interface that applies rigorous constraints but may be slow and inflexible. The main options are:

Perform no input editing. For short programs, or for test runs of proposed program code during debugging, such an approach might be acceptable. Remember, though, that inappropriate data can be fatal to a program. If one of the objectives of the program is to capture data that are transient or difficult to gather, the programmer should ask whether the risk of data loss is worth the time saved in coding. This risk is particularly high if one of the actions of the program is to change or update data that are in permanent storage.

Perform checks of data reasonableness and type validation. *Reasonableness tests* can be built into the program text. One such technique is *range checking.* For example, a numeric entry for a date should include an entry for month that is greater than or equal to 1 and less than or equal to 12. *Type validation* involves verifying, for example, that an entry for the numeric day of the month includes no alphabetic characters. Range checking and type validation should be done before processing of the input data begins.

Range checking allows for inputs to be corrected before any results have been returned. One advantage of performing these tests is that the casual user is notified, through the use of error messages, about any incorrect entries. Thus, the training cycle is shortened.

Verify each input item. The ideal input editing scheme would include procedures for checking each data input item in relation to what data are required for usable results. Such checking would include verifying that entries do not exceed some specified length, rejecting entries that are out of specified ranges, rejecting entries that are of the incorrect data type, and checking for invalid characters. More extensive prompting may be done, such as prompting 'IS THIS CORRECT?' after an entry and while the user is still in control. Then, the previous input may be reentered if a "No" is entered. Previous correct entries may be saved to a file and used to prompt subsequent program runs.

USER MESSAGES

Another aspect of the user's "window" is that certain processing functions may slow execution of that portion of the program. In such situations, the user may feel that some inappropriate entry has disrupted processing or that some further entry is necessary for processing to continue. When processing is apt to be lengthy and will not require any further user inputs, the message 'PLEASE WAIT' can be displayed. For more extensive processing, a progress chart may be displayed and updated for the user's benefit as each processing phase is executed. (Recall that the Pascal compiler displays its progress in similar fashion.) A straightforward way of providing a status report for the user is to display a running total of the number of records processed, for example.

It is often good practice to provide some means for the user to halt processing if desired, and then continue at will. When processing has been halted by a user command, a message such as 'CONTINUE?' or 'PRESS ANY KEY TO CONTINUE' is appropriate. Remember, though, that display of such messages slows actual program processing.

In case of a user-requested program halt, intermediate results should be displayed, if possible. After all, it may be that only a partial run is desired but that the intermediate results are significant. Also, the user should be given the ability to resume processing, if desired, at the point where the halt occurred.

One potential problem stems from the tendency for users to become confused by particularly long menu-driven programs. Such programs may contain a main menu and other menus that are subordinate to it. These menus typically appear one at a time. This control technique is known as *nested menus.* Some messages are necessary in this case to notify the user where the program is in terms of the hierarchy of processing steps defined by the various menus. In this situation, a display line at the bottom of each subordinate menu might say 'PRESS <RETURN> FOR MASTER COMMAND DIRECTORY', or at the top say 'MAIN MENU OPTION 3—PRINT REPORT'.

User messages and control procedures recognize that program execution is controlled by people. With microcomputers occupying only a portion of desks used for other activities, it may be necessary to halt processing to answer the telephone or attend a meeting. In a time-sharing environment, in which many terminals share a central computing resource, processing speeds can vary widely depending upon the number of users. In such situations, keeping the user informed of the program's progress is essential.

THE DISPLAY SCREEN

The display screen is an important tool for interacting with the user. This display represents the user's "window," as pointed out at the beginning of this chapter. Thus, producing a program that is user-friendly requires that control be exercised over data entry—and also that care be taken in the placement and visual appearance of prompts and messages on the screen. The display is also a programmer's tool in that it can be used to help the user organize the problem he or she is trying to solve.

In the programming examples encountered so far in this book, the console display has been treated as if it were a printer, with successive output lines displayed as if running down the page, in effect. The console display, however, has many more formatting capabilities than a printer does, and Pascal offers some procedures for using this potential.

The **PAGE** procedure is used to start a new page, or display area, on the output device. A new page may be started on the display by giving the predeclared file name **OUTPUT**, which is associated with the display device, as a parameter for the procedure PAGE:

```
PAGE(OUTPUT);
```

This new page starts with the cursor appearing at the upper left corner of the display. On some computers, the previous page is erased and a blank screen presented. Presenting a new page to the user is a helpful technique for signalling, for example, the beginning of a new question, the next page of a report, the next menu in a series of nested menus, and so on.

The procedure PutTitle presented in Figure 5-2 uses the PAGE feature to begin a new display page and may be passed a parameter that holds the title, a string value, for the page.

```
(***************************************************************************)
(*                                                                         *)
(*          PROCEDURE TO ERASE SCREEN AND DISPLAY Title AT THE TOP --      *)
(*  PROCEDURE TO BE CALLED WHEN A NEW DISPLAY PAGE AND TITLE ARE NEEDED    *)
(*                                                                         *)
(***************************************************************************)
PROCEDURE PutTitle(Title:STRING);
BEGIN
  PAGE(OUTPUT);                                    (* clear the screen *)
  WRITELN(Title);                                     (* display title *)
  WRITELN('----------------------------------------');    (* underline *)
  WRITELN;                                              (* skip a line *)
END;
```

Figure 5-2. Procedure PutTitle.

Each time a new page is required, PutTitle may be called and passed the page title as a parameter.

Once the new display page has been created, the programmer must be able to specify exactly where the cursor is to be positioned on the display, so that user prompts and messages, as well as input fields, may be organized visually. To understand how this aspect of control may be exercised, consider some basic characteristics of the display device.

A microcomputer display device can show a limited number of characters on each line. This line width is typically 40 or 80 characters. The display also is limited to a fixed number of lines, typically 24. Each character position on the display can be located uniquely by specifying first its *character position,* or horizontal position (column), and then its *line number,* or vertical position (row). These two *coordinates* traditionally are referred to as the *X axis* value and the *Y axis* value, where X is the character position and Y is the line number. Figure 5-3 illustrates these relationships.

Character positions are numbered from 0 on the extreme left of the display to 39 on the right for a 40-column display, 79 on the right for an 80-column display. Lines are numbered from 0 at the top to 23 at the bottom for a 24-line display. Thus, on a 40-column display device with 24 lines, the coordinates for the point at the top left of the display are:

```
X is 0 and
Y is 0,
or X, Y coordinates of 0,0
```

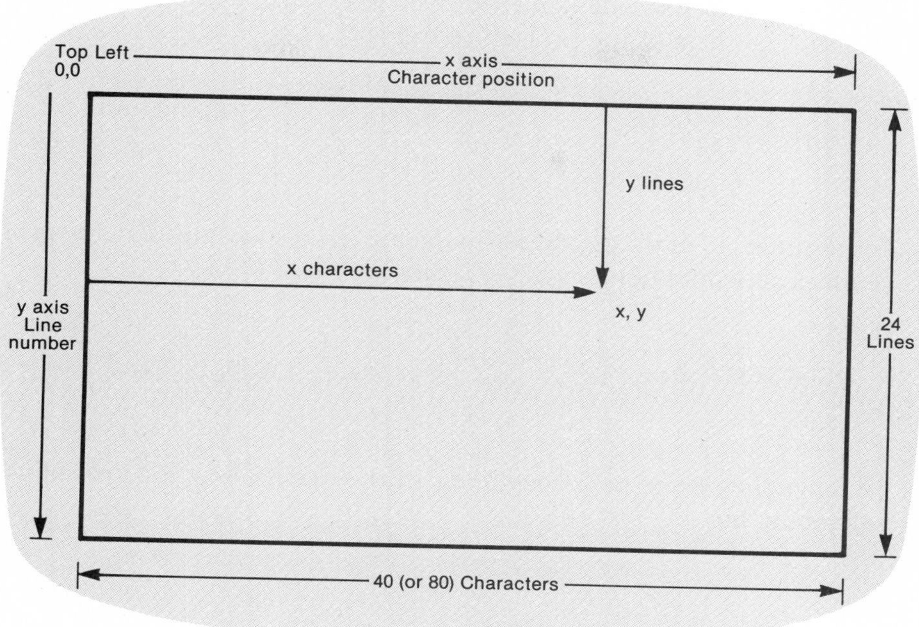

Figure 5-3. Position on the face of a CRT can be specified by coordinates that refer to the vertical and horizontal axes of the screen.

Accordingly, the coordinates of the point at the bottom right of the display are:

```
X is 39 and
Y is 23,
or X, Y coordinates of 39, 23
```

Bear in mind that the screen location of the cursor indicates the point at which the next character to be displayed will appear. To give the programmer control over exact cursor position, UCSD Pascal offers the procedure **GOTOXY**. Arguments corresponding to the X and Y coordinates for desired screen location must be given when calling the GOTOXY procedure. The form of the procedure call is:

```
GOTOXY(X,Y);
```

For example, to move the cursor to the top left display position, the procedure call would be:

```
GOTOXY(0,0);
```

To move the cursor to the beginning of the twelfth line, the procedure call would be:

```
GOTOXY(0,11);
```

Remember that the character position and line number are counted from 0 rather than from 1. So, in the above example, the Y coordinate of the twelfth line is 11.

The procedure AskValue presented in Figure 5-4 asks the user for an input at screen coordinates X,Y. This procedure may be called any time a new entry must be prompted. (Note the use of VAR in the procedure header to return the value of Answer to the calling block.)

DESIGN OF PROGRAM *BalancePlus*

In Chapter 4, the *BalanceCheckbook* program is developed to give the user the ability to enter a starting balance, enter various debits and credits, and have the program calculate a final balance on the account. However, this program serves only to computerize a simple manual process. A checkbook is actually a type of ledger system. To use a checkbook to manage money, it is necessary to categorize, or classify, debits and credits to indicate the reason for the transaction. In the manual process of posting entries to the check register, each check is identified by the name

```
(****************************************************************************)
(*                                                                          *)
(*          ASK THE USER FOR A REAL NUMBER AT COORDINATES X,Y --            *)
(*    PROCEDURE TO BE CALLED EACH TIME ANY DOLLAR AMOUNT MUST BE KEYED      *)
(*                                                                          *)
(****************************************************************************)
PROCEDURE AskValue(X,Y:INTEGER;Question:STRING;VAR Answer:REAL);
BEGIN
  REPEAT
   GOTOXY(X,Y);           (* screen location determined by parameters passed *)
   WRITE(Question,' ');                  (* Question must be passed as argument *)
   READLN(Answer);                            (* user makes entry at keyboard *)
  UNTIL OK;         (* calls the function OK, which is either TRUE or FALSE *)
END;
```

Figure 5-4. Procedure AskValue.

of the payee and the purpose of the expenditure. Credits and deposits are posted, with the sources of each indicated. Managing money, preparing budgets, and keeping books of account all require that expenses and income be classified by categories such as meals, lodging, transportation, etc.

To allow your friend with the home computer to categorize these entries, and to implement a more friendly user interface, you develop a new program called *BalancePlus.* Design considerations for this program, particularly as they relate to the user interface, are discussed below. Program control structures and code that implement selections and repetitions specified by the design are presented, along with the program text, in Chapter 6.

Some added features that improve the user interface provide preliminary program specifications:

Data input editing. User inputs to the program must be edited to make sure that entries are valid.

Second-chance input. The user should be allowed to try again when entering data. This feature would allow the user to correct keystroke and other input errors as such errors are discovered on input.

Menu selection. Multiple-choice options should be offered for data entry.

Page headings. Titles should be placed on each display page to indicate the operation that is being performed.

Tabular reporting. Printed output should be displayed in a concise, columnar format.

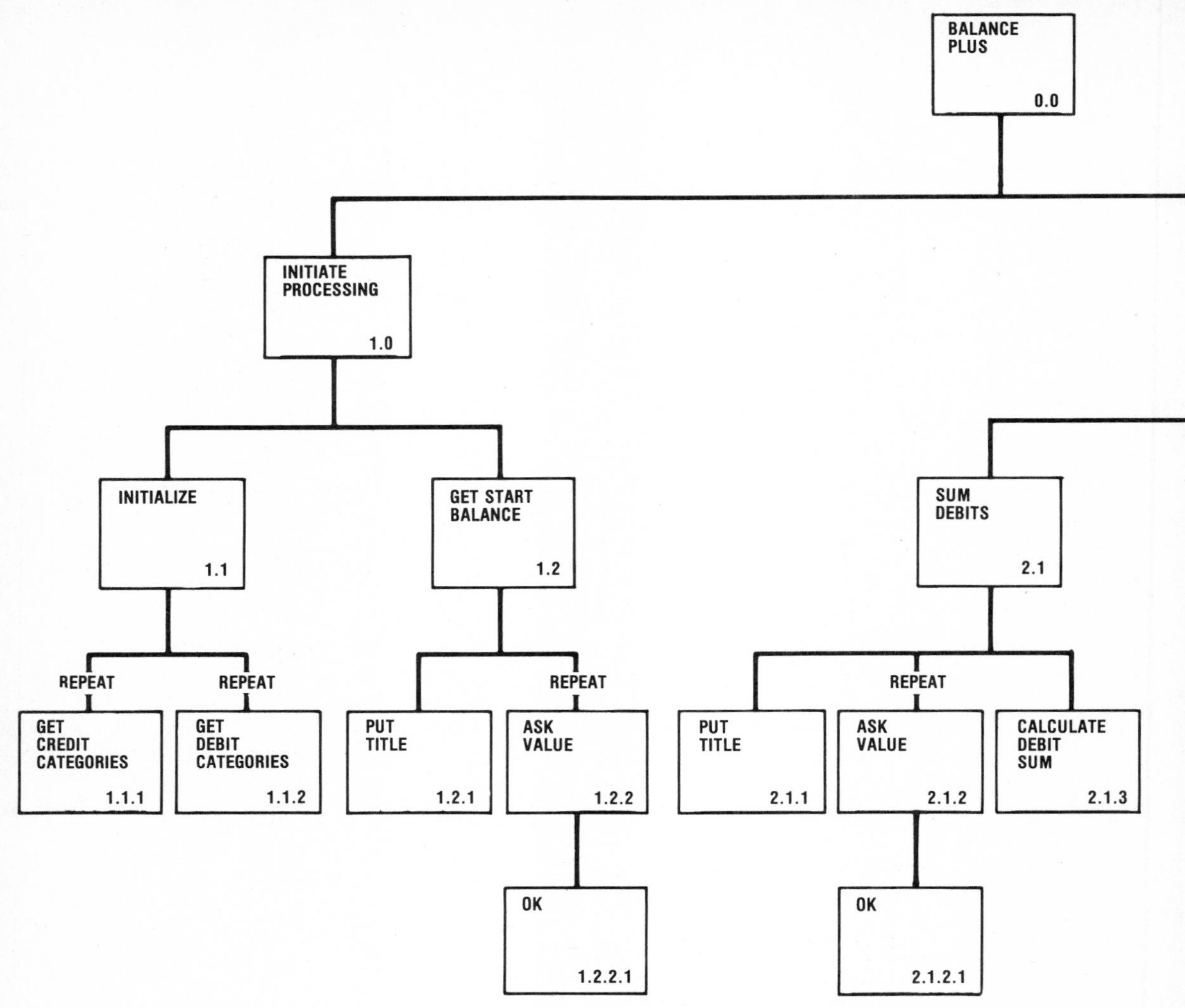

The main body of the *BalancePlus* program can be almost identical to the corresponding section of *BalanceCheckbook*. The reason for the similarity is that the two programs share much the same logical design. The difference lies in the physical implementation. Accordingly, the user interface is primarily a physical consideration. The main body of *BalancePlus* contains the following procedure calls:

```
BEGIN
  Initialize;
  GetStartBalance;
  SumDebits;
  SumCredits;
  CalculateCurrentBalance;
END.
```

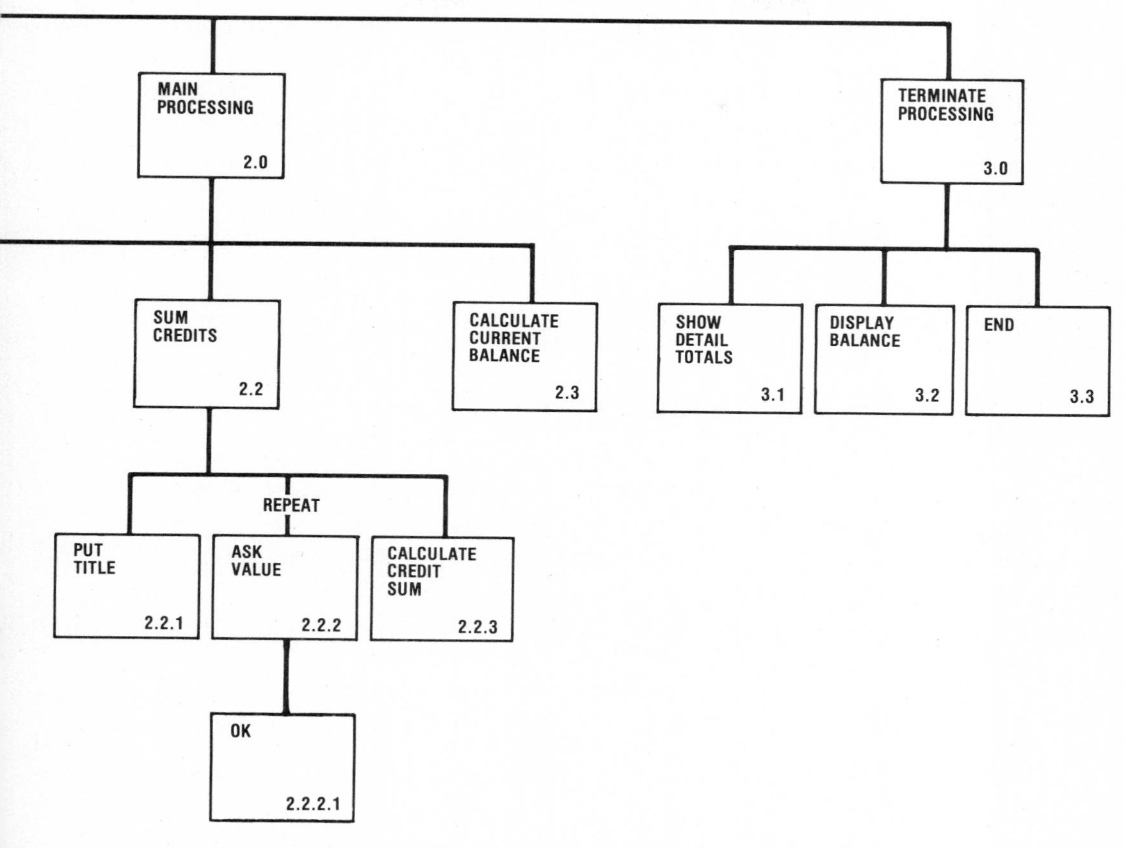

Figure 5-5. Structure chart for program *BalancePlus.*

Logically, main processing begins with SumDebits. The procedures Initialize and GetStartBalance implement the initialization module. The tasks contained in the program modules are presented in a structure chart in Figure 5-5.

A new procedure, Initialize, is added to prompt user selections for processing options. The tasks involved are getting debit and credit categories from the user and clearing all working variables. The procedure also calls the GetDebitCategories and GetCreditCategories, which allow the user to specify the names of up to five categories each for debits and credits. The actual user input selection is implemented by invoking the function AskCategory, which displays a menu of category options and gets a numbered response from the user. The initialization module and the corresponding user inputs are completed by the execution of GetStartBalance.

The termination module consists of the output statements in CalculateCurrentBalance and the program END statement.

Summary

The user interface sets a style for the program by forming a convenient and useful "window" through which the user views and reacts to the program. Factors to be considered in designing the user interface are the user's familiarity with the application area and with the target computer system. Volume of data to be processed, frequency of program use, and degree of skill of the individual who actually enters data are additional factors to be weighed.

The program gives support to the user through prompts. The program may be either self-documenting or have external documentation associated with it. Basic types of user program controls are command-driven and prompt-driven techniques. Trade-offs must be considered in evaluating these alternative user interface strategies. Specific prompt-driven approaches are the use of menus and yes/no responses. These represent forms of multiple-choice processing.

Providing formats for data input is another feature of a user interface. Such formats include free-form, ask-and-answer, and fill-in-a-form.

Some degree of input editing should be done to be sure that the input data are valid and likely to produce usable results. Messages can be generated to keep the user informed of the program's progress and to avoid confusion.

A new page may be caused on the display screen by passing the predeclared identifier OUTPUT to the PAGE procedure. This new page will appear with the cursor in the top left corner.

The display device usually is addressed by reference to a coordinate system of 40 (or 80) horizontal positions by 24 vertical positions. Screen locations are defined by two coordinates, one for the character position, or X axis, and one for the line number, or Y axis. The screen location of the cursor indicates where the next character is to appear. Cursor control is accomplished through use of GOTOXY.

Features to be incorporated in the program *BalancePlus* include: data input editing, second chance input, menu selection, page headings, and tabular reporting.

Review Questions

1. What is meant by the user interface and why is it so important to good program design?
2. Write a short program that draws a geometric object (a hexagon, for example) using only WRITE or WRITELN and GOTOXY statements.
3. What factors must be considered in deciding how much external documentation is desirable for a given program?
4. What is the basic difference between programs that are command-driven and those that are prompt-driven?
5. What are some techniques used in prompt-driven programs?

Pascal Practice

1. Write a narrative describing how the Pascal editor and compiler address the user (programmer) interface.
2. Write a short program that draws a geometric object (a hexagon, for example) using only WRITELN and GOTOXY statements.

Key Terms

1. user-friendly
2. package
3. programming style
4. application area
5. target computer system
6. user interface
7. prompting
8. documentation
9. self-documenting
10. external documentation
11. user's guide
12. user's manual
13. trade-off
14. command-driven
15. prompt-driven
16. error checking
17. scan
18. parse
19. error message
20. menu
21. yes/no prompting
22. default condition
23. multiple-choice processing
24. free-form
25. delimiter
26. feedback
27. ask-and-answer
28. fill-in-a-form
29. highlighting
30. validate
31. input editing
32. overhead
33. reasonableness test
34. range checking
35. type validation
36. nested menu
37. character position
38. line number
39. coordinate
40. X axis
41. Y axis

Pascal Library

1. PAGE
2. OUTPUT
3. GOTOXY

6 IMPLEMENTING PROGRAM CONTROLS

OBJECTIVES

On completing the reading and other learning assignments in this chapter, you should be able to:

- ☐ Describe the role of logical tests in coding loops and iterations.
- ☐ Explain how logical tests may be implemented by Boolean comparisions.
- ☐ Describe the uses of the BOOLEAN data type in Pascal.
- ☐ Use the Pascal control structures IF . . THEN and CASE . . OF.
- ☐ Use the looping and repetition control structures FOR . . DO and WHILE . . DO.
- ☐ Explain the use of arrays and how reference is made to array elements.
- ☐ Tell how programs may be entered and debugged by testing individual modules.

PROGRAM CONTROL STRUCTURES

Recall that the limited set of control structures used in writing programs in a structured language like Pascal involves sequences, selections, and repetitions. Sequences are implemented by the sequence of program statements in the absence of other control structures. Selections in Pascal are implemented through the control structures IF . . THEN . . ELSE and CASE . . OF. Repetitions, or loops, are implemented by REPEAT . . UNTIL, FOR . . DO, and WHILE . . DO.

A series of selections may be used to implement menus for user options, or *multiple-choice processing.* Such selections may take the form of condition tests, or *logical tests.* Selections that involve user input to logical tests typify interactive processing. Of course, both interactive and batch programs may use selections based on logical tests of values presented to the program.

Repetitions, although found in interactive programs, are the basis of batch processing. An item is input, processed through the loop instructions, and then program control returns to the beginning of the loop; the second item is input and processed, and so on until all items in the batch have been processed. Logical tests also may be used to terminate program loops.

LOGICAL COMPARISONS AND THE BOOLEAN DATA TYPE

Such tests are a form of Boolean logic, which provides rules for comparison of data values by evaluating statements that are either true or false. Figure 6-1 gives a table of frequently used logical comparisons and their corresponding symbols in Pascal program text.

Recall that the equal sign (=) in Pascal is used to invoke a comparison, or test of equality. The result derived from evaluating a Pascal program statement containing such a comparison results in one of two values—**TRUE** or **FALSE**. Logical comparisons also may be made with any of the symbols shown in Figure 6-1.

LOGISTICAL COMPARISONS AND THEIR SYMBOLS IN PASCAL PROGRAM TEXT

EQUAL TO	=
NOT EQUAL TO	<>
GREATER THAN	>
LESS THAN	<
GREATER THAN OR EQUAL TO	>=
LESS THAN OR EQUAL TO	<=

Figure 6-1. Boolean comparisons and symbols.

The following example uses a logical comparison to terminate a loop:

```
BEGIN
  WRITELN('ENTER SPACE BAR TO READ THE NEXT MESSAGE.');
   REPEAT
    READ(Character);
   UNTIL Character = ' ';
  WRITELN('THIS IS THE NEXT MESSAGE.');
END;
```

The above loop does not terminate unless the user enters a space bar. The UNTIL statement makes a logical comparison of each entry to determine whether a space bar has been entered. The UNTIL, then, awaits a result of TRUE for the expression:

```
Character = ' '
```

Often it is useful in writing Pascal programs to create a variable or a function that can have only one of two values, TRUE or FALSE. For this purpose, Pascal includes the **BOOLEAN** data type. BOOLEAN is a predefined type, like INTEGER, and identifies a given variable or function as having one of two values—TRUE or FALSE.

Program statements that evaluate logical comparisons or conditions that result in either TRUE or FALSE values may be referred to as Boolean comparisons, or logical tests.

The program block presented in Figure 6-2 is taken from the example program at the end of this chapter and illustrates both a logical test used to control the termination of a loop and the assignment of a BOOLEAN value based on another logical test.

In the example in Figure 6-2, the loop set up by REPEAT . . UNTIL terminates when either a <SPACE BAR> or a <RETURN> is entered by the user. If a return is entered, processing control proceeds to the next

```
(**************************************************************************)
(*                                                                        *)
(*     FUNCTION TO ALLOW THE USER TO CHANGE AN ANSWER OR TO CONTINUE      *)
(*                                                                        *)
(**************************************************************************)
FUNCTION OK:BOOLEAN;               (* value of function to be TRUE or FALSE *)
VAR
 Character:CHAR;
 Message:STRING;                                (* declare local variables *)
BEGIN
 Message := 'ENTER (RETURN) IF OK, (SPACE BAR) TO CHANGE ANSWER';
  REPEAT
   WRITE(Message);
   READ(KEYBOARD,Character);              (* READ without echoing character *)

 (* first logical test: *)
  UNTIL (Character = ' ') OR EOLN(KEYBOARD); (* EOLN(KEYBOARD) is (RETURN) *)

(* second logical test: *)
 IF EOLN(KEYBOARD) THEN OK := TRUE

 ELSE OK := FALSE;
END;                                               (* END OF FUNCTION OK *)
```

Figure 6-2. Function OK.

program statement, which sets a value of TRUE for the function. Otherwise, a value of FALSE is assigned. This function may be called at appropriate points in the program to implement logical tests to determine whether the user wishes to change an answer or continue. If the function returns a value of TRUE, the user wishes to continue. If the function returns a value of FALSE, the user has chosen to change an entry.

IF . . THEN and CASE . . OF

An **IF . . THEN** program statement is used in the function OK to test the value entered by the user and specify a condition that must be met before a processing step can occur. This is a form of selection, or alternative, processing. One of the uses of logical tests is to trigger processing alternatives.

The most general form of the IF . . THEN program statement is:

```
IF logical test THEN statement;
                    (* and optionally: *)
IF logical test THEN statement ELSE statement;
                    (* semicolon not allowed before ELSE *)
```

When compound statements are employed, the form is:

```
IF logical test THEN
 BEGIN
  program statement;
  ..
  program statement  (* semicolon not required before END *)
 END                 (* semicolon not allowed before ELSE *)
ELSE
 BEGIN
  program statement;
  ..
  program statement  (* semicolon not required before END *)
 END;
```

ELSE may be used to specify an optional, alternate condition and its corresponding program statement. BEGIN and END are required only when more than one statement is used following THEN or following ELSE.

No semicolons appear before or after THEN and ELSE. Semicolons are used to separate statements, and the IF . . THEN . . ELSE construction is evaluated by the compiler as a single statement.

The statement or compound statement following ELSE is skipped if the logical test in the IF statement is TRUE and is executed only if that logical test is FALSE.

Programmers soon find that IF . . THEN . . ELSE statements tend to multiply like rabbits once introduced into a program. It is not unusual for algorithms to require IF . . THEN . . ELSE IF . . THEN . . ELSE, and this is only the beginning. The words **AND** and **OR** also are permissible for combining simple logical tests into compound tests. Also, the word **NOT** will reverse the truth value of the logical test it precedes. The possible combinations can become complex and do not contribute to program clarity.

Instead of the potential complications of IF . . THEN . . ELSE, Pascal has another control structure that provides an orderly means for selecting the results of conditions. It also may require fewer lines of program text. This alternative control structure is known as **CASE . . OF**.

CASE . . OF gives the programmer the ability to specify all possible options for a given condition, along with a processing action for each. In this way, it appears the ideal method for implementing menus and more complex forms of multiple-choice processing.

This structure has the following form:

```
CASE expression OF
 selector : program statement;
 selector : program statement;
  ..
 selector : program statement;    (* semicolon optional *)
END;
```

The options in this structure are called *case selectors.* There is no semicolon after the line that contains CASE because it serves as a delimiter like BEGIN. Accordingly, an END; reserved word must appear at the end of the block. The options listed can include some or all of the possible values that can occur for the expression given in the header. If all possible values are not given, values encountered for which there is no selector will cause no processing. (This possibility can be eliminated by restricting the range of values that may result from evaluating the CASE expression.)

The differences between coding with IF . . THEN and ELSE or with CASE . . OF can be illustrated by considering a function that implements a yes/no user option:

```
FUNCTION Yes(Question:STRING):BOOLEAN;
VAR
 Answer:CHAR;
BEGIN
 WRITE(Question);
 REPEAT
  READ(Answer);
 UNTIL (Answer = 'Y') OR (Answer = 'N');
(***************************************************************************)
(*                                                                         *)
(*        FUNCTION ASSIGNED A VALUE IN STATEMENTS THAT GO HERE             *)
(*                                                                         *)
(***************************************************************************)
END;
```

Notice that a portion of the above program block is missing. This portion is where a value must be assigned for the function, based on certain conditions. Performing this assignment with an IF . . THEN structure could be accomplished by:

```
IF Answer = 'Y' THEN Yes := TRUE
ELSE Yes := FALSE;
```

On the other hand, the same processing may be implemented by:

```
CASE Answer OF
'Y' : Yes := TRUE;
'N' : Yes := FALSE;
END;
```

Note particularly that, on encountering either structure, no processing occurs until the user responds by keying 'Y' or 'N'. Of course it also would be possible to achieve the same result with the following statement, which includes an implicit Boolean test:

```
Yes := (Answer = 'Y');
```

LOOPING AND REPETITION CONTROL

The implementation of menus and other multiple-choice processing schemes frequently requires that actions be repeated a number of times, depending on the value of some logical test. The construction REPEAT . . UNTIL is useful for this purpose. Two other Pascal control structures provide for other kinds of looping and repetition control. These are FOR . . DO and WHILE . . DO.

FOR . . DO

The Pascal control structure **FOR . . DO** is used for repetition, or iteration, control and is known as a *counting loop.* A counting loop is a series of program statements repeated a specific number of times, as determined by the value of a *counter variable.* A range for this counter variable is specified by a starting value and an ending value. Then, each time the series of program statements in the loop is executed, the value of the counter variable is *incremented,* or advanced to the next counter value, until the ending value is reached. For example, the following loop causes 'THIS LINE WILL BE DISPLAYED TEN TIMES' to be displayed on the console ten times:

```
FOR LoopCounter := 1 TO 10 DO
WRITELN('THIS LINE WILL BE DISPLAYED TEN TIMES');
```

The counter variable, LoopCounter in this case, must have been declared previously. Further, the counter variable must be of a data type that implies counting. Data types that imply counting are said to be *scalar,* or *ordinal,* and include INTEGER, CHARacter, and BOOLEAN (and any user-defined scalar types, such as Weekday in a prior example). Examples of data types that do not imply counting would be REAL and STRING. (STRING refers to a string of characters. 'C' is a CHARacter; 'CAT' is a STRING.) These last two data types do not have any sequence implied in the values they define. For example, it would be possible to set a counter with the CHARacter type, since Pascal requires that it be possible to "count" from 'A' to 'Z'. However, if STRING were used, there is no clearly defined way of counting from 'CAT' to 'DOG'.

The beginning value for the counter variable (1 in the previous example) must be of the same data type as the ending value (10) and must be lower in value so that each iteration of the loop can increment the counter by increasing it one scalar unit. If the beginning value exceeds the ending value, the body of the loop will be skipped.

To provide for situations in which a "count-down" is appropriate, Pascal allows **DOWNTO** to be substituted for **TO**, as in:

```
FOR LoopCounter := 10 DOWNTO 1 DO
WRITELN('THE COUNTDOWN STANDS AT ',LoopCounter,' AND COUNTING.');
```

LoopCounter may be included as a variable name to be output in the WRITELN statement, as shown in the above example, because this variable always contains a value corresponding to the current status of the counter. In this way, it is treated like any other variable.

The form of the FOR .. DO structure, then, is:

```
FOR CounterVariable := StartValue TO EndValue DO
    (* where StartValue is the starting point and EndValue is the
                ending point of the range of CounterVariable *)
  statement (or compound statement with BEGIN and END);
```

BEGIN and END must appear only when a compound statement is used—that is, when multiple statements are to be repeated. The expression that contains the counter variable, of course, is another form of logical test that controls the sequence of processing.

WHILE . . DO

The Pascal control structure **WHILE . . DO** is similar to the previously introduced structure REPEAT . . UNTIL. WHILE . . DO says, in effect, as long as a certain logical test is TRUE, perform certain processing steps, then repeat the test. This form of loop is controlled, not by a counter, but by a continuing condition, or result, of a logical comparison. For example:

```
BEGIN
 I := 1;             (* I is an integer value used as a counter *)
  WHILE I < 25 DO
   BEGIN
    WRITELN('THIS IS LINE NUMBER ',I);
    I := I + 1;                          (* increment the counter *)
   END;
END;
```

This loop prints lines from 1 to 24. The statements within this program block will be executed again every time this comparative condition is found to be TRUE. Notice that the processing within the loop changes the value of the variables in the original logical test. Unlike the FOR . . DO structure, WHILE . . DO requires that the action of the loop change the value of the variables used in the comparison. Otherwise the activating condition always would be TRUE, and an infinite loop would result.

The important thing to remember in using this control structure is that the action of the loop must alter the value of the conditional expression, or logical comparison, that initiates it.

The form of the WHILE .. DO control structure is:

```
WHILE ConditionalExpression DO          (* a logical,
                                           or Boolean, comparison *)
  statement (or compound statement with BEGIN and END);
```

BEGIN and END are required only when a compound statement is used. Note that the logical test is stated in the first line of the WHILE . . DO construction. By comparison, in the REPEAT . . UNTIL construction, the conditional expression is encountered at the end of the loop, in the UNTIL statement. This distinction means that a WHILE . . DO program block may never be executed if the logical test is never met. However, a REPEAT . . UNTIL program block will be executed at least once because its program statements are encountered before the termination condition is evaluated. Unlike REPEAT . . UNTIL and FOR . . DO, the program must have initialized all variables in the conditional expression prior to encountering WHILE, or the result may be invalid.

WHILE . . DO and REPEAT . . UNTIL, then, are nearly identical loop control structures, distinguished from one another only by the location of the loop's exit condition test—after WHILE (at the beginning of the loop) or after UNTIL (at the end of the loop).

The example function AskCategory in Figure 6-3 is taken from the program at the end of this chapter and uses FOR . . DO and REPEAT . . UNTIL loops to implement a menu format for prompting user entries.

```
(*************************************************************************)
(*                                                                       *)
(*    SHOW A MENU OF THE AVAILABLE CATEGORY NAMES FOR CREDITS OR DEBITS  *)
(*                  AND ASK FOR THE DESIRED CATEGORY NUMBER              *)
(*                                                                       *)
(*************************************************************************)
FUNCTION AskCategory(NumberOfCategories:INTEGER;
                      CategList:CategArray):INTEGER;
VAR
 Counter,
 Answer:INTEGER;
BEGIN
  WRITELN;
  FOR Counter := 0 TO NumberOfCategories DO          (* display all Categs *)
   WRITELN(Counter:8,'. ',CategList[Counter]);                (* as a menu *)
  WRITELN;                                                 (* skip a line *)
   REPEAT
    WRITE('':8);                                       (* tab 8 spaces *)
    WRITE('ENTER CATEGORY (FROM 0 TO ',NumberOfCategories,') ');
    READLN(Answer);                                       (* READ Answer *)
   UNTIL (Answer IN [0..NumberOfCategories]);      (* check for valid range *)
  AskCategory := Answer;                     (* return result of function *)
 END;
```

Figure 6-3. Function AskCategory.

A coined type used in this example, CategArray, is explained below. The UNTIL statement implements a range checking technique that is explained in depth in Chapter 8. The formatting (:8) in the WRITE and WRITELN statements is used to control the appearance of the output display and also is covered in Chapter 8. Array references with brackets ([ ]) are covered below.

ARRAYS

The order of processing is determined by program control structures. The ways that groups of data items are referenced by the program form *data structures.* Pascal provides a means for referencing a group of data items that are all of the same data type. This *predefined data structure* is known as an *array.*

When dealing with many different data items within a program, it would be particularly inconvenient to coin a variable name for each data item. Instead, array structures allow the programmer to organize data items into categories within the computer's memory space.

Arrays are declared within the VARiable declaration section of the program, where each **ARRAY** is given a name and type. Simply stated, an array is a group of one or more variables of the same data type. It is possible to declare an ARRAY OF INTEGER, an ARRAY OF REAL, an ARRAY OF STRING, and so on. Such arrays are known as *one-dimensional arrays.* It is also possible to declare an ARRAY OF ARRAY, or a *multi-dimensional array.*

One of the conveniences of employing arrays is that individual data items, or *elements* of the array, are held in memory and referenced by *location* within the array. Thus, an *array name,* which is common to all elements of the array, combined with a specific location within the array, serve to specify uniquely a single data item. The location of a data item within an array is designated by a scalar value, commonly a number, called an *index.* The index of a data item is shown in program text as an array *subscript,* a number enclosed in brackets ([ ]).

For example, without the array structure, 10 REAL variables might be declared as follows:

```
VAR
 Credit1Total,
 Credit2Total,
 Credit3Total,
 Credit4Total,
 Credit5Total,
 Credit6Total,
 Credit7Total,
 Credit8Total,
 Credit9Total,
 Credit10Total: REAL;
(* 10 separate variables, all of REAL type *)
```

Since all 10 of these variables share the same data type, a single array declaration may be substituted instead of the 10 declarations above:

```
VAR
 CreditTotals: ARRAY[1..10] OF REAL;   (* single array declaration *)
```

In this example, the array CreditTotals contains 10 elements of type REAL. The elements of CreditTotals are indexed, numbered 1 to 10. The expression [1..10] indicates the *range* of the subscript. Based on this declaration, then, the 10 elements of ARRAY CreditTotals can be referred to as:

```
CreditTotals[1]
CreditTotals[2]
CreditTotals[3]   ..   CreditTotals[10]
```

This chapter's program example includes a coined array type, CategArray. The purpose of this type definition is to allow array variables to be passed as parameters to procedures and functions within the program. This was done in the above example AskCategory. The array variable CategArray holds string values that correspond with category names input by the user. An integer constant, MaximumCateg, is declared to restrict the number of categories the user may enter. (The size of an array is not variable during execution of the program.) The definitions look like this:

```
CONST
 MaximumCateg = 5;
TYPE
 CategArray = ARRAY[0..MaximumCateg] OF STRING;
```

One of the functions of the input section of the program is to gather entries for debit and credit category names. These entries are held in arrays of type CategArray that are declared as follows:

```
VAR
 DebitCategoryList,
 CreditCategoryList:CategArray;
```

Similarly, arrays also are used in the program to hold category totals:

```
VAR
 DebitTotals,
 CreditTotals: ARRAY[0..MaximumCateg] OF REAL;
```

Although the array index (as in [1]) often is a single integer value, note that an index also can be defined by any expression that produces a result having a value of the proper data type defined for that subscript in the array declaration. To illustrate, valid expressions for referring to elements in the array CreditTotals might be:

```
CreditTotals[ 1 + 2 ]                              (* refers to element 3 *)
CreditTotals[ (4 DIV 2) + 1 ]                      (* refers to element 3 *)
CreditTotals[ X * Y + Z ]                          (* refers to element ?,
                                                     depending upon the
                                                    current values of the
                                                     variables X, Y, and Z. *)
```

Of course, the index must fall within the subscript range declared for the array. Therefore, all of the following references to elements of Credit-Totals cause errors to occur:

```
CreditTotals[ 14 ]
CreditTotals[ 12 * 2 - 4 ]    (* result of evaluating the expression is 20 *)
CreditTotals[ X * Y + Z  ]       (* if X = 12, Y = 2, and Z = -4, as above *)
```

The declared subscript range of an array is quite flexible. The index need not be an integer but may be of any scalar type. For example, all of the following declarations are valid:

```
VAR
 AlphaArray : ARRAY['A'..'Z'] OF STRING;          (* first element would be
                                                          AlphaArray['A'] *)

 ResponseCount : ARRAY[FALSE..TRUE] OF INTEGER;
                        (* first element would be ResponseCount[FALSE] *)

 DaysWorked : ARRAY[(Monday,Tuesday,Wednesday,Thursday,Friday)] OF BOOLEAN;
                          (* first element would be DaysWorked[Monday] *)
```

Array References

In certain situations, the name of an array may be used without a subscript.

The subscript is omitted when performing assignment or equality tests on two arrays of the same declared size and type. For example, two arrays that are identical in size and type might be declared in the following way:

```
VAR
 AccountNameArray,
 CustomerList : ARRAY[1..20] OF STRING;
```

Given the above declarations, the following are valid statements:

```
AccountNameArray := CustomerList;
                 (* assigns contents of CustomerList to AccountNameArray *)

IF AccountNameArray = CustomerList THEN program statement;
   (* tests for equality between arrays AccountNameArray and CustomerList *)
```

The subscript also is omitted when passing an entire array as an argument to a procedure or function. For example, a program might contain the following definitions and declarations:

```
TYPE
 MasterAccountList = ARRAY[0..1024] OF STRING;

VAR
 Array1, Array2, Array3 : MasterAccountList;
```

In this example, a new type is coined, MasterAccountList. Then, in the VAR declaration, three arrays are declared as being of the MasterAccountList type. The program also might contain the following procedure header:

```
PROCEDURE Update(VAR ArrayParameter : MasterAccountList);
```

The parameter ArrayParameter is declared as being of type MasterAccountList. Hence, the procedure Update acts only on arrays that are of type MasterAccountList. Notice that for arrays to be used as arguments to a procedure (or function), the arrays must have a data type defined in the TYPE section that defines the array size and type. VAR is necessary in the formal declaration if it is desired to change the array in the calling procedure.

To continue with the example, given the above declarations and definitions, the following statements are valid, even though no subscripts are specified:

```
Update(Array1);   (* call procedure Update with parameter Array1 *)
Update(Array2);   (* call procedure Update with parameter Array2 *)
```

As previously stated, arrays of arrays are said to be multi-dimensional. In general, the same subscript rules apply to multi-dimensional arrays as those just illustrated. Other features of multi-dimensional arrays are covered in Chapter 14.

ENTERING AND DEBUGGING *BalancePlus*

The example programs in this book build one upon the other. Also, as new features and subprograms are added, the amount of program text grows. Although keying in program text is time-consuming, it is one of the basic ways to build proficiency in Pascal.

Considerable effort has been taken to be sure that the example program text is free of both logical and syntactical errors. However, even experienced programmers can introduce typographical errors into program text, inadvertently omit program statements, and so on. Encountering and correcting such errors is the first step toward mastering program debugging techniques.

Syntactical errors, of course, will be caught by the compiler. It is possible, though, to have a typographical error that compiles successfully. Such errors can show up as unexpected results from program execution, including incorrect values returned from test data and program halts caused by invalid ranges.

A good approach to entering a large program is to enter and compile modules, or smaller subprograms, one at a time. A procedure may be entered and compiled by including a PROGRAM header, BEGIN and END delimiters, and perhaps adding WRITELN statements to display intermediate results. Global variables used by the procedure must be declared and input statements or explicit values provided. If the procedure depends on arguments being passed to its parameters, explicit values or READLN statements must be added. If calls to other procedures or functions are made, these may be substituted with test values that are of the expected type and within the expected range.

Using this technique, additional modules may be added. Thus, the program is built up gradually and tested after the addition of each module. Debugging a program by modules may be compared to the task of laying bricks. First, you test the bricks and mortar. Then, you test the walls, one at a time. Finally, you test the house.

Figure 6-4 presents sample program text for testing the procedure SumDebits in *BalancePlus*. Other subprograms may be entered and tested in similar fashion. The process of debugging and devising test data is covered in depth in Chapter 10.

Of course, you can use comments (* *) to enclose statements or parts of statements that you want removed temporarily from compilation. However, comments cannot be nested; that is, the syntax (* (* *) *) would be incorrect.

PROGRAM *BalancePlus*

The program text for *BalancePlus* is presented in Figure 6-5. Comments appear frequently throughout the program text to clarify the processing actions caused by the program statements. A few additional coding

```
PROGRAM TestBalancePlus;

CONST
 MaximumCateg = 5;

VAR
 DebitSum:REAL;              (* declare global variables used by SumDebits *)
 DebitTotals:ARRAY[0..MaximumCateg] OF REAL;

 PROCEDURE SumDebits;
 VAR
  Amount:REAL;
  Choice:INTEGER;
 BEGIN
  REPEAT                                               (* UNTIL Amount = 0 *)
   WRITELN('ENTER DEBIT AMOUNT.'); (* skip PutTitle and prompt next READLN *)
   READLN(Amount);                        (* substitute for call of AskValue *)
   DebitSum := DebitSum + Amount;                     (* add to debit total *)
   WRITELN;
   WRITELN('':8,'    DEBIT SUMMARY IS $',DebitSum:8:2); (* show debit total *)
   IF Amount <> 0 THEN
    BEGIN
     Choice := 1;            (* substitute explicit value for AskCategory *)
     DebitTotals[Choice] := DebitTotals[Choice] + Amount;
            (* above adds the debit to the total for the selected category *)
    END;
  UNTIL Amount = 0;
 WRITELN('--- END OF DEBITS ---');
 END;
BEGIN                                                 (* main test program *)
 DebitSum := 0;                                     (* initialize variables *)
 DebitTotals[1] := 0;
 SumDebits;                                             (* call procedure *)
END.                                                 (* end test program *)
```

Figure 6-4. Program *TestBalancePlus*, used to enter and test a portion of the *BalancePlus* program.

---

techniques not yet encountered are included in the program. A brief explanation of each follows, and references are given, where appropriate, to the portions of the book that treat these techniques in greater depth.

LENGTH(StringExpression) This predeclared integer function causes the actual length in characters to be computed for the string variable specified. In this program, the statement is used to calculate

Figure 6-5. Program *BalancePlus*.

```
(* NOTE: Program text areas carried over from BalanceCheckbook are shaded. *)

PROGRAM BalancePlus;

CONST MaximumCateg = 5; (*defines a program-wide max. number of categories *)

(* THE FOLLOWING DATA TYPE DEFINITION IS DONE TO ALLOW VARIABLES OF THE
    TYPE CategArray TO BE PASSED AS PARAMETERS TO PROCEDURES OR FUNCTIONS. *)

TYPE
 CategArray = ARRAY[0..MaximumCateg] OF STRING;      (* for category names *)

VAR
 StartBalance,
 DebitSum,
 CreditSum,
 CurrentBalance:REAL;                  (* same variables as in BalanceCheckbook *)

 HowManyDebitCategories,
 HowManyCreditCategories:INTEGER;                   (* counters for categories *)

 DebitCategoryList,
 CreditCategoryList:CategArray;   (* two arrays to hold list of categories *)

 DebitTotals,
 CreditTotals:ARRAY[0..MaximumCateg] OF REAL;         (*  declare arrays of
                                                          category totals *)
(*************************************************************************)
(*                                                                       *)
(*   PROCEDURE TO ERASE SCREEN AND DISPLAY CENTERED Title AT THE TOP --  *)
(*   PROCEDURE TO BE CALLED WHEN A NEW DISPLAY PAGE AND TITLE ARE NEEDED *)
(*                                                                       *)
(*************************************************************************)
PROCEDURE PutTitle(Title:STRING);
CONST ScreenWidth = 40;              (* assume screen is 40 columns wide *)
VAR
 StartPosition:INTEGER;       (* declare variable to hold the calculation  *)
BEGIN
  PAGE(OUTPUT);                                     (* clear the screen *)
  StartPosition := (ScreenWidth DIV 2) - (LENGTH(Title) DIV 2);
  GOTOXY(StartPosition,1);        (* move cursor to position on second line *)
  WRITELN(Title);                                      (* display title *)
  WRITELN('---------------------------------------');        (* underline *)
  WRITELN;                                             (* skip a line *)
END;

(*************************************************************************)
(*                                                                       *)
(*       FUNCTION TO ALLOW THE USER TO CHANGE ANSWER OR TO CONTINUE      *)
(*                                                                       *)
(*************************************************************************)
FUNCTION OK:BOOLEAN;              (* value of function to be TRUE or FALSE *)
VAR
 Character:CHAR;
 Message:STRING;                               (* declare local variables *)
BEGIN
 Message := 'ENTER (RETURN) IF OK, (SPACE BAR) TO CHANGE ANSWER';
  REPEAT
   GOTOXY(0,22);
   WRITE(Message);
   READ(KEYBOARD,Character);
  UNTIL (Character = ' ') OR EOLN(KEYBOARD);
 IF EOLN(KEYBOARD) THEN OK := TRUE
 ELSE OK := FALSE;
 GOTOXY(0,22);
 WRITE('':LENGTH(Message));                        (* erase user message *)
END;
```

```
(*************************************************************************)
(*                                                                       *)
(*          ASK THE USER FOR A REAL NUMBER AT COORDINATES X,Y --         *)
(*    PROCEDURE TO BE CALLED EACH TIME ANY DOLLAR AMOUNT MUST BE KEYED   *)
(*                                                                       *)
(*************************************************************************)
PROCEDURE AskValue(X,Y:INTEGER;Question:STRING;VAR Answer:REAL);
BEGIN
  REPEAT
   GOTOXY(X,Y);
   WRITE(Question,' ');
   READLN(Answer);
  UNTIL OK;                                (* calls the function OK, above *)
GOTOXY(X,Y+1);                              (* cursor to next display line *)
END;
(*************************************************************************)
(*                                                                       *)
(*      GET THE NAMES OF THE CREDIT CATEGORIES AND PUT INTO AN ARRAY;    *)
(*      TERMINATE WHEN 5 ARE ENTERED OR WHEN USER ENTERS JUST A RETURN   *)
(*                                                                       *)
(*************************************************************************)
PROCEDURE GetCreditCategories;
VAR
 Temp:STRING;          (* local variable declared to hold temporary value *)
BEGIN
  PutTitle('CREDIT CATEGORY NAMES');            (* call procedure PutTitle *)
  CreditCategoryList[0] := 'MISCELLANEOUS CREDITS     ';
  HowManyCreditCategories := 0;
  WRITELN('Credit Category 0 : MISCELLANEOUS CREDITS');
   REPEAT
    WRITE('Credit Category ',HowManyCreditCategories + 1,' ? ');
    READLN(Temp);                   (* any response accepted until <RETURN> *)
    IF Temp <> '' THEN                             (* IF any answer THEN... *)
     BEGIN
(*the following fills the answer with spaces until it is 25 characters long*)
      WHILE(LENGTH(Temp)<25) DO Temp := CONCAT(Temp,' '); (*pad with spaces*)
      HowManyCreditCategories := HowManyCreditCategories + 1;
      CreditCategoryList[HowManyCreditCategories] := Temp; (* save in list *)
     END;
   UNTIL (Temp = '') OR (HowManyCreditCategories = MaximumCateg);
  WRITELN;
END;
(*************************************************************************)
(*                                                                       *)
(*      GET THE NAMES OF THE DEBIT CATEGORIES AND PUT INTO AN ARRAY      *)
(*                                                                       *)
(*************************************************************************)
PROCEDURE GetDebitCategories;
VAR
 Temp:STRING;          (* declare local variable to hold temporary value *)
BEGIN
  PutTitle('DEBIT CATEGORY NAMES');             (* call procedure PutTitle *)
  DebitCategoryList[0] := 'MISCELLANEOUS DEBITS      ';
  HowManyDebitCategories := 0;
  WRITELN('DEBIT CATEGORY 0 : MISCELLANEOUS DEBITS');
   REPEAT                                                 (* UNTIL done *)
    WRITE('DEBIT CATEGORY ',HowManyDebitCategories + 1,' ? ');
    READLN(Temp);                   (* any response accepted until <RETURN> *)
    IF Temp <> '' THEN                             (* IF any answer THEN... *)
     BEGIN
(*the following fills the answer with spaces until it is 25 characters long*)
      WHILE (LENGTH(Temp) < 25) DO Temp := CONCAT(Temp,' ');   (*pad spaces*)
      HowManyDebitCategories := HowManyDebitCategories + 1;
      DebitCategoryList[HowManyDebitCategories] := Temp;
     END;
   UNTIL (Temp = '') OR (HowManyDebitCategories = MaximumCateg);
  WRITELN;
END;
(*************************************************************************)
(*                                                                       *)
(*             ASK FOR THE BEGINNING BALANCE OF THE ACCOUNT              *)
(*                                                                       *)
(*************************************************************************)
```

```
PROCEDURE GetStartBalance;
BEGIN
  PutTitle('ACCOUNT STARTING BALANCE');          (* call procedure PutTitle *)
               (* the following calls AskValue and passes parameters to it *)
  AskValue(8,6,'ENTER STARTING BALANCE $',StartBalance);
END;
(***************************************************************************)
(*                                                                         *)
(*   SHOW A MENU OF THE AVAILABLE CATEGORY NAMES FOR CREDITS OR DEBITS     *)
(*   AND ASK FOR THE DESIRED CATEGORY NUMBER                               *)
(*                                                                         *)
(***************************************************************************)
FUNCTION AskCategory(NumberOfCategories:INTEGER;
                     CategList:CategArray):INTEGER;
VAR
 Counter,
 Answer:INTEGER;
BEGIN
  WRITELN;
  FOR Counter := 0 TO NumberOfCategories DO           (* display all categs *)
   WRITELN(Counter:8,'. ',CategList[Counter]);                 (* as a menu *)
  WRITELN;                                                  (* skip a line *)
   REPEAT                                         (* UNTIL Answer in range *)
    WRITE('':8);                                          (* tab 8 spaces *)
    WRITE('ENTER CATEGORY (FROM 0 TO ',NumberOfCategories,') ');
    READLN(Answer);                                        (* READ Answer *)
   UNTIL (Answer IN [0..NumberOfCategories] );      (* check for valid range *)
  AskCategory := Answer;                       (* return result of function *)
 END;
(***************************************************************************)
(*                                                                         *)
(*      GET EACH DEBIT AND ITS CATEGORY AND ADD IT TO THE TOTALS           *)
(*                                                                         *)
(***************************************************************************)
PROCEDURE SumDebits;
VAR
 Amount:REAL;
 Choice:INTEGER;
BEGIN
  REPEAT                                              (* UNTIL Amount = 0 *)
   PutTitle('DEBIT ENTRIES');                            (* call PutTitle *)
   AskValue(8,6,'  ENTER DEBIT AMOUNT $ ',Amount);     (* get debit Amount *)
   DebitSum := DebitSum + Amount;                    (* add to debit total *)
   WRITELN;
   WRITELN('':8,'   DEBIT SUMMARY IS $ ',DebitSum:8:2); (* show debit total*)
   IF Amount <> 0 THEN
    BEGIN
     Choice := AskCategory(HowManyDebitCategories,DebitCategoryList);
            (* above presents debit category menu and gets user's choice *)
     DebitTotals[Choice] := DebitTotals[Choice] + Amount;
          (* above adds the debit to the total for the selected category *)
    END;
  UNTIL Amount = 0;
 WRITELN('--- END OF DEBITS ---');
END;
(***************************************************************************)
(*                                                                         *)
(*      GET EACH CREDIT AND ITS CATEGORY AND ADD IT TO THE TOTALS          *)
(*                                                                         *)
(***************************************************************************)
PROCEDURE SumCredits;
VAR
 Amount: REAL;
 Choice: INTEGER;
BEGIN
  REPEAT                                              (* UNTIL Amount = 0 *)
   PutTitle('CREDIT ENTRIES');                           (* call PutTitle *)
   AskValue(8,6,' ENTER CREDIT AMOUNT $ ',Amount);    (* get credit Amount *)
   CreditSum := CreditSum + Amount;                        (* add to total *)
   WRITELN;
   WRITELN('':8,'    CREDIT SUMMARY IS $ ',CreditSum:8:2); (*display total*)
   IF Amount <> 0 THEN
```

```
    BEGIN
     Choice := AskCategory(HowManyCreditCategories,CreditCategoryList);
             (* above presents credit category menu and gets user's choice *)
     CreditTotals[Choice] := CreditTotals[Choice] + Amount;
           (* above adds the credit to the total for the selected category *)
    END;
  UNTIL Amount = 0;
 WRITELN('--- END OF CREDITS ---');
END;
(**********************************************************************)
(*                                                                    *)
(*   THE FOLLOWING PROCEDURE WILL DISPLAY TOTALS FOR DEBITS AND CREDITS   *)
(*   THAT HAVE BEEN ENTERED UNDER EACH CATEGORY, AS WELL AS GRAND TOTALS  *)
(*                                                                    *)
(**********************************************************************)
PROCEDURE ShowDetailTotals;
VAR
 Counter:INTEGER;
 Underline:STRING;
BEGIN
 Underline := '----------------------------------------';
                           (* list the summaries for each category of debit *)
 WRITELN;
 WRITELN('--DEBITS--');                                  (* WRITE heading *)
 FOR Counter := 0 TO HowManyDebitCategories DO         (* for each category *)
  WRITELN(DebitCategoryList[Counter],                 (* show category name *)
          DebitTotals[Counter]:14:2);                 (* and category total *)
  WRITELN(Underline);                                        (* underline *)
  WRITELN('DEBIT TOTAL',DebitSum:28:2);                     (* show total *)
                          (* list the summaries for each category of credit *)
  WRITELN;
  WRITELN('--CREDITS--');                                (* WRITE heading *)
  FOR Counter := 0 TO HowManyCreditCategories DO       (* for each category *)
   WRITELN(CreditCategoryList[Counter],               (* show category name *)
           CreditTotals[Counter]:14:2);               (* and category total *)
   WRITELN(Underline);                                       (* underline *)
   WRITELN('CREDIT TOTAL',CreditSum:27:2);                  (* show total *)
   WRITELN;
END;
(**********************************************************************)
(*                                                                    *)
(*  SHOW TOTALS FOR DEBIT/CREDIT CATEGORIES AND SHOW ACCOUNT BALANCE      *)
(*                                                                    *)
(**********************************************************************)
PROCEDURE CalculateCurrentBalance;
BEGIN
  PutTitle('TOTAL ACCOUNT ACTIVITY');                      (* call PutTitle *)
  WRITELN('BEGINNING BALANCE       $',StartBalance:14:2);
  ShowDetailTotals;
  CurrentBalance := StartBalance - DebitSum + CreditSum;
  WRITELN('YOUR ACCOUNT BALANCE IS $',CurrentBalance:14:2);
END;
(**********************************************************************)
(*                                                                    *)
(*  INITIALIZE SOME PROGRAM VARIABLES AND GET DEBIT/CREDIT CATEGORIES     *)
(*                                                                    *)
(**********************************************************************)
PROCEDURE Initialize;
VAR
 Number:INTEGER;
BEGIN
 FOR Number := 0 TO MaximumCateg DO
  BEGIN
   DebitTotals[Number] := 0;
   CreditTotals[Number] := 0;                               (* clear totals *)
  END;
DebitSum := 0;
CreditSum:= 0;                                      (* initialize variables *)
GetCreditCategories;
GetDebitCategories;
END;
```

```
(***********************************************************************)
(*                                                                    *)
(*                        MAIN PROGRAM BLOCK                          *)
(*                                                                    *)
(***********************************************************************)
BEGIN                  (* this BEGIN is for main program instructions *)
 Initialize;
 GetStartBalance;                         (* call procedures declared above *)
 SumDebits;
 SumCredits;
 CalculateCurrentBalance;
END.                                             (* END of PROGRAM *)
```

Figure 6-5. (Conclusion)

screen positions based upon the length of a message to be printed. Further uses of this technique are covered in Chapter 6: Coding Program Output.

READ(KEYBOARD,VariableName) This statement causes an input to be read from the keyboard without screen display and places that input in the variable name specified. The predefined input device KEYBOARD is used to inhibit the *echoing* of the entered characters to the screen.

EOLN(KEYBOARD) Calling this function is a way of sensing a <RETURN>. EOLN stands for end-of-line. The program tests for this condition to see if a <RETURN> has been entered at the keyboard.

CONCAT((* list of strings *)) CONCAT is an abbreviation of *concatenate,* to link together. CONCATenate is a Pascal function that causes the contents of the string variables or constants given within the parentheses to be combined. In *BalancePlus,* this function is used to *pad* the user's answer with spaces until it is exactly 25 characters wide. The CONCATenate function is discussed in greater depth in Chapter 8.

WRITELN(VariableName:X:Y) X and Y in this expression are *length specifiers* for the format of real data output. In this program, X refers to the total number of digits that are to appear in a dollar amount, and Y refers to the number of decimal places. Length specifiers and other means of formatting output are presented in Chapter 8.

IN IN allows a statement to test whether an item is included in a set of items. Sets are covered elsewhere. The result is Boolean—either TRUE or FALSE.

Summary

Program control structures consist of sequences, selections, and repetitions. Selections and repetitions may be dependent upon logical tests. Logical tests often employ the principles of Boolean logic. Pascal provides the BOOLEAN data type, which defines values as either TRUE or FALSE. One Pascal implementation of the use of logical tests is the IF . . THEN . . ELSE control structure, although the CASE . . OF structure also may be used to perform the same processing. Looping and repetition control, also sometimes necessary for multiple-choice processing, may be implemented by the FOR . . DO and WHILE . . DO constructions, as well as by the previously introduced REPEAT . . UNTIL construction.

Arrays are a convenient method for storing large amounts of data. An array is a group of variables of the same data type. Arrays may be one-dimensional or multi-dimensional.

Data items in an array are called elements of the array. Location of elements is defined by the array name, combined with a subscript enclosed in brackets. This subscript is the array index of the element. An array declaration includes a subscript range definition that is enclosed in brackets.

A subscript may be any expression that produces results of the same data type as the declared index. Subscripts also may be expressions that produce values in the declared range. Subscripts are omitted when performing assignment or equality tests on two arrays of the same declared size and type. The subscript also is omitted when passing an entire array as an argument to a procedure or function.

Longer programs should be entered and tested as a series of individual modules.

The *BalancePlus* program introduces the Pascal terms LENGTH, IN, READ(KEYBOARD), EOLN, CONCAT, and length specifiers in the WRITELN statement.

Review Questions

1. How may logical tests be implemented by Boolean comparisons?
2. What is the difference between a Boolean comparison and the use of the BOOLEAN data type in Pascal?
3. What is the form of an IF . . THEN . . ELSE construction, and how does it implement conditional branching within a program?
4. How are case selectors used in the CASE . . OF construction?
5. Why might the CASE . . OF construction be preferred over a long IF . . THEN construction?
6. What omissions from the program text would cause incorrect processing of a CASE . . OF program block?
7. What is the form of the FOR . . DO construction?
8. How could improper coding of the counter variable in a FOR . . DO program block cause incorrect processing?
9. What is the effect of employing the reserved word DOWNTO instead of TO in a FOR . . DO construction?
10. What is the form of the WHILE . . DO construction?
11. How does the logical test given in a WHILE . . DO structure differ from the condition given in a REPEAT . . UNTIL structure, and how are the processing actions of each different?
12. What is meant by an array, and how is reference made to array elements in program text?
13. How may individual program modules be entered and tested?

Pascal Practice

1. Using the Yes function example in the text, convert the OK function in *BalancePlus* so that it asks the user 'IS THIS CORRECT?' after each entry.
2. Given an array of integers, write a procedure to display the data in 6-column tabular form:

   Item1 Item2 Item3 Item4 Item5 Item6

   Item7 Item8 Item9 Item10 Item11 Item12, and so on.

3. Write a program that uses the columnar display procedure you've developed. The declaration section of the program should include:

```
CONST
 MaxData = 100;

VAR
 DataArray : ARRAY[1..MaxData] OF INTEGER;
```

The main program block should allow user input of data into the array and output of results in tabular format at the printer.

Key Terms

1. multiple-choice processing
2. logical test
3. case selector
4. counting loop
5. counter variable
6. increment
7. scalar
8. ordinal
9. data structure
10. predefined data structure
11. array
12. one-dimensional array
13. multi-dimensional array
14. element
15. location
16. array name
17. index
18. subscript
19. range
20. echo
21. concatenate
22. pad
23. length specifier

Pascal Library

1. BOOLEAN
2. IF . . THEN
3. ELSE
4. NOT
5. AND
6. CASE . . OF
7. FOR . . DO
8. TO
9. DOWNTO
10. WHILE . . DO
11. ARRAY . . OF
12. LENGTH
13. READ(KEYBOARD)
14. EOLN
15. CONCAT
16. IN

7 DESIGNING USEFUL OUTPUTS

OBJECTIVES

On completing the reading and other learning assignments for this chapter, you should be able to:

- ☐ Explain the importance of considering the factors of value and permanence in designing physical outputs.
- ☐ Use several common output formats, including answers to specific questions, lists, specific reports, and general reports.
- ☐ Tell what factors must be considered in designing outputs for convenience and clarity.
- ☐ Describe the physical constraints of display devices, including design criteria for outputs to CRTs and printers.
- ☐ Give examples of other output devices used to produce hard copy.
- ☐ Describe guidelines used for designing device-independent outputs.
- ☐ Give additional design considerations for the output function.

VALUE AND PERMANENCE OF OUTPUT

The logical design of a program specifies the content of the information to be produced. However, programs often must be designed to accommodate multiple physical output options from a single program execution. Tasks involved in specifying physical output include:

- Determine what specific data items are to be presented.
- Design a format in which to present those data.

These tasks may be influenced by one overall consideration: What is the value and permanence of the information to be presented? The value and permanence of information are matters of degree and fall somewhere between these two extremes:

- Critical information may be added to permanent records. An example would be sales totals for a company's products made available for study and analysis by top managers. Such data would be stored for long-term reference as part of the company's operations history.
- Transient data serve an interim use. An example would be a subtotal displayed on a calculator. Such a result typically would be used as a basis for further action and then discarded.

These extremes typify the two basic forms of output: *document* and *nondocument.* Document outputs, or *hard copy,* are relatively permanent records and are produced on an output medium such as paper. Printers produce document outputs. Nondocument outputs are transient; no permanent record is created. A CRT display is an example of a nondocument output.

Beyond the consideration of output medium, the determination of the value and permanence of the output also affects its content. Some judgment must be made as to how exhaustive the presentation should be. For example, will the output provide details of all transactions or extract summaries from those data?

Once output content has been determined, it may appear in one of the following forms:

- Answers to specific questions
- Lists
- Specific reports
- General reports.

Answers to specific questions. One kind of output is a simple *answer to a question.* For example:

Question: What is the first-year interest received on a bank deposit of $10,000 earning 10 percent compounded quarterly?

Answer: Total first-year interest is $1038.13.

Many of the tasks involved in personal computing fall into this category.

Lists. An example of a *list* format would be a printed output of client names and addresses. Another example would be a simple form of inventory exception report that gives a count and description of each item to be restocked.

Specific reports. A *specific report* output implies some kind of pre-existing format. An invoice that a company renders its customers is an example. The invoice uses a pre-existing form that already includes printing areas for information such as company name, address, and column headings for item number, quantity, description, unit amount, and extensions. The computer program must be coded so that data items are printed according to the exact layout of the invoice form. Other specific output requirements may be needed to meet specific demands. For example, traditional accounting practice would call for a single underscore beneath subtotals and a double underscore beneath the total. Specific reports often are based upon an organization's existing manual forms and procedures. Format requirements of specific reports are relatively inflexible.

General reports. The format of a *general report* varies from one program run to another based upon specific selections made by the user during each run. A sales analysis report, for example, may offer the user options for listing sales volume data—by region, by salesperson, by product line, and so on. These data may be grouped or processed further according to combinations of options—for example, listing sales volume by product line for each region.

The subprograms that implement the options for a general report must be designed anticipating variations in output requirements. Categories of output data are determined, of course, by the logical design of the program. The physical design of the output format must be appropriate for all combinations of data items likely to appear.

Another design consideration for a general report format is the level of detail to be output. The variables within a sales analysis program, for example, may contain data down to the level of individual sales transactions. Although this comprehensive store of data may be necessary to fulfill all possible processing options, rarely must output be listed at the transaction level. Further, a truly informative report should be as concise as possible. Therefore, a practical design approach would be to provide summaries by category as the program's default condition. More detailed output, then, could be offered as a user option at run time.

PHYSICAL DESIGN FOR CONVENIENCE AND CLARITY

Well-designed output documents have some key features that are not related directly to main processing tasks but that make the document itself more readable and intelligible. These features include:

- Show the date of the program run. Some applications also may require indication of the exact time of the program run.
- Number the pages of a report. Numbering pages is particularly important for reports printed out on continuous forms that are to be broken apart.
- Space output lines attractively. Don't try to fit too much on a page.
- Consider numbering items that appear in a list. This feature is especially helpful if the list takes up most of a page.
- Provide headings at the top of each page. Begin each report section on a new page. Provide subheadings for report sections of longer reports.
- Present lists in tabular, or columnar, format where possible. Be sure that captions line up with the items those captions describe.
- Provide headings for each column. Break up long lists of figures with subtotals that represent categories of items, if possible.

Many of these features also apply to design of attractive screen displays. For all types of output, two additional guidelines should be helpful:

- When possible, identify the question being answered. Display or print a summary of the question immediately before showing the answer. Highlight menu items selected.
- Underline or otherwise highlight key items. The eye should go quickly to the most important items.

These features should be included routinely in program outputs.

PHYSICAL CONSTRAINTS OF DISPLAY DEVICES

A typical microcomputer system has a CRT display device and a printer. Combined with the keyboard, the CRT, or video display terminal, serves as the console for data displays that are temporary. The printer, on the other hand, is used primarily to create permanent records.

Time-sharing terminals may have either a CRT or a printer as a display device but seldom have both. Other types of output devices, such as plotters, are beyond the scope of this book. Data storage devices also may be used for output. File management techniques for both input and output are covered in the next chapter.

Beyond requirements for content and format of output, the selection of an output device for a particular application depends on the physical constraints imposed by the device. A general description of output devices and characteristics follows.

CRT Displays

As discussed in the previous chapter, the screen of a CRT, or a video display terminal, can be thought of as a *matrix,* or grid system, typically 80 characters wide (40 characters on many devices) and 24 lines high. The position of any point on the screen, therefore, can be specified by reference to this matrix. A pair of coordinates specifies each point. One coordinate gives the X axis position (0–79 on 80-character displays, 0–39 on 40-character displays); and one coordinate gives the Y axis position (0–23). This pair of coordinates can be used to specify the location of the cursor and, hence, the position of output characters.

A new line may be specified at any point on the screen, at any time. In other words, points on the CRT matrix are *randomly addressable;* display positions may be accessed in any order. The exact method of this access, as implemented in hardware, varies with display device. Usually some *control character,* a byte of information that does not correspond with any other in the alphanumeric character set, is sent from the computer to the display device to signal that a change in cursor position follows. In machines running UCSD Pascal, the GOTOXY procedure causes the appropriate control characters to be output to reset the display. Once a starting point is specified, output is sequential by columns and rows until a new origin is selected.

With this degree of cursor control, the programmer can cause the cursor to *tab* from left to right, advancing by groups of spaces. Tabbing is particularly useful in formatting columnar displays. Tabbing from right to left, or *backtab,* is also possible. The cursor may move up or down, advancing the display page as it does so. This technique is known as *scrolling.*

The relative freedom of positioning outputs on CRT display devices requires that the programmer be aware of the exact position of the cursor at any point in the program. Starting an output line too close to the right edge of the screen generally causes text to *wrap around* to the beginning of the next writing line. From the standpoint of coding, the basic difference between WRITELN and WRITE becomes important in keeping track of cursor position: WRITELN advances the cursor to the beginning of the next available line, and WRITE is used for successive outputs on a single line. A sample output layout form for CRT displays is shown in Figure 7-1.

Figure 7-1. Sample output layout form for CRT display.

```
              1111111111222222222233333333333
    0123456789012345678901234567890123456789
 0
 1
 2                LYMAN LAMPS
 3           INVENTORY CONTROL REPORT
 4          -------------------------
 5
 6      PART                          NO. IN
 7      NO.     DESCRIPTION           STOCK
 8     ----------------------------------
 9
10     XX-XXX XXXXXXXXXXXXXXXXXXX XXXXX
11
12     XX-XXX XXXXXXXXXXXXXXXXXXX XXXXX
13
14     XX-XXX XXXXXXXXXXXXXXXXXXX XXXXX
15
16
17     PRESS <SPACE BAR> TO RETURN TO
18                 MAIN MENU
19
20
21
22
23
```

Once lines of text have been displayed on the CRT, individual lines may be erased selectively by *overwriting* the line with blanks (spaces). This technique is used in the *BalancePlus* program. Overwriting previously displayed entries is particularly useful, for example, in the output of forms that have been filled in based on prior responses. The user's new entries are made to overwrite only those entries that must be changed or updated.

CRT displays often have a set of *graphic characters,* such as arrows, that may be used to highlight displayed items. Often these devices also have a *blink* feature that causes characters to be written and erased repeatedly. Another feature is *reverse characters,* used for highlighting, that are displayed in the screen background color and surrounded by a bright box.

Most microcomputers provide for some advanced screen display features by performing some functions in response to certain characters that are written to the console device. These characters are usually in the ASCII control set (values from 0 to 31). Some of these features are:

- Erase screen
- Erase from current position to end-of-screen
- Erase line
- Erase from current position to end-of-line
- Move up one line
- Move down one line
- Back up one character.

You should consult the system manual for the particular system you are working with for a list of these characters.

For example, to erase line 7 on a particular machine, you would use:

```
GOTOXY(0,6);
WRITE(CHR (29));
```

The machine for which this example is written has defined the character equivalent of CHR(29) as the erase-line feature.

One obvious consideration is that information output to a CRT screen will disappear when the screen is cleared (as is done by the PAGE procedure), when the computer is reset, when the display is scrolled off the top, or when the power to the system is turned off. Except in the case of certain CRT devices that project large images on wall screens, the number of users that can view the display is limited. Usually, CRT displays are used to communicate temporary data to a single user during a program run. For this reason, the CRT is the ideal device for display of interactive messages.

Printers

Printers generally use paper as an output medium. Unlike the random addressability of the CRT display, most printers (except those adapted for graphics applications, for example) are restricted to advancing across and down the page in serial fashion. Once printed, a line of text is not erased or overwritten.

The typical printer has a larger writing area than a CRT. Line widths vary from approximately 80 to 200 horizontal spaces, with 132 being typical for production work. A paper form measuring 8½ by 11 inches generally has 66 writing lines, or six lines per inch. Continuous-feed forms, of course, may be used to output multiple pages.

Some printers allow input of control characters that cause tabbing from left to right and *line-feed* for advancing down the page. Most printers do not have provisions for tabbing left, or backtabbing. On many printers, the programmer must implement tabbing by printing individual blanks (space bar). On these printers, characters are output in sequence as each character arrives at the printer. A new line is begun as an end-of-line is reached or when a line-feed instruction is received. A line-feed is caused at the end of a WRITELN statement, for example, or when a <RETURN> is encountered in output of a text file.

In designing outputs for printers, the programmer must be aware of character position and line count at each point in the program. For example, in writing code for output of headings at the top of each page, a running count of lines previously output must be maintained so that the exact position of the starting point for the next page may be determined. Printers allow variable spacing between lines, just as typewriters do; and line spacing must be taken into account, both in determining line count and in designing for attractiveness.

For these reasons, the printer is used primarily as a device for creating documentation such as formal reports. It is generally poor programming practice to ask questions of the user on the printer. If a console with a CRT is available to the system, and if input is to be required of the user at the console, then it is appropriate that prompts and questions also appear at the console. It is particularly awkward to use *line printers* for this purpose, since such devices, unlike *character printers,* display only completed lines, not individual characters as typed.

Character and line printers are shown in Figure 7-2.

Other Hard Copy Devices

Other types of hard copy devices include:

- Electrostatic, or laser printers
- Computer output microforms (COM)
- Plotters.

Electrostatic, or laser printers. These are high-speed, high-quality printing devices. Approximately 20,000 lines per minute can be produced by a laser printer.

Computer output microforms (COM). COM machines, or *film recorders,* are used to output alphanumeric and graphic data to *microfilm* or to sheet film called *fiche.* Such outputs are said to be of *archival* quality because a film record will outlast a paper document. Also, these formats are suitable for reference-quality storage because they are so compact. A fiche can hold the equivalent of 200 pages of printed matter.

Plotters. These devices are specifically designed for *graphics* output. A plotter makes line drawings on paper or film material with a *stylus,* a pen-like device, under program control. Plotters and other graphics output devices render images that have been *digitized,* or converted into numeric coordinates.

Many types of printers, and particularly *dot matrix* and *ink-jet* printers, have the ability to reproduce graphics as well as alphanumeric data. Graphics may be included in engineering drawings or business charts and graphs, to name just two common application areas. Electrostatic and laser printers can produce publication-quality graphics. COM machines

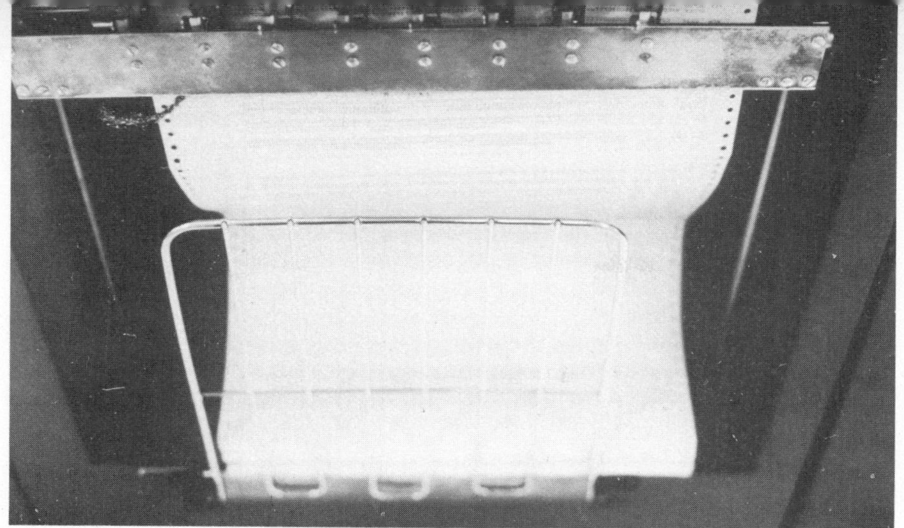

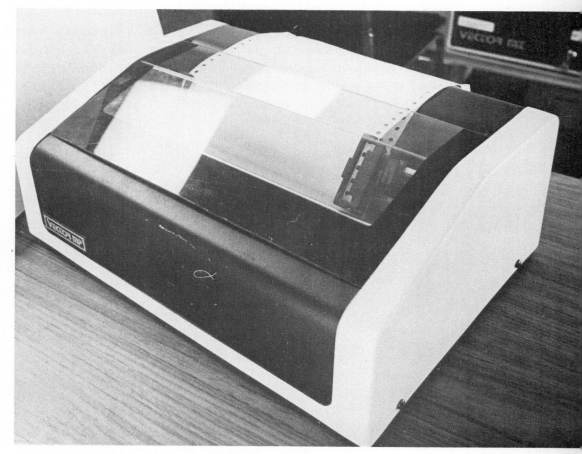

Figure 7-2. Output printing devices. Character printer (above) and line printer (below)

and film recorders may be equipped to produce graphics on color film for special applications.

Physical design considerations for such devices are, of course, highly specialized, particularly for graphic outputs. Apart from printers and CRTs, output devices most commonly in use with microcomputers are desk-top film recorders (that make film hard copies of the CRT display) and plotters.

Representative hard copy devices are pictured in Figure 7-3.

DESIGN FOR DEVICE INDEPENDENCE

Output formats should be as independent as possible from specific hardware features. The *portability* of your program from one computer system to another may be enhanced by this approach. Also, hardware changes to the system you are using may be easier to implement.

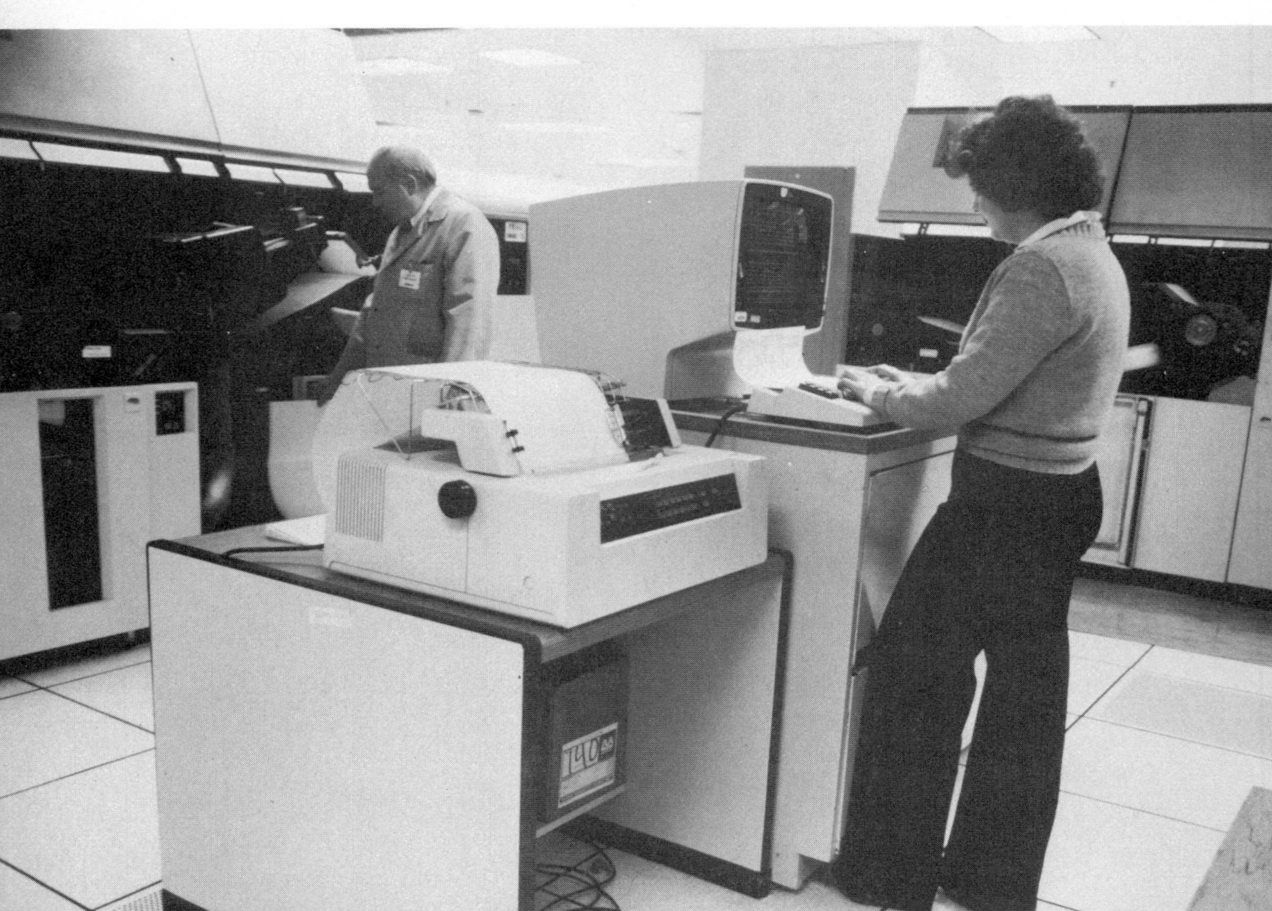

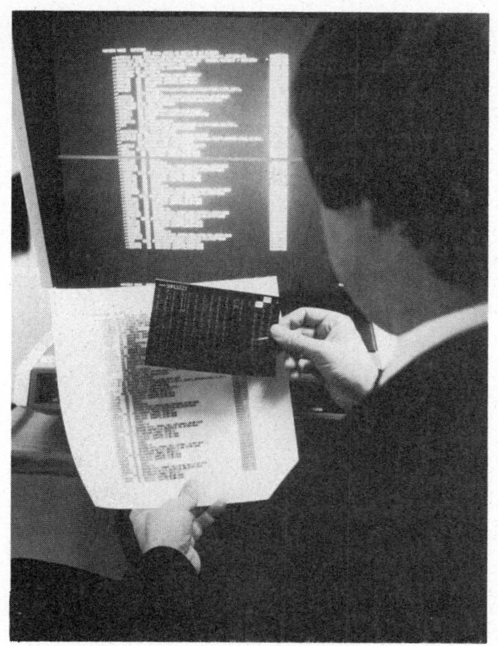

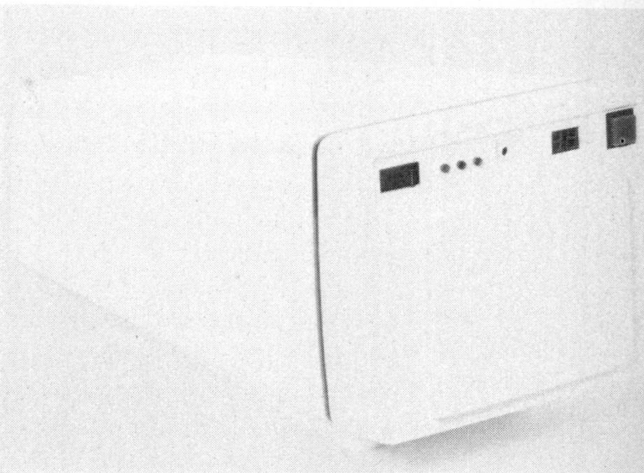

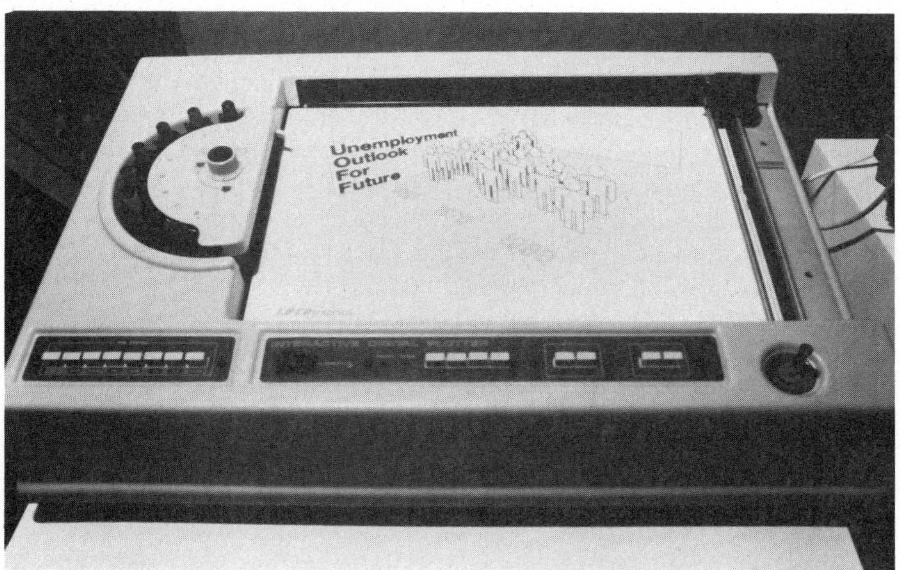

Figure 7-3. Hard copy devices: Laser printer (left) (Photo by Liane Enkelis) and Computer Output Microform (COM) (above) (Photos by Liane Enkelis at McDonnell Douglas Automation, St. Louis) Film recorder (right) (Celtic VFR 2000 Computer Camera ™) Plotter (below) (Photo by Liane Enkelis)

One convenient and practical approach is to design your formats by assuming that the output device is a printer that has an output matrix corresponding with the CRT. For example, if the CRT has a matrix of 40 by 24 addressable characters, you would not exceed these dimensions on any given printer page. Further, all cursor movements on the CRT would be executable also on the printer. Backtabbing and scrolling upward would not be used, for example. Thus, the narrowest constraints of both output devices would be accommodated by your output design. You could make the choice of output device, then, a user option at program run time.

The above approach may, of course, be ruled out by special features required by a particular application. Graphics applications often must use special hardware features of output devices. Heavily interactive programs with screen prompting should not be constrained by the serial, or linear, nature of printers. Or, often a report will require the full width of a printed page.

Coding the output sections of a program requires meticulous attention. Characters must be counted and precise calculations made for character positions and form layout. Careful attention to this design phase, however, may save time in the long run by cutting down on rework to overcome user problems with readability or formatting. Output reports that support business applications are expected to be concise, correct, and neat in appearance. Care in initial design can help eliminate later problems or redesign requirements.

Also, when later changes are needed, well-organized output code also assists the programmer in responding to user requests. Output formats almost always are affected in some way by changes to the program text. Bear in mind that the physical appearance of your program outputs is the first impression that can encourage, or discourage, the user of your program.

DESIGNING *BasicAccounting*

This program is based on the *BalancePlus* program in the preceding chapter. Design considerations are presented here and program coding is discussed in Chapter 8. An overall design objective is to provide greater flexibility for the user. One way this objective is accomplished is to pay particular attention to the design of the physical output of the program. Specific features that can enhance the program's usefulness include:

- Data input of the various categories of data may occur at the user's discretion, or in random order. The program should allow entry of data items in any sequence. This pattern of input is encountered frequently due to the nature of certain business practices. The importance of this consideration in program design is discussed in depth in Chapter 8.
- Report options are given for presentation of data in different formats. In the example program, summary information may be extracted to derive percentages of input items to a category total and to represent these percentages in graphic form.
- Physical layout of the report is attractive and coherent. A tabular format with column headings and underscores enhances readability.
- Device output options are presented. The output section of the program is designed to display results on either the console or the printer.

Program Output

Given the above design criteria, the physical design of program outputs can be developed.

Sample outputs for *BasicAccounting* are shown in Figures 7-4 through 7-7. Figure 7-4 shows the result of the Sum option. Figure 7-5 shows the result of the Percent option. Figure 7-6 shows the result of the BarGraph option. Sample session displays are shown in Figures 7-7A through 7-7G.

```
                        TOTAL ACCOUNT ACTIVITY
------------------------------------------------------------------------------

CATEGORY                AMOUNT
------------------------------------------------------------------------------
BEGINNING BALANCE  $   1000.00

--DEBITS--
MISC. DEBITS            150.00
CAR                     197.02
HOUSE                   735.00
FOOD                    350.00
CLOTHING                250.00
------------------------------------------------------------------------------
DEBIT TOTAL            1682.02

--CREDITS--
MISC. CREDITS           100.00
HARRY'S INCOME         2000.00
PAT'S INCOME            500.00
------------------------------------------------------------------------------
CREDIT TOTAL           2600.00

ACCOUNT BALANCE IS $   1917.98
                     =========
```

Figure 7-4. Output from the *Sum* report option in *BasicAccounting*.

```
                        TOTAL ACCOUNT ACTIVITY
------------------------------------------------------------------------------

CATEGORY                AMOUNT  PERCENT
------------------------------------------------------------------------------
BEGINNING BALANCE  $   1000.00

--DEBITS--
MISC. DEBITS            150.00    8.92%
CAR                     197.02   11.71%
HOUSE                   735.00   43.70%
FOOD                    350.00   20.81%
CLOTHING                250.00   14.86%
------------------------------------------------------------------------------
DEBIT TOTAL            1682.02     100%

--CREDITS--
MISC. CREDITS           100.00    3.85%
HARRY'S INCOME         2000.00   76.92%
PAT'S INCOME            500.00   19.23%
------------------------------------------------------------------------------
CREDIT TOTAL           2600.00     100%

ACCOUNT BALANCE IS $   1917.98
                     ==========
```

Figure 7-5. Output from the *Percent* report option in *BasicAccounting*.

```
                            TOTAL ACCOUNT ACTIVITY
--------------------------------------------------------------------------------

CATEGORY                    AMOUNT  PERCENT CHARTED
--------------------------------------------------------------------------------
BEGINNING BALANCE  $      1000.00

--DEBITS--
MISC. DEBITS                150.00    8.92% ****....................................
CAR                         197.02   11.71% *****...................................
HOUSE                       735.00   43.70% *****************.......................
FOOD                        350.00   20.81% ********................................
CLOTHING                    250.00   14.86% ******..................................
--------------------------------------------------------------------------------
DEBIT TOTAL                1682.02     100%

--CREDITS--
MISC. CREDITS               100.00    3.85% **......................................
HARRY'S INCOME             2000.00   76.92% *******************************.........
PAT'S INCOME                500.00   19.23% ********................................
--------------------------------------------------------------------------------
CREDIT TOTAL               2600.00     100%

ACCOUNT BALANCE IS $       1917.98
                        ==========
```

Figure 7-6. Output from the *BarGraph* report option in *BasicAccounting*.

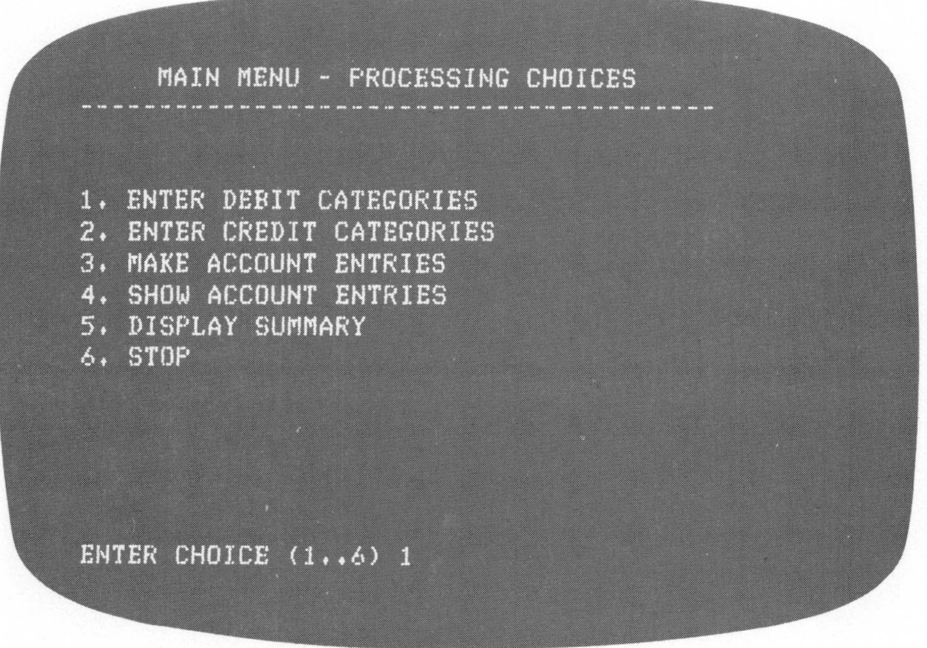

MAIN MENU - PROCESSING CHOICES
1. ENTER DEBIT CATEGORIES
2. ENTER CREDIT CATEGORIES
3. MAKE ACCOUNT ENTRIES
4. SHOW ACCOUNT ENTRIES
5. DISPLAY SUMMARY
6. STOP
ENTER CHOICE (1..6) 1

Figure 7-7A. Main menu. User selects option 1.

```
     ENTRY OF DEBIT CATEGORY NAMES
----------------------------------------

DEBIT CATEGORY 0 : MISC. DEBITS
DEBIT CATEGORY 1 ? CAR
DEBIT CATEGORY 2 ? HOUSE
DEBIT CATEGORY 3 ? FOOD
DEBIT CATEGORY 4 ? CLOTHING
DEBIT CATEGORY 5 ?
```

Figure 7-7B. Result of selecting main menu option 1. All categories have been entered, followed by a <RETURN>.

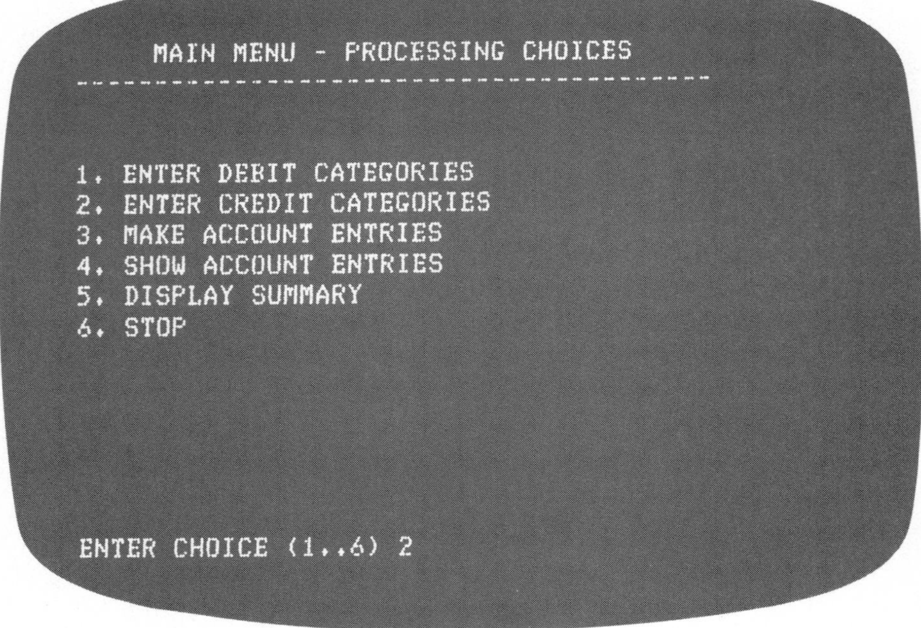

Figure 7-7C. Main menu. User selects option 2.

```
     ENTRY OF CREDIT CATEGORY NAMES
-----------------------------------------

CREDIT CATEGORY 0 : MISC. CREDITS
CREDIT CATEGORY 1 ? HARRY'S INCOME
CREDIT CATEGORY 2 ? PAT'S INCOME
CREDIT CATEGORY 3 ?
```

Figure 7-7D. Result of selecting main menu option 2. Entry of credit categories is complete.

```
     MAIN MENU - PROCESSING CHOICES
-----------------------------------------


1. ENTER DEBIT CATEGORIES
2. ENTER CREDIT CATEGORIES
3. MAKE ACCOUNT ENTRIES
4. SHOW ACCOUNT ENTRIES
5. DISPLAY SUMMARY
6. STOP


ENTER CHOICE (1..6) 3
HAS AN ACCOUNT FILE BEEN CREATED ? (Y/N) N
ACCOUNT FILE CREATED
DO YOU WANT TO ADD AN ACCOUNT ENTRY ? (Y/N) Y
```

Figure 7-7E. Main menu. User selects option 3 and answers the resulting prompts.

ENTER ITEM NUMBER 1

DEBIT OR CREDIT? (D/C) D

DEBIT AMOUNT $ 197.02

<RETURN> IF OK;<SPACE> TO CHANGE ANSWER

Figure 7-7F. Result of selecting main menu option 3. Entry type and amount are entered. Prompt at bottom allows user to change answer.

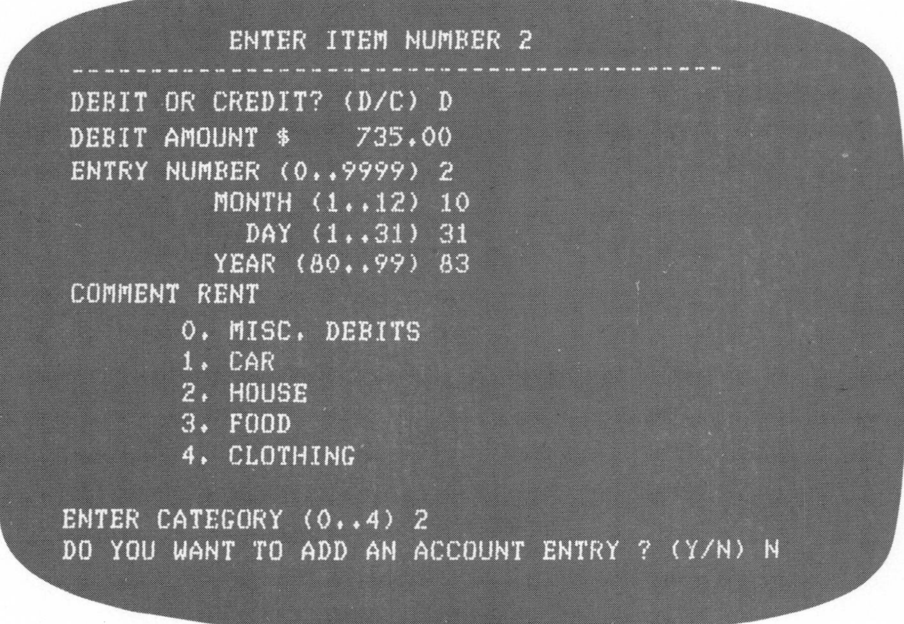

ENTER ITEM NUMBER 2
DEBIT OR CREDIT? (D/C) D
DEBIT AMOUNT $ 735.00
ENTRY NUMBER (0..9999) 2
MONTH (1..12) 10
DAY (1..31) 31
YEAR (80..99) 83
COMMENT RENT
0. MISC. DEBITS
1. CAR
2. HOUSE
3. FOOD
4. CLOTHING
ENTER CATEGORY (0..4) 2
DO YOU WANT TO ADD AN ACCOUNT ENTRY ? (Y/N) N

Figure 7-7G. Result of selecting main menu option 3. All items for one debit entry are completed.

Summary

Programs may be designed to accommodate multiple physical output options from a single program execution. Output content must address the specific need indicated by the output option.

Tasks involved in specifying physical output include determining what specific data items are to be presented and designing a format in which to present those data.

An overall consideration is the value and permanence of the information to be presented, which falls somewhere between two extremes: critical information added to permanent records and transient data for interim use.

Once output content has been fixed, it may appear in one of the following forms: an answer to a question, lists, specific reports, and general reports.

Well-designed output documents have key features for readability. The programmer should show the date of the program run, number the pages of a report, space output lines attractively, number items that appear in a list, provide headings at the top of each page, present lists in tabular format, and provide headings for each column.

These features also apply to design of attractive screen displays. A CRT screen can be thought of as a matrix of coordinates. For all types of output, the programmer should identify the question being answered and highlight key items.

Unlike the random addressability of the CRT display, most printers are restricted to advancing across and down the page in serial fashion. Once printed, a line of text is not erased or overwritten. The typical printer has a larger writing area than a CRT.

In designing outputs for printers, the programmer must be aware of character position and line count at each point in the program. Printers allow variable spacing between lines, just as typewriters do. The printer is used primarily as a device for creating documentation such as formal reports. It is generally poor programming practice to ask questions of the user on the printer.

Your program portability may be enhanced by designing for device independence. Also, hardware changes may be easier to implement.

Review Questions

1. What tasks are involved in designing physical outputs?
2. What overall consideration applies to the design of physical outputs?
3. What are the main types of output formats, and what are some examples of each?
4. What physical design features may be included in output formats for convenience and clarity?
5. What physical constraints are imposed by CRT displays?
6. What physical constraints are imposed by printers?
7. Besides printers, what other devices may be used to obtain hard copy output?
8. What output device is preferred for displaying prompts for user inputs?
9. What approach may be used for designing relatively device-independent output formats?
10. What is meant by program portability, and how may it be affected by the choice of output device?

Pascal Practice

1. Review the user's guide for the computer system you are using. What specific design constraints are imposed by the console device? By the printer?
2. Re-examine the sample displays presented in Figures 7-4 through 7-7. How do these display formats compare with those offered on the output devices you are using?
3. Assume that you are using a small portable microcomputer that has only one output capability—a single line of text shown on a matrix-type display. The matrix allows display of up to 20 characters on a single line. Returning to the sample displays for *BalancePlus,* which outputs could be modified for this small computer? Sketch a sequence of such matrix displays and explain what design problems are imposed by the device.

Key Terms

1. document
2. nondocument
3. hard copy
4. answer to a question
5. list
6. specific report
7. general report
8. matrix
9. randomly addressable
10. control character
11. tab
12. backtab
13. scroll
14. wrap around
15. overwrite
16. graphic character
17. blink
18. reverse character
19. line-feed
20. line printer
21. character printer
22. electrostatic
23. laser printer
24. computer output microform (COM)
25. microfilm
26. fiche
27. archival
28. plotter
29. graphics
30. stylus
31. digitize
32. portability

8 CODING PROGRAM OUTPUT

OBJECTIVES

On completing the reading and other learning assignments for this chapter, you should be able to:

- ☐ Use Pascal coding techniques for formatting outputs, including the use of long integers and length specifiers.
- ☐ Tell how truncation, scientific notation, and exponentiation are treated in Pascal program text.
- ☐ Use the predeclared function LENGTH to determine the number of characters in a string variable and the function POS to determine the position of a character within a string.
- ☐ Use the CONCAT function to concatenate string variables.
- ☐ Use the COPY function and the procedures INSERT and DELETE to manipulate string variables.
- ☐ Explain how approximations are derived with the TRUNC and ROUND functions.
- ☐ Explain the use of the EXIT procedure.
- ☐ Explain the use of enumeration types in Pascal.
- ☐ Describe how the reserved word SET is used.
- ☐ Tell what operations may be performed on sets of values.
- ☐ Demonstrate how specific devices may be referenced in output statements.

CODING TECHNIQUES FOR FORMATTING OUTPUT

By comparison with other programming languages, Pascal provides few convenient means for formatting outputs. This characteristic of Pascal should cause you to pay particular attention to learning to use the tools that are available.

Recall that the PAGE procedure is used to clear the screen and begin a new page. UCSD Pascal adds the GOTOXY extension for cursor control. Other capabilities, including UCSD extensions provided to enhance data formatting, are explained below.

WRITE and WRITELN

The principal means of displaying data from a Pascal program is the use of the WRITE or WRITELN statements. Data to be output by these statements are specified within a pair of parentheses following WRITE or WRITELN. *Literal data* to be output, or *string constants*, appear between single quotation marks. Contents of data items (such as variables and constants) may be output by specifying the corresponding name in the WRITE or WRITELN statements. Data to be output by these statements may be of the following types: INTEGER, REAL, and CHARacter, as well as the UCSD extensions STRING and **long INTEGER**.

On most microcomputers, the allowable range for a data item of type INTEGER is from −32,768 to +32,767. UCSD Pascal offers the extension long INTEGER, which allows an integer to be declared as having up to 36 digits. The number of digits in the largest possible integer value is shown within brackets in the declaration. The form of the declaration is:

```
VAR
 VariableName: INTEGER[Z];
```

In the above declaration, Z can be any integral value from 1 to 36. The declaration of long integers is not restricted to the VAR declaration. A long integer may appear in any declaration that types a data item, as in a parameter list. Long INTEGER values and INTEGER values are interchangeable for most uses. However, like arrays, a particular long INTEGER size must be defined as a TYPE if it is to be used as a parameter. For example:

```
TYPE
 Long8 = INTEGER[8];
```

Once this definition has been made, parameters may be defined as being of this coined type:

```
PROCEDURE XYZ(L:Long8);
```

Further, it is not possible to assign directly a long INTEGER value to an INTEGER variable. The assignment statement must call the **TRUNC**ate function. TRUNC is a predeclared function that returns an INTEGER value for a long INTEGER or REAL argument. For example:

```
VAR
 I:INTEGER;
 L:INTEGER[8];
```

Given the above declaration, a *truncated* form of the value contained in L may be assigned to the variable I as follows:

```
I := TRUNC(L);
```

In addition, the MOD operation (for calculating the remainder of an integer division) cannot be used with long integers. Data items of type INTEGER, REAL, CHARacter, STRING, or long INTEGER may be given *length specifiers* in the WRITE or WRITELN statements, as demonstrated in the

BalancePlus program. For data of type INTEGER, long INTEGER, CHARacter, or STRING, the form of the statement with length specifier is:

```
WRITELN(VariableName:X); (* same format for WRITE *)
```

In the above example, X is a positive integer (or an integer variable or expression) that specifies the length, in characters, for the output of the contents of the variable. From the standpoint of formatting outputs, the length specifier gives the programmer the ability to control exactly the number of characters that are to be output for a given data item. (Some exceptions are noted below.)

If no length specifier is given, WRITE or WRITELN produce only the number of characters required to display the contents of the data item. Real numbers are an exception and use scientific notation as a default in the absence of length specifiers. Note especially that, if numeric data are too large to fit in the specified length, the length specifier is ignored. This is particularly important in producing tabular reports in which large numbers might not fit the columnar format. For example:

```
X := 1234;
WRITE(X:2);
```

This output statement produces a result of 1234. The length specifier is ignored. Remember that the length specifier operates independently of the actual length of the value stored. Values that are shorter than the specified length are padded with blanks appearing to the left until the specified length is filled. Stored values of type STRING that exceed the length specified are truncated, or shortened, to fit the number of spaces given in the length specifier. Characters on the right do not appear in the displayed value. For example:

```
TempStr := 'ABCDE';
WRITE(TempStr:2);
```

This output statement causes the displayed value to be truncated to AB.

To illustrate further how output statements handle numeric data, assume that your program contained the following:

```
WRITELN('THE COUNT IS ',Count:3);
```

This statement causes the literal expression 'THE COUNT IS ' to be output, followed by the contents of the variable Count, using three spaces. If the current contents of Count were the value 32, the output line would look like this:

```
THE COUNT IS ƀ32
           (* ƀ represents blank, or space bar *)
```

The value 32 is padded with one space to bring the length of the output item to three spaces. On the other hand, if the current value of Count were 22146, exceeding the specified output length, the length specifier would be ignored:

```
THE COUNT IS 22146
```

Clearly, the programmer must anticipate the maximum number of spaces that are likely to appear in each output item.

The length specifier often is used to align values at a particular column position on a report. For example:

```
WRITELN('ASSET:',Asset:20);
WRITELN('SALVAGE VALUE:',Salvage:12);
```

If Asset holds a value of 567 and Salvage holds 123, these output statements would produce:

```
ASSET:                        567
SALVAGE VALUE:                123
```

Recall that data of the REAL type are numbers that contain a decimal point and possibly a fractional portion. The length specifier for REAL data output has the form:

```
WRITELN(VariableName:X:Y);
                         (* same format for WRITE *)
```

In this expression, X specifies the total number of characters to appear—including the decimal point. Y specifies how many of those characters, or digits, represent the fractional portion of the number, that is, how many digits appear to the right of the decimal point. For example, consider the following statement:

```
WRITELN('THE RATIO IS ',Ratio:6:3);
```

If the current value of Ratio were 64.5349, the above statement would cause the output to look like this:

```
THE RATIO IS 64.535
```

Notice that the usual mathematical procedure of *rounding* to the next decimal place occurs. (Rounding is discussed later in this chapter in connection with the programming example.) The number 64.5349 is approximated more closely by 64.535 than by 64.534. Remember, though, that rounding is an approximation. Accordingly, small margins of error may be introduced when using real numbers. Bear in mind also that rounding or truncation of a real number occurs with relation to the fractional part, not by dropping digits to the left of the decimal.

Pascal provides another means for output of real numbers that is derived from *scientific notation.* Scientific notation in mathematics is a way of writing large real numbers in concise form as factors of some exponent of 10. For example, the number 1,372,000,000 would be written in scientific notation as:

1.372×10^9

In Pascal program text, the same number would be written:

```
1.372E+09
```

The E stands for *exponent* of, or power of, 10. A negative number appearing as an exponent is used to represent small fractional numbers. For example, the number 0.0000000024 in scientific notation would be written:

2.4×10^{-9}

In Pascal, the same number would be written:

```
2.4E-09
```

Output statements in Pascal that give no length specifier or only one length specifier for REAL data items cause the data to be output in scientific notation. The allowable range of real numbers varies with the computer system. A typical microcomputer allows a range of 10^{-38} to 10^{38}.

Report Format Example

Using the techniques described so far, a brief example illustrates how report formats may be created. Suppose you had written a program that includes the following variable declarations:

```
VAR
 BorrowerName:STRING;
 LoanAmount:REAL;
 Rate:REAL;
```

You wish to create a report in the following format:

```
BORROWER:(20 characters) LOAN AMOUNT:$(8 digits) INTEREST RATE:(4 digits)%
```

The output section of the program using the WRITELN statement would look like this:

```
WRITELN('BORROWER:',BorrowerName:20,'ƀLOANƀAMOUNT:$',LoanAmount:9:2,
        'ƀINTERESTƀRATE:',Rate:4:1,'%');
                                        ( * ƀ represents space bar *)
```

Assume that the current values of the variables are:

```
BorrowerName  HASKELLƀE.ƀSTEPHENS
LoanAmount    120311.65
Rate          11.3
```

The output line, then, would look like this:

```
BORROWER:ƀHASKELLƀE.ƀSTEPHENSƀLOANƀAMOUNT:$120311.65ƀINTERESTƀRATE:11.3%
```

Note that the value stored in BorrowerName in this case is 19 characters long because the period and internal blanks are counted as characters. The output statement, therefore, pads the string display out to 20 spaces by adding a blank on the far left. The output statement also shows that the programmer has inserted spaces in the literal outputs 'ƀLOANƀAMOUNT' and 'ƀINTERESTƀRATE' so that values and captions do not run together. Thus, a more attractive spacing is achieved.

The same result can be obtained with a series of WRITE statements, as in:

```
WRITE('BORROWER:',BorrowerName:20);
WRITE('ƀLOANƀAMOUNT:$',LoanAmount:9:2);
WRITE('ƀINTERESTƀRATE:',Rate:4:1:,'%');
WRITELN;        (* needed to advance to next writing line *)
```

Use of a length specifier causes data items to be *justified*, or lined up, to the extreme right of the writing area, or *field*, specified. In printing reports, it is standard practice to right-justify numerical outputs and to left-justify text or alphabetic outputs. A sample report showing justification of text and numerical data is shown in Figure 8-1.

```
                    SAMPLE REPORT

ABC COMPANY                              $1234.56
BETA INDUSTRIES                            789.10
OMEGA MINES                               5678.91
```

ALPHANUMERIC DATA LEFT-JUSTIFIED | **NUMERIC DATA RIGHT-JUSTIFIED**

Figure 8-1. Sample report showing text and alphanumeric data left-justified, numeric data right-justified.

The action of the length specifier makes it easy to right-justify data items, but it is comparatively difficult to provide for left justification. One way to implement left justification of text strings is to pad each string variable with blanks (spaces) on the right until the string reaches a specified length.

Manipulation of Strings

The Pascal function LENGTH allows the programmer to obtain a count of the number of characters currently in a string variable. This function is useful for procedures designed to pad output lines with spaces, as demonstrated in the *BalancePlus* program. This function has the form:

```
SomeValue := LENGTH(StringExpression);
```

The function returns to the calling block a single numeric value that is an integer representing the number of characters in the string specified by the string expression given within the parentheses. Using the string variable from the report example above, a use of LENGTH would be:

```
SomeValue := LENGTH(BorrowerName);
```

For the BorrowerName 'HASKELL E. STEPHENS', the function would return the single integral value of 19. This value then could be used, for example, as a basis for padding the string with spaces. Strings in UCSD Pascal may have lengths ranging from 0 to 255.

POSition is a predeclared function that returns the starting numeric position of a given string within a larger string. The form is:

```
SomeValue := POS(TargetString, OtherString);
```

If TargetString cannot be found within OtherString, a value of 0 is returned. The following example illustrates the use of POS:

```
Temp := 'ABCXYZ';

I := POS('XYZ',Temp);
```

The value returned by the POS function above will be 4.

CONCATenate is a predeclared function that returns a single string value that is the result of linking, or concatenating, a series of strings specified within the CONCAT statement. The form of the CONCAT statement is:

```
StrResult := CONCAT(StringName1,StringName2,StringName3);

                    (* and so on for any number of
                              strings to be concatenated *)
```

Any number of strings may be linked in this way. String constants rather than string names also may be specified by enclosing the string constant in single quotation marks (' '). An example of the use of CONCAT is:

```
PROCEDURE LinkSentence;
VAR
 ResultString:STRING;
 PlaceHolder:STRING;
BEGIN
 PlaceHolder := 'W IT';
 ResultString := CONCAT('NO',PlaceHolder,' IS C','LEAR.');
END;
```

The single string value that would result from running the procedure LinkSentence would be:

```
NOW IT IS CLEAR.
```

Another Pascal function useful for formatting outputs is **COPY**. The COPY function is of the form:

```
Result := COPY(StringName,N,M);
                (* where N is a character position
                   and M is a length in characters *)
```

The COPY function returns a single string value that is the result of copying a series of characters from the designated string, starting at the Nth character position, as counted from the left, and including the next M characters. Consider the following example:

```
LastName := COPY(BorrowerName,12,8);
```

For the BorrowerName 'HASKELL E. STEPHENS', the above COPY statement returns the single string value 'STEPHENS'.

LENGTH, CONCAT, and COPY are Pascal functions that operate on string parameters. Two Pascal procedures, **INSERT** and **DELETE**, also may be used to manipulate characters within string variables (not within literals or string constants).

The form of the INSERT procedure is:

```
INSERT(SourceStringExpression,DestinationStringName,N);

      (* where N is a character position
                       in the second string *)
```

The INSERT procedure causes the characters in the first string given, the source string, to be inserted in the second, or destination, string. The insertion occurs at the character position N, as counted from the left in the destination string. An example of INSERT would be:

```
PROCEDURE Speak;
VAR
 Sentence,
 Negative:STRING;
BEGIN
 Sentence := 'THIS IS FRENCH.';
 Negative := 'NOT ';
 INSERT(Negative,Sentence,9);
END;
```

Running procedure Speak produces the following value from the string Sentence:

```
'THIS IS NOT FRENCH.'
```

The action of the DELETE procedure deletes a specified number of characters from a string, beginning at a specified character position within the string. The DELETE procedure has the form:

```
DELETE(StringName,N,M);  (* where N is character position,
                            and M is a count of characters to be deleted *)
```

Using a variable from the previous example, a DELETE statement would look like this:

```
DELETE(Sentence,1,8);
```

Assume, then, that the current Sentence string value is:

```
'THIS IS FRENCH.'
```

The example DELETE procedure would change the value of Sentence to:

```
'FRENCH.'
```

Note that INSERT and DELETE will change an existing string. Therefore, the DestinationString used in INSERT and StringName used in DELETE refer to variables (not constants or literals). On the other hand, LENGTH, COPY, CONCAT, and POS can use any string expression as an argument.

CODING *BasicAccounting*

Some additional Pascal features are required to implement the design objectives developed in Chapter 7. These are:

- Enumeration types
- Subrange types
- Sets
- Writing to a device
- ROUND function
- EXIT procedure.

Enumeration Types and Subrange Types

As previously discussed, besides the use of predefined types such as INTEGER, the programmer may coin types in Pascal. Coined enumeration and subrange types define data types that are *scalar.* To restate the definition of scalar data, scalar values are those that imply counting. Further, a scalar data type has a known range and number of possible values. Of the predefined types in Pascal, INTEGER, BOOLEAN, and CHARacter are all scalar. REAL and STRING, however, are not scalar because the number of possible values in each type are indeterminate.

The number of values may be said to be indeterminate for REAL data, for example, because the number of possible values for fractional numbers of this type is practically limitless. To illustrate, consider the difference between a piano and a trombone. A piano has 88 keys. The range and number of tones that can be produced on the piano is fixed and known. The tones of the piano, therefore, have a scalar relationship to one another. The trombone, on the other hand, may produce a limitless number of tones. The tones produced are continuously variable—moving the trombone slide only slightly produces a different tone—and the number of possible positions is indeterminate, even though the upper and lower range of tones is limited. Accordingly, the tonal values produced by the trombone are not scalar. The ways to define new scalar types include:

- Subrange
- Enumeration.

Subrange. A *subrange* type is defined in program text by two constants separated by the (. .) symbol. This symbol has the meaning in Pascal "through and including." An example of the syntax of this type definition would be:

```
TYPE
 DozenOrLess = 0..12;
```

The subrange defines lower and upper limits for the range of possible values. The first constant to appear defines the lower limit. Counting is implied by the (. .) symbol, indicating that possible values increase to an upper limit, as defined by the second constant.

Enumeration. An *enumeration* is a list of all the possible identifiers appearing in the type definition. The identifiers are values coined by the programmer. These identifiers appear within parentheses in the type definition and are separated by commas. The order of appearance also implies an ordering of value from lowest to highest. For example, if the programmer knows that a particular variable can have only three values, an enumeration may be used to name those values explicitly:

```
VAR ShirtSize : (Small,Medium,Large);
```

Subsequent program statements, then, could make use of the ordering implied in the enumeration:

```
IF ShirtSize > Small THEN
           (* or *)
FOR ShirtSize := Small TO Large DO
```

If enumeration types were not possible, the programmer would have to resort to declaring ShirtSize as an integer and assigning numeric values to each possible size. For long or complex enumerations, such an approach would not be practical, nor would it have the clarity and ease of use of a coined enumerated type. Enumeration is one more feature of Pascal that allows the programmer to produce meaningful program statements by coining names.

In *BasicAccounting*, a data type called ReportChoices is defined with an enumeration. The type definition indicates the possible values:

```
TYPE
 ReportChoices = (Sum,Percent,BarGraph);
```

Sets

A *set* is a mathematical concept that groups values according to some common property or rule. Values contained within a given set are said to be *members* of the set. For example, the set of planets of the solar system includes Mercury, Venus, Earth, Mars, etc. The set of the moons of Jupiter includes Io, Europa, Callisto, and Ganymede. The set of celestial objects in the solar system includes all the planets, the moons of Jupiter, the Sun, etc. Figure 8-2 is a diagram that represents these relationships.

Pascal offers the reserved term **SET** that is used to type variables whose values, or members, form a set. It often is useful to categorize certain data in sets, and to add members to, and remove members from, those sets. It also may be necessary to determine whether a given data item is a member of a given set. Pascal provides for all of these operations.

Variables may be declared to be of type SET in the variable declarations section of the program. A set must consist of scalar values. Accordingly, it is possible to have a SET OF CHAR, a SET OF BOOLEAN, or a SET OF INTEGER. Because their members would not be scalar, it is not possible to have a SET OF REAL or a SET OF STRING.

A set variable may be thought of as a list with a check mark beside each item of the list that is present. Check marks may be added to or subtracted from the list. Also, the list may be tested to see if an item is

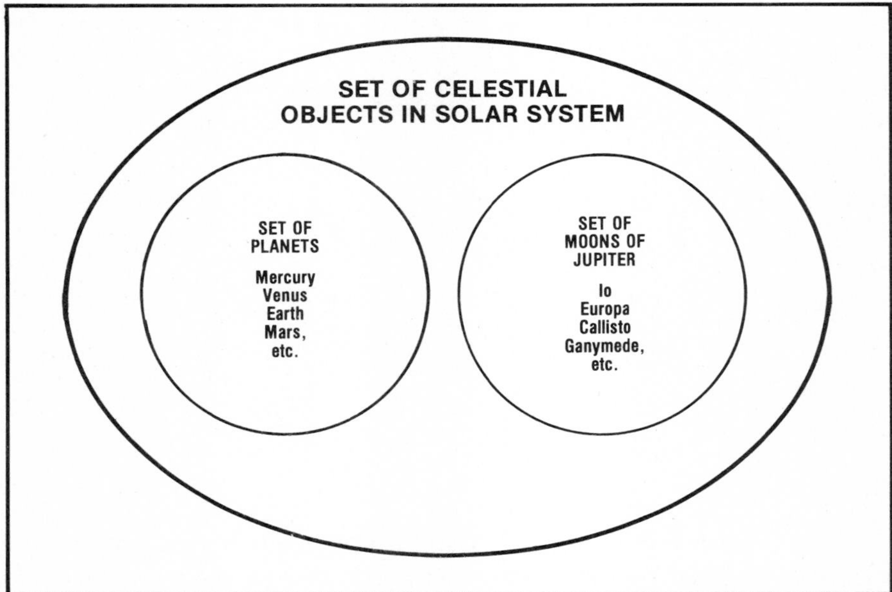

Figure 8-2. A Venn diagram is a graphic way of showing the relationship of members to sets that contain them.

checked. This analogy is illustrated further in Figure 8-3 and in the table in Figure 8-5, which lists operations that may be performed on sets.

Additionally, any duplicate members that are added to a set merge into the existing members; sets do not contain duplicates.

In the *BasicAccounting* program, an enumeration type, ReportChoices, is defined to specify allowable choices for report format. The set variable ReportSet, a SET OF ReportChoices, then is declared to hold a value corresponding with the choice made by the user for summary data, percentages, or bar graphs.

```
TYPE
 ReportChoices = (Sum,Percent,BarGraph);    (* report format choices *)
VAR
 ReportSet: SET OF ReportChoices;    (* users choices *)
```

	SET OF ALPHABETIC CAPITALS	SET OF LOWERCASE LETTERS	SET OF CHARACTERS
A	✓		✓
B	✓		✓
C	✓		✓
D	✓		✓
E	✓		✓
f		✓	✓
g		✓	✓
h		✓	✓
i		✓	✓
j		✓	✓
1			✓
2			✓
3			✓
4			✓
5			✓

Figure 8-3. Lists can be used to illustrate the concept of logical tests applied to sets. Check marks indicate which items are present.

The procedure AskReportType assigns values to ReportSet based on prompted user inputs. This assignment is controlled by CASE selectors corresponding with the user inputs. This procedure is presented in Figure 8-4.

During the output processing phase of the program, the value of ReportSet is tested, using the set operation IN, to see which report option the user has chosen:

```
IF Percent IN ReportSet THEN    (* print a table of percentages *)

IF BarGraph IN ReportSet THEN              (* display a bar graph *)
```

Variables of type SET may be assigned values from other sets, or from *set constants.* A set constant is a set whose members are fixed and may not be added to or removed from the set within the program. A set constant may be coded using the syntax given in the examples below. The members of the set constant are contained within brackets ([ ]) and may be defined through the use of the (. .) syntax, implying a range of values; or sets may be enumerated explicitly. Some set constants are illustrated in the following examples:

```
VAR
  NumberSet, BigSet, OddSet : SET OF INTEGER;
```

Given the above declaration, the following program statements are valid:

```
NumberSet := [ 1 .. 10 ];           (* set contains 1,2,3,4,5,6,7,8,9,10 *)
BigSet := [ 1 .. 10,12,23 ]; (* set contains 1,2,3,4,5,6,7,8,9,10,12,23 *)
OddSet := [ 1,3,5,7,9 ];                       (* set contains 1,3,5,7,9 *)
```

Operations may be performed on entire sets. Figure 8-5 shows symbols used in Pascal program text to cause these operations to be performed.

```
(************************************************************************)
(*                                                                      *)
(*      ASK USER WHAT FORM REPORT IS TO TAKE, SET VARIABLE ReportSet    *)
(*                                                                      *)
(************************************************************************)
PROCEDURE AskReportType;
VAR
 Choice:INTEGER;
BEGIN
(* show user a menu of choices for report format *)
 PutTitle('SELECTION OF DATA FORMAT');
 WRITELN;
 WRITELN('1. DATA SUM');
 WRITELN('2. DATA SUM AND PERCENTAGES');
 WRITELN('3. DATA SUM, PERCENTAGES, AND BAR GRAPH');
 Choice := AskChoice(0,10,'ENTER CHOICE ',1,3);
(* now convert answer (1,2,3) into ReportSet values *)
  CASE Choice OF
   1:ReportSet := [Sum];
   2:ReportSet := [Sum,Percent];
   3:ReportSet := [Sum,Percent,BarGraph];
  END;
END;
```

Figure 8-4. Procedure AskReportType.

SET OPERATIONS IN PASCAL

+	Adds members of one set to another (adds check marks)
−	Removes members of one set from another (removes check marks)
*	Produces the intersection (set of all numbers in common) of two sets (The check marks in both lists are combined.)
=	Tests two sets for equality (Are both lists checked the same?)
<>	Tests two sets for inequality (Are the lists checked differently?)
<=	Tests to see if one set is contained in another (Are all the check marks in a given list among the check marks in another?)
>=	Tests to see if one set contains another (same as <= but looking the other way)
IN	Tests to see if a given value is a member of a given set (Is a given item checked?)

Figure 8-5. Symbols used for set operations in Pascal program text.

To illustrate operations performed on sets, consider the following Boolean expression:

```
['Y','y'] = ['Y','y','N','n']
```

The expression is TRUE because the set on the left is contained in the set on the right. Similarly, the following expression also is TRUE because the two sets are not equal:

```
[SMALL,LARGE] <> [MEDIUM,LARGE]
```

The following expression tests whether the element on the left is contained in the set on the right:

```
'A' IN ['A'..'Z']
```

The expression is TRUE since the character 'A' is contained within the set of characters defined by 'A' through 'Z'.

A set constant also may be associated with an identifier in the CONST declaration section. For example:

```
YesNoSet = ['Y','y','N','n']
```

Writing to a Device

As mentioned earlier in this book, Pascal regards all system peripherals, or devices, as files. The structure of files is discussed in depth in Chapter 9. The UCSD Pascal operating system predeclares the files **PRINTER:** and **CONSOLE:** for use in any output operations referring to those devices. To write to a selected device, you must pass a reference to the desired device to a WRITE or WRITELN statement as its first argument. In *BasicAccounting*, the selection is done through a variable OutDevice, which is associated with a file named 'CONSOLE:' or 'PRINTER:', depending on the user's selection. A file that is to receive output from WRITE or WRITELN statements must be of the predefined type TEXT.

ROUND and EXIT

Not previously encountered are the **ROUND** function and the **EXIT** procedure. Both are used in *BasicAccounting*.

The statement in the example program that calls the ROUND function is:

```
NumberOfStars := ROUND(Ratio * 40);
```

This function returns a value for a given real number that has been rounded to the nearest whole number. The variable Ratio in this case represents a real number, which is multiplied by the total width of a bar graph to determine the length of a bar that corresponds to Ratio. The bar is represented in physical output by an integral number of stars, or asterisks (*).

(When a REAL argument is given to TRUNC, its action resembles that of ROUND. However, no rounding takes place; the fractional part simply is abandoned.)

The example of the EXIT procedure in the program is:

```
EXIT(PROGRAM);
```

The EXIT function causes the named procedure to terminate, and if the reserved word PROGRAM is used, the program is halted. In the example program, EXIT is used as a way to terminate what otherwise would be an infinite loop. EXIT can be used in any procedure or function to exit from any other procedure or function. Thus, a called procedure can cause the calling procedure to exit.

Program Text

The program text of *BasicAccounting* is presented in Figure 8-6. Key procedures and processing actions are explained in program comments.

Figure 8-6. Program *BasicAccounting*.

```
    (* NOTE:  Program text areas carried over from BalancePlus are shaded. *)

PROGRAM BasicAccounting;
CONST
 MaximumCateg = 10;             (* maximum number of debit/credit categories *)

TYPE
 CategArray = ARRAY[0..MaximumCateg] OF STRING;              (* category names *)
 ReportChoices = (Sum,Percent,BarGraph);              (* report format choices *)

VAR
 ReportSet: SET OF ReportChoices;                               (* users choices *)

 StartBalance,
 DebitSum,
 CreditSum,
 CurrentBalance:REAL;                             (* variables from BalancePlus *)

 PageWidth,                                   (* variable to hold screen width *)
 HowManyDebitCategories,                                   (* category counter *)
 HowManyCreditCategories:INTEGER;                          (* category counter *)

 DebitCategoryList,
 CreditCategoryList:CategArray;                 (* arrays as in BalancePlus *)

 DebitTotals,
 CreditTotals:ARRAY[0..MaximumCateg] OF REAL;              (* category totals *)

 OutDevice:TEXT;                              (* declare output file for reports *)

 Underline:STRING;                             (* will hold underline characters *)

 Printing,            (* used to test if an output is to CONSOLE or PRINTER *)
 FileOpen:BOOLEAN;       (* used to test if an output file is already open *)
                                         (* see Chapter 9 for more on files *)
(***************************************************************************)
(*                                                                         *)
(*    PROCEDURE TO ERASE SCREEN AND DISPLAY A CENTERED TITLE AT THE TOP    *)
(*                                                                         *)
(***************************************************************************)
PROCEDURE PutTitle(Title:STRING);
VAR
 EndPosition:INTEGER;           (* declare variable to hold the calculation *)
BEGIN
 PAGE(OUTPUT);                          (* clear the screen or start new page *)
 EndPosition := (PageWidth DIV 2) + (LENGTH(Title) DIV 2);
 WRITELN(Title:EndPosition);                                 (* display title *)
 WRITELN(Underline:PageWidth);                                   (* underline *)
 WRITELN;                                                      (* skip a line *)
END;
```

```
(**************************************************************************)
(*                                                                        *)
(*          PROCEDURE TO CENTER A MESSAGE ON THE OUTPUT DEVICE            *)
(*                                                                        *)
(**************************************************************************)
PROCEDURE PageCenter(Title:STRING);
VAR
 EndPosition:INTEGER;         (* declare a variable to hold the calculation *)
BEGIN
 EndPosition := (PageWidth DIV 2) + (LENGTH(Title) DIV 2);
 WRITELN(OutDevice,Title:EndPosition);
END;
(**************************************************************************)
(*                                                                        *)
(*      PROCEDURE TO DRAW AN UNDERLINE ACROSS THE OUTPUT DEVICE PAGE      *)
(*                                                                        *)
(**************************************************************************)
PROCEDURE PageUnderline;
BEGIN
 WRITELN(OutDevice,Underline:PageWidth);
END;
(**************************************************************************)
(*                                                                        *)
(*   PROCEDURE TO START A NEW PAGE; DISPLAY A CENTERED TITLE AT THE TOP   *)
(*                                                                        *)
(**************************************************************************)
PROCEDURE NewPage(Title:STRING);
BEGIN
 PAGE(OutDevice);                    (* clear the screen or start new page *)
 PageCenter(Title);
 PageUnderline;                                              (* underline *)
 WRITELN(OutDevice);                                       (* skip a line *)
END;
(**************************************************************************)
(*                                                                        *)
(*       FUNCTION TO ALLOW THE USER TO CHANGE ANSWER OR TO CONTINUE       *)
(*                                                                        *)
(**************************************************************************)
FUNCTION OK:BOOLEAN;
VAR
 Character:CHAR;
 Message:STRING;
BEGIN
 Message := '(RETURN) IF OK;(SPACE) TO CHANGE ANSWER';
  REPEAT
   GOTOXY(0,22);
   WRITE(Message);
   READ(KEYBOARD,Character);
  UNTIL (Character = ' ') OR EOLN(KEYBOARD);
 IF EOLN(KEYBOARD) THEN OK := TRUE
 ELSE OK := FALSE;
 GOTOXY(0,22);
 WRITE('':LENGTH(Message));                              (* erase message *)
END;
(**************************************************************************)
(*                                                                        *)
(*                     WAIT FOR USER TO PRESS A KEY                       *)
(*                                                                        *)
(**************************************************************************)
PROCEDURE AwaitAnyKey;
VAR
 AnyChar:CHAR;
BEGIN
 IF NOT Printing THEN
  BEGIN
   WRITELN;
   WRITE('PRESS ANY KEY TO CONTINUE');
   READ(AnyChar);
  END;
END;
```

```
(****************************************************************************)
(*                                                                          *)
(*           ASK THE USER FOR A REAL NUMBER AT COORDINATES X , Y            *)
(*                                                                          *)
(****************************************************************************)
PROCEDURE AskValue(X,Y:INTEGER;Question:STRING;VAR Answer:REAL);
BEGIN
  REPEAT
   GOTOXY(X,Y);
   WRITE(Question,' ');
   READLN(Answer);
  UNTIL OK;
 GOTOXY(X, Y + 1);
END;
(****************************************************************************)
(*                                                                          *)
(*    GET THE NAMES OF THE CREDIT CATEGORIES AND PUT THEM INTO AN ARRAY     *)
(*                                                                          *)
(****************************************************************************)
PROCEDURE GetCreditCategories;
VAR
 Temp:STRING;
 Counter:INTEGER;
BEGIN
 PutTitle('ENTER CREDIT CATEGORY NAMES');
(* show all categories currently saved *)
 FOR Counter := 0 TO HowManyCreditCategories DO
  WRITELN('CREDIT CATEGORY ',Counter,' : ',CreditCategoryList[Counter]);
(* if list is already full, tell user and don't allow any more entries *)
 IF HowManyCreditCategories = MaximumCateg THEN
  BEGIN
   WRITELN;
   WRITELN('NO MORE ROOM IN LIST');
   AwaitAnyKey;
  END
 ELSE
  REPEAT
   WRITE('CREDIT CATEGORY ',HowManyCreditCategories + 1,' ? ');
   READLN(Temp);
   IF Temp <> '' THEN
    BEGIN
     WHILE(LENGTH(Temp) < 20) DO Temp := CONCAT(Temp, ' ');
     HowManyCreditCategories := HowManyCreditCategories + 1;
     CreditCategoryList[HowManyCreditCategories] := Temp;
    END;
  UNTIL (Temp = '') OR (HowManyCreditCategories = MaximumCateg);
 WRITELN;
END;
(****************************************************************************)
(*                                                                          *)
(*    GET THE NAMES OF THE DEBIT CATEGORIES AND PUT THEM INTO AN ARRAY      *)
(*                                                                          *)
(****************************************************************************)
PROCEDURE GetDebitCategories;
VAR
 Temp:STRING;
 Counter:INTEGER;
BEGIN
 PutTitle('ENTER DEBIT CATEGORY NAMES');
(* show all categories currently saved *)
 FOR Counter :=0 TO HowManyDebitCategories DO
  WRITELN('DEBIT CATEGORY ',Counter,' : ',DebitCategoryList[Counter]);
(* if list is already full, tell user and don't allow any more *)
  IF HowManyDebitCategories = MaximumCateg THEN
  BEGIN
   WRITELN;
   WRITELN('NO MORE ROOM IN LIST');
   AwaitAnyKey;
  END
 ELSE
```

```
  REPEAT                                                          (* until done *)
   WRITE('DEBIT CATEGORY ',HowManyDebitCategories + 1,' ? ');
   READLN(Temp);
   IF Temp <> '' THEN
    BEGIN
     WHILE(LENGTH(Temp) < 20) DO Temp := CONCAT(Temp, ' ');
     HowManyDebitCategories := HowManyDebitCategories + 1;
     DebitCategoryList[HowManyDebitCategories] := Temp;
    END;
  UNTIL (Temp = '') OR (HowManyDebitCategories = MaximumCateg);
 WRITELN;
END;
(***************************************************************************)
(*                                                                         *)
(*               ASK FOR THE BEGINNING BALANCE OF THE ACCOUNT              *)
(*                                                                         *)
(***************************************************************************)
PROCEDURE GetStartBalance;
BEGIN
 PutTitle('ACCOUNT STARTING BALANCE');
 AskValue(8,6,'ENTER STARTING BALANCE $',StartBalance);
END;
(***************************************************************************)
(*                                                                         *)
(*  ASK THE USER FOR A NUMBER FROM Min TO Max, AND REPEAT UNTIL OBTAINED   *)
(*                                                                         *)
(***************************************************************************)
FUNCTION AskChoice(X,Y:INTEGER;Q:STRING;Min,Max:INTEGER):INTEGER;
VAR
 Answer:INTEGER;
BEGIN
  REPEAT
   GOTOXY(X,Y);
   WRITE(Q,' (FROM ',Min,' TO ',Max,') ');
   READLN(Answer);
  UNTIL Answer IN [Min..Max];   (* note use of the set function IN to ensure
                                   that the integer read lies within range *)
 AskChoice := Answer;
END;
(***************************************************************************)
(*                                                                         *)
(*     SHOW A "MENU" OF THE AVAILABLE CATEGORY NAMES FOR CREDIT OR DEBIT   *)
(*                 AND ASK FOR THE DESIRED CATEGORY NUMBER                 *)
(*                                                                         *)
(***************************************************************************)
FUNCTION AskCategory(NumberOfCategories:INTEGER;
                    CategList:CategArray):INTEGER;
VAR
 Counter,
 Answer:INTEGER;

BEGIN
 WRITELN;
 FOR Counter := 0 TO NumberOfCategories DO       (* display all categories *)
  WRITELN(Counter:8,'. ',CategList[Counter]);       (* menu display format *)
 AskCategory := AskChoice(10,22,'ENTER CATEGORY',0,NumberOfCategories);
END;
(***************************************************************************)
(*                                                                         *)
(*        GET EACH DEBIT AND ITS CATEGORY, AND ADD IT TO THE TOTALS        *)
(*                                                                         *)
(***************************************************************************)
PROCEDURE SumDebits;
VAR
 Amount:REAL;
 Choice:INTEGER;
BEGIN
  REPEAT
   PutTitle('DEBIT ENTRIES');
   AskValue(8,6,'  ENTER DEBIT AMOUNT $ ',Amount);      (* get debit amount *)
```

```
    DebitSum := DebitSum + Amount;                        (* add to debit total *)
    WRITELN;
    WRITELN(' ':8,'    DEBIT SUMMARY IS $ ',DebitSum:8:2);     (* show total *)
    IF Amount <> 0 THEN
     BEGIN
      Choice := AskCategory(HowManyDebitCategories,DebitCategoryList);
      (* above presents a menu of debit categories and prompts users choice *)
      DebitTotals[Choice] := DebitTotals[Choice] + Amount;
              (* above adds the debit to the total for the selected category *)
     END;
   UNTIL Amount = 0;
 WRITELN('--- END OF DEBITS ---');
 END;
(**************************************************************************)
(*                                                                        *)
(*        GET EACH CREDIT AND ITS CATEGORY, AND ADD IT TO THE TOTALS      *)
(*                                                                        *)
(**************************************************************************)
PROCEDURE SumCredits;
VAR
 Amount:REAL;
 Choice:INTEGER;
BEGIN
  REPEAT
   PutTitle('CREDIT ENTRIES');
   AskValue(8,6,' ENTER CREDIT AMOUNT $ ',Amount);    (* get credit amount *)
   CreditSum := CreditSum + Amount;                        (* add to total *)
   WRITELN;
   WRITELN(' ':8,'    CREDIT SUMMARY IS $ ',CreditSum:8:2);     (*show total*)
   IF Amount <> 0 THEN
    BEGIN
     Choice := AskCategory(HowManyCreditCategories, CreditCategoryList);
   (* above presents a menu of credit categories and prompts users choice *)
     CreditTotals[Choice] := CreditTotals[Choice] + Amount;
          (* above adds the credit to the total for the selected category *)
    END;
  UNTIL Amount = 0;
 WRITELN('--- END OF CREDITS ---');
END;
(**************************************************************************)
(*                                                                        *)
(*       THIS PROCEDURE WILL DRAW A BAR GRAPH, USING STARS **** TO SHOW   *)
(*        DATA, AND FINISHING THE LINE WITH DOTS ......................   *)
(*                                                                        *)
(**************************************************************************)
PROCEDURE DrawBar(NStars,GraphWidth:INTEGER);
VAR
 Position:INTEGER;
BEGIN
 FOR Position := 1 TO GraphWidth DO
  IF Position <= NStars THEN
   WRITE(OutDevice,'*')                                  (* show bar graph *)
  ELSE
   WRITE(OutDevice,'.');                             (* fill out with dots *)
END;
(**************************************************************************)
(*                                                                        *)
(*       THIS PROCEDURE WILL DISPLAY AMOUNTS AS EITHER 1. RAW DATA,       *)
(*       2. PERCENTAGE OF TOTAL, OR 3. A BAR GRAPH 40 CHARACTERS LONG.    *)
(*       NOTE THAT THE BAR GRAPH IS NOT DRAWN UNLESS THE PERCENTAGES      *)
(*       ALSO ARE PRINTED.                                                *)
(*                                                                        *)
(**************************************************************************)
PROCEDURE ShowData(Amount,Total:REAL);
VAR
 I,
 NumberOfStars:INTEGER;
 Ratio,
 Pct:REAL;
BEGIN
 IF Total <> 0 THEN                               (* avoid division by zero *)
```

```
   BEGIN
    Ratio := Amount / Total;                    (* calculate ratio of item to total *)
    Pct := Ratio * 100;                                   (* calculate percentage *)
    NumberOfStars := ROUND(Ratio * 40);                    (* length of bar graph *)
    WRITE(OutDevice,Amount:10:2);                                 (* show amount *)
    IF Percent IN ReportSet THEN
     BEGIN
      WRITE(OutDevice,Pct:8:2,'% ');                (* show percentage to total *)
      IF BarGraph IN ReportSet THEN
       DrawBar(NumberOfStars,40);                       (* bar graph, show scale *)
     END;
   END;
  WRITELN(OutDevice);                                             (* finish line *)
 END;
(**************************************************************************)
(*                                                                        *)
(*    THIS PROCEDURE WILL DISPLAY THE TOTALS FOR THE DEBITS AND CREDITS   *)
(*    THAT HAVE BEEN ENTERED UNDER EACH CATEG, AS WELL AS GRAND TOTALS.   *)
(*                                                                        *)
(**************************************************************************)
PROCEDURE ShowDetailTotals;
VAR
 Cat:INTEGER;                                                  (* category index *)
BEGIN
(* list the summaries for each category of debit *)
 WRITELN(OutDevice);                                               (* skip a line *)
 WRITELN(OutDevice,'--DEBITS--');                               (* write heading *)
 FOR Cat := 0 TO HowManyDebitCategories DO                  (* for each category...*)
  BEGIN
   WRITE(OutDevice,DebitCategoryList[Cat]);               (*display category name *)
   ShowData(DebitTotals[Cat],DebitSum);                           (* format data *)
  END;
 PageUnderline;                                                     (* underline *)
 WRITE(OutDevice,'DEBIT TOTAL          ',DebitSum:10:2);            (*show total*)
 IF Percent IN ReportSet THEN                                (* if user wants pct *)
  WRITE(OutDevice,'100% ':10);                                       (* show 100% *)
 WRITELN(OutDevice);
(* list the summaries for each category of credit *)
 WRITELN(OutDevice);
 WRITELN(OutDevice,'--CREDITS--');                              (* write heading *)
 FOR Cat := 0 TO HowManyCreditCategories DO                 (* for each category...*)
  BEGIN
   WRITE(OutDevice,CreditCategoryList[Cat]);                   (* show categ name *)
   ShowData(CreditTotals[Cat],CreditSum);                         (* format data *)
  END;
 PageUnderline;                                                     (* underline *)
 WRITE(OutDevice,'CREDIT TOTAL         ',CreditSum:10:2);           (*show total*)
 IF Percent IN ReportSet THEN                                (* if user wants pct *)
  WRITE(OutDevice,'100% ':10);                                       (* show 100% *)
 WRITELN(OutDevice);                                               (* finish line *)
 WRITELN(OutDevice);                                               (* skip a line *)
END;
(**************************************************************************)
(*                                                                        *)
(*      ASK USER WHAT FORM REPORT IS TO TAKE, SET VARIABLE ReportSet      *)
(*                                                                        *)
(**************************************************************************)
PROCEDURE AskReportType;
VAR
 Choice:INTEGER;
BEGIN
(* show user a menu of choices for report format *)
PutTitle('SELECTION OF DATA FORMAT');
WRITELN;
WRITELN('1. DATA SUM');
WRITELN('2. DATA SUM AND PERCENTAGES');
WRITELN('3. DATA SUM, PERCENTAGES, AND BAR GRAPH');
Choice := AskChoice(0,10,'ENTER CHOICE ',1,3);
(* now convert answer (1,2,3) into ReportSet values *)
```

```
  CASE Choice OF
   1:ReportSet := [Sum];
   2:ReportSet := [Sum,Percent];
   3:ReportSet := [Sum,Percent,BarGraph];
  END;
END;
(***********************************************************************)
(*                                                                     *)
(*             ASK NAME OF OUTPUT FILE (PRINTER, CONSOLE)              *)
(*      NOTE: FOR DISCUSSION OF FILE OPERATIONS, REFER TO CHAPTER 7    *)
(*                                                                     *)
(***********************************************************************)
PROCEDURE AskOutputDevice;
BEGIN
 IF FileOpen THEN CLOSE(OutDevice);         (* must close if already open *)
 PutTitle('OUTPUT FILE SELECTION');
 WRITELN;
 WRITELN('1. DISPLAY ON CONSOLE');
 WRITELN('2. DISPLAY ON PRINTER');
  CASE AskChoice(0,8,'Choice',1,2) OF
   1:BEGIN
      REWRITE(OutDevice,'CONSOLE:');
      Printing := FALSE;
      PageWidth := 40;                       (* set width of display line *)
     END;
   2:BEGIN
      REWRITE(OutDevice,'PRINTER:');
      Printing := TRUE;                (* set a flag for later program use *)
      PageWidth := 80;                          (* set width of print line *)
     END;
  END;
 FileOpen := TRUE;
END;
(***********************************************************************)
(*                                                                     *)
(*      SHOW TOTALS FOR DEBIT / CREDIT CATEGORIES AND SHOW ACCT BALANCE  *)
(*                                                                     *)
(***********************************************************************)
PROCEDURE CalculateCurrentBalance;
VAR
 Temp:STRING;
BEGIN
 AskReportType;                                 (* get format for output *)
 AskOutputDevice;
 NewPage('TOTAL ACCOUNT ACTIVITY');                  (* new page, heading *)
 WRITE(OutDevice,'CATEGORY                   AMOUNT');        (* write heading *)
 IF Percent IN ReportSet THEN
  WRITE(OutDevice,'PERCENT ':10);                       (* write heading *)
 IF BarGraph IN ReportSet THEN
  WRITE(OutDevice,'CHARTED');                           (* write heading *)
 WRITELN(OutDevice);                                      (* finish line *)
 PageUnderline;                                             (* underline *)

 WRITELN(OutDevice,'BEGINNING BALANCE  $',StartBalance:10:2);
 ShowDetailTotals;
 CurrentBalance := StartBalance - DebitSum + CreditSum;
 WRITELN(OutDevice,'ACCOUNT BALANCE IS $',CurrentBalance:10:2);
 WRITELN(OutDevice,'==========':30);           (* = for double underscore *)
(* give user time to look at data before main menu appears again *)
 AwaitAnyKey;
END;                                       (* only if Printing is FALSE *)
(***********************************************************************)
(*                                                                     *)
(*     INITIALIZE SOME PROGRAM VARIABLES AND GET DEBIT/CREDIT CATEGS   *)
(*                                                                     *)
(***********************************************************************)
PROCEDURE Initialize;
VAR
 Number:INTEGER;
BEGIN
 FOR Number := 0 TO MaximumCateg DO
```

```
    BEGIN
     DebitTotals[Number] := 0;                                  (* clear totals *)
     CreditTotals[Number] := 0;
     DebitCategoryList[Number] := '';                   (* clear category names *)
     CreditCategoryList[Number] := '';
    END;
   StartBalance := 0;                                           (* clear totals *)
   DebitSum := 0;
   CreditSum := 0;
   CreditCategoryList[0] := 'MISC. CREDITS       ';            (* 20 chars long *)
   DebitCategoryList[0] :=  'MISC. DEBITS        ';            (* 20 chars long *)
   HowManyDebitCategories := 0;
   HowManyCreditCategories := 0;
   PageWidth := 40;                                   (* set default page width *)
   FileOpen := FALSE;         (* default condition of display file is closed *)
   Underline := '';
   FOR Number := 1 TO 80 DO Underline := CONCAT(Underline,'-');
  END;
(***************************************************************************)
(*                                                                         *)
(*                        MAIN PROGRAM BLOCK                               *)
(*                                                                         *)
(***************************************************************************)
BEGIN                     (* this BEGIN is for the main program instructions *)
 Initialize;
  REPEAT                      (* main menu repeats until user stops program *)
   PutTitle('MAIN MENU - PROCESSING CHOICES');
   WRITELN;
   WRITELN('1. ENTER STARTING BALANCE');
   WRITELN('2. ENTER DEBIT CATEGORIES');
   WRITELN('3. ENTER CREDIT CATEGORIES');
   WRITELN('4. ENTER DEBITS');
   WRITELN('5. ENTER CREDITS');
   WRITELN('6. DISPLAY SUMMARY');
   WRITELN('7. STOP');
   CASE AskChoice(0,15,'ENTER CHOICE',1,7) OF
    1:GetStartBalance;
    2:GetDebitCategories;
    3:GetCreditCategories;
    4:SumDebits;
    5:SumCredits;
    6:CalculateCurrentBalance;
    7:EXIT(PROGRAM);                   (* predeclared function for program halt *)
   END;
  UNTIL FALSE;                                       (* creates infinite loop *)
END.                                                  (* end of program text *)
```

Figure 8-6. (Conclusion)

Summary

Pascal provides for output of real numbers in a form similar to scientific notation. Output statements that give a single length specifier, or no specifier, for REAL data items cause the data to be output in scientific notation.

The predeclared function LENGTH may be passed a string value argument and will return an integral value corresponding with the number of characters in the string. The POS function, when passed arguments for a character and a string variable, returns an integral value for the position of the character within the string.

The CONCAT function concatenates, or links, a series of string values passed to it to form a single string value.

The functions TRUNC and ROUND are useful for deriving approximations of REAL values.

The COPY function and the INSERT and DELETE procedures are used to manipulate string values.

The EXIT procedure is passed the name of a program block and causes processing in that block to terminate.

A set may be defined in Pascal by enumerating its members or by defining the lower and upper limits, or subrange, of the values that may be contained in it. Subranges must be defined with scalar data types.

Pascal allows operations to be performed on entire sets. These operations include addition, subtraction, intersection, test of equality, test of inequality, and so on. The reserved word IN may be used to test whether a given data item is contained in a set.

The UCSD Pascal operating system predeclares the file names PRINTER: and CONSOLE: for use in output statements that will write to these devices.

Review Questions

1. What is meant in Pascal by a long INTEGER, and how is this data type used?
2. What is the syntax of a WRITE or WRITELN statement that includes a length specifier?
3. What Pascal data type may require a length specifier of the form :X:Y when output by a WRITE statement, and what is the meaning of this specifier?
4. What are rounding and truncation, and how can rounding and truncation introduce errors?
5. What syntax is used to represent scientific notation in Pascal?

6. What is the form of the program statements for LENGTH and POS, and how is each used with reference to string variables?
7. What is the form of the CONCAT function, and how is it used?
8. What is the form of the COPY function, and how is it used?
9. What is the form of the program statements for the procedures INSERT and DELETE, and how is each used?
10. What is meant by typing by enumeration and typing by subrange, and how is each used in program text?
11. What is the use of the Pascal type SET?
12. What operations may be performed on sets?

Pascal Practice

1. Compare the program text for *BalancePlus* presented in the previous chapter with the *BasicAccounting* program text. How do the logical designs of the two programs compare?
2. Change *BasicAccounting* so that the output reports can be written to a file on a diskette as well as to the CONSOLE or PRINTER. (You may wish to read relevant sections of Chapter 9 on files before trying this.)
3. Change the maximum number of user categories in *BasicAccounting* from 10 to 20. Why is some limit on the number of categories a good idea? What impact does increasing the number of allowable categories have on program execution?
4. Add user prompts to *BasicAccounting* for the current date and display the date in the report title.
5. Using the string functions CONCAT, COPY, POS and LENGTH, write a single statement to change any string containing a name in the form 'Firstname M. Lastname' to the form 'Lastname, Firstname M.' (You may need more than one line for this statement.)

Key Terms

1. literal data
2. string constant
3. truncate
4. length specifier
5. round
6. scientific notation
7. exponent
8. justify
9. field
10. scalar
11. subrange
12. enumeration
13. set
14. member
15. set constant

Pascal Library

1. long INTEGER
2. TRUNC
3. LENGTH
4. POS
5. CONCAT
6. COPY
7. INSERT
8. DELETE
9. SET
10. IN
11. PRINTER:
12. CONSOLE:
13. ROUND
14. EXIT

9
SAVING AND USING INFORMATION

OBJECTIVES

On completing the reading and other learning assignments for this chapter, you should be able to:

- ☐ Explain how the concept of a transaction implies data structure.
- ☐ Describe the use of RECORD in Pascal and tell how fields are related to records.
- ☐ Demonstrate the use of the WITH . . DO construction in specifying records and fields to be operated upon.
- ☐ Explain how FILE is used to type records for storage and access.
- ☐ Demonstrate the use of the predeclared file variables INPUT and OUTPUT.
- ☐ Demonstrate how files are created and opened by REWRITE and reopened by RESET.
- ☐ Give some characteristics of files that reside on diskette.
- ☐ Use properly the Pascal procedures GET, PUT, SEEK, and CLOSE.
- ☐ Describe the use of the file formats TEXT, CODE, and DATA.
- ☐ Describe the file access methods: serial, sequential, and direct (random).

DATA STRUCTURES: RECORDS AND FILES

A related series of data items processed as an integrated entity forms a *data structure.* A data structure, in turn, is an extension of the underlying logic of the program.

All variables of the same data type have certain properties in common. However, this typing is independent of the structure in which those variables are stored. Data structures are needed for grouping and accessing variables as members of meaningful sets, as in the capturing, storage, and retrieval of transaction data. Recall that an array is a predefined data structure in Pascal for grouping and referencing elements held in memory.

Suppose a program required that data representing 10 checking account entries reside in memory. One way to implement this data structure would be to declare five array variables, each consisting of 10 elements. The five array variables correspond with the different data items contained in each check:

```
VAR
 Number:ARRAY[1..10] OF INTEGER;
 Amount:ARRAY[1..10] OF REAL;
 Date:ARRAY[1..10] OF STRING;
 Payee:ARRAY[1..10] OF STRING;
 Description:ARRAY[1..10] OF STRING;
```

The typing in these declarations enforces certain distinctions among data items. Names of payees cannot be entered by mistake into the Amount variable, for example. There is, however, a fundamental relationship among this group of data items that is not defined so far in the program text. That is, a set of data items, consisting of one corresponding element from each array, provides all data for a single check. The check is the basis for a meaningful grouping of the data items. It records a set of data items generated by a single transaction, or act of doing business.

Although it is possible to access each array element independently, it may be necessary to perform certain operations that affect all data items that refer to a single check. Accessing array elements individually each time this is required would involve a tedious coding task.

RECORDS

Pascal provides the reserved word **RECORD** that may be used to associate data items in groups. Any number of data items may be included in a *record*, and the data items may be of various types. A common use of records, but by no means the only one, is to group related data items according to transaction relationships. A transaction might involve a check, an electric bill, a job application, an insurance claim, a purchase in a store, and so on. Another typical use of records is to group data items collected within a certain time period, such as a series of measurements made during one trial of a scientific experiment.

Although a practical application of the Pascal term RECORD is to categorize data, data items within a record need not be related. The relationship of data items in a record is arbitrary, as defined by the programmer. Teachers of mathematics are fond of warning students not to "mix apples and oranges," but data items of coined types Apple and Orange could be included in a record, along with INTEGER, CHARACTER, REAL, STRING, and BOOLEAN, as well as other coined types, such as Rocket, Blue, and Book. The point is, defining records is a powerful tool for structuring data; the concept of a record is so flexible that the programmer may implement any relationships required by the logic of the program.

In Pascal program text, RECORD is a TYPE. However, it is not a predefined type because the programmer may define a record consisting of any data items, of any type. (An exception is FILE, discussed later in this chapter.) For example, all data for a single check, or transaction, could be grouped as a RECORD in the TYPE definition section of the program:

```
TYPE
 Check = RECORD
  Number:INTEGER;
  Amount:REAL;
  Date,
  Payee,
  Description:STRING;
 END;
```

In the above TYPE definition, Check is the coined type; and Number, Amount, Date, and so on, are fields within records of this type.

Continuing with the checking example, defining checks as records would allow a program to operate on a batch of checks as an array of records. Each array element would be of type Check. Given the above definition of type Check, the following variable declaration types the array variable CheckBatch with the previously coined record type Check:

```
VAR
 CheckBatch:ARRAY[1..100] OF Check;
```

This declaration creates, as a variable, an array of 100 records of type Check. To access a single element, or transaction, within an array of records, the individual record is specified by the array name and subscript. In other words, the name of the first record, or check, in the array CheckBatch is CheckBatch[1]. This record contains a single, related group of five data items: Number, Amount, Date, Payee, and Description.

The term RECORD may be used to declare a single variable as being of the RECORD type. This is done in the variable declaration section of the program. For example:

```
VAR
 TotalReceipts : RECORD
                   Date : STRING;
                   Amount : REAL;
                  END;
```

This declaration means that the variable TotalReceipts is itself a record that contains the *fields* Date and Amount. Fields are data items within records. This declaration defines a record type that has no type name associated with it.

Declaring a RECORD in the TYPE section creates a new type that may be assigned to any number of variables in the VAR declaration section of the program. Declaring a variable as a RECORD in the VAR section without a previous TYPE definition restricts the use of that record type to the single variable for which it was defined.

FIELDS

Individual fields, or data items, within records are referred to in program statements by expressions of the form:

```
RecordName.FieldName
```

Thus, the individual fields within the first record in CheckBatch would be:

```
CheckBatch[1].Number
CheckBatch[1].Amount
CheckBatch[1].Date
CheckBatch[1].Payee
CheckBatch[1].Description
```

Fields within records may, in turn, be records. For example, rather than have the Date field within a given record contain a single string (such as '2-15-85'), it would be possible to define a record type that would contain the month, day, and year as separate fields:

```
TYPE
 DateType = RECORD
  Month,
  Day,
  Year:INTEGER;
 END;
```

Then, a record of type DateType might be contained as a field within a record of type Check. Accordingly, the definition of a type Check record must be changed to look like this:

```
TYPE
 Check = RECORD
  Number:INTEGER;
  Amount:REAL;
  Date:DateType;
  Payee,
  Description:STRING;
 END;
```

Reference to fields within records that are themselves fields within larger records has the form:

```
RecordName.FieldName.FieldName
```

For example, the value stored in the variable Month in the first check in the batch is accessed by the following reference:

```
CheckBatch[1].Date.Month
```

Giving a separate reference for each field that must be operated on by the program can be a tedious coding task. For example, consider the following group of program statements:

```
BEGIN
 CheckBatch[1].Number := 1;
 CheckBatch[1].Amount := 12.45;
 CheckBatch[1].Date.Month := 2;
 CheckBatch[1].Date.Day := 15;
 CheckBatch[1].Date.Year := 1985;
 CheckBatch[1].Payee := 'ABC OIL CO.';
 CheckBatch[1].Description : = 'GASOLINE';
END;
```

For handling such situations, Pascal offers a syntactic shortcut, the **WITH . . DO** construction.

WITH . . DO

This construction gives the programmer the ability to specify a record and then list program statements relating to fields within that record without having to repeat the record name. The form of this construction is:

```
WITH RecordReference,OptionalRecordReference DO
 BEGIN
  program statement;
   ..
  program statement;
 END;
```

Note that, within the WITH . . DO header, more than one record or field reference may be given, separated by commas. A record reference such as "RecordName,FieldName" would allow all following program statements to reference fields within the record or field named. Alternatively, the record definition given in the header may specify only RecordName, in which case program statements may refer to many fields within the same record. *Nested records,* or fields within fields, may be specified by record definitions of the form:

```
WITH RecordReference,FieldReference,FieldReference,FieldReference DO
                                    (* for any number of levels *)
```

It is important to remember that this construction does not cause any processing to take place. It is only a means for referring to the records and fields that are to be operated upon.

To return to the CheckBatch example, it would be possible to code program statements referring to the first record in the array CheckBatch:

```
WITH CheckBatch[1] DO
 BEGIN
  Number := 1;
  Amount := 12.45;
  Payee := 'ABC OIL CO.';
  Description := 'GASOLINE';
 END;
```

Since the field Date is itself a record, program statements relating to it may be nested within the above block as follows:

```
WITH CheckBatch[1] DO
 BEGIN
  Number := 1;
  Amount := 12.45;
  Payee := 'ABC OIL CO.';
  Description := 'GASOLINE';
   WITH Date DO
    BEGIN
     Month := 2;
     Day := 15;
     Year := 1985;
    END;
 END;
```

However, to simplify the program text, the optional record reference syntax may be used instead in the header:

```
WITH CheckBatch[1],Date DO
 BEGIN
  Number := 1;
  Amount := 12.45;
  Payee := 'ABC OIL CO.';
```

```
    Description := 'GASOLINE';
    Month := 2;
    Day := 15;
    Year := 1985;
  END;
```

Note that BEGIN and END are required only when a compound statement is used. For a single program statement, the reference above could be made as:

```
WITH CheckBatch[1] DO WITH Date DO Month := 2;
```

An alternate format would be:

```
WITH CheckBatch[1],Date DO Month := 2;
```

A special need for caution should be pointed out regarding the use of WITH . . DO. The programmer must be aware of any duplications among field names within the record and data names used in other nested WITH statements or elsewhere in the program. An ambiguity would arise in the CheckBatch example if there were a global variable Number as well as a field of that name. In this case, the record name given in the WITH statement would supercede, but such constructions are to be used carefully. In general, if WITH statements are nested, the reference in the *last* WITH statement supercedes. Such situations provide yet another reason why you should choose variable names that are distinct as well as descriptive.

FILES

A *file* may be thought of as an array of elements that all share the same data type and that reside on a diskette. For example, customer bills might exist as records. The programmer could coin a record type, INVOICE, to define the fields to be contained within each record. Fields could contain customer name, address, customer number, item descriptions, amounts, extensions, and so on. In Pascal, the reserved word **FILE** may be used to declare a collection of records residing on an auxiliary storage device, such as a diskette. For example, a file declaration could create an array of customer bills, or records of type Invoice, that is to be saved on diskette.

In the previous example, CheckBatch is declared as an array of records. Recall that all entries in an array reside in memory. Unlike an array, a file exists outside of, or external to, memory; and any desired records must be brought into memory explicitly by the program. To handle records in this way, a *file variable* must be declared in the variable declaration section of the program. This declaration indicates to the compiler that records identified by the file variable name are to be stored outside of memory on a storage device. A file variable may not be included in a record definition, as stated above, because records are always contained *within* files. File variables sometimes are referred to as *complex data structures.*

Before data can be used in a program, the data must reside in the computer's main memory. When you declare a variable, you are actually naming a location within memory that is to hold the values of that variable. The array CheckBatch is declared as a variable. Accordingly, all of the elements of that array reside in memory. The retention of the array CheckBatch in memory is represented in a diagram in Figure 9-1.

The declaration of a variable of type FILE enables you to name a memory location that is to store, not an entire array of records, but a single record. This area of memory is known as a *file buffer.* Typically, the rest of the file exists on some storage device that is external to the computer's main memory. These are *external files.* Frequently, the amount of information in a file exceeds the capacity of the computer's memory. This storage method is diagrammed in Figure 9-2.

To process records contained in a file, you may cause the program to access individual records in the file and read those portions into active memory for processing. You also may cause the reverse to occur, saving the contents of memory to an external device.

In practical terms, a file is a group of records that is saved to some storage medium, such as a diskette. The range for the number of records within the file, then, would be from zero, or no records in the file, to the maximum number of records allowed by the storage device.

Most of the discussion in this chapter refers to this kind of file. Recall, however, that UCSD Pascal gives a broader meaning to the term file.

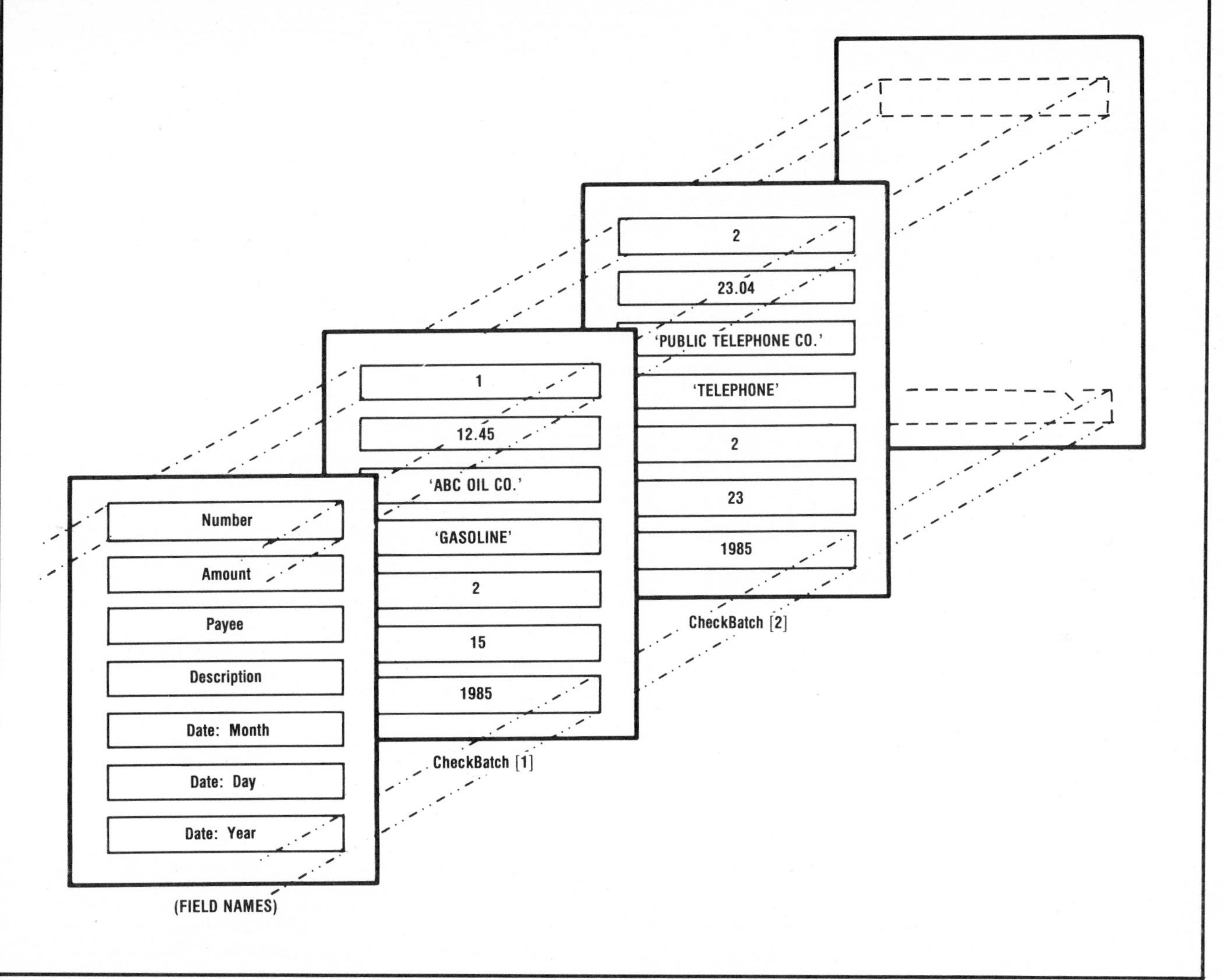

Figure 9-1. An array of records resides in memory. Each element of the array CheckBatch contains one record. Each record, in turn, contains the fields shown.

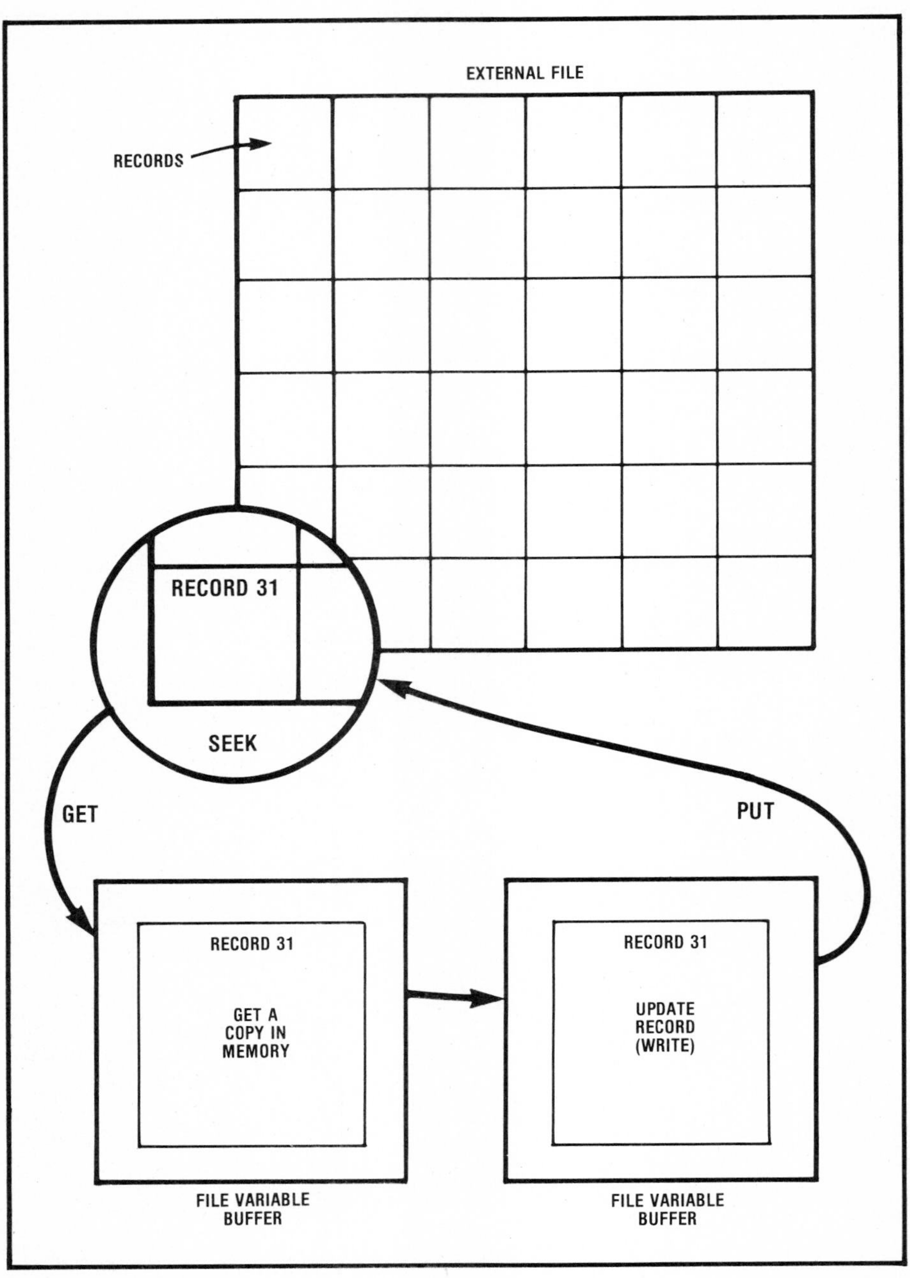

Figure 9-2. File operations and the file variable.

Pascal regards all system peripherals as files. Whether data are output to the display, input from the keyboard, output to the printer, or input/output to storage devices, many of the basic programming techniques for access are the same regardless of device. As stated previously, this data structure is device-independent in Pascal.

To rephrase the definition, FILE is a data type used to allow the programmer to associate a memory area with an external file. File variables for files of *formatted records,* that is, records explicitly typed within the program, have declarations of the form:

```
VAR
  FileName: FILE OF SomeType;
```

Files declared as above are called *typed files* because a data type is associated with the file variable. File variable declarations that omit a data type are known as *untyped files.* Untyped files are discussed in depth in Chapter 14.

Transaction data may exist as formatted records; for example:

```
VAR
  CheckFile: FILE OF Check;
```

In this example, CheckFile is the file variable created by the declaration. Note the distinction here: In the previous example, CheckBatch is the variable name of an array whose elements are records. The entire CheckBatch array resides in memory. By contrast, CheckFile is the program's name for an external group of records, only one of which might be in memory at a time.

To restate the distinction between arrays of records and files, typically an entire array of records resides in memory during program execution. From the standpoint of the compiler, the array is a group of ordered storage locations in memory. A file, on the other hand, typically exists on a storage device external to the computer's memory. Inherent in the use of FILE within program text is the ability to cause individual records to be brought into memory from the external file for processing. These records also may be written, in turn, to another external file.

Input/Output

The UCSD Pascal compiler predeclares two file names for use by the program. These files are named **INPUT** and **OUTPUT**. The compiler assigns the file name INPUT to the keyboard and OUTPUT to the console display. The programmer may reassign these file names to any device through program statements.

The file names INPUT and OUTPUT are implicit—or contained in, without being shown in—certain program statements. For example, the READ and WRITE statements are translated by the compiler as if the statements were written:

```
READ(INPUT,DataList);
WRITE(OUTPUT,DataList);
```

The use of file variables provides the programmer with a great deal of flexibility in performing *input/output*, or *I/O* operations, moving data into main memory to be processed and moving the results back out. For example, the programmer may assign a file variable name like Printer to the printer. Output operations to the printer then could be accomplished by the program statement:

```
WRITE(Printer,DataList);
```

The Pascal compiler predefines two types that may be associated with file variables. These predefined types are **TEXT** and **INTERACTIVE**. Both of these types refer to I/O devices that are character-oriented, that is, devices that process data one character at a time. The INPUT file (keyboard) is predeclared as being of the INTERACTIVE type. The OUTPUT file (console) is predeclared as type TEXT.

The distinction between these two types lies in how data are accessed. When a TEXT file is opened by a RESET statement (as explained below), the first character in the file is read into memory automatically.

The first character of an INTERACTIVE file, on the other hand, is not read in automatically as a result of RESET. The INTERACTIVE type usually implies keyboard entry, since the RESET procedure could not be completed, and thus no further programming steps could be processed, until the user had entered a character.

Creating, Opening, and Closing Files

A file is said to exist in one of two states: *open* or *closed.* When a file is open, data transfer can occur. No transfer operations can be performed on a closed file.

Pascal procedures are available for creating, opening, and closing files on storage devices. **REWRITE** creates a new file and opens it. **RESET** opens an existing file. **CLOSE** closes a file so that no further data access may occur until the file is reopened with a RESET procedure.

A CLOSE always should be performed if a file has been written to during the program. This practice ensures that the new data are retained on file. If no writing has been done, the CLOSE need not be performed explicitly, since the compiler closes all files at program termination. Of course, if the same file variable is to be associated with a different file, the first file must be closed before the file variable can be used to open another external file. The form of the REWRITE and RESET program statements is identical:

```
REWRITE(FileVariableName,FileNameString);
RESET(FileVariableName,FileNameString);
```

In both statements, the first FileVariableName appearing within the parentheses is the file variable name as it is declared in the variable declaration section of the program. The FileNameString is a string of characters that specifies a name for the physical file on the storage medium as it is known to the operating system. In program text, the string may be shown enclosed in single quotation marks or may be contained in a STRING variable. An example would be:

```
REWRITE(DataFile,'#4:NewFile.DATA');
```

The syntax #4: refers to the *device number* upon which the file NewFile.DATA is to be found. (For more information on these device assignments, consult the user's guide for the system you are using.) The suffix .DATA, discussed later in this chapter, is an optional file name extension that refers to an untyped file. The file variable DataFile will be associated with the external file NewFile.DATA until it is closed.

Diskette Files

The operating system assigns a dedicated space on the storage medium, such as a magnetic diskette, for use as a *file directory.* The format of this directory is created when a blank diskette is *initialized* by the operating system upon command from the computer operator.

The directory is an index, or *lookup table,* that contains file names and the actual locations of those files on the diskette. The directory serves as a guide to the operating system for the physical locations of files on the diskette. Other information in the directory includes the date each file was created and its length, which is used by the operating system to inform the operator of the current status of storage space on the diskette. The UCSD Pascal operating system refers to file length in *blocks,* units of 512 characters. Recall that a character is coded in one byte, or eight bits, of information. Thus, a block encompasses 4,096 bits of data.

The file directory is dynamic. That is, it is updated each time a file is closed. Thus, the directory always reflects the current status of all closed files on the diskette.

Diskette capacities are limited by the size of the storage medium. Capacity also is limited on most microcomputer systems by a maximum number of data entries in the device directory. In practice, a diskette is filled to capacity as soon as either of the two limits is reached. For example, a typical microcomputer system has a disk format with a capacity of 280 blocks. On the same system, the number of directory entries on a given disk may not exceed 77. Approximately four blocks are required for the directory, and two more blocks are reserved by the operating system. Therefore, it would be possible, theoretically, to store a single long file of approximately 274 blocks on a diskette. However, if all files were as short as one block each, the operating system would find the disk full at 77 blocks, since only that number of directory entries is allowed. (From an operational standpoint, it is not good practice to load a diskette to capacity. Doing so eliminates your flexibility in reading and rewriting files. A good operating guideline would be to try to use no more than 80 percent of the storage capacity of the working copy of a diskette, for example.)

The FileNameString referred to in REWRITE or RESET procedures is a string of characters that is identical to the name of the file in the directory on the storage medium. REWRITE causes the FileNameString to be entered in the directory for the first time when the file is closed and causes the variable given by FileVariableName to be associated with that external storage name. When a REWRITE is performed, a new file containing no records is created. The new file may receive data as directed by output statements (such as WRITE and PUT, discussed below) that reference the file variable given in the program.

When a RESET procedure is performed, the operating system searches the directory for the file on the diskette specified by FileNameString, opens it, and causes it to be associated with the file variable named in the RESET procedure call. Then, the stored file may be accessed by an input statement (such as READ or GET, discussed below) or written to by an output statement, both of which must specify the file variable given in the program. RESET cannot be used to open a new file but must refer to an existing file.

When an existing file is opened with the RESET procedure, with the exception of INTERACTIVE files, the first record in the file is read automatically into the system's main memory. You must bear this fact in mind when trying to keep track of which record is currently being accessed. When the first record is read in, it is stored in a portion of that file variable (FileVariableName) named in the RESET statement. If a file already has been opened with RESET and is still open, the following form causes the file to reread the first record of the file and then point to the second record:

```
RESET(FileVariableName);
                        (* without the external name *)
```

The File Variable

The file variable is actually a highly structured record. It contains fields that point to, or indicate the location of, the next position in the file, a flag or indicator for the *end-of-file,* and a buffer area used in transfers to and from the actual device.

To access the record currently contained in a file variable, a specific syntax must be used. This syntax involves the use of the file variable name with a caret symbol (^). The caret following a variable name in Pascal has the meaning *the content of*. When a file variable name appears followed by the caret symbol, it becomes syntactically equivalent to a RECORD name. A portion of the file variable is used as the buffer, or storage, area for the data values from the file that are currently residing in memory.

The file variable acts as a "window" for the program. It associates the portion of the file residing in memory with the rest of the file stored in the external device. The form of the file variable reference is:

```
FileVariableName^
```

The data content of a specific field within a record is referred to by:

```
FileVariableName^.FieldName
```

Nested fields are referred to by adding field names (.FieldName) to this syntax until the desired level is reached.

Note the distinction between the uses of the file variable. When the file variable syntax with the caret symbol (FileName^) is used, the reference is to the *data* contained within a record (or field) currently residing in memory. Recall that the buffer area in the file variable holds the contents of a single record.

In general, when referring to the name of a file, or when referring to the entire file, the file variable name is used. Again, when referring to the data content of a specific record or field within a file, or the specific data contained under the file variable name in memory, the file variable syntax with the caret symbol is used.

GET and PUT

To restate the operations involved in the RESET procedure: A RESET statement causes a file variable to be associated with an external file. The file is opened on an external device, and the first record in the file (unless of type INTERACTIVE) is read into memory and held under the name of the file variable specified in the RESET statement. Once the RESET procedure has been executed, the next record in the file may be accessed by passing the file variable as a parameter to the **GET** procedure.

The GET procedure is used to access the next sequential record in the file and read it into memory. The file variable, which contains a pointer to the next record in the file, is passed as a parameter to the procedure. The GET procedure is of the form:

```
GET(FileVariableName);
```

Suppose the array CheckBatch, consisting of 10 records of type Check, is to be saved on diskette. The file variable name that has been given to this type of record is CheckFile. Recall that the array name CheckBatch refers to records residing in memory. By contrast, the file variable CheckFile is used in program statements that refer to an external file. The file variable points to the next record to be read into memory from that file. The file variable and caret syntax, CheckFile^, is used to refer to the data contained in the current record.

To restate the relevant definitions and declarations:

```
TYPE
 Check = RECORD
  Number:INTEGER;
  Amount:REAL;
  Date:DateType;
  Payee,
  Description:STRING;
 END;

VAR
 CheckFile: FILE OF Check;
```

Given the above, the external file that is to contain the records on the diskette is created and opened by:

```
REWRITE(CheckFile,'DiskFile1');
```

Notice that the external file name need not be identical to the file variable name used by the program. Once the above statement has been executed, the references in the program are to the file variable name, regardless of what the external file name is. The first record in the array CheckBatch may be saved to the diskette by the following statements:

```
CheckFile^ := CheckBatch[1];
PUT(CheckFile);
```

These statements may be repeated in a program loop, incrementing the array subscript until each record in the array has been saved as an individual record in CheckFile.

Note the use of the **PUT** procedure to save a record that currently resides in memory to an existing file. This procedure is of the form:

```
PUT(FileVariableName);
```

An external file name must have been specified with the file variable by a previous REWRITE or RESET statement that opened the file. A series of PUT statements specifying the same file variable causes records to be saved in serial fashion on the diskette. Files built up in this way, with records appearing one after another in chronological order, are referred to as *serial access* files. Serial access files that are written in some logical order to coincide with processing requirements are known as *sequential access* files.

Suppose that another program requires that 10 records previously saved in this way be read into memory one at a time for processing. The file would be opened for access by:

```
RESET(MyFile,'DiskFile1');
```

Notice that the string referring to the external file name is identical to the one given in the REWRITE statement that created the file. The file variable given, on the other hand, need not be the same, since the RESET statement reestablishes a correspondence between the file variable name used in the program and the external file name. Remember, however, that the file variable given must be of the same type as the records residing in the external file. If this is not the case, unpredictable things can occur. For example, records of type Check should not be read in using a file variable of type Invoice because the data would be meaningless without the proper structure.

Execution of the above RESET statement would open the file and cause the first record, originally CheckBatch[1], to be read into memory. The data contained in this record then would be available in memory for processing by the program. The program would refer to this data as MyFile^. When the program is ready for the next record to be read in, the program statement would be:

```
GET(MyFile);
```

This statement would cause the next record, originally CheckBatch[2], to be read into memory. The next GET statement that refers to MyFile would access CheckBatch[3], and so on.

SEEK

Some versions of Pascal allow only serial access to files. However, processing operations in many applications frequently require access to records that are not adjacent to one another. The accessing of records individually, in any order, is referred to as *direct access*, or *random access*.

To provide for access to records in random order, UCSD Pascal offers the SEEK procedure. This procedure allows the programmer to specify explicitly the location of any record within a file as being the next record to be accessed by the program. Recognize, however, that the SEEK procedure only points to the record to be read in. The procedure does not cause the record to be input. A subsequent GET or PUT procedure must follow the SEEK procedure to access the record. The form of the SEEK procedure is:

```
SEEK(FileVariableName,RecordNumber);
```

In this statement, RecordNumber is a positive integer, ranging from zero to the maximum value allowed for an integer on your computer. The integral value of RecordNumber refers to the position of a record within the file according to the sequence of records in that file. Remember, though, that the number of the first record in a file is zero (0). Therefore, the number of the tenth record, for example, is 9. Either a GET or a PUT procedure always must be performed after a SEEK procedure has been executed. Other program statements may be encountered between SEEK and GET (or PUT), but an access must occur before another SEEK procedure can be performed, or an error results. After a GET statement, you must SEEK the same record again before performing a PUT to update the existing record. The additional SEEK is required because GET and PUT statements advance the file pointer to the next serial record.

CLOSE

The CLOSE procedure is used to mark a file CLOSED. There are two forms of this procedure:

```
CLOSE(FileVariableName);
```

```
CLOSE(FileVariableName,Option);
```

The action caused by the first form, without any option given, depends upon how the file was opened originally. The possible results are:

- If the file was opened with RESET, it simply is declared closed to further access by the program.
- If the file was opened with REWRITE, the file thus created ceases to exist.

However, a wider range of actions can be specified by the following options, which may be passed as parameters to the CLOSE procedure: **LOCK**, **PURGE**, or **CRUNCH**. The possible results are:

- If the file was opened with REWRITE and closed with the LOCK option, the operating system designates the file *permanent.* In this case, the end-of-file is set just after the highest record placed in the file.
- If the file was opened with either REWRITE or RESET and closed with the PURGE option, the file ceases to exist.
- If the file was opened with either REWRITE or RESET and closed with the CRUNCH option, an end-of-file is designated as the current next-record position, and any previously existing records appearing after that point are discarded.

File Formats TEXT, CODE, and DATA

Pascal defines formats that restrict the kinds of operations that can be performed on files. As mentioned previously, program text files are given the **.TEXT** suffix after the file name when they are created with the editor. Once a program text file has been compiled, the file name for the resulting code file has the suffix **.CODE**. File operations thus are restricted and file typing enforced. A compilation cannot be performed on any file format but a TEXT file, for example. An eXecute command can be performed only on a file that has been formatted as a CODE file.

Files created by the user through FILE type definitions within a program are termed **DATA** files. Data files do not have any particular naming convention and may have any legal name up to 15 characters long. This format means that the Pascal operating system associates no predefined data structures with the file. Further, the existence of a DATA file implies that the user has knowledge of the data structure of that file.

When accessing a DATA file, it is always up to the programmer to be aware of the record structure of the file. The Pascal compiler does not verify the structure of DATA file records when they are used. Therefore, care must be taken to define such records properly.

WITH . . DO and the File Variable

Earlier in this chapter, the WITH . . DO construction is demonstrated as a syntactic shortcut for references to records in program statements. These same operations also may be performed on files of records.

When using the WITH . . DO construction with files, the form of the statements is the same as that previously given, except that the file variable with caret syntax must be used to refer to the data in the file.

It may be helpful to think of the file variable and caret syntax as the *file buffer pointer,* because this syntax serves as an indicator to the data in the buffer area of the file variable. The construction has the form:

```
WITH FileName^ DO
BEGIN
 program statement;
  ..
 program statement;
END;
```

Of course, BEGIN and END are required only when a compound statement is used. As is the case with using this construction with arrays of records, the WITH . . DO statement itself does not cause any processing to occur.

FILE MANAGEMENT

The principal methods for accessing files include:

- Serial access
- Sequential access
- Direct, or random access.

In practice, an existing file is not always *searched,* or accessed for specific data, in the same way it was created, or built up. In Pascal, all files are created as serial access files. These files are built up chronologically, with one record following the other on the storage medium in the order the records are written. Serial access refers to the physical order of access to records on the storage medium. Nothing is implied about the content of, or logical relationships among, those records.

Sequential access can be thought of as a special case of serial access. Sequential files also are stored in serial fashion. However, sequential files are ordered also by a logical sequence according to the content of the files. This sequence is determined by the program that causes the files to be written. For example, a file of records representing cancelled checks written to a diskette in the order in which the checks were received by the bank is a serial file. There is no order to the appearance of a given record except a chronological one, the order of receipt.

On the other hand, a program might first *sort* checks into check number order, with the lowest check number first, followed in sequence to the highest. The program then might save the check records to an external file in check number order. The result would be a sequential file. In general terms, a sequential file is one in which the logical order and the physical order of records are the same. Program coding techniques for implementing sorts are presented in the next chapter.

Direct, or random access, as previously explained, allows the program to indicate which record in a file is to be read or written next. In Pascal, random access is implemented by the SEEK procedure. Bear in mind, however, that the physical structure of data files in Pascal is always serial. The SEEK procedure provides a way of pointing to arbitrary records within files instead of having to search for them serially.

Random access with SEEK presupposes that the programmer has some knowledge of the location of the desired record in the file. Since SEEK is performed solely by record number, no information about the content of the file can be obtained without actually performing a GET and inspecting the values that have been read in. Performing random access operations without prior knowledge of record contents may be highly inefficient, since many records may have to be searched until the desired record is found. It is generally more efficient to perform random access operations on sequential files, since some correspondence exists between the physical location of a record and its logical sequence in the group of records.

Physical characteristics of storage devices are a major factor in the choice of file handling technique. High speed disk systems, using *rigid* or *hard disks,* are efficient media for implementing random access methods. Sequential files often are associated with magnetic tape systems. Further study of the physical characteristics of storage devices and more advanced techniques of file organization can assist you in designing programs for efficient file management.

Serial Access Example

To illustrate how program text implements serial access, the following statements open an existing file and read in records one at a time until the end of the file is reached. (Recall that the file variable CheckFile is declared as a FILE OF Check.)

```
RESET(CheckFile,'MyChecks');
WHILE NOT EOF(CheckFile) DO GET(CheckFile);
```

RESET attempts to read in the first record in the file. If the file is empty, an end-of-file condition already exists and no processing can occur. For this reason, the WHILE NOT construction is used with the Pascal function EOF. When a file variable is passed as a parameter to the EOF function, the function returns a value of False as long as no end-of-file is found. When the end-of-file is encountered, a value of TRUE is returned. Notice that the WHILE NOT construction tests for this condition before loop processing occurs.

Suppose, then, that the processing of the program causes a new record to be created. The new record is written at the end of the existing file by:

```
PUT(CheckFile);
```

The file now has one more record than it did when it was opened. The end-of-file is advanced to the end of the new record. Then, the file may be closed and made permanent by:

```
CLOSE(CheckFile,LOCK);
```

Random Access Example

To illustrate random access, consider the following example. Assume a variable has been declared to hold an integer value for the record position:

```
VAR
 RecPos:INTEGER;
```

Program statements, then, would be:

```
BEGIN
 RecPos := 0;
 RESET(CheckFile,'MyChecks');
  REPEAT
   SEEK(CheckFile,RecPos);
   GET(CheckFile);
   RecPos := RecPos + 10;
  UNTIL EOF(CheckFile);
END;
```

These statements cause every tenth record in CheckFile to be accessed. This approach could be used to increase the speed of a search through a file that is organized sequentially. Note that the form of this search is still serial, but by steps larger than one record at a time.

The following example is a search for a specific record. These statements quickly find and get the twenty-fifth record in CheckFile. The contents of this record are then assigned to the variable NewCheck for processing by the program:

```
BEGIN
 RESET(CheckFile,'MyChecks');
 SEEK(CheckFile,24);        (* records numbered from zero *)
 GET(CheckFile);
 IF NOT EOF(CheckFile) THEN
  BEGIN
   NewCheck := CheckFile^;    (* file buffer pointer used *)
  END;
END;
```

Note that the file buffer pointer, CheckFile^, is used in the assignment statement because it is the data content of the record that must be assigned to the variable NewCheck.

Assuming that the file is still open, it would be possible to "jump" from the twenty-fifth record back to GET the second record in the file by:

```
BEGIN
 SEEK(CheckFile,1);
 GET(CheckFile);
 IF NOT EOF(CheckFile) THEN
  BEGIN
   NewCheck := CheckFile^;
  END;
END;
```

Remember that the first record number is zero, so the number of the second record is 1. Remember also that a SEEK must be followed by GET or PUT. Also, a SEEK must separate each GET and PUT if updating in place is desired. SEEK only performs a computation and points to the record specified. The EOF function cannot return a value for the end-of-file condition unless GET has been performed already.

File and record data structures are incorporated in the program design of *AccountManagement,* presented in the next chapter. This program is derived from the previous program *BasicAccounting.*

Summary

A related series of data items processed as an integrated entity forms a data structure. Type definitions enforce certain distinctions among data items. Data items often are grouped by transaction. Transactions may be represented in records.

Any number of data items may be included in a record, and the data items may be of various types. Data items within a record need not be related. The relationship of data items in a record is purely arbitrary, as defined by the programmer.

In Pascal program text, the term RECORD may be used to define a formatted RECORD type. Variables also may be declared to be of type RECORD. Data items within records are fields. Fields within records may, in turn, be records.

The WITH . . DO construction gives the programmer the ability to specify a record and then list program statements relating to fields within that record without having to repeat the record name.

A file is an array of records that all share the same type and reside on an external storage device. To create a file, a file variable must be declared in the variable declaration section of the program, and the file must be opened and closed.

To process records contained in a file, you may cause the program to access portions of the file (records) and read those portions into active memory for processing. You also may cause the reverse to occur, saving a record in memory to an external device.

In practical terms, a file is a group of records that are saved to some storage medium like a diskette. The UCSD operating system also regards all system peripherals as files.

The Pascal compiler predeclares two file variables for use by the program. These files are named INPUT (for the keyboard) and OUTPUT (for the console). The programmer may reassign these file variables to any device through program statements. File variables may be of predefined types INTERACTIVE (for the INPUT file) and TEXT (for the OUTPUT file), or some user-defined type.

REWRITE creates a new file for writing. RESET opens an existing file for reading or writing. CLOSE closes a file.

A file directory is created when a blank diskette is initialized by the operating system upon command from the computer operator. The UCSD Pascal operating system refers to file length in blocks, units of 512 characters.

When a file variable name appears followed by the caret symbol (^), it refers to the current contents of the data buffer area in the file variable. The file variable is used as a storage buffer for a single record from the file that is residing currently in memory.

The GET procedure is used to access the next record in series in the file and read it into memory. A record that currently resides in memory may be saved to an existing file through use of the PUT procedure.

The SEEK procedure allows the programmer to specify explicitly the location of any record within a file as being the next record to be accessed by the program. A subsequent GET or PUT procedure must follow the SEEK procedure to access the record.

The CLOSE procedure may be called with one of the following options: LOCK, PURGE, or CRUNCH.

File formats in Pascal include: TEXT, for program text; CODE, for compiled machine code; and DATA, for user files.

In Pascal, all files are created as serial access files. Sequential files are serial files that are ordered also by a logical sequence according to the content of the files. Direct, or random, access searches a file in any order specified by the programmer. In UCSD Pascal, random access is implemented by the SEEK procedure.

Review Questions

1. How may records correspond to transactions?
2. How is a RECORD defined in Pascal program text?
3. How are fields related to records?
4. What is the form of the WITH . . DO construction, and what is its principal use in program text?
5. What is the form of a FILE type declaration?
6. How may files of records differ from arrays of records?
7. What default devices are associated with the predeclared file names INPUT and OUTPUT, and what predefined type is associated with each?
8. What is the form of the REWRITE and RESET statements, and how do the actions caused by these statements differ?
9. What does the term block mean in relation to files stored on diskette?
10. How are the procedures GET, PUT, SEEK, and CLOSE used?
11. What options may be used with the CLOSE procedure, and how is each used?
12. What is the main reason for formatting files as TEXT, CODE, and DATA?
13. What are the three principal file access methods?

Pascal Practice

1. Given the following program text, write an alternate version that uses the WITH . . DO construction to code these statements in the shortest possible way:

```
TYPE
 NumRec = RECORD
  Number1,
  Number2,
  Number3 : INTEGER;
 END;

VAR
 X,Y,Z : NumRec;

BEGIN
 Z.Number1 := X.Number1 + Y.Number1;
 Z.Number2 := X.Number2 + Y.Number2;
 Z.Number3 := X.Number3 + Y.Number3;
END;
```

2. Write a routine to compare the first record of a file with the remaining records of the same file. (Note: Pascal allows you to use = to test for equality and < > to test for inequality between entire records if the two records are of the same type.)

Key Terms

1. data structure
2. record
3. field
4. nested record
5. file
6. file variable
7. complex data structure
8. file buffer
9. external file
10. formatted record
11. typed file
12. untyped file
13. input/output (I/O)
14. open
15. close
16. device number
17. file directory
18. initialize
19. lookup table
20. block
21. end-of-file
22. caret
23. serial access
24. sequential access
25. direct access
26. random access
27. permanent
28. file buffer pointer
29. searched
30. sort
31. rigid disk
32. hard disk

Pascal Library

1. RECORD
2. WITH . . DO
3. FILE
4. INPUT
5. OUTPUT
6. TEXT
7. INTERACTIVE
8. REWRITE
9. RESET
10. GET
11. PUT
12. SEEK
13. CLOSE
14. LOCK
15. PURGE
16. CRUNCH
17. CODE
18. DATA

10
TESTING AND DEBUGGING

OBJECTIVES

On completing the reading and other learning assignments for this chapter, you should be able to:

- ☐ Describe how program testing and debugging may be anticipated in program design.
- ☐ Explain the use of test program modules.
- ☐ Describe the methods of module testing, integration testing, and function testing.
- ☐ Demonstrate the use of top-down and bottom-up approaches to incremental testing.
- ☐ Find typographical errors, misplaced variable references, and uninitialized variables in Pascal programs.
- ☐ Explain how test data are developed.
- ☐ Demonstrate debugging techniques, including coding memory dumps and execution traces and performing program desk checking and hypothesis testing.
- ☐ Describe the use of the predeclared Pascal functions SUCCessor and PREDecessor.
- ☐ Describe the use of the procedure STRing.
- ☐ Use correctly the MODulus operation.

ANTICIPATING ERRORS

Entering and compiling a long program in its entirety almost always produces unexpected results. Even though syntactical errors may have been caught by the compiler, certain typographical errors may remain. Additionally, logical errors, or flaws in program design, do not appear until a program or module is executed.

As discussed briefly in Chapter 6, good programming practice requires that programs be entered and built up in stages, one module at a time. This process is referred to as *incremental testing.* By contrast, *nonincremental testing* is the entering, compiling, and test execution of a program in its entirety.

In general, a systematic approach encompasses the following steps:

- Include testing and debugging routines in program design.
- Develop test data as part of the program design activity.
- Enter, compile, test, and debug program modules incrementally.
- Test and debug integrated program segments.
- Test the program as a functional system, based on evaluation of results from a user's point of view.

Learning to test and debug programs involves analysis of human nature. Perhaps surprisingly, most programmers make the same types of errors over and over again. In testing and debugging your own programs, you must learn to evaluate your own techniques of "explaining" problems to a computer in programming language.

THE GOAL OF TESTING

The immediate goal of testing is to cause a given module or program to fail. Testing techniques that focus on successful executions may mask certain kinds of errors rather than disclose them. In other words, to isolate errors, you must devise situations that cause probable errors to occur. Anticipating errors is part of the program design phase. Testing is the process of error detection. Debugging involves isolating the problem that caused an error and solving it.

Program Design Considerations

Unlike some other programming languages, UCSD Pascal provides only limited built-in debugging features. Beyond the compiler's detection of syntactical errors, the programmer is notified of program errors only if they are serious enough to cause a program halt. Many of these errors amount to failed input or output operations, which cause the program to stop and an error message and numeric code to be displayed. (Specific I/O errors are presented in Chapter 13.)

Given this limited capability, the programmer must design error-checking features into modules or programs to be tested. This process may be thought of as planting clues for the deductive debugging process. In practical terms, this means inserting statements or procedures that specifically implement test features. Test methods vary, depending on the application. Some specific testing tools are presented below.

As an overall aid to testing, you may coin a variable that serves as a debugging switch, indicating whether the program is being run in a test mode. For example:

```
VAR
 Debug : BOOLEAN;
```

Given this declaration, you may toggle the switch by inserting the following:

```
Debug := TRUE;     (* set Debug mode *)
```

Or, you may prompt at the beginning of program execution:

```
WRITE('DO YOU WANT DEBUGGING? Y/N ');
READLN(Answer);
Debug := (Answer = 'Y');
```

If this switch is provided, program statements that implement tests may be enabled selectively by:

```
IF Debug THEN      (* test statement *)
```

PROGRAM ENTRY AND TEST TECHNIQUES

Physical methods of program entry vary depending on the computer environment. In mainframe installations employing time-sharing terminals, program coding and entry may be distinctly different functions. Typically, program modules are assigned to members of software development teams. Coding these modules takes the form of completing coding sheets. Then, the coding sheets are captured separately in a batch operation, perhaps by a data entry group.

Increasingly, program development is done on individual microcomputers. In such situations, program coding and entry occur in one step as interactive sessions using a text editor.

Regardless of the entry method used, the principles of program testing remain the same. It may be possible to code an entire program in a single session, especially with the help of a text editor. However, if modules are entered and tested incrementally, the time required to track errors during the debugging phase is reduced considerably.

Types of Testing

The principal methods of testing may be categorized as:

- Module
- Integration
- Function.

Module testing. This method involves entry and testing of individual program modules. *Module testing* is also referred to as *unit testing.*

Integration testing. The process of combining modules to test the interfaces between those modules is *integration testing.* Different program test strategies deal with the order in which modules are combined. *Top-down* testing is performed by entering and testing the most general program modules first. With reference to a structure chart, general modules are the highest levels on the chart. Integration proceeds progressively by adding lower-level modules. *Bottom-up* testing occurs in reverse: Low-level, or detailed, modules are tested individually and then integrated.

Function testing. Testing the program as a whole with data derived from anticipated application conditions is *function testing.* Using this approach, the program may be evaluated from a user's perspective. Even though test data are derived from the application, the data may be devised purposely to fall out of expected ranges or data types.

INCREMENTAL TESTING

In practice, the testing of modules and integration testing proceed in parallel. Once a module is completed and tested, another module may be added and the two modules tested as a unit, and so on.

Applying top-down testing, the highest-level modules are coded first. Lower-level modules are included in the code as *stubs.* That is, procedure or function headers are included to satisfy the compiler's requirement for declarations, but the block contains no program statements, or at most, contains "dummy" data. For example, a low-level procedure might be coded:

```
PROCEDURE CrunchData;
BEGIN
END;
```

The appearance of this stub enables fully coded high-level modules to include calls to CrunchData. Of course, the call will do nothing but allow processing control to proceed to the next block.

In general, the input segment of the program is tested first, then the output segment. Finally, the processing segment is coded and tested. However, when reports or formatted displays are to be produced, the report format module may be coded and executed first, displaying blanks for data output fields. Modules that generate the data may be added as incremental testing progresses.

Applying bottom-up testing involves the individual coding and testing of low-level modules. Since lower-level modules frequently depend on global data or upon arguments passed from other program blocks, test modules may have to be developed to generate the data. These test modules are referred to as *drivers.*

COMMONLY ENCOUNTERED ERRORS

Three kinds of errors frequently encountered are presented here by way of example:

- Typographical errors
- Misplaced variable references
- Uninitialized variables.

Typographical errors. Strictly syntactical errors are caught by the compiler as invalid statements, undefined variable names, missing identifiers, and so on. However, some typographical errors introduced in coding or entry may compile successfully. For example, assuming that the variable I has been declared as an integer for use as a subscript, the following reference might be expected:

```
Amount := Value[I];
```

However, the programmer intended to code:

```
Amount := Value[1];
```

Also, such errors may be introduced in making program changes. These errors are difficult to detect with visual inspection of the text file, and the programmer may pass over that same section of the program several times before discovering the error.

Misplaced variable references. Such references are coding mistakes in which the programmer uses a variable outside of its scope. For example:

```
PROGRAM Test;
VAR
 I, J : INTEGER;

PROCEDURE DoIt;
BEGIN
 FOR I := 1 TO 10 DO Something;
END;                              (* end of procedure *)

BEGIN                             (* main program *)
 FOR I := 1 TO 20 DO
  BEGIN
   DoIt;
  END;
END.                              (* end of program *)
```

In this example, the global variable I is used both within the procedure DoIt as well as in the main program. However, the main program calls DoIt from a loop controlled by I. Instead of looping 20 times, the main loop will repeat infinitely: Each time DoIt is called, the variable I will be used as a loop control with an exit value of 11. Then, the main program loop will increment I and call DoIt again, and so on.

The solution in this case is to make the variable I in the procedure DoIt a local variable by declaring it within the procedure.

In general, it is safer to declare local variables because their scope can be tracked more easily than global variables. Counter variables in particular should be declared locally. As an alternative, a global temporary variable may be declared if it is used selectively.

Uninitialized variables. It is good practice to initialize all variables to 0 or to their desired initial values in a separate initialization section of the program. Remember that an uninitialized variable can have literally any possible value. Occasionally, a program will execute correctly for a period of time before some spurious error appears. What happens is that the variable's memory location has contained some acceptable value quite by accident. Then, some difference in the program environment causes that location to contain some other erroneous value.

As a general rule, initialize variables explicitly and make no assumptions about their values unless they are initialized in the current block. After all, no harm is caused by initializing a variable twice. Variables of type INTEGER or REAL should be assigned values of 0. STRING variables should be set to ''. CHAR variables should be set to ' ' or CHR(0).

DEVISING TEST DATA

Test data are developed concurrently with program design. In identifying program inputs and specifying input formats, data items to be presented to the program are identified along with their expected ranges and data types. Program design devises data structures for use in processing and storing these data items.

Test data must be generated that exercise program modules with both probable and improbable inputs. In general, three kinds of test values should be applied, presenting a variety of:

- Ranges
- Data types
- Processing sequences.

Ranges. Common trouble spots when dealing with numeric values (INTEGER or REAL) are *range errors,* also referred to as *bounds,* or *limits,* errors. For example, a subrange may define expected values as 1 . . 100. What happens when 0 is input? Values of 0 also may occur unexpectedly, as the result of some operation, for example. Division (DIV or /) by 0 is particularly troublesome and is made more likely if a variable name appears in the program text as the divisor. Division by 0 is undefined and results in a *fatal error,* or error causing a program halt.

Array indexes and loop counters also are susceptible to range errors. If a list is to contain 100 items, what happens when the number 101 is encountered as a list reference?

Unexpected negative numeric values are another cause of errors. Again, the negative value may result from the evaluation of an expression. Such a mistake might not be apparent from an inspection of the program text, and the programmer may not realize that such values can result under certain circumstances.

The bounds of each data item to be input should be tested. A systematic approach would be to choose a value for each of the following:

- Value at the lower boundary of the range
- Value at the upper boundary of the range
- Value that is less than the lower boundary
- Value that is greater than the upper boundary.

Clearly, testing with values at the midpoint of an expected range is contrary to the goal of testing. Midpoint values may be the least likely to cause errors.

Data types. In Pascal, supplying test data from different categories amounts to testing TYPE definitions. What happens, for example, when alphabetic data are input to a numeric field? Any input editing designed to protect against such inadvertent input must be tested with erroneous data. A common user input error might be to transpose fields in entering a transaction record, resulting in a mismatch of data types. For example, transposing input fields might result in the attempt to place a Name in an Amount field.

Processing sequences. The programmer should attempt to foresee the results of inappropriate user selections that affect the order of processing. For example, if the user is presented a menu of processing options, it might be possible to select the PRINT REPORT option before the ENTER TRANSACTION DATA option. In general, attempting a WRITE before the corresponding READ has been performed is a commonly encountered program bug.

DEBUGGING TECHNIQUES

The programmer may devise debugging tools by embedding test statements and procedures in the program. These statements may be enabled by toggling a switch such as Debug, discussed above. Specifically, program debugging features include:

- Memory dumps
- Execution traces
- Selective logic isolation.

In addition, errors may be found by:

- Program desk checking
- Hypothesis testing.

Memory dumps. Output statements, or *memory dumps*, may be included at key points in the program to track the changing values of variables. One objective of doing so is to verify that expected values result when test data are input or when conducting a functional evaluation of the program with actual application data.

The procedure SumUp includes WRITELN statements that enable the inspection of intermediate values:

```
PROCEDURE SumUp;
VAR
 I , J : INTEGER;
  BEGIN
   WRITELN('PROCEDURE SUMUP');                              (* debug *)
   FOR I := 1 TO 20 DO
    BEGIN
     WRITELN('I = ',I,',VALUE[I] = ',Value[I]);            (* debug *)
     J := J + Value[I];
     WRITELN('TOTAL = ',J);                                 (* debug *)
    END;                                                  (* END FOR *)
  END;                                                  (* END SumUp *)
```

The output from SumUp with debugging statements might look like this:

```
PROCEDURE SUMUP
I = 1,VALUE[1] = 10
TOTAL = 6231
I = 2,VALUE[I] = 23
TOTAL = 6254
..    (* and so on for values of I from 3 to 20 *)
```

The above display indicates that the value of J was never initialized to 0. The displayed values for Total could have been produced only if some random value were held in J when the loop began. The addition of dumping code demonstrates the error much more clearly than trying to find the error by visual inspection of the program text.

Execution traces. The first WRITELN statement in SumUp is an *execution trace:*

```
WRITELN('PROCEDURE SUMUP');
```

This tracing information is inserted in the program text immediately after the first BEGIN in each procedure or function. As the program executes, the flow of processing control may be tracked from one block to the next. If an error causes a program halt, the last block name displayed is the place to begin an inspection of the text file. Tracing is helpful in monitoring execution of calculation or processing steps that contain no other output statements.

Selective logic isolation. Some portions of a program may be nested so deeply or used so infrequently that devising test data to activate those portions is difficult. In particular, when a code portion must handle a system error or a file error, often it is easier to force the error to occur by modifying logical tests surrounding the code portion. For example, consider the following:

```
IF FileNotFound THEN
 BEGIN
  WRITELN('ERROR--PROGRAM WILL STOP');
  EXIT(PROGRAM);
 END;
```

In this case, it is possible to place comment delimiters around the conditional statement so that the subsequent statement executes for test purposes:

```
(* IF FileNotFound THEN *)
```

Alternatively, logical expressions within complex conditional expressions can be modified selectively by inserting constant TRUE/FALSE values:

```
IF FileNotFound (* AND HaveData = TRUE *) THEN
```

Program desk checking. This method of troubleshooting amounts to visual inspection, known as *desk checking,* of the text file. The technique of the walkthrough, discussed previously in evaluating logical designs, may be used in tracking the flow of processing control.

Large software development teams often have one programmer review another programmer's code during the debugging phase. An objective view can isolate some kinds of errors rapidly, especially if it is true that programmers tend to repeat their own mistakes.

Hypothesis testing. When other systematic debugging methods fail to isolate the problem, it may be possible to form a hypothesis, or tentative description, about the source of trouble. Experience shows that certain kinds of errors produce particular results, as in the value for Total encountered in running SumUp. The hypothesis, then, must be tested in some way that causes a clearly defined processing result only if the hypothesis is true. *Hypothesis testing* is almost always more productive than going after the source of the problem on a trial-and-error basis.

These testing and debugging techniques should prove useful in entering and testing the example program *AccountManagement.*

PROGRAM *AccountManagement*

The design objective of the previous example program, *BasicAccounting,* is to provide for greater user flexibility, primarily through the application of report format options. As an extension of the material presented in Chapter 9, a desirable feature is to be able to save data grouped by transaction to an external file. This provides practical data storage, allowing convenient reference to individual items on a long-term basis. Specific program design features include:

- The user is able to make entries grouped by transaction. This is done by declaring records for debits or credits that include fields for amount, number, description, date, and so on.

- Records so created are saved to a master account file. The external file provides long-term storage and allows convenient access to account detail for reference by the user at any time. The external file name of the master file is 'ACCOUNT.DATA', which is known to the program as the file variable AcctFile.
- Subsequent program executions use and update the master file, providing a continuity of data storage format and allowing the addition of entries over time without having to reconstruct any information.
- Category totals, a feature provided in previous programs, now are saved to a separate file. This file has the external file name 'ACCOUNT.INFO' and is known to the program as the file variable InfoFile. The file is, in effect, a sublist of summary data that have been extracted from the detail in the master account file.

Additional Pascal features used in the program include:

- The predeclared function **SUCC**essor. (A similar function, **PRED**ecessor, is explained below but does not appear in the program text).
- The predeclared procedure **STR**ing
- The operation **MOD**ulus
- Another use of the LENGTH function.

SUCC and PRED

These two predeclared functions are used to increment or decrement any scalar value—that is, to return the next value, or to the previous value, in a series for any given value. These functions may be used to step through values in an ordered series. The current value is passed as an argument to the function. SUCCessor returns the next higher-ordered value, while PREDecessor returns the next lower-ordered value. These functions are useful especially in manipulating variables that are declared with an enumeration type. In fact, use of SUCC and PRED is the only way to "count" through an enumeration (other than by a FOR . . DO loop).

In the example program, the SUCC function is used in instances to increment counter variables.

For example, if the current value of a counter variable, Counter, were 12, the following statement would write a value of 13:

```
WRITE(SUCC(Counter));
```

Similarly, writing the PRED function would display a value of 11. Note that calling the SUCC function has the same effect, when the counter is of type INTEGER, as the expression:

```
Counter + 1
(* PRED would return Counter - 1 *)
```

Note that these functions do not alter the variable passed to them. Rather, they return a value based on the variable value.

Recall that these functions may be used with any scalar type. Suppose, in the above example, that Counter were declared with an enumeration type:

```
Counter : (A,B,C,D,E,F,G,H,I,J);
```

Now, if the current value of Counter were E, passing it as a parameter to SUCC would return a value of F and PRED would return a value of D.

The value returned by these functions is undefined beyond the range of the variable. If the range of Counter is A . . J, and the current value of Counter is J, the value returned by SUCC is undefined as there is no enumerated value that has a higher order than J. Assigning this value to Counter would cause a fatal error resulting in program termination.

STRing

There are instances in coding program text in which it is necessary to work with a data value in one instance as a number, as in performing some calculation, and in another instance as a string, as in formatting an output field. The predeclared procedure **STR**ing returns a string value for the integer argument passed to it.

For example, suppose a program that generates a client list has a variable ClientNumber. Arithmetic operations must be performed on this variable in calculating record positions in a sequential file. Accordingly, ClientNumber is declared as an INTEGER. However, in calculating output field sizes for a report, occasionally it might be necessary to convert the value contained in ClientNumber as a string, so that it could be passed as a parameter to functions like CONCAT or LENGTH that operate only on strings. If the current value of ClientNumber were 10036, the following procedure call would return a string value of '10036':

```
STR(ClientNumber,OutputString);
```

MODulus

MODulus is an arithmetic operation that calculates the remainder resulting from integral division. That is, if one integer is divided by another, the result must also be an integer (contain no fractional part), and the remainder is an integer also (including zero, of course).

For example, the expression "5 MOD 2" would result in a value of 1. Dividing 5 by 2 produces a remainder of 1.

This operation is used in the procedure ShowAccountEntries in the example program. The MOD operation is used in a condition test to determine the status of the line count on the output device. If the remainder of dividing the current line number by the maximum lines allowed per page is 0, the display page is full and it is time to start a new page.

Figure 10-1 shows the text for a program *Columns* that employs the MOD operation. This program demonstrates the printing of data in vertical, rather than horizontal, columns. *Columns* prints out the indexes that would serve to print out data arrays of varying lengths in proper columnar order.

LENGTH

The following arithmetic calculation is used in the sample program:

```
20 - LENGTH(StringName);
```

```
PROGRAM COLUMNS;

VAR

       X,ROW_POSN,INDEX,LEFTOVER,PERCOLUMN:   INTEGER;
       COLS,ITEMS,LINES:                INTEGER;
       MORE:                            BOOLEAN;

 PROCEDURE PRINT_COLUMNS;
 BEGIN
  IF ITEMS > 0 THEN
   BEGIN
    INDEX :=1;                          (* INIT COLUMN INDEX *)
    LINES :=1;                          (* INIT LINE COUNT *)
    PERCOLUMN := ITEMS DIV COLS;        (* CALC # PER COLUMN *)
    LEFTOVER  := ITEMS MOD COLS;        (* CALC # TO BE DISTRIBUTED
                                           AMONG LONGER COLUMNS *)
    FOR X := 1 TO ITEMS DO
     BEGIN
      WRITE(INDEX:4);                   (* DISPLAY INDEX *)
      ROW_POSN := X MOD COLS;
      IF ROW_POSN > 0 THEN              (* ROW_POSN=0 MEANS LINE (ROW) DONE *)
       BEGIN
        INDEX := INDEX + PERCOLUMN;     (* SKIP TO NEXT COLUMN VALUE *)
        IF (ROW_POSN <= LEFTOVER) THEN  (* IF THIS COLUMN WILL HAVE EXTRA, *)
         INDEX := INDEX + 1;            (* ..MUST INCREMENT NEXT VALUE *)
       END                              (* END IF *)
      ELSE                              (* ROW_POSN IS ZERO, END OF ROW *)
       BEGIN
        WRITELN;                        (* END OF ROW, START NEW LINE *)
        LINES := LINES + 1;             (* COUNT LINES *)
        INDEX := LINES;                 (* SET INDEX TO START OVER HIGHER *)
       END                              (* END ELSE *)
     END                                (* END FOR *)
   END                                  (* END IF *)
  ELSE MORE := FALSE                    (* STOP LOOP *)
END;                                    (* END PROCEDURE *)

BEGIN                                   (* M A I N   PROGRAM *)
 MORE:=TRUE;                            (* INITIALIZE FLAG *)
 WHILE MORE DO
  BEGIN
   WRITELN;                             (* SPACE BETWEEN PRINTOUTS *)
   WRITELN;                             (* SPACE BETWEEN PRINTOUTS *)
   WRITE('ENTER NUMBER OF ITEMS AND COLUMNS - ');
   READLN(ITEMS,COLS);                  (* ASK FOR 2 VALUES, SEP BY SPACE *)
   PRINT_COLUMNS;                       (* CALL PROCEDURE TO PRINT LIST *)
  END                                   (* END WHILE *)
END.                                    (* END PROGRAM *)
```

Figure 10-1. Program *Columns.* Note differences in coding style, including all uppercase letters, and uses of underscore character in identifiers.

Since LENGTH is an integer function, it may appear in calculations. This calculation is used to determine how many characters must appear after the StringName to make the field width equal to 20. Since the length of StringName is less than or equal to 20, the resulting value will range from 0 (if the string is 20 characters long) to 20 (if the string is empty). This calculation allows the programmer to control the appearance of output fields. It is necessary in this case because it is standard practice to left-justify, or add trailing blanks to, alphanumeric fields.

Records in *AccountManagement*

Several RECORD definitions are made in the example program. The two main data structures are defined as records to hold individual transaction data: the detail entries for the master account file and the summary sublist saved as a file.

The account detail file consists of sequential records of type EntryRec. These are formatted records that are defined to contain the following fields: EntryType, EntryCode, Number, Date, Amount, and Comment. Each of these fields is declared with a data type. Note also that the field Date is itself a record, containing separate fields for month (mm), day (dd), and year (yy).

The master file AcctFile is declared as a FILE OF EntryRec so that access to the file uses records containing all the fields named.

The file InfoFile, the summary sublist, is declared to contain only one record. That record is an array of two items, one for Debit and one for Credit. These array elements, in turn, are records in themselves, each being of type DbCrInfo. This record includes a name (either 'DEBIT' or 'CREDIT'), a category counter, a list of category names, an array of category totals, and a summary total. When the file InfoFile is accessed, the first (and only) record contains all of the summary data for both Credit and Debit.

In this program, these two file variables are treated differently. The records in AcctFile are read into memory one at a time, and all operations on those data are done directly on the file variable itself, using the file variable contents (AcctFile^) where appropriate. On the other hand, when InfoFile is accessed, the program assigns the data in that file variable to another variable of the same type, namely Info. The form of the assignment statement is:

```
Info := InfoFile^;
```

In this case, the assignment to another variable is more illustrative than practical. However, consider a case in which you want to GET the first record in a file, then compare it with other records in the file. You could not use the file variable for this purpose, since every time you accessed a different record from the file, the content of the file variable would change. Therefore, you would have to use an assignment statement like the one shown above to hold an "image" of the record in some other memory location for purposes of making logical comparisons within the program.

Enumeration Types in *AccountManagement*

References to Debit and Credit entries are more efficient in this program than those encountered in *BasicAccounting.* The reason for this is that an enumeration type is used to categorize entries:

```
TYPE
 DebCred = (Debit,Credit);
```

A variable of type DebCred then is defined to hold a value of either Debit or Credit. Recall that *BasicAccounting* duplicated entire program blocks, processing Debit and Credit entries separately with similar procedures. Consolidating these similar procedures simplifies the program. For example, the procedures GetDebitCategories and GetCreditCategories have been combined into a single procedure, GetCategories. The parameters Debit and Credit then are passed to the procedure. Similarly, individual totals and category lists have been combined for more compact and efficient program text.

Program Text

The program text of *AccountManagement,* shown in figure 10-2, is a derivation of *BasicAccounting.* Portions incorporated from that program are shown in shaded areas.

Figure 10-2. Program *AccountManagement*.

```
  (* NOTE:  Program text areas carried over from BasicAccounting are shaded.*)

PROGRAM AccountManagement;
CONST
 MaximumCateg = 10;           (* maximum number of debit/credit categories *)

TYPE
 CategArray = ARRAY[0..MaximumCateg] OF STRING;           (* category names *)
 ReportChoices = (Sum,Percent,BarGraph);           (* report format choices *)

(*  establish a RECORD type for dates *)

mmddyy = RECORD
 mm,                                                               (* month *)
 dd,                                                                 (* day *)
 yy:INTEGER;                                                        (* year *)
END;

  (*establish enumeration type that defines DEBIT and CREDIT as data values*)

DebCred = (Debit,Credit);

                 (* define a subrange value to hold category code values *)

CodeType = 0..MaximumCateg;

(* define a RECORD type to hold the data for each entry in the master file *)

EntryRec = RECORD
 EntryType:DebCred;                                (* type is credit/debit *)
 EntryCode:CodeType;                                     (* category codes *)
 Number:INTEGER;                                        (* number of entry *)
 Date:mmddyy;                                             (* date of entry *)
 Amount:REAL;                                           (* amount of entry *)
 Comment:STRING[20];                    (* description may be 20 chars long *)
END;

(* define a RECORD type to hold common information for both debits/credits *)

DbCrInfo = RECORD
 Name:STRING[6];                        (* holds string 'CREDIT' OR 'DEBIT' *)
 HowManyCategories:INTEGER;    (* category counter for both debits/credits *)
 CategoryList:CategArray;                           (* list of category names *)
 Totals:ARRAY[0..MaximumCateg] OF REAL;                  (* category totals *)
 Sum:REAL;                                                           (* sum *)
END;
   (* define a RECORD type to hold debit and credit summaries; note use of
                  enumeration type DebCred to specify the array bounds *)

InfoType = ARRAY[DebCred] OF DbCrInfo;

VAR
 ReportSet: SET OF ReportChoices;                           (* users choices *)

 StartBalance,
 CurrentBalance:REAL;                           (* variables from BalancePlus *)
               (* new record formats require declarations to set up files *)

 Info:InfoType;
 AcctFile:FILE OF EntryRec;                            (* file for account data *)
```

```
 InfoFile:FILE OF InfoType;  (* file for categories, totals--summary data  *)
 ItemCount:INTEGER;                            (* count of entries on file *)
 AccountOpen:BOOLEAN;        (* flag to indicate when account file is open *)
 PageWidth,                               (* variable to hold screen width *)
 LinesPerPage,
 LineNumber:INTEGER;      (* page control variables for report formatting *)

 OutDevice:TEXT;                          (* declare output file for reports *)

 Underline:STRING;                          (* will hold underline characters *)

 Printing,
 FileOpen:BOOLEAN;       (* used to test if an output file is already open *)
(***************************************************************************)
(*                                                                         *)
(*   PROCEDURE TO ERASE SCREEN AND DISPLAY A CENTERED TITLE AT THE TOP    *)
(*                                                                         *)
(***************************************************************************)
PROCEDURE PutTitle(Title:STRING);
VAR
 EndPosition:INTEGER;           (* declare variable to hold the calculation *)
BEGIN
 PAGE(OUTPUT);                         (* clear the screen or start new page *)
 EndPosition := (PageWidth DIV 2) + (LENGTH(Title) DIV 2);
 WRITELN(Title:EndPosition);                              (* display title *)
 WRITELN(Underline:PageWidth);                                (* underline *)
 WRITELN;                                                   (* skip a line *)
END;
(***************************************************************************)
(*                                                                         *)
(*           PROCEDURE TO CENTER A MESSAGE ON THE OUTPUT DEVICE           *)
(*                                                                         *)
(***************************************************************************)
PROCEDURE PageCenter(Title:STRING);
VAR
 EndPosition:INTEGER;         (* declare a variable to hold the calculation *)
BEGIN
 EndPosition := (PageWidth DIV 2) + (LENGTH(Title) DIV 2);
 WRITELN(OutDevice,Title:EndPosition);
END;
(***************************************************************************)
(*                                                                         *)
(*     PROCEDURE TO DRAW AN UNDERLINE ACROSS THE OUTPUT DEVICE PAGE        *)
(*                                                                         *)
(***************************************************************************)
PROCEDURE PageUnderline;
BEGIN
 WRITELN(OutDevice,Underline:PageWidth);
END;
(***************************************************************************)
(*                                                                         *)
(*   PROCEDURE TO START A NEW PAGE; DISPLAY A CENTERED TITLE AT THE TOP    *)
(*                                                                         *)
(***************************************************************************)
PROCEDURE NewPage(Title:STRING);
BEGIN
 PAGE(OutDevice);                      (* clear the screen or start new page *)
 PageCenter(Title);
 PageUnderline;                                               (* underline *)
 WRITELN(OutDevice);                                        (* skip a line *)
END;
(***************************************************************************)
(*                                                                         *)
(*      FUNCTION TO ALLOW THE USER TO CHANGE ANSWER, OR TO CONTINUE        *)
(*                                                                         *)
(***************************************************************************)
FUNCTION OK:BOOLEAN;
VAR
 Character:CHAR;
 Message:STRING;
BEGIN
```

```
 Message := '<RETURN> IF OK;<SPACE> TO CHANGE ANSWER';
  REPEAT
   GOTOXY(0,22);
   WRITE(Message);
   READ(KEYBOARD,Character);
  UNTIL (Character = ' ') OR EOLN(KEYBOARD);
 IF EOLN(KEYBOARD) THEN OK := TRUE
 ELSE OK := FALSE;
 GOTOXY(0,22);
 WRITE('':LENGTH(Message));                              (* erase message *)
END;
(***************************************************************************)
(*                                                                         *)
(*                     WAIT FOR USER TO PRESS A KEY                        *)
(*                                                                         *)
(***************************************************************************)
PROCEDURE AwaitAnyKey;
VAR
 AnyChar:CHAR;
BEGIN
 IF NOT Printing THEN
 BEGIN
  WRITELN;
  WRITE('PRESS ANY KEY TO CONTINUE');
  READ(AnyChar);
 END;
END;
(***************************************************************************)
(*                                                                         *)
(*          ASK THE USER FOR A REAL NUMBER AT COORDINATES X , Y            *)
(*                                                                         *)
(***************************************************************************)
PROCEDURE AskValue(X,Y:INTEGER;Question:STRING;VAR Answer:REAL);
BEGIN
  REPEAT
   GOTOXY(X,Y);
   WRITE(Question,' ');
   READLN(Answer);
  UNTIL OK;
 GOTOXY(X, Y + 1);
END;
(***************************************************************************)
(*                                                                         *)
(*   GET THE NAMES OF THE CATEGORIES AND PUT THEM INTO AN ARRAY IN Info;   *)
(*   (THIS PROCEDURE REPLACES BOTH GetCreditCategory AND GetDebitCategory  *)
(*   BY USING THE VARIABLE Kind TO BE EITHER Credit OR Debit)              *)
(*                                                                         *)
(***************************************************************************)
PROCEDURE GetCategories(Kind:DebCred);
VAR
 Temp:STRING;
 Counter:INTEGER;
BEGIN
 WITH Info[Kind] DO                (* WITH..DO shortcut for field reference *)
  BEGIN
   PutTitle(CONCAT('ENTRY OF ',Name,' CATEGORY NAMES'));
                                     (* show all categories currently saved *)
FOR Counter := 0 TO HowManyCategories DO
 WRITELN(Name, ' CATEGORY ',Counter,' : ',CategoryList[Counter]);
    (* if list is already full, tell user and don't allow any more entries *)
 IF HowManyCategories = MaximumCateg THEN
  BEGIN
   WRITELN;
   WRITELN('NO MORE ROOM IN LIST');
   AwaitAnyKey;
  END
 ELSE
  REPEAT                   (* display next category number with SUCC procedure *)
   WRITE(Name,' CATEGORY ',SUCC(HowManyCategories),' ? ');
   READLN(Temp);
   IF Temp <> '' THEN
```

```
   BEGIN
    WHILE(LENGTH(Temp) < 20) DO Temp := CONCAT(Temp, ' ');
                  (* increment number of categories with SUCC procedure *)
    HowManyCategories := SUCC(HowManyCategories);
    CategoryList[HowManyCategories] := Temp;           (* save in list *)
   END;
  UNTIL (Temp = '') OR (HowManyCategories = MaximumCateg);
 WRITELN;
 END;
END;
(***************************************************************************)
(*                                                                         *)
(*  ASK THE USER FOR A NUMBER FROM Min TO Max, AND REPEAT UNTIL OBTAINED   *)
(*                                                                         *)
(***************************************************************************)
FUNCTION AskChoice(X,Y:INTEGER;Q:STRING;Min,Max:INTEGER):INTEGER;
VAR
 Answer:INTEGER;
BEGIN
 REPEAT
  GOTOXY(X,Y);
  WRITE(Q,' (',Min,'..',Max,') ');
  READLN(Answer);
 UNTIL (Answer >= Min) AND (Answer <= Max);
 AskChoice := Answer;
END;
(***************************************************************************)
(*                                                                         *)
(*    SHOW A "MENU" OF THE AVAILABLE CATEGORY NAMES FOR CREDIT OR DEBIT    *)
(*                 AND ASK FOR THE DESIRED CATEGORY NUMBER                 *)
(*                                                                         *)
(***************************************************************************)
FUNCTION AskCategory (Kind:DebCred) :INTEGER;
VAR
 Counter,
 Answer:INTEGER;
BEGIN
 WITH Info[Kind] DO
  BEGIN
  WRITELN;
  FOR Counter := 0 TO HowManyCategories DO      (* display all categories *)
  WRITELN(Counter:8,'. ', CategoryList[Counter]);          (* menu format *)
  AskCategory := AskChoice(10,22,'ENTER CATEGORY',0, HowManyCategories);
  END;
END;
(***************************************************************************)
(*                                                                         *)
(*     THIS PROCEDURE WILL DRAW A BAR GRAPH, USING STARS **** TO SHOW      *)
(*     DATA, AND FINISHING THE LINE WITH DOTS ......................       *)
(*                                                                         *)
(***************************************************************************)
PROCEDURE DrawBar(NStars,GraphWidth:INTEGER);
VAR
 Position:INTEGER;
BEGIN
 FOR POSITION := 1 TO GraphWidth DO
  IF POSITION <= NStars THEN
   WRITE(OutDevice,'*')                              (* show bar graph *)
  ELSE
    WRITE(OutDevice,'.');                         (* fill out with dots *)
END;
(***************************************************************************)
(*                                                                         *)
(*       THIS PROCEDURE WILL DISPLAY AMOUNTS AS EITHER 1. RAW DATA,        *)
(*      2. PERCENTAGE OF TOTAL, OR 3. A BAR GRAPH 40 CHARACTERS LONG       *)
(*                                                                         *)
(***************************************************************************)
PROCEDURE ShowData(Amount,Total:REAL);
VAR
 I,
```

```
 NumberOfStars:INTEGER;
 Ratio,
 Pct:REAL;
BEGIN
 IF Total <> 0 THEN
  BEGIN
   Ratio := Amount / Total;         (* calculate ratio of item to total *)
   Pct := Ratio * 100;                          (* calculate percentage *)
   NumberOfStars := ROUND(Ratio * 40);           (* length of bar graph *)
   WRITE(OutDevice,Amount:10:2);                         (* show amount *)
   IF Percent IN ReportSet THEN            (* if percent display is wanted *)
    BEGIN
     WRITE(OutDevice,Pct:8:2,'% ');            (* show percentage to total *)
     IF BarGraph IN ReportSet THEN               (* if bar graph is wanted *)
      DrawBar(NumberOfStars,40);                 (* bar graph, show scale *)
   END;
 END;
 WRITELN(OutDevice);                                     (* finish line *)
END;
(***************************************************************************)
(*                                                                         *)
(*    THIS PROCEDURE WILL DISPLAY THE TOTALS FOR THE DEBITS AND CREDITS    *)
(*    THAT HAVE BEEN ENTERED UNDER EACH CATEG, AS WELL AS GRAND TOTALS.    *)
(*                                                                         *)
(***************************************************************************)
PROCEDURE ShowDetailTotals;
VAR
 X:INTEGER;
 Kind:DebCred;
BEGIN
(* list the summaries for each category of credit or debit *)
 FOR Kind := Debit TO Credit DO
  WITH Info[Kind] DO
   BEGIN
    WRITELN(OutDevice);                                   (* skip a line *)
    WRITELN(OutDevice,'--',Name,'S--');                 (* write heading *)
    FOR X := 0 TO HowManyCategories DO              (* for each category...*)
     BEGIN
      WRITE(OutDevice,CategoryList[X]);            (* display category name *)
      ShowData(Totals[X],Sum);                              (* format data *)
     END;
   PageUnderline;                                           (* underline *)
 (* show total *)
   WRITE(OutDevice,Name, ' TOTAL        ',Sum:10:2);
   IF Percent IN ReportSet THEN                     (* if user wants pct *)
    WRITE(OutDevice,'100% ':10);                            (* show 100% *)
    WRITELN(OutDevice);                                   (* finish line *)
   END;
 WRITELN(OutDevice);                                      (* skip a line *)
END;
(***************************************************************************)
(*                                                                         *)
(*      ASK USER WHAT FORM REPORT IS TO TAKE, SET VARIABLE ReportSet       *)
(*                                                                         *)
(***************************************************************************)
PROCEDURE AskReportType;
VAR
 Choice:INTEGER;
BEGIN
(* show user a menu of choices for report format *)
 PutTitle('SELECTION OF DATA FORMAT');
 WRITELN;
 WRITELN('1. DATA SUM');
 WRITELN('2. DATA SUM AND PERCENTAGES');
 WRITELN('3. DATA SUM, PERCENTAGES, AND BAR GRAPH');
 Choice := AskChoice(0,10,'ENTER CHOICE ',1,3);
(* now convert answer (1,2,3) into ReportSet values *)
 CASE Choice OF
  1:ReportSet := [Sum];
  2:ReportSet := [Sum,Percent];
  3:ReportSet := [Sum,Percent,BarGraph];
```

```
 END;
END;
(*************************************************************************)
(*                                                                       *)
(*              ASK NAME OF OUTPUT FILE (PRINTER, CONSOLE)               *)
(*                                                                       *)
(*************************************************************************)
PROCEDURE AskOutputDevice;
BEGIN
 IF FileOpen THEN CLOSE(OutDevice);          (* must close if already open *)
 PutTitle('OUTPUT FILE SELECTION:');
 WRITELN;
 WRITELN('1. DISPLAY ON CONSOLE');
 WRITELN('2. DISPLAY ON PRINTER');
  CASE AskChoice(0,8,'Choice',1,2) OF
   1:BEGIN
      REWRITE(OutDevice,'CONSOLE:');
      Printing := FALSE;
      PageWidth := 40;                           (* set width of display line *)
      LinesPerPage := 20;
     END;
   2:BEGIN
      REWRITE(OutDevice,'PRINTER:');
      Printing := TRUE;                  (* allows time for device to print *)
      PageWidth := 80;                             (* set width of print line *)
      LinesPerPage := 60;
     END;
  END;
 FileOpen := TRUE;
END;
(*************************************************************************)
(*                                                                       *)
(*     FUNCTION TO ASK A YES/NO QUESTION, WAIT FOR Y OR N AND <RETURN>     *)
(*                                                                       *)
(*************************************************************************)
FUNCTION Yes(Question:STRING):BOOLEAN;
VAR
 Answer:CHAR;
BEGIN
  REPEAT
   WRITE(Question,' ? (Y/N) ');      (* show the question with ? and options *)
   READLN(Answer);                         (* get Answer, await <RETURN> *)
  UNTIL Answer IN ['Y','N'];                  (* test if answer is in set *)
 Yes := (Answer = 'Y');         (* if answer is Y, then Yes function is TRUE *)
END;
(*************************************************************************)
(*                                                                       *)
(*       PROCEDURE TO ASK ALL THE DATA FOR A SINGLE TRANSACTION, OR        *)
(*       ACCOUNT ENTRY; THE FILE IS AcctFile --SO THE FILE POINTER         *)
(*       VARIABLE IS AcctFile^                                             *)
(*                                                                       *)
(*************************************************************************)
PROCEDURE GetAcctEntry;
VAR
 TempString:STRING;
 TempChar:CHAR;
BEGIN
 WITH AcctFile^ DO
  BEGIN
   STR(SUCC(ItemCount),TempString);       (* convert ItemCount+1 to STRING *)
   PutTitle(CONCAT('ENTER ITEM NUMBER ',TempString));          (* put title *)
(* first, ask if entry is Debit or Credit *)
   REPEAT
    GOTOXY(0,2);                                  (* go to start of line *)
    WRITE('DEBIT OR CREDIT? (D/C) ');       (* ask user if Debit or Credit *)
    READ(TempChar);                                        (* read answer *)
    CASE TempChar OF                                  (* interpret answer *)
     'D':EntryType := Debit;
     'C':EntryType := Credit;
    END;
   UNTIL TempChar IN ['D','C'];          (* test; if answer no good, redo *)
(* get amount and category for item *)
```

```
   WITH Info[EntryType] DO
    BEGIN
     AskValue(0,3,CONCAT(Name,' AMOUNT $ '),Amount);           (* get Amount *)
     Sum := Sum + Amount;                                    (* add to total *)
    END;
   Number := AskChoice(0,4,'ENTRY NUMBER',0,9999);             (* ask number *)
   WITH Date DO
    BEGIN
     mm := AskChoice(9,5,'MONTH',1,12);     (* pass parameters to function *)
     dd := AskChoice(11,6,'DAY',1,31);            (* note restrictions on *)
     yy := AskChoice(9,7,'YEAR',80,99);                (* possible values *)
    END;
   GOTOXY(0,8);                      (* advance writing position on display *)
   WRITE('COMMENT ');                       (* ask for description of entry *)
   READLN(Comment);                                    (* get description *)
   GOTOXY(0,9);                  (* advance to next writing line on display *)
   EntryCode := AskCategory(EntryType);                   (* get category *)
   WITH Info[EntryType] DO
    Totals[EntryCode] := Totals[EntryCode] + Amount;       (* sum category *)
   END;
END;
(*************************************************************************)
(*                                                                       *)
(*        PROCEDURE TO OPEN THE ACCOUNT FILE IF NOT ALREADY OPEN;        *)
(*           FILE WILL BE CREATED IF IT DOES NOT ALREADY EXIST.          *)
(*                                                                       *)
(*************************************************************************)
PROCEDURE OpenAccountFile;
BEGIN
 ItemCount := 0;
 IF NOT AccountOpen THEN                            (* test: Is file open? *)
  BEGIN
   IF Yes('HAS AN ACCOUNT FILE BEEN CREATED') THEN
    BEGIN
     RESET(InfoFile,'ACCOUNT.INFO');         (* open file and read in entry *)
     Info := InfoFile^;        (* move data into another variable (note ^) *)
     WRITELN('SUMMARY FILE LOADED');
     RESET(AcctFile,'ACCOUNT.DATA');         (* open file and read in entry *)
     WRITE('ACCOUNT FILE OPENED');
     WHILE NOT EOF(AcctFile) DO          (* read all records temporarily... *)
      BEGIN
       ItemCount := SUCC(ItemCount);
       GET(AcctFile);
      END;
     WRITELN(', ',ItemCount,' ENTRIES FOUND ');               (* show count *)
    END
   ELSE                               (* file not created yet, so do it now *)
    BEGIN
     REWRITE(AcctFile,'ACCOUNT.DATA');        (* create account detail file*)
     REWRITE(InfoFile,'ACCOUNT.INFO');             (* create summary file *)
     WRITELN('ACCOUNT FILE CREATED');        (* tell user what's happening *)
    END;
   AccountOpen := TRUE;                                      (* set a flag *)
  END;
END;
(*************************************************************************)
(*                                                                       *)
(*      PROCEDURE TO GET NEW ENTRIES FOR ACCOUNT FILE AND KEEP TOTALS     *)
(*                                                                       *)
(*************************************************************************)
PROCEDURE MakeAccountEntries;
BEGIN
 OpenAccountFile;                                   (* open file for data *)
 WHILE Yes('DO YOU WANT TO ADD AN ACCOUNT ENTRY') DO
  BEGIN
   GetAcctEntry;                                    (* ask for entry data *)
   PUT(AcctFile);                       (* save entry to master account file *)
   ItemCount := SUCC(ItemCount);                 (* increment item count *)
  END;
 CLOSE(AcctFile,LOCK);              (* close master file and make permanent *)
 SEEK(InfoFile,0);                       (* point to beginning of info file *)
 InfoFile^ := Info;                       (* move variable to file variable *)
```

```
 PUT(InfoFile);                                    (* put file variable to disk *)
 CLOSE(InfoFile,LOCK);                                  (* close and lock file *)
 AcctOpen := FALSE;                        (* set flag to indicate closed file *)
END;
(****************************************************************************)
(*                                                                          *)
(*     SHOW THE CONTENTS OF THE CURRENT AcctFile RECORD ON CONSOLE OR       *)
(*     ON PRINTER (AS DETERMINED BY OutDevice)                              *)
(*                                                                          *)
(****************************************************************************)
PROCEDURE ShowEntry;
BEGIN
 WITH AcctFile^ DO
  BEGIN
   WITH Info[EntryType] DO
    BEGIN
     WRITE(OutDevice,Name:6,' ');                             (* display Name *)
     WITH Date DO
      WRITE(OutDevice,mm:2,'/',dd:2,'/',yy,' ');              (* display Date *)
      WRITE(OutDevice,Number:3,' ');                        (* display Number *)
      IF Printing THEN
       BEGIN
        WRITE(OutDevice,CategoryList[EntryCode],' ');
(* left justify description string and fill to 20 character field *)
        WRITE(OutDevice,Comment,'':(20-LENGTH(Comment)));
       END
      ELSE
       WRITE(OutDevice,CategoryList[EntryCode]:6,' ');
      IF EntryType = Debit THEN
      WRITE(OutDevice,'(')           (* use brackets () to show Debit amounts *)
     ELSE
      WRITE(OutDevice,' ');          (* no () for Credits, but space needed *)
     WRITE(OutDevice,Amount:8:2);               (* specify output and length *)
     IF EntryType = Debit THEN
      WRITE(OutDevice,')');                (* add right bracket for Debits *)
     WRITELN(OutDevice);                                      (* skip a line *)
    END;
 END;
END;
(****************************************************************************)
(*                                                                          *)
(*      PROCEDURE TO SHOW ENTRIES THAT ARE ON MASTER ACCOUNT FILE           *)
(*                                                                          *)
(****************************************************************************)
PROCEDURE ShowAccountEntries;
BEGIN
 LineNumber := 0;
 AskOutputDevice;             (* see if printer or console desired display *)
 IF NOT AccountOpen THEN                               (* test file open flag *)
  BEGIN
   RESET(AcctFile,'ACCOUNT.DATA');              (* open file if not already *)
   RESET(InfoFile,'ACCOUNT.INFO');                (* open summary file, too *)
   Info := InfoFile^;                  (* move file var into other variable *)
   AccountOpen := TRUE;                                           (* set flag *)
  END;
 RESET(AcctFile);                                       (* get first record *)
 PAGE(OutDevice);                                    (* start new display page *)
 WHILE NOT EOF(AcctFile) DO            (* GET sets EOF if no more records *)
  BEGIN
(* if the remainder of LineNumber divided by LinesPerPage is zero,
then a new page must be started--following starts new page, also *)
   IF(LineNumber MOD LinesPerPage) = 0 THEN           (* test:Is page full?*)
    BEGIN
     IF NOT Printing THEN                                   (* if on console...*)
      IF LineNumber > 0 THEN                        (* and if not first line *)
       AwaitAnyKey;                                 (* pause before new page *)
     IF Printing THEN                                       (* if on printer...*)
      BEGIN
(* show heading--this takes two lines of program text: *)
       WRITELN(OutDevice,'    -TYPE- --DATE-- NBR ------CATEGORY------',
                    ' ------COMMENT------- --AMOUNT--');
       WRITELN(OutDevice);                                    (* skip a line *)
      END
```

```
      ELSE                                     (* display format for console *)
       PutTitle('    -TYPE- --DATE-- NBR -CAT.- --AMOUNT--');
      END;
      LineNumber := SUCC(LineNumber);               (* increment line number *)
      WRITE(OutDevice,LineNumber:2,' ');              (* number display line *)
      ShowEntry;                            (* call procedure to display entry *)
      GET(AcctFile);                       (* get next record from master file *)
     END;
    IF NOT Printing THEN
     AwaitAnyKey;
    CLOSE(AcctFile);                 (* no LOCK needed since nothing changed *)
    CLOSE(InfoFile);                 (* no LOCK needed since nothing changed *)
    AccountOpen := FALSE;                                         (* set flag *)
END;
(*************************************************************************)
(*                                                                       *)
(*     SHOW TOTALS FOR DEBIT / CREDIT CATEGORIES AND SHOW ACCT BALANCE     *)
(*                                                                       *)
(*************************************************************************)
PROCEDURE CalculateCurrentBalance;
VAR
 Temp:STRING;
BEGIN
 AskReportType;                                  (* get format for output *)
 AskOutputDevice;
 NewPage('TOTAL ACCOUNT ACTIVITY');                 (* new page, heading *)
 WRITE(OutDevice,'CATEGORY                 AMOUNT');        (* write heading *)
 IF Percent IN ReportSet THEN
  WRITE(OutDevice,'PERCENT ':10);                          (* write heading *)
 IF BarGraph IN ReportSet THEN
  WRITE(OutDevice,'CHARTED');                              (* write heading *)
 WRITELN(OutDevice);                                       (* finish line *)
 PageUnderline;                                              (* underline *)
 WRITELN(OutDevice,'BEGINNING BALANCE  $',StartBalance:10:2);
 ShowDetailTotals;
 CurrentBalance := StartBalance - Info[Debit].Sum + Info[Credit]Sum;
WRITELN(OutDevice,'ACCOUNT BALANCE IS $',CurrentBalance:10:2);
 WRITELN(OutDevice,'==========':30);   (* = for double underscore *)
(* give user time to look at data before main menu appears again *)
 AwaitAnyKey;
END;
(*************************************************************************)
(*                                                                       *)
(*                  INITIALIZE SOME PROGRAM VARIABLES                    *)
(*                                                                       *)
(*************************************************************************)
PROCEDURE Initialize;
VAR
 X :INTEGER;
 Kind:DebCred;
BEGIN
 FOR Kind := Debit TO Credit DO
  WITH Info[Kind] DO
   BEGIN
    Sum := 0;                                             (* clear totals *)
    HowManyCategories := 0;

    CASE Kind OF                                      (* establish names *)
     Credit:Name := 'CREDIT';
     Debit :Name := 'DEBIT';
    END;

    FOR X := 0 TO MaximumCateg DO                     (* clear categories *)
     BEGIN
      Totals[X] := 0;
      CategoryList[X] := '';
     END;
    CategoryList[0] := CONCAT('MISC. ',Name,'S');          (* init categ 0 *)
    WHILE LENGTH(CategoryList[0]) < 20 DO                (* 20 chars long *)
     CategoryList[0] := CONCAT(CategoryList[0],' ');
    END;
```

```
  AccountOpen := FALSE;                                (* set file status flag *)
  StartBalance := 0;                                        (* clear totals *)
  PageWidth := 40;                                  (* set default page width *)
  FileOpen := FALSE;        (* default condition of display file is closed *)
  Underline := '';
  FOR X := 1 TO 80 DO Underline := CONCAT(Underline,'-');
 END;
(**************************************************************************)
(*                                                                        *)
(*                        MAIN PROGRAM BLOCK                              *)
(*                                                                        *)
(**************************************************************************)
BEGIN                    (* this BEGIN is for the main program instructions *)
 Initialize;
  REPEAT                    (* main menu repeats until user wants it to stop *)
   PutTitle('MAIN MENU - PROCESSING CHOICES');
   WRITELN;
   WRITELN('1. ENTER DEBIT CATEGORIES');
   WRITELN('2. ENTER CREDIT CATEGORIES');
   WRITELN('3. MAKE ACCOUNT ENTRIES');
   WRITELN('4. SHOW ACCOUNT ENTRIES');
   WRITELN('5. DISPLAY SUMMARY');
   WRITELN('6. STOP');
   CASE AskChoice(0,15,'ENTER CHOICE',1,6) OF
    1:GetCategories(Debit);                     (* pass parameter to procedure *)
    2:GetCategories(Credit);
    3:MakeAccountEntries;
    4:ShowAccountEntries;
    5:CalculateCurrentBalance;
    6:EXIT(PROGRAM);                (* predefined function for program halt *)
   END;
  UNTIL FALSE;                                      (* creates infinite loop *)
END.                                                   (* end of program text *)
```

Figure 10-2. (Conclusion)

Summary

Entering and testing program modules one at a time is referred to as incremental testing. Nonincremental testing is the entering, compiling, and test execution of a program in its entirety.

In planning for testing and debugging, the programmer should: include testing and debugging routines in program design; develop test data as part of the program design activity; enter, compile, test, and debug program modules incrementally; test and debug integrated program segments; and test the program as a functional system, based on evaluation of results from a user's point of view.

The immediate goal of testing is to cause a given module or program to fail. Testing is the process of error detection. Debugging involves isolating the problem that caused an error and solving it.

UCSD Pascal provides only limited built-in debugging features. The programmer must design error-checking features into modules or programs to be tested by inserting statements or procedures that specifically implement test features.

Regardless of the method used to enter a program or module, the principles of program testing remain the same. The principal methods of testing may be categorized as module, integration, and function testing.

Module testing, also known as unit testing, involves entry and testing of individual program modules.

The process of combining modules to test the interfaces between those modules is integration testing. Incremental test methods include top-down and bottom-up integration testing.

Testing the program as a whole with data derived from anticipated application conditions is function testing.

Top-down testing codes the most general, or high-level, modules and substitutes stubs for lower-level modules. Bottom-up testing integrates lower-level modules that are interfaced by drivers substituted for higher-level modules.

Three kinds of errors frequently encountered are typographical errors, misplaced variable references, and uninitialized variables.

Values for test data should be accumulated according to ranges, categories, and ordered sets.

Debugging techniques in program text include test statements for memory dumps and execution traces. Additionally, errors may be found by program desk checking and hypothesis testing.

Pascal features introduced in this chapter include SUCCessor, PREDecessor, STRing, MODulus, and use the LENGTH function in calculations.

Review Questions

1. What is the difference between incremental and non-incremental testing?
2. What is the difference between testing and debugging?
3. What is the goal of testing, and how does it contribute to debugging a program or module?
4. What are three principal methods of testing, and how are they applied?
5. What are two approaches to integration of program modules, and what are the characteristics of each?
6. What are three kinds of commonly encountered errors, and how may each be prevented?
7. What criteria should be used to develop test data?
8. What debugging tools may be included in program text?
9. What is meant by the process of hypothesis testing?
10. What is the purpose of maintaining two file variables (AcctFile and InfoFile) in the *AccountManagement* program?
11. How are records in AcctFile and InfoFile handled differently within the program?
12. How does the enumeration type DebCred in *AccountManagement* simplify the procedures from *BasicAccounting?*
13. When might it be appropriate to assign the content of a file variable to a temporary variable?
14. How is the EOF function used?
15. What is the usage of the SUCC and PRED functions?
16. What is the usage of the STR procedure?
17. What processing actions are caused by the MOD operation?

Pascal Practice

1. Develop a set of test data for *AccountManagement.* Pay particular attention to ranges and data types. How do ordered sets of test data apply to the files in the program?
2. Insert statements for execution traces and memory dumps for the modules called in the MAIN PROGRAM of *AccountManagement.* Insert stubs for lower-level modules and enter and compile the program using top-down integration. Test addition of each new module with the data developed in the first exercise.
3. Write a brief program that calls *Columns* as a procedure. The program should gather a group of names into an array and then print them out in vertical columnar format. Note that the original *Columns* program must be modified to display STRING values rather than array indexes.

Key Terms

1. incremental testing
2. nonincremental testing
3. module testing
4. unit testing
5. integration testing
6. function testing
7. top-down
8. bottom-up
9. stub
10. driver
11. range error
12. bounds error
13. limits error
14. fatal error
15. memory dump
16. execution trace
17. desk checking
18. hypothesis testing

Pascal Library

1. EOF
2. SUCC
3. PRED
4. STR
5. MOD

11 REARRANGING AND MAINTAINING INFORMATION

OBJECTIVES

On completing the reading and other learning assignments for this chapter, you should be able to:

- ☐ Explain the function of file processing and tell how master files are updated from transaction files.
- ☐ Tell why it is necessary to rearrange data to create and maintain lists.
- ☐ Describe the actions of sorting techniques to create ordered lists including: selection in order, bubble sort, sift, and Shell's sort.
- ☐ Describe how files may be processed by merging.
- ☐ Describe trade-offs involved in designing data structures and using search techniques in those structures.
- ☐ Explain the uses of serial lists, sequential lists, and linked lists.
- ☐ Describe list maintenance considerations for various kinds of lists.
- ☐ Demonstrate the use of the pointer variable in Pascal program text in implementing linked lists and tree structures.
- ☐ Describe how the hierarchical structure of trees may be applied.
- ☐ Explain the principles of linear search, linked search, and binary search.
- ☐ Describe the characteristics of random files, sorted files, linked files, and hashed files, as well as the search techniques that apply to each.

FILE PROCESSING

Data are a key resource in any organization. This data resource is maintained in files, which, collectively, represent both the history and the current status of business operations. In essence, application programs are written to create and maintain files. In general, individual files may be categorized as either transaction files or master files.

Transaction files are built from records created by business activities. Typically, transaction files are created from temporary serial files. These serial files are created by the act of capturing data. For example, serial files may be built up as retail sales transactions are entered at point-of-sale terminals in a department store. At least initially, such a file has no particular order. At most, the temporary serial file is structured chronologically, in the order of data input. For processing within information systems, transactions often are arranged into an ordered sequence. Because the raw data of business transactions are represented in transaction files, such files may be thought of as *detail files.* Collectively, transaction files represent the history of business activities.

Master files, on the other hand, are used for long-term retention of data, often in a form that is necessary for routine processing. Data from transaction files are *posted* to, or entered into, master files. This processing updates master files. To use the department store example, data from sales transactions would be posted periodically to customer master account files used to produce statements. Collectively, master files are maintained to represent the current status of the business.

Once the master file has been updated from the transaction file, the transaction file may be retained for backup, allowing reconstruction if master files are destroyed. Transaction files also must be retained to preserve the *audit trail,* the means of tracing any transaction back to its source.

In transforming data from transaction files, summary information may be *extracted,* or derived, and the order of data items may be changed. In general, the order of a transaction file is a serial, physical one that does not change; the transaction file is used once in posting data and then archived. Master files, by contrast, generally must be maintained continuously in some logical order. A retail store master file for customers might be maintained in account number order, for example. This logical order is determined by application processing requirements.

One important processing consideration is to determine whether a job is to be executed interactively or whether groups of transactions or groups of jobs are to be accumulated and then run as a *batch.* An example of a batch application would be the periodic execution of a payroll program in which all employee time reports are entered to transaction files and then processed against the master payroll file. In an interactive session, a person and a computer transmit messages to one another and also respond to the content of the messages. An example would be an airline reservation system in which passenger seats are sold on a first-come, first-served basis.

FILE ORGANIZATION AND STRUCTURE

Organizing files involves placing structured data, or records, into some logical order. File design is an important requirement for your overall program design. Design considerations include:

- What is the structure, or logical order (if any), that is used to store the data to be presented to the program?
- Must this structure, or logical order, be rearranged for efficient processing?
- Must data items or results be rearranged to produce the required outputs?
- At what point during program execution is it most efficient for this rearrangement to occur?

Certain data structures, including arrays and files, may be thought of as *lists.* A special case of lists that implies a hierarchy is the *tree.* Rearrangement of data to create ordered lists is accomplished by sorting.

The actual physical processing for sorting data into lists may be accomplished by a variety of programming techniques. The design decision centers around considerations of when sorting should be performed and what type of sort must be applied. These considerations, in turn, involve trade-offs of processing efficiency and the ease of maintaining the order of the list.

The programmer often has to work with files that exist in arbitrary order or that were designed by someone else. For example, a sales analysis program might have to derive data from existing transaction files.

Then, too, your program may make use of a master file originally created for another application, under a logical order that does not correspond with the one you want. It is necessary, then, to understand how list orders may be created through sorting.

SORTING

Sorting may seem to be an intuitive process, since it is a familiar task. Finding a name in a telephone book relies on the fact that the book is sorted in alphabetical order. Even small children can sort objects by size or group them by color.

Computer sorting is an extension of logical comparison. Two data items are compared. If a given item is greater than the other, it is placed in a higher order in the output list, and the other is placed in a lower order. Repeated comparisons eventually can result in a correctly ordered output list.

Devising the most efficient means of sorting a group of data items, however, can be a formidable task. Arriving at some algorithm for performing a sort may be a crucial decision in designing an efficient program. Data required by the program may have been input and stored in random order. The programmer must rely on the computer's ability to rearrange data so that efficient processing can occur and the desired results can be extracted. For this reason, it is important for you to be aware of several techniques for accomplishing sorts and to become acquainted with the trade-offs inherent in each technique.

Sorting techniques that are complex from a programming standpoint may yield exceptionally fast program execution times. On the other hand, sorts that are easy to program may be inordinately time-consuming in execution.

There are two basic actions required in sorting a group of items. First, two items in the list are selected and compared. Second, the two items are either left as is, or their positions in the list are swapped. The comparison can be simple, as in the sorting of a list of integers, in which the comparison is simply subtraction. Or, the comparison may be complex, as in the comparison of two records of type Check. In the case of a complex record, it may be necessary to select one or more fields as the *key* upon which the comparison is to be made.

Once the comparison has been made, if swapping is required, Pascal can make the swap easy to code. If the data items are Pascal RECORDs, they can be swapped directly. For example:

```
TYPE
 Check = RECORD
  Number : INTEGER;
  Amount : REAL;
  Date,
  Payee,
  Description : STRING;
 END;

VAR
 A, B, Temp : Check;
 Swap : BOOLEAN;
```

Given the above, it would be possible to code:

```
IF Swap THEN
 BEGIN
  Temp := A;
  A := B;
  B := Temp;
 END;
```

Depending upon the kind of list required, the sort key may be the field Number (to sort by check number), Date (to sort chronologically), or Payee (to sort by payee).

The means by which the items to be compared are selected depends upon the sort algorithm applied. Three such algorithms are discussed in this chapter.

A fast sorting method that suits the application is one of the programmer's most valuable tools. Numerous sorting methods exist. In fact, sorting is an area of active research among theorists in computer science. It is sufficient here to describe some basic methods and give examples of how these methods are implemented in program text. Four general methods are presented, along with trade-offs associated with each. These four methods are:

- Selection in order
- Bubble sort
- Sift, or shuttle sort
- Shell's sort.

Selection in Order

If a list does not need to be ordered in its entirety, desired data items may be extracted from the list in the order needed for processing. This approach may be referred to as *selection in order.*

For example, a short, unstructured client list may contain 50 entries. For purposes of generating a report, account totals for clients numbered 1 to 10 may be required. The *record key,* the client number field in this case, may be examined within each record in the file. Searching is begun with client number 1. When that key is found, the account total is extracted from the appropriate field in the record for that client. Then, a search is made for the next ordered record key, and the process is repeated. As each desired data item (the account total) is found, it is placed in a sublist, which may take the form of an array in memory or a temporary file on a diskette.

This technique is useful mainly for small lists from which summaries or a limited amount of data must be extracted. It is important for the approximate size of the resulting sublist to be known before the sort is initiated so that the required memory or file space may be allocated.

Selection in order may be used when deriving reports from unstructured data. Within a group of data items, the lowest ordered item remaining in the list may be found and displayed. The program must keep track of what items have been displayed already in seeking the lowest ordered item remaining.

Bubble Sort

A straightforward technique for sorting lists is the *bubble sort.* This technique scans an entire list repeatedly and also is referred to as the *standard exchange method.* As the list is scanned, higher ordered items are caused to rise to the top, or migrate to the end, of the list, like bubbles rising to the surface.

As the list is scanned, each item is tested to determine its value in relation to its successor. When two adjacent items are found to be out of the desired order, their positions within the list are reversed, or swapped. This testing and swapping process continues through the list. The list is scanned repeatedly until it is found to be in order. Since each scan places one more item in its final position, the length of the scan is reduced by one item with each pass. Thus, each pass scans only the sublist of unordered items. The sort is complete when scanning the list reveals that no further swaps are necessary. Accordingly, the result of the bubble sort is a list sequenced from lowest ordered item at the beginning to highest ordered item at the end (or *vice versa* if descending order is desired).

For example, suppose a bubble sort is to be performed on the following list of characters. The desired result is a list in alphabetic order. The form of the list before it is sorted looks like this:

```
A C B
```

The first scan would test the relationship between the first pair of items, A and C. This test discloses that A and C are ordered correctly with respect to each other, so no swap is performed. Continuing the first scan through the list, the next pair of items to be tested is C and B. This test discloses that C and B are out of the desired order, and the items are swapped, resulting in the following list:

```
A B C
```

One more scan of the list determines that no further swaps are required; the list is in order.

Although this example illustrates the basic principle of the bubble sort, its simplicity is deceptive in that only a single pass through the list is required to achieve the desired order. Ordinarily, a bubble sort requires a large number of passes, or scans, through the list to sort the data.

The number of passes required varies depending upon how close the original list is to the desired order. Each pass through the list will require K – 1 comparisons, where K is the number of items that have not been placed in final positions by previous passes.

If N represents the number of items in the list, the maximum number of comparisons is defined by:

$$[N(N-1)] \div 2$$

To illustrate, consider the list:

```
Z Y X Q R T U L M A B C
```

```
ZYXQRTULMABC
XX
YZXQRTULMABC
 XX
YXZQRTULMABC
  XX
YXQZRTULMABC
   XX
YXQRZTULMABC
    XX
YXQRTZULMABC
     XX
YXQRTUZLMABC
      XX
YXQRTULZMABC
       XX
YXQRTULMZABC
        XX
YXQRTULMAZBC
         XX
YXQRTULMABZC
          XX
YXQRTULMABCZ

END OF PASS 1
11 SWAPS
11 COMPARISONS
   THIS PASS
11 COMPARISONS TOTAL

YXQRTULMABCZ
XX
XYQRTULMABCZ
 XX
XQYRTULMABCZ
  XX
XQRYTULMABCZ
   XX
XQRTYULMABCZ
    XX
XQRTUYLMABCZ
     XX
XQRTULYMABCZ
      XX
XQRTULMYABCZ
       XX
XQRTULMAYBCZ
        XX
XQRTULMABYCZ
         XX
XQRTULMABCYZ

END OF PASS 2
10 SWAPS
10 COMPARISONS
   THIS PASS
21 COMPARISONS TOTAL

XQRTULMABCYZ
XX
QXRTULMABCYZ
 XX
QRXTULMABCYZ
  XX
QRTXULMABCYZ
   XX
QRTUXLMABCYZ
    XX
QRTULXMABCYZ
     XX
QRTULMXABCYZ
      XX
QRTULMAXBCYZ
       XX
QRTULMABXCYZ
        XX
QRTULMABCXYZ

END OF PASS 3
9 SWAPS
9 COMPARISONS
  THIS PASS
30 COMPARISONS TOTAL

QRTULMABCXYZ
^^
QRTULMABCXYZ
 ^^
QRTULMABCXYZ
  ^^
QRTULMABCXYZ
   XX
QRTLUMABCXYZ
    XX
QRTLMUABCXYZ
     XX
QRTLMAUBCXYZ
      XX
QRTLMABUCXYZ
       XX
QRTLMABCUXYZ

END OF PASS 4
5 SWAPS
8 COMPARISONS
  THIS PASS
38 COMPARISONS TOTAL

QRTLMABCUXYZ
^^
QRTLMABCUXYZ
 ^^
QRTLMABCUXYZ
  XX
QRLTMABCUXYZ
   XX
QRLMTABCUXYZ
    XX
QRLMATBCUXYZ
     XX
QRLMABTCUXYZ
      XX
QRLMABCTUXYZ

END OF PASS 5
5 SWAPS
7 COMPARISONS
  THIS PASS
45 COMPARISONS TOTAL
```

There are 12 items in this list. Since two items are evaluated in each comparison, N – 1 comparisons, or 11, are required for the first pass through the list. For this particular list, 10 passes are required to put the list in alphabetic order, for a total of 65 comparisons. Note that, since this example was in nearly inverse order, the number of comparisons required is only one less than the maximum, as defined by the above formula. The order of the list as it would appear after each comparison for 10 passes is shown in Figure 11-1. For purposes of illustration, an x appears under items that must be swapped and a ^ appears under items that are found to be in the desired order.

The requirement for numerous scans is the primary drawback of the bubble sort. However, this method is relatively easy to code and requires a small amount of memory space in comparison with alternative methods. Therefore, bubble sorts are most appropriate when a small list is to be sorted and when processing speed is not critical. Because of the number

```
QRLMABCTUXYZ
^^
QRLMABCTUXYZ
 XX
QLRMABCTUXYZ
  XX
QLMRABCTUXYZ
   XX
QLMARBCTUXYZ
    XX
QLMABRCTUXYZ
     XX
QLMABCRTUXYZ

END OF PASS 6
5 SWAPS
6 COMPARISONS
  THIS PASS
51 COMPARISONS TOTAL
```

```
QLMABCRTUXYZ
XX
LQMABCRTUXYZ
 XX
LMQABCRTUXYZ
  XX
LMAQBCRTUXYZ
   XX
LMABQCRTUXYZ
    XX
LMABCQRTUXYZ

END OF PASS 7
5 SWAPS
5 COMPARISONS
  THIS PASS
56 COMPARISONS TOTAL
```

```
LMABCQRTUXYZ
^^
LMABCQRTUXYZ
 XX
LAMBCQRTUXYZ
  XX
LABMCQRTUXYZ
   XX
LABCMQRTUXYZ

END OF PASS 8
3 SWAPS
4 COMPARISONS
  THIS PASS
60 COMPARISONS TOTAL
```

```
LABCMQRTUXYZ
XX
ALBCMQRTUXYZ
 XX
ABLCMQRTUXYZ
  XX
ABCLMQRTUXYZ

END OF PASS 9
3 SWAPS
3 COMPARISONS
  THIS PASS
63 COMPARISONS TOTAL
```

```
ABCLMQRTUXYZ
^^
ABCLMQRTUXYZ
 ^^
ABCLMQRTUXYZ

END OF PASS 10
NO SWAPS
2 COMPARISONS
  THIS PASS
65 COMPARISONS TOTAL
```

Figure 11-1. Bubble sort example showing status of list at each comparison for 10 passes. (x represents items that must be swapped and ^ represents items found in the desired order.)

of passes required, bubble sorts are slow in processing long lists. This is especially true if an item in the list appears at a point distant from its correct position in the final order; a given item migrates only one position toward its destination with each swap.

Bubble Sort Example

The following procedure implements a bubble sort on a list of N characters that are found in a previously declared array named List. The resulting list is in alphabetic order. The procedure BubbleSort uses a global array variable:

```
VAR
 List : ARRAY[1..N] OF CHAR;
```

The procedure, then, is:

```
PROCEDURE BubbleSort(N:INTEGER);
VAR
 AnySwaps: BOOLEAN;      (* declare a flag to indicate when sort is done *)
 TempChar: CHAR;       (* variable to hold the character being exchanged *)
 I: INTEGER;                              (* variable for loop counter *)
BEGIN
 REPEAT                                      (* scan list repetitively *)
  AnySwaps := FALSE;                        (* set exchange flag FALSE *)
  FOR I := 1 TO N-1 DO           (* scan list from first to next-to-last *)
   BEGIN
    IF List[I] > List[I+1] THEN                   (* are items in order? *)
     BEGIN
       AnySwaps := TRUE;                                     (* set flag *)
       TempChar := List[I];                                   (* do swap *)
       List[I] := List[I+1];        (* move second item to first position *)
       List[I+1] := TempChar;   (* move first item to second; swap done *)
     END;
   END;
  N := N-1;                       (* make next pass 1 comparison shorter *)
 UNTIL NOT AnySwaps;                      (* if no exchanges, sort complete *)
END;
```

Sift

The *sift* is a variation of the bubble sort and may be referred to as the *shuttle sort* or *linear insertion with exchange.* Unlike the bubble sort, the sift does not use fixed sequences of comparison. Sift proceeds in a manner identical to the bubble sort until a swap is made. The item that is moved lower then is compared in backward fashion to each preceding item in the list. This reverse comparison continues until a lower ordered item is found. Thus, the item is caused to move as close to the beginning of the list as possible. Then, the sequence of comparisons reverses again and resumes at the point at which the first swap was made.

The least number of comparisons performed by a sift is $N-1$. The maximum number of comparisons is given by:

$$(N-1)^2 \div 2$$

Sift Example

The following procedure implements a sift on an alphabetic array List of N items:

```
PROCEDURE Sift;
VAR
 I, J : INTEGER;
 TempChar : CHAR;
BEGIN
 FOR I := 1 TO N-1 DO               (* pass through list forward *)
  BEGIN
   J := I;                          (* hold current position in J *)
   WHILE J > 0 DO               (* do once at least--more if swap *)
    BEGIN
     IF List[J] > List [J+1] THEN         (* if swap needed... *)
      BEGIN
       TempChar := List[J];
       List[J] := List[J+1];
       List[J+1] := TempChar;                     (* swap done *)
       J := J-1;               (* decrement J for backward scan *)
      END
     ELSE J := 0;                         (* no swap; set flag *)
   END;                                           (* END WHILE *)
 END;                                               (* END FOR *)
END;                                          (* END PROCEDURE *)
```

The application of the sift to the previous example is illustrated in Figure 11-2. For the given list, the sift seems more efficient than the bubble sort, since just one pass is required. However, the number of comparisons (62) is about the same.

Shell's Sort

Shell's sort is a further enhancement of bubble and sift techniques. This technique is named for Donald L. Shell, who originally formulated it. Shell's sort first partitions the list into segments with a defined *gap* between the segments. Then, the bubble sort technique is applied by comparing, not adjacent entries, but entries that are separated by the gap. Items that are out of order with respect to one another are swapped, as in the bubble sort, but at the distance of the gap. A backward scan, as in the sift, is then initiated that involves the items already compared. The effect is that items far out of order tend to move quickly to their approximate ordered positions.

Figure 11-3 shows the progress of a version of Shell's sort applied to the same list presented above. Note that Shell's sort scans fewer entries

```
ZYXQRTULMABC    YZXQRTULMABC    XYZQRTULMABC    QXYZRTULMABC    QRTXYZULMABC    QRXYZTULMABC
XX               XX               XX               XX                 XX             XX
                XX               XX               XX                XX             XX
                                XX               XX                XX             XX
                                                ^^                ^^             ^^
```

Figure 11-2. Sift example showing one pass and 62 comparisons. (x represents items that must be swapped and ^ represents items found in the desired order.)

than the bubble sort in the earlier passes because the gap is large. Notice also that, as the sort progresses, the gap between segments is made smaller. The last pass is made with the gap equal to just one position so that the entire list is treated as a single, continuous segment. In this case, when the gap is equal to 1, the order of comparisons is identical to a sift.

When the number of items (N) in a list is expressed as an exponent of 2, the number of passes required is:

$$\log_2 N$$

For long lists that are far out of the desired order, Shell's sort is more efficient than either the bubble sort or the sift because items that are far away from their destinations are placed quickly in positions that approximate the final order. In this example, Shell's sort requires three passes and just 26 comparisons.

The Shell's sort offers a favorable trade-off between simplicity of programming and fast execution. Not only does it work well on long lists, but it also makes fairly efficient use of memory space.

```
QRTUXYZLMABC   LQRTUXYZMABC   LMQRTUXYZABC   ALMQRTUXYZBC   ABLMQRTUXYZC
      XX              XX              XX              XX              XX
     XX              XX              XX              XX              XX
    XX              XX              XX              XX              XX
   XX              XX              XX              XX              XX
  XX              XX              XX              XX              XX
 XX              XX              XX              XX              XX
XX              XX              XX              XX              XX
               ^^              XX              XX              XX
                              XX              XX              XX
                                             ^^              ^^
                                                            ABCLMQRTUXYZ

                                                            END OF PASS 1
                                                            56 SWAPS
                                                            62 COMPARISONS THIS PASS
                                                            62 COMPARISONS TOTAL
                                                            --------------------
```

```
GAP := 6
ZYXQRTULMABC
x     x
UYXQRTZLMABC
 x     x
ULXQRTZYMABC
  x     x
ULMQRTZYXABC
   x     x
ULMARTZYXQBC
    x     x
ULMABTZYXQRC
     x     x
ULMABCZYXQRT

END OF PASS 1
6 SWAPS
6 COMPARISONS
  THIS PASS
6 COMPARISONS TOTAL
```

```
GAP := 3
ULMABCZYXQRT
x  x
ALMUBCZYXQRT
 x  x
ABMULCZYXQRT
  x  x
ABCULMZYXQRT
   ^  ^
ABCULMZYXQRT
    ^  ^
ABCULMZYXQRT
     ^  ^
ABCULMZYXQRT
      x  x
   x  x
^  ^
ABCQLMUYXZRT
       x  x
    ^  ^
ABCQLMURXZYT
        x  x
     ^  ^
ABCQLMURTZYX

END OF PASS 2
7 SWAPS
13 COMPARISONS
   THIS PASS
15 COMPARISONS TOTAL
```

```
GAP := 1
ABCQLMURTZYX
^^
ABCQLMURTZYX
 ^^
ABCQLMURTZYX
  ^^
ABCQLMURTZYX
   xx
  ^^
ABCLQMURTZYX
    xx
   ^^
ABCLMQURTZYX
     ^^
ABCLMQURTZYX
      xx
     ^^
ABCLMQRUTZYX
       xx
      ^^
ABCLMQRTUZYX
        ^^
ABCLMQRTUZYX
         xx
        ^^
ABCLMQRTUYZX
          xx
         xx
        ^^
ABCLMQRTUXYZ

END OF PASS 3
7 SWAPS
18 COMPARISONS
   THIS PASS
26 COMPARISONS TOTAL
```

Figure 11-3. Shell's sort showing 3 passes through list. (x represents items that must be swapped and ^ represents items found in the desired order.)

Shell's Sort Example

The following program block sorts N elements of the array List into alphabetic order. Note especially the similarity to the statements in the procedure BubbleSort.

```
PROCEDURE ShellSort;
VAR
 Gap,
 I, J : INTEGER;
 TempChar: CHAR;
BEGIN
 Gap := N DIV 2; (* first, make gap equal to half list length *)
 WHILE Gap > 0 DO                          (* repeat until gap is 0 *)
  BEGIN
   FOR I := 1 TO N-Gap DO                   (* loop through the list *)
    BEGIN
     J := I;                           (* save list pointer into J *)
     WHILE J > 0 DO          (* J is index for secondary search *)
      BEGIN
       IF List[J] > List[J+Gap] THEN       (* if swap needed... *)
        BEGIN
         TempChar := List[J];
         List[J] := List[J+Gap];
         List[J+Gap] := TempChar;                     (* swap done *)
         J := J - Gap;                           (* scan backwards *)
        END
       ELSE J := 0;                   (* no swap; set J = 0 as flag *)
      END;                                      (* END WHILE J > 0 *)
    END;                                                (* END FOR *)
   Gap := Gap DIV 2;                         (* divide Gap in half *)
  END;                                        (* END WHILE Gap > 0 *)
END;                                              (* END PROCEDURE *)
```

MERGING

A *merge* is a processing operation that combines the content of two ordered lists to achieve a single, ordered list. In the merging of two ordered files, two records, the lowest ordered record from each input file, are compared. Then, the lower ordered record of the two is written to an output list. This process is repeated until all records in the input files have been read.

It is usually most efficient to perform a merge after sorting. For example, it might be necessary to merge two lists that were created under different circumstances or during different program executions. Another common use of the merge, especially for microcomputer applications, occurs when there is not enough memory to perform a single sort on a long file. In this case, it is possible to divide the file into sublists, sort and save each sublist separately, then merge the sublists to a single output file.

LISTS

A list is a serial arrangement of data items. Forms that lists may take include:

- Unstructured lists
- Sequential, or ordered, lists
- Linked lists.

Lists may be held in memory during program execution or may be maintained as external files and accessed as record structures.

Unstructured Lists

In perhaps the simplest form of list, the physical order of data items corresponds with the order in which those items are input. Recall that this is the basic form of the serial file. The order of the items in the list is seemingly random, or unpredictable from the programmer's viewpoint. For practical purposes, a *serial list* must be treated as unstructured if its structure is not known. For example, transaction records may be input as the transactions occur. However, you may not be justified in assuming a strictly chronological order for those records, since entries may have been omitted and added later, or entered out of the order in which transactions actually took place. A diagram that illustrates how data items might appear in a serial list is shown in Figure 11-4.

Unstructured lists often are printed in their original form as accounting journals—which are nothing more than detailed, chronological lists of transactions. Such printouts may be needed for audit purposes; these transaction journals can serve as elements of audit trails.

The only other report that may be derived readily from an unordered list is a summary of the list. Specific fields from each record can be extracted and the content summarized. For example, in a checkbook management program that processes a list of check records, the program could read in all values from the check amount fields and compute a running total. If, however, the report format that must be produced requires a listing by payee, further processing would have to be done. The records would have to be ordered logically, perhaps in alphabetical order, sorting by the string values contained in the payee fields. Of course, once this sorting has been performed, the result is no longer an unstructured list.

To obtain summary information from a serial-access list, data items must be *extracted.* The program may have to scan an entire file to find a specific item. Since the order of the records in the file is unpredictable, records must be read in, one after another in serial fashion, and tested for the desired data. To produce an alphabetical list of payees from the above checkbook example, the program would have to scan the payee field of each record in the file and test for string values beginning with 'A'. Once the lowest string value has been found and output, the entire file must be scanned again to find the next lowest value, keeping track,

Serial List
(Chronological Order)

RECORD NUMBER	CLIENT NUMBER	CLIENT NAME	DATE WRITTEN
1	004	Charlie's Cab	06–24–85
2	003	Alpha Corp.	06–25–85
3	001	Craft Sales	06–26–85
4	002	Beta Industries	06–27–85

Figure 11-4. Order of data items in a serial list.

of course, of the values that were output previously. This series of processing steps must be repeated until each payee field in each record has been output. Accordingly, this approach (selection in order) is impractical for unstructured lists, unless the lists are quite short.

The principal advantage of serial lists is simplicity. The creation of such a list is straightforward and no special processing must be done to maintain the order of the list. Serial lists are useful when:

- The number of data items in the list is small.
- Summary information only is to be derived from the list.
- Only a single type of data is to be extracted from the list.
- Chronology must be maintained; all entries in the list are to be displayed or operated upon just as those entries are found in the list, as in following an audit trail.

Sequential Lists

A *sequential list* has some logical order, although that order may not be appropriate for all processing tasks that must be performed on the data items in the list. A straightforward implementation of this kind of list is a sequential access file in which the physical order of data items coincides with a logical order. For example, records containing client names stored as a file in alphabetical order could be accessed in serial fashion for processing to produce a report that outputs those names in alphabetical order. A diagram showing the physical order of data items in a sequential list is given in Figure 11-5.

This kind of file structure is relatively easy to use. Besides the ability to process all items in the list in some order, a sequential list also may be searched efficiently. Unlike the process of searching an unstructured list, searching a sequential list does not require the scanning of all data items. A list maintained in alphabetical order, for example, need only be scanned within a relatively limited range of records to find an item beginning with a given series of alphabetic characters. Also, the extremely fast binary search technique may be used on ordered lists. An example of binary search is presented in Chapter 14.

The same file operations may be performed on sequential lists as on serial lists. The difference is that a sequential list has an order that corresponds with some program requirement, typically an output requirement for report format. The most efficient use of a given sequential list, however, is restricted to operations that correspond with the particular logical order of the list. A client list maintained in alphabetical order is no more efficient in producing a report ordered by client number than an unstructured list would be. This is the difficulty in selecting a single method of organization for a sequential list. If information must be organized in a variety of ways—as demanded by different report format options, for example—limiting the file organization to a single logical order also limits the processing options that can be performed efficiently.

As in the example of a client list, the list may be ordered alphabetically by client name. However, reports based on processing this list may require a variety of formats. For instance, records within the list may contain other fields that must be searched—the name of the company president, the client number, the assigned line of credit, and the outstanding balance on the account. The sales department may want a list of company presidents, ordered alphabetically by the name of each individual. The accounting department may want a report listing company names in a numerical order beginning with the highest outstanding account balance. Clearly, having the source list ordered alphabetically by company name offers no advantage in either case.

A sequential list is most appropriate when a single logical ordering scheme is required. In other words, a sequential list should be maintained

Sequential List
(Physically Ordered by Client Number)

RECORD NUMBER	LOGICAL ORDER BY CLIENT NUMBER	CLIENT NAME	DATE WRITTEN
1	001	Craft Sales	06-26-85
2	002	Beta Industries	06-27-85
3	003	Alpha Corp.	06-25-85
4	004	Charlie's Cab	06-24-85

Figure 11-5. Relationship of data items in a sequential list.

in a logical order that corresponds to its most frequent use, or processing order. Maintaining payroll data in a sequential access file in order of employee number is a good example.

List maintenance for sequential lists. In practice, a list structure is selected, a large number of data items are placed in the list, and then periodic changes must be made to update the list. New items must be added and older items may have to be deleted.

Of course, changes may be made at random anywhere within an unstructured list. New items merely are added to the end of the list. The logical order of a sequential list, however, must be maintained continuously. Processing done to preserve the logical order of a list is known as *list maintenance.*

For example, a sequential list may have a chronological structure that coincides with some other logical structure. Such a list might be created by the input of checks to a checkbook program in the order in which checks are written. The chronological order coincides with the check number, implying a sequential structure. However, this logical structure becomes more difficult to maintain when it is necessary to input a check that is not in check number order, at some later time. Such a list offers no mechanism for saving records out of order, and a sort would have to be performed to reorder the list after input of the new item.

Some file management technique, then, is required to preserve the logical order of the list when items must be input out of the corresponding physical order. The order of items in the list must be reinstated as each new item is input, or the entire list must be reordered after all inputs have been entered. In either case, list maintenance operations are necessary to preserve the order of items in the list for further processing.

Linked Lists

As discussed earlier in this chapter, a client number field may be used for ordering records. A data field that may be compared with a desired field to find a related group of data items is known as a key, or record key. Multiple relationships among data items in a list may be indicated by relationships among keys called *pointers,* or *links.* A pointer or link is an element in an array, or a field in a record that relates a given element or record to the next element or record in some desired order. Lists whose structure is disclosed by the relationships among these links are called *linked lists.*

The discussion thus far has concentrated on ordering the physical relationship of data items so that their sequence coincides with some logical order. The actual data items within such lists are not altered by the process of sorting the items into a new physical order. The resulting physical order discloses the logical order. Then, processing is executed in physical order, or sequentially, accessing one record after another.

Linked lists do not depend on the physical order of data items to determine structure. The pointer is numeric information that corresponds with the physical location of the next data item in the list in some logical order.

When data items in memory are linked, the pointer contains a value corresponding with a memory address or array index for the next item. When data items are stored externally in files, the pointer contains a value for the record number of the next data item in the file for the desired order.

Links may be used, for example, to maintain a relationship of alphabetical order among client names in a list:

```
CRAFT SALES
BETA INDUSTRIES
ALPHA CORPORATION
CHARLIE'S CAB CO.
```

A pointer field may be added to a record of client data for Alpha Corporation. The record is contained in a file with other client records. The pointer field within the record for Alpha Corporation contains a numeric value corresponding with the physical location, or record position, of Beta Industries, the next record in alphabetical order. Accordingly, the record for Beta Industries may be located anywhere within the file. This record would contain a pointer to the next record, Charlie's Cab Company. The record for Charlie's Cab would contain a pointer to Craft Sales, and so on. The last pointer in the list does not have a record to point to, and its value is set to a special value that cannot correspond to the location of a record. In linked lists, there must be some value for links that signals this end-of-list condition.

To process the records in alphabetical order, it is necessary to find the first record in the list. The pointer to the first item in the list is contained in a separate *directory file,* which is usually maintained for linked lists. When the Alpha Corporation record has been processed, a SEEK is done for the record position indicated by the pointer in that record, and a GET brings the record into memory. These steps are repeated for all records in the file until a test for the value of the pointer shows it to be the end of the linked list.

A similar chain of links may structure this same client list in numerical order. For example, the client numbers may be:

```
CRAFT SALES          001
BETA INDUSTRIES      002
ALPHA CORPORATION    003
CHARLIE'S CAB CO.    004
```

A separate start-of-list pointer must contain a pointer indicating the physical location of the first record in order of client number, the record for Craft Sales. As previously stated, this pointer may be contained in a directory. Only one such pointer is required for each desired order. The Craft Sales record would have a field containing a pointer to Beta Industries. The pointer in the Beta Industries record would give the location of Alpha Corporation, and the pointer for client number in Alpha would point to Charlie's Cab. If this were the end of the list in client number order, the client number pointer in Charlie's Cab would be set to indicate the end-of-list.

In this way, several relationships may be maintained within the same list without affecting the physical order of the list in any way. The records may contain other fields having pointers to the next records in alphabetical order by name of company president, in numerical order by outstanding credit balance, and so on.

Of course, if the file is reordered physically, the links must be updated or they become meaningless. However, the physical order of data items in a linked list need not change and may be completely unstructured. The physical locations of the records are significant only as pointer values. The pointers link the records. Multiple pointers may be used to disclose multiple relationships. An example diagramming these relationships in a linked list for client records is given in Figure 11-6. In effect, a linked list is a sequential list whose order is found by chaining through its links rather than by accessing each record in physical order.

Searches within linked files are relatively efficient compared with searches in unordered serial lists but are less efficient than searching

START #3

Linked List
(Client Number Order)

RECORD NUMBER	CLIENT NUMBER	CLIENT NAME	DATE ENTERED	LINK TO NEXT
1	004	Charlie's Cab	06-24-85	NIL
2	003	Alpha Corp.	06-25-85	#1
3	001	Craft Sales	06-26-85	#4
4	002	Beta Industries	06-27-85	#2

START #2

Linked List
(Alphabetic Order by Client Name)

RECORD NUMBER	CLIENT NAME	LINK TO NEXT
1	Charlie's Cab	#3
2	Alpha Corp.	#4
3	Craft Sales	NIL
4	Beta Industries	#1

Figure 11-6. Relationships among data items in a linked list, including several pointers for each item.

sequential lists. Some processing *overhead* is introduced in following the pointer to each entry before the entry can be processed. Lists also may be *double-linked,* so that links exist in each record to point to both the next record and the previous record in the desired order. Double linking can serve to reduce processing overhead.

In a list stored as a file, the link is the physical record number of the next item in logical order. In UCSD Pascal, the SEEK command is used to search for the record indicated by the link. The record then is accessed by the GET procedure. Search techniques are discussed in depth later in this chapter.

For lists in memory, Pascal allows numeric values for links to be held as *pointer variables.* The pointer variable stores a value, or pointer, corresponding with the memory location of a data item. Since the physical structure of the linked list is serial, records may be added at the end of the list or in unused portions within the list and deleted within the list if the appropriate pointers are added or revised.

Pointer variables and linked lists. Pointer variables may be used in Pascal to hold values for links. The pointer variable is used when a linked list is in *dynamic memory.* Dynamic memory is a portion of memory that the programmer may allocate with the **NEW** procedure, explained below. The value of the pointer variable corresponds with the memory location of a given data item.

The pointer variable allows the programmer to maintain pointers to physical memory locations of data items within lists linked in memory without having to be aware of the exact numeric addresses of those memory locations. By contrast, the physical locations of data items linked in an external file is straightforward. The programmer knows, for example, that the first record in the file is in record position zero and that the tenth record in the file is in record position nine.

However, when attempting to link data items residing in memory, the programmer often does not know, nor is there a reason to know, the actual physical memory locations of data items. A typical microcomputer may have 65,000 memory locations. The addresses of these memory locations are irrelevant, since the compiler associates variable names with data in corresponding memory locations. The programmer, then, need only refer to data items by variable names.

Pointer variables differ from other variables in a program. Variables are memory locations that contain data. A variable name, or identifier, is used in program text as if it were the particular data item. A pointer variable, on the other hand, is a memory location that contains the address of a particular data item. Of course, the content of a given pointer variable may be changed to contain some other memory address, just as values of other variables may be changed by program statements.

To access the data item pointed to by the pointer variable, then, it is necessary to use a syntax that indicates clearly that it is not the pointer to the data item that is being referred to, but the data item itself. This is done through use of the caret syntax (^). When referring to the data item in the location whose address is held in the pointer variable, the syntax is:

```
PointerVariableName^
```

The caret syntax must be used any time a pointer variable name is to be used to access a data item. When it refers to the actual memory address held in the pointer variable itself, the name of the pointer variable is used without the caret. The syntax without the caret is used only in operations in which the programmer desires to change the address held in the pointer variable or to compare the content of the pointer variable with other pointer values.

Pointer variables may point to data items of any type. A pointer is declared as pointing to a specific type of data. There is one exception: Pointer variables may not point to file variables. For example, a pointer may point to a data item of type INTEGER, REAL, or RECORD.

The form of the pointer variable declaration is:

```
VAR
 PointerVariableName:^SomeType;
```

Pointer declarations may occur in either the TYPE definition section or in the VARiable declaration section of the program.

For example, a list of integers that is to reside in memory may have pointers declared as follows:

```
VAR
 IntPointer:^INTEGER;
```

The fact that this pointer variable points to an integer data value somewhere in memory does not mean that the pointer variable itself is of type INTEGER. Basically, all pointers are addresses. Accordingly, the caret in the above declaration indicates that the type declaration relates to the data item pointed to, rather than to the value stored in the pointer variable itself.

Another example of a pointer variable declaration might be:

```
VAR
 StringPointer:^STRING;
```

The pointer variable occupies only enough memory to hold a value for a memory address. The fact that the pointer points to a STRING data value somewhere in memory has no bearing on the size of the memory portion allocated to the pointer variable itself.

The distinction between data names and pointer names. For a named data item, the compiler assigns a memory location (or sequence of locations) to hold the data item. References within the application program (such as to variable names) are translated to memory accesses using a pointer to the data item. Such pointers are internal and cannot be inspected easily or manipulated by the programmer.

The relationship between a pointer and its data is diagrammed in Figure 11-7. Pointers can swap values (addresses) with identically typed pointers.

The NEW procedure. As each variable is declared within a program, the compiler sets aside a certain amount of memory space to hold the values that are to be assigned to the variable name. Once all variables

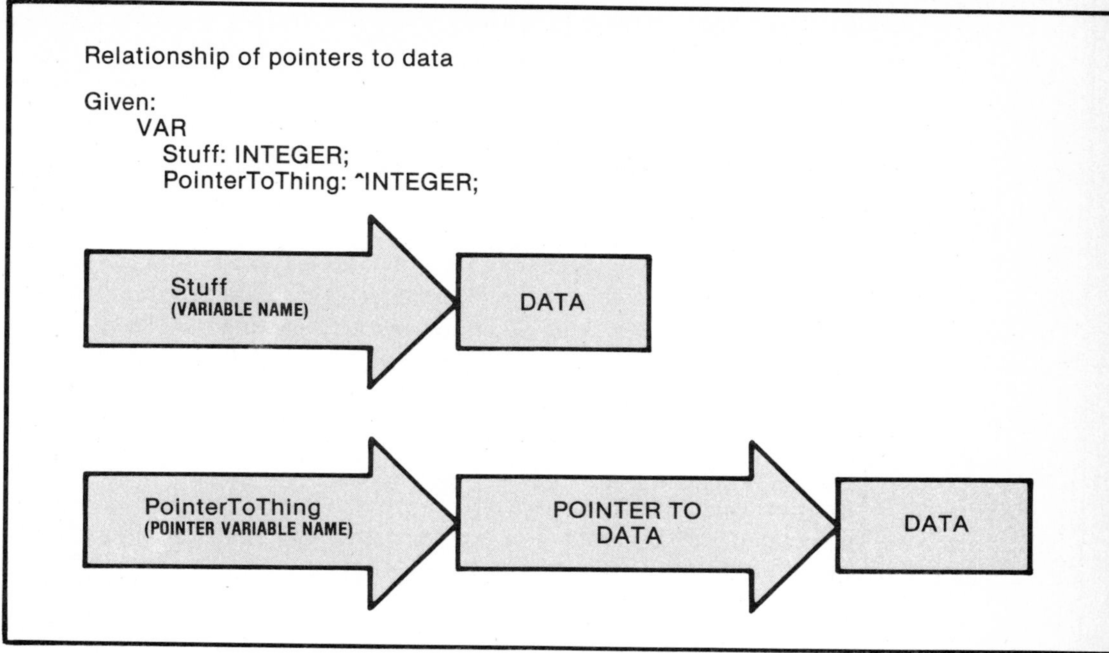

Figure 11-7. Pointers hold information on the location of a data item rather than the data item itself.

have been declared, the remaining unallocated memory space is used as temporary storage for operations carried out by the program. This unallocated memory is referred to as dynamic memory because space within it is allocated in dynamic, or constantly changing, fashion during program execution. The programmer may control the use of the dynamic portion of memory through the use of certain procedures that return pointers. These pointers are used to permit reference to the portions of memory that have been allocated for a given variable or data structure.

The declaration of a pointer variable assigns memory to hold the pointer but does not assign space for the corresponding data value. That is, no memory space allocation is made for the data—only for the pointer. Allocation of memory for the data referred to by a pointer variable must be done explicitly by the programmer and is accomplished by using the predeclared procedure NEW. The form of the procedure call is:

```
NEW(PointerVariableName);
```

No caret is used with the pointer variable name in the above statement. The pointer variable itself receives a value (address) from the procedure. When the NEW procedure is executed, the following actions are caused:

- An area of memory large enough to hold the type of data associated with the pointer variable, as defined in a previous pointer declaration, is set aside. For example, more memory space would be required for long string data than would be required for integers.
- The address, or beginning location, in memory set aside for the data then is stored in the pointer variable. The only information the programmer needs about the location of the data is the name of the pointer variable. Note particularly that no other variable name is associated with the data. The pointer is the only key to accessing such dynamically allocated data in program statements.

Implementing linked lists with pointer variables. Linked lists that are to reside in memory must group data items through use of the RECORD type, rather than by simple types. A record structure is required so that the data items and one or more pointers to other records in the list may be treated as a single group of associated items.

A type definition for a linked list is illustrated in this example:

```
TYPE

 ClientPointer = ^ClientList;

 ClientList = RECORD
  ClientName:STRING;
  ClientNumber:INTEGER;
  ClientPresident:STRING;
  AccountBalance:REAL;
  NextClient:ClientPointer;
 END;
```

Notice that the TYPE ClientPointer is defined as a pointer to the type ClientList. However, the type ClientList has not yet been defined in the program text. This is an exception allowed in Pascal for defining pointers to types before the types have been defined.

ClientList is the data type for the record structure containing client data. Each record of this type has the same format. The pointer field NextClient will be used to point to the next record in the list in some logical order. Memory space for ClientList is allocated through repeated use of the NEW procedure.

List maintenance for linked lists. As previously stated, multiple relationships may be maintained within the same group of data items in a linked list. List maintenance for linked lists is accomplished by updating the values of pointers to indicate additions, deletions, or changes to the list. In other words, the physical locations of data items do not change; only the values of pointers given within those data items change to maintain logical relationships or to disclose new ones.

Of course, maintaining a current linked list means linking each new entry into the list as it is entered. Values for all affected links in the list must be updated accordingly. This maintenance can require sophisticated techniques, depending on the number and complexity of logical relationships that must be maintained.

This complexity may be illustrated even with the relatively straightforward list given above containing records for Alpha Corporation, Beta Industries, Charlie's Cab Company, and Craft Sales. Suppose the user were to enter a new record for Apex Chemicals. In physical location, this new entry is merely added to the end of the list. In the series of alphabetical links, Apex would fall between Alpha Corporation and Beta Industries. However, the alphabetic pointer in the Alpha Corporation record currently points to Beta Industries. The alphabetic pointer in Alpha, then, must be updated to point to the location of the Apex Chemicals record. The value of the alphabetic pointer to Beta Industries must be assigned to the pointer in the Apex Chemicals record. Links must be updated for each logical relationship that is to be maintained in the file. Each new entry to the list must be linked into the list for each relationship desired, and the links in other records in the list updated.

A new entry to a linked list will fall into logical order, for any given relationship, at the beginning of the list, at the end, or somewhere within the list. Different maintenance techniques are required for each of these situations.

If a new entry falls in logical order at the beginning of the list, the pointer indicating the start of the list must be changed to point to the new entry. The pointer in the new entry must be set to the value corresponding with the position of the former first entry. All other links for this relationship in the list remain unchanged. A diagram illustrating these relationships is presented in Figure 11-8. Note that the reserved word **NIL** is used for the value of the pointer at the end-of-list.

If a new entry falls in logical order at the end of the list, the pointer in the former last item must be reassigned from NIL to the value of the physical location of the new entry. The value of the pointer in the new entry must be set to NIL. All other links for this relationship remain unchanged.

If a new entry falls in logical order somewhere within the list, the value of the pointer in the record that is to precede the current entry, or is lower in logical order, must be changed to point to the new entry. The former value of the preceding item's pointer must be reassigned to the pointer in the new entry. This is illustrated in Figure 11-9.

An example Pascal program that implements a linked list with pointer variables is presented in Figure 11-10. *LinkIt* also uses the NEW procedure for dynamic memory allocation. Note that the linked list has a "dummy" first entry that serves as the first entry pointer. A layout example of memory allocation created by *LinkIt* is presented in Figure 11-11. This layout assumes that the list starts at memory address 100 and that each entry has a length of 86 bytes.

TREES

Another important storage technique for logical ordering of data items is the tree. Trees enforce a hierarchical structure in a group of data items. By contrast, any given relationship within a linked list is linear; no hierarchy of items is implied other than the sequential order disclosed by the relationship.

Data items in a tree structure are related by *branching.* In a *binary tree,* each data item is connected to up to two other data items that, in turn, are connected to other data items, and so on. The resulting structure resembles a tree when represented in a diagram; however, data trees usually are drawn with the "base" of the tree at the top and branches "growing" downward. This is illustrated in Figure 11-12.

The base of the tree, at the top of the diagram, is referred to as its *root.* Points at which branches occur are known as *nodes.* The highest

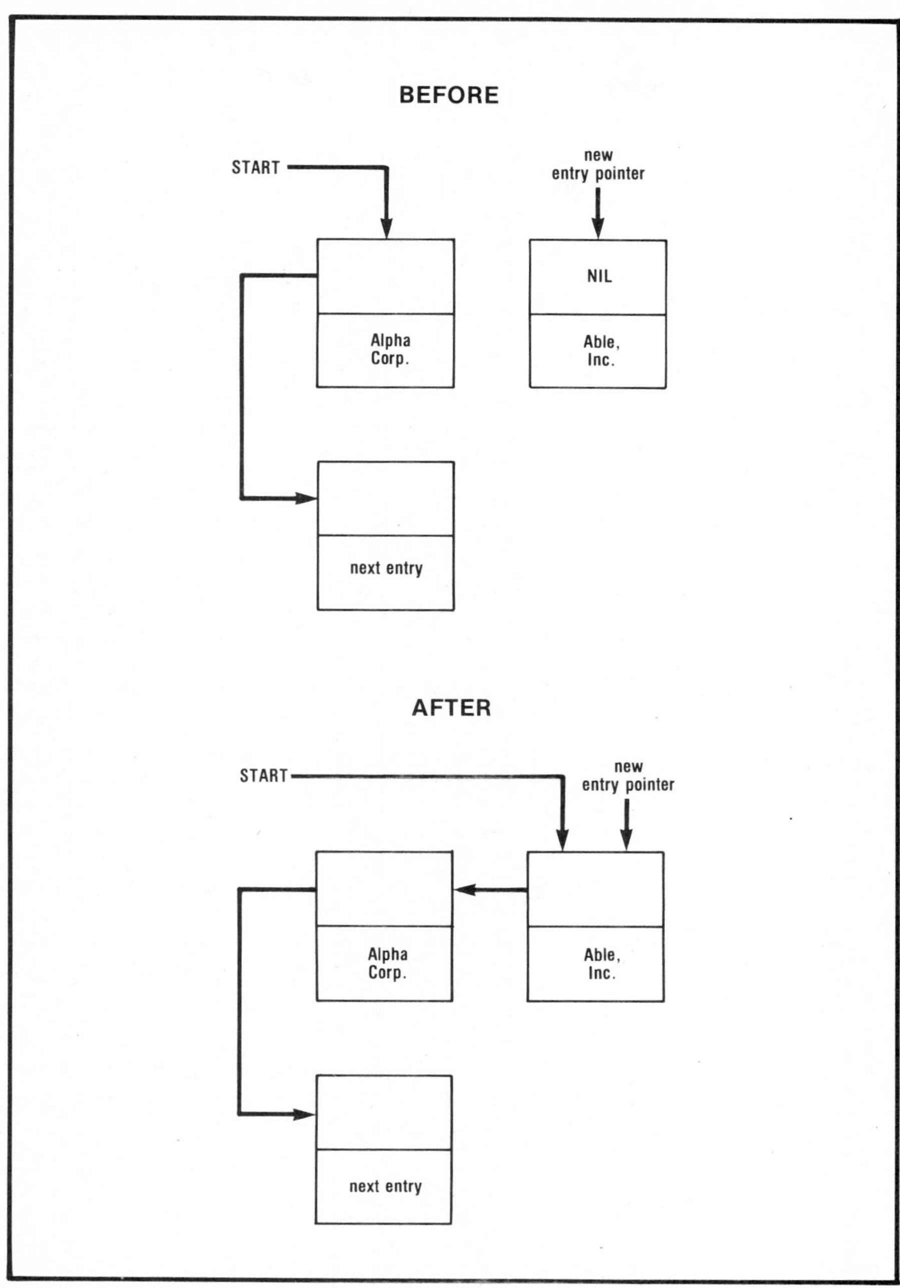

Figure 11-8. List maintenance for new item at beginning of linked list.

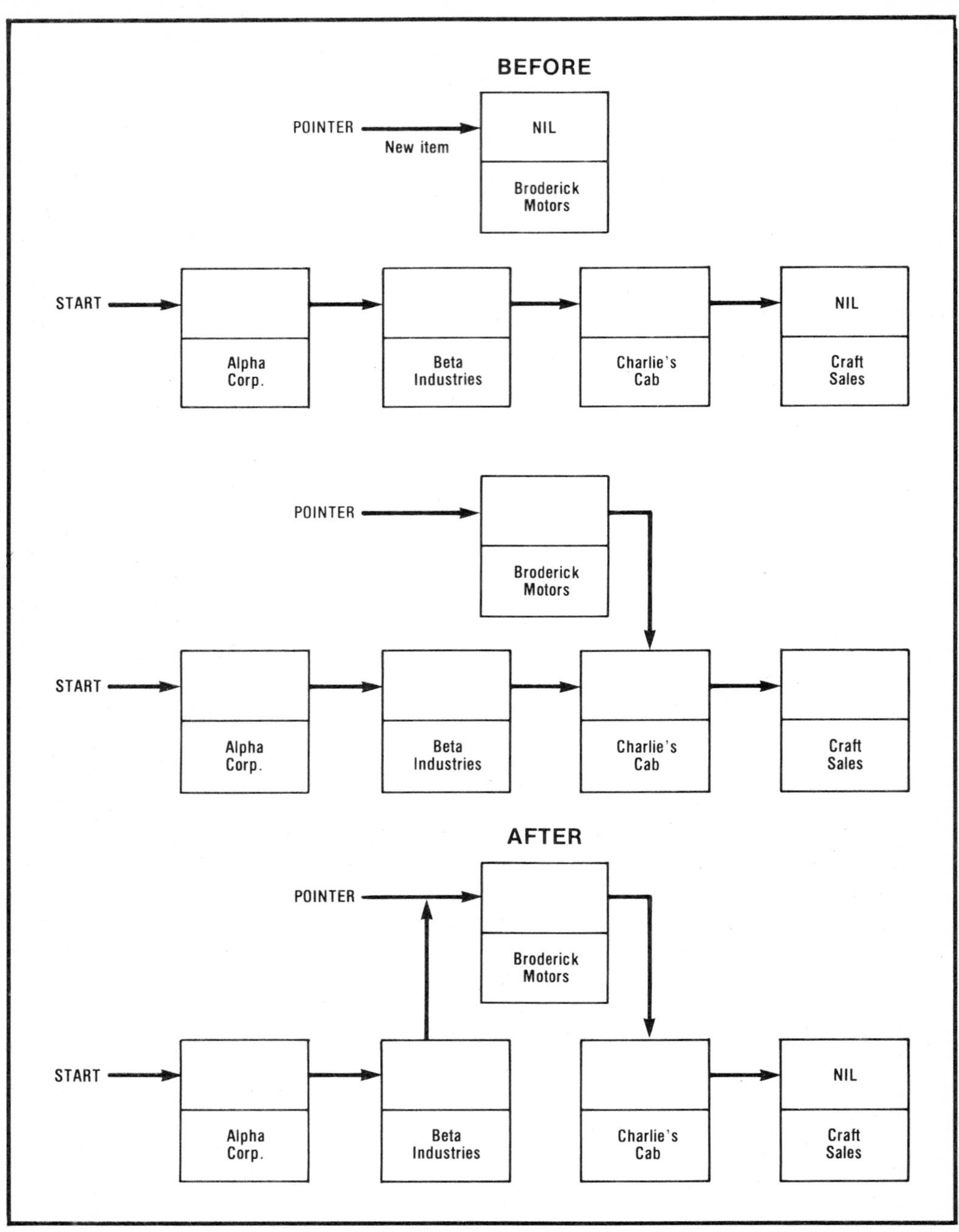

Figure 11-9. List maintenance for new data item in middle of linked list.

Figure 11-10. Program *LinkIt.* Note differences in coding style—all uppercase letters and use of braces syntax ({ }) for comments.

```
PROGRAM LINKIT;

TYPE

CLIENTREC = RECORD
 NAME:STRING;
 NUMBER:INTEGER;
 LINK:^CLIENTREC;
END;

VAR

START_OF_LIST,
NEXT,
CURRENT,
NEWENTRY:^CLIENTREC;             {POINTER VARIABLES FOR CLIENT RECORDS}
NEW_NAME:STRING;                 {TEMPORARY STORAGE FOR NEW CLIENT NAME}

PROCEDURE INIT_LIST;
BEGIN
 NEW(START_OF_LIST);             {FIRST GET A DUMMY ENTRY AT START-OF-LIST}
 WITH START_OF_LIST^ DO          {CLEAR VALUES}
  BEGIN
   NAME:='';                     {SET NAME TO NULL STRING}
   NUMBER:=0;                    {NUMBER TO ZERO}
   LINK:=NIL;                    {NO CURRENT LINK}
  END;
 END;

PROCEDURE LINK_NEW_ENTRY;
BEGIN
 CURRENT:=NIL;                        {START WITH DUMMY VALUE FOR CURRENT}
 NEXT:=START_OF_LIST;                 {SET NEXT TO START OF THE LIST}
 WHILE (NEXT <> NIL)                  {WHILE NOT AT END OF CHAIN...}
 AND (NEW_NAME > NEXT^.NAME) DO       {AND NAME POSITION NOT FOUND YET...}
  BEGIN
   CURRENT:=NEXT;                     {SAVE POINTER TO NEXT}
   NEXT:=NEXT^.LINK;                  {CHAIN TO THE NEXT ENTRY}
  END;
 NEW_ENTRY^.LINK:=NEXT;               {POINT NEW ENTRY TO NEXT}
 CURRENT^.LINK  :=NEW_ENTRY;          {POINT CURRENT TO NEW ENTRY}
END;

PROCEDURE ASK_NEW_ENTRY;
BEGIN
 WRITE('ENTER CLIENT NAME ');          {ASK FOR CLIENT NAME}
 READLN(NEW_NAME);                     {GET NAME INTO TEMP VARIABLE}
 IF NEW_NAME <> '' THEN                {IF VALID NAME THEN PROCESS:}
  BEGIN
   NEW(NEW_ENTRY);                     {ACQUIRE SPACE FOR NEW ENTRY}
   NEW_ENTRY^.NAME := NEW_NAME;        {SAVE NAME INTO NEW ENTRY}
   WRITE('ENTER CLIENT NUMBER ');      {ASK FOR CLIENT NUMBER}
   READLN(NEW_ENTRY^.NUMBER);          {READ CLIENT NUMBER INTO NEW ENTRY}
  END;
END;
```

```
PROCEDURE SHOW_CLIENTS;
BEGIN
 NEXT:=START_OF_LIST^.LINK;              {POINT TO FIRST ENTRY}
  WHILE NEXT <> NIL DO                   {IF NOT AT END OF LIST:}
   WITH NEXT^ DO
    BEGIN
     WRITELN(NUMBER:4,'  ',NAME);        {DISPLAY ENTRY}
     NEXT:=NEXT^.LINK;                   {GET POINTER TO NEXT}
    END;
 END;

BEGIN
 INIT_LIST;                              {INITIALIZE START_OF_LIST}
  REPEAT                                 {REPEAT UNTIL NAME IS NULL STRING}
   ASK_NEW_ENTRY;                        {GET A NEW ENTRY}
   IF NEW_NAME <> '' THEN                {IF VALID NAME THEN..}
    LINK_NEW_ENTRY;                      {LINK NEW ENTRY INTO LIST}
  UNTIL NEW_NAME = '';                   {DONE}
 SHOW_CLIENTS;                           {SHOW THE LIST}
 RELEASE(START_OF_LIST);                 {GIVE BACK MEMORY}
END.
```

Figure 11-10. (Conclusion)

MEMORY ADDRESS	CLIENT NAME	CLIENT NUMBER	ADDRESS LINK
100	<none>	<0>	358
186	Craft Sales	001	NIL
272	Beta Industries	002	444
358	Alpha Corp.	003	272
444	Charlie's Cab	004	186

StartOfList: 100

"DUMMY" FIRST ENTRY

Figure 11-11. Memory layout diagram for program *LinkIt.*

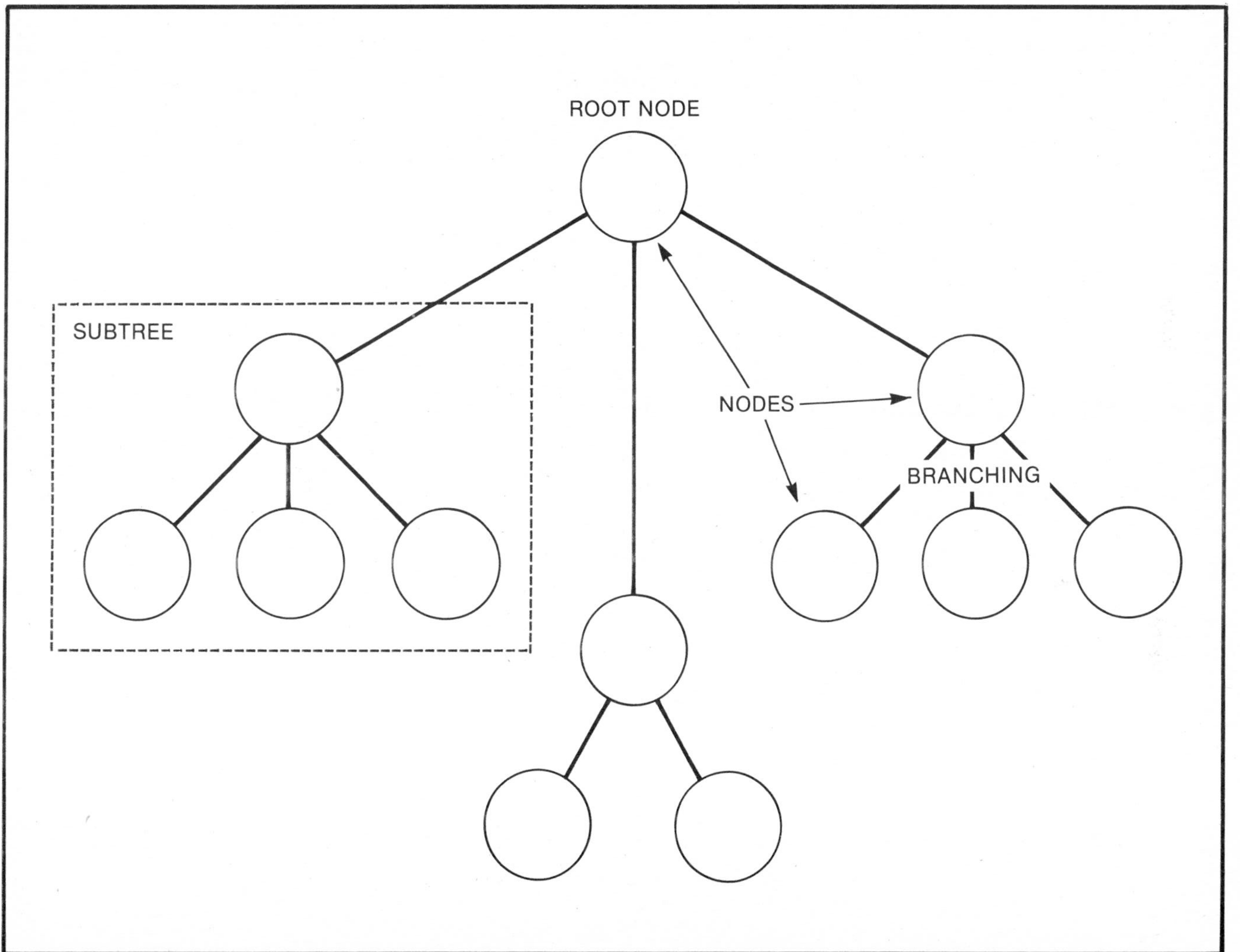

Figure 11-12. Data maintained in a tree structure.

entry in the hierarchy is called the *root node.* Groups of nodes below and connected to a given node are referred to as *subtrees.*

Tree structures are useful for storage of data items that have some inherent hierarchical relationship, as in the organizational relationships among company officers. Tree structures in which each node has branches leading to at most two nodes below it are binary trees. Such trees may be used to represent a series of Boolean comparisons that yield either true or false results. A program having yes/no responses might have data items corresponding with alternate answers stored in a tree structure.

The tree structure in Figure 11-13 shows how a linear relationship, the alphabetical order of a group of names, may be stored in a tree. Note that the alphabetic relationship between any given node and the other items in the list is maintained by the relationship between each node and the node above it. Further, each node must point to the two nodes beneath it.

To implement such a tree in program text, you define a record type that structures data items for each node, as well as pointers to establish the relationship of the node to the other nodes in the tree. For the example given in Figure 11-13, the pointers for each node might be named LeftNode and RightNode. LeftNode would indicate the location of the data item that precedes the node in logical order, and RightNode would indicate the location of the node that follows in logical order. This scheme would establish the alphabetical order desired.

By using pointers to the subtrees for each node, a tree may be implemented in much the same way as a linked list. The data items in the tree may reside as records in memory, with corresponding pointer variables to allocated memory space. Or, the tree may be maintained as a group of records in a file structure. Pointers, then, would identify record positions, as in linked lists.

DESIGN TRADE-OFFS

Factors that determine what structure should be used for storing a group of data items include:

- What logical order is required by later processing steps in the program or other programs that make use of the data?
- What output formats are required?

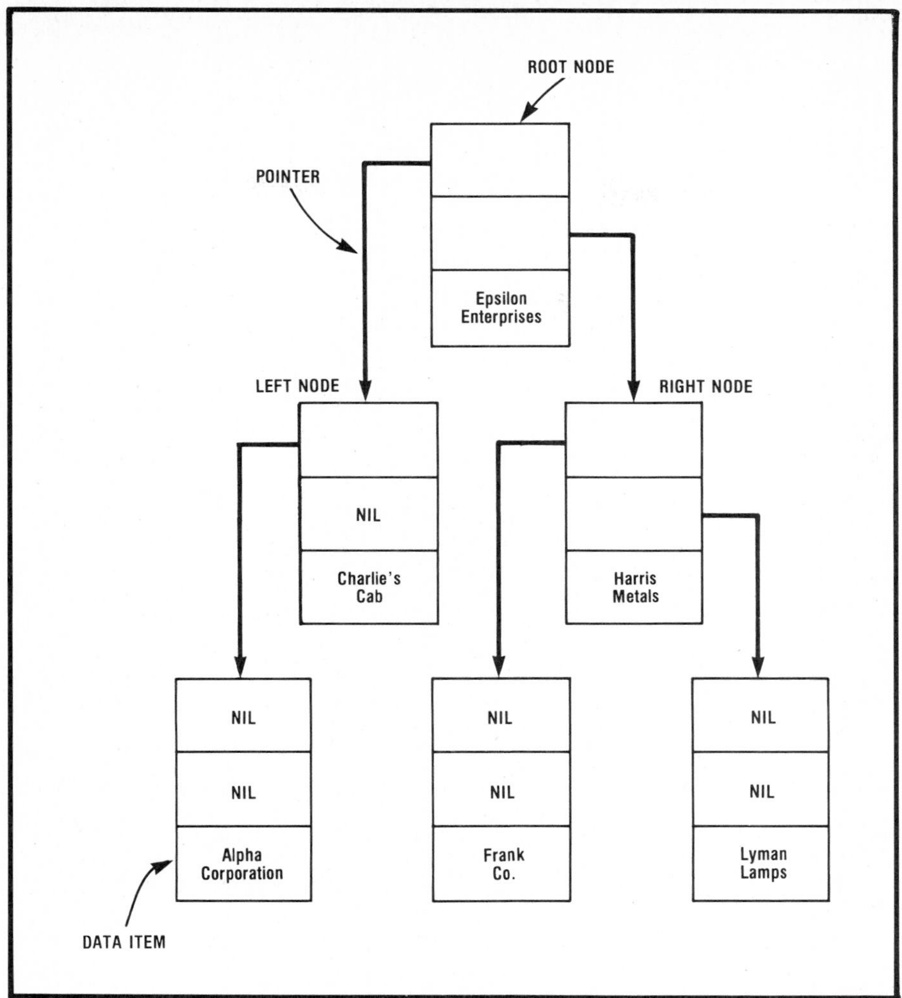

Figure 11-13. Data items in alphabetical order maintained in a tree structure through binary links.

- How much processing must be done to order the data for these formats?
- What is the impact on the program execution time and user interface if this processing is done at the time of input?
- What is the impact if the rearrangement is done just prior to main processing?
- What is the impact if the rearrangement is done during the output phase of the program?

Management of files, including techniques chosen for list maintenance, must take into account the following factors:

- What is the order of data items created by the input functions of data capture and storage?
- What is the order of data items that results from rearranging the items into a convenient structure?
- What order is implied by the need to extract data from the reordered list, as in generating a report?

Note that these three factors correspond with the three main logical phases of a program: input, processing, and output. Accordingly, the order of data items may change several times during program execution. Trade-offs of performing sort operations, for example, involve questions of how much processing time is required to reorder each item, and at what processing phase it is most efficient (or least disruptive) to use that time.

One of the most important considerations in designing a program that must manage data is the evaluation of the trade-off between the difficulty of maintaining a list and the difficulty of retrieving information from that list. You may choose a straightforward maintenance scheme in which items are added to the end of a list on input. It becomes a significant programming task, then, to rearrange the list into some logical order.

As discussed previously, rearranging data items may be accomplished by sorting. The processing time that may be required to perform a sort is an important factor in determining how lists are to be structured initially and how those lists will be maintained.

For example, sorting check records into check number order is apt to be time-consuming. It would be possible to perform this processing on input, testing the record key for each check to determine its relation to previously stored records and saving the record only when the correct logical order is known. Such an approach would be justified if the user inputs a few checks on an occasional basis. If, however, the user will input hundreds or thousands of checks, insertion-in-order, or preordering, on input is not practical. Input would be slow and tedious. In this situation, it would be preferable to save the check records in chronological order of input, then perform the sorting in a batch operation on the entire file after all inputs have been entered.

EXTRACTING USEFUL INFORMATION FROM LISTS

Reports derived from lists or trees may require either summary information or specific information. Specific data must be extracted from the list and saved or output. If summary information is required, only the relevant data needed to derive the summary are selected, and the summary itself is saved or output.

The consideration of whether summary or detailed data are required helps determine how a list is maintained and what method is used to extract data from the list. Methods used to locate and extract data from lists are search techniques.

If the source data used to generate a report reside on an external file in some order that differs from the report order, data extracted from the file for output or for deriving summaries must be held in memory or in temporary files until results can be displayed. If, on the other hand, source data are stored in the order in which the data are required for output, the required data items may be accessed in sequence and displayed immediately. This straightforward method eliminates the need to hold intermediate results in memory or in secondary storage and is useful especially on microcomputers that have limited memory and diskette space for temporary storage of report lists.

A sequential list may be accessed in sequence for this purpose, or a linked list may be accessed in the order indicated by the links. A tree may be accessed by following the steps in the hierarchy in the order required to disclose a particular relationship.

For situations in which the required data cannot be accessed in order without performing intermediate processing steps, some form of sublist first must be derived from the source list. For example, a report might be a listing of account balances for all clients in a given sales territory. The master client list must be searched first for all clients in the particular sales territory. Then, that sublist must be saved and processing must be performed on it to produce the listing for the report. If the number of client records to be produced in the sublist is relatively small, the entire list may be held in memory during program execution. However, a longer list requires a separate external file to hold the records that are extracted by the search.

In some cases, the size of the sublist may not be predictable. Saving the sublist to a file would be the safest approach to avoid the possibility of running out of memory during program execution. The decision to hold an intermediate list in memory or save it to a temporary file depends on the anticipated size of the list.

SEARCH TECHNIQUES

The particular technique used for a search within a list depends on how that list is ordered. Another consideration, of course, is what information is needed from the list. Search techniques include:

- Linear search
- Linked search
- Binary search.

Linear Search

In a *linear search,* each data item in the list is accessed and examined individually, beginning with the item in the first physical location in the list and proceeding serially to the last physical item. This approach may scan an entire file. If summary information to be produced must include data from each record in the file, a linear search may be as effective as any other. However, if specific data must be extracted from selected records in the file, a linear search begins to resemble the task of "looking for a needle in a haystack," since there is no way of predicting where in the file the desired data may be found. A linear search is appropriate if any of the following hold true:

- The file to be searched is relatively small.
- Only summary information is required.
- The sequence of processing corresponds with the order of a sequential access file.
- The ordering of records in the file to be searched is unpredictable.

Linked Search

A *linked search* is similar to a linear search, except that it is performed in the logical order indicated by the links in each record rather than in physical order. Accordingly, the speed and efficiency of a linked search is comparable to that of a linear search, with only slight additional overhead required to locate each record from its indicated link.

Binary Search

Files that have a known physical order, such as sequential files, may be accessed by *binary search*. In such cases, binary search is far faster and more efficient than linear search.

Since the items in the list or file exist in some order, an estimate may be made about where in the list the desired item is located. Alternatively, the midpoint of the list may be chosen as a default. Then, the list is sampled at the estimated position. The value of the data item stored at that position is tested against the value desired. If the sampled item is equal to the value desired, the search is over. If not, one of two conditions must exist: The desired item is lower in order in the list, or it is higher. The value of the sampled item should indicate the relative position of the desired item.

Based on this information, another estimate is made for the probable position of the desired item in the list. The estimate may correspond to the midpoint between the current position in the list and the beginning or ending positions in the list, depending on which position is estimated to be closer to the desired item. The data item at the new estimated position is then sampled, and a revised estimate is made based on the value obtained.

The search is said to be binary because a decision is made at each estimated position whether to search either higher or lower in the list order to find the desired item. The range of possible positions to be searched decreases with each new estimate, until the desired item is found. Binary search is basically a process of successive partitioning of the list into smaller and smaller lists until the target is found.

For example, suppose a file contains 100 client records, ordered alphabetically by client name. It is known, then, that the first record contains a field for client name whose string value is closest to 'A'. The last record has a client name string value that is closest to 'Z'. If the record to be searched is Matthew Scientific Corporation, an estimated position for this record within the list might be at record position 50. If record 50 is sampled and the value of the string in the client name field is Tyler Marine Development, it becomes apparent that the desired record position must fall in the range of record positions 0 to 49, since Matthew is lower in alphabetic order than Tyler.

Accordingly, an estimate is made at the midpoint of this range, at record position 24. Sampling this record, the client name field yields Dixie Products. The desired record must, therefore, fall in the range of record positions 25 to 49. Again, the midpoint of the range, this time 37, is sampled, and the client field contains Martin Investments. The possible range now has been narrowed to record positions 38 to 49. Sampling at record position 43, the value is Norbert Chemical. The range narrows to record positions 39 to 42. The desired record, in this case, is found at the next midpoint, record position 40.

In this example, the desired record is found in accessing the file only five times. If a linear search had been performed, the record Matthew Scientific Corporation, at record position 40, would have been found on the forty-first attempt.

A binary search is extremely efficient in finding specified entries in large, ordered files. The maximum number of samples is bounded by:

$$\log_2 N$$

This expression represents the base-2 logarithm of the number of entries to be searched. For example, a given entry may be found in a file of a million records in approximately 19 attempts, on the average. A linear search, on the other hand, requires a number of attempts that averages half the number of records in the file. Therefore, a linear search of a file of a million records would have to sample approximately 500,000 records before finding the desired entry.

The necessity of maintaining the source list in logical order may outweigh the advantages gained in a binary search technique. This is the principal trade-off that must be examined when considering application of a binary search.

No counterpart exists for performing binary searches in linked lists, since no convenient means exists to determine where a midpoint record position would be. Each pointer would have to be sampled in a linked search to disclose the order of the list.

Directory Files

The above search techniques may be used either in lists in memory or in external files. Files, however, may contain far greater amounts of data than lists in memory. Additionally, the relationships among linked records in a file may be quite complex. The size and complexity of a file may require not only that the file be maintained in a logical order—through linking or sorting—but also that a separate, smaller, directory file be maintained. The directory file exists solely to make the process of searching the larger file more efficient.

Directory files may contain an entry for the pointer to the first record in each relation in the linked file. Accessing the directory file is the first step in a linked search to find the starting point for a given logical order. Once the location of the first record in the relation is found in the directory file, accessing the pointer in each record in the linked file yields the next record in the relation, and so on.

For example, a directory file for a linked client list might have three entries that point to the first records in three separate relations: alphabetical order of client name, client number order, and alphabetical order of company president name. However, if a list of employees for each client also is maintained in a linked file, the corresponding directory would contain an entry for each client. Each client entry in the directory would be a pointer to the first employee record for that client in the linked file. Pointers within employee entries in the linked file would maintain the logical order of employee entries. This form of linked list is a simplified example of a *relational database.*

Relational Databases

A relational database is a collection of files or data structures that have internal links as well as external links to other files or data structures. *Database management* software is designed to allow the user to specify new relations among items in the database and to access those items according to the relations so defined. The physical location of items in the database remains unchanged. With database techniques, it is possible to maintain multiple logical orders, or relations, among data items from what amounts to a single physical list. Several file access techniques may be applied by the database management software to access the data, depending upon the relationships required by the user.

Database techniques can be sophisticated and are beyond the scope of this book. However, you should be aware that packaged database management software is available for microcomputers, and it is almost certain that you will encounter these techniques in a practical programming environment.

SEARCH TECHNIQUE TRADE-OFFS

Generally, file structures fall into these broad categories:

- Random files
- Sorted files
- Hashed files
- Linked files.

The best, or fastest and most efficient, file search technique depends on the structure of the file to be searched and the specific data desired.

Random Files

Random files consist of records in unpredictable order. The only feasible search technique in such a file is the linear search. As stated above, a linear search requires an average number of attempts equal to half the total number of records in the file.

Sorted Files

Sorted files are sequential access files. Processing has been performed on the data items in the file so that their physical order coincides with the logical order required for the kind of search to be done. Binary searches are highly efficient in this kind of file. Frequently, it is worth the additional processing to sort a file into sequential order so that binary searches may be used. In some cases, linear searches are performed on sorted files if the order of the search corresponds with the logical order of the data.

A special case of the sorted file has not yet been discussed. In what may be thought of as a *preordered file,* a certain fixed number of record positions is allocated according to some anticipated number of total entries. The actual number of total entries may not be known. As each new record is entered, that record is placed in its correct physical location within the file. Other locations contain no information, or invalid information, as a placeholder. Such a file always may be processed in sequential fashion or by direct access to a given location, even though a complete set of records may not yet exist.

For example, a client list may be anticipated to have a maximum of 1,000 entries. If the list were to be maintained in numerical order by client number, possible client record positions would range from 0 to 999.

Client numbers could correspond with these record positions. As each new client is assigned, the corresponding record would be entered at the corresponding numeric position in the list. Deletions from the list are straightforward, since there is no need to fill every position in the list. The number of the deleted entry would contain no record.

Accordingly, such ordered lists are relatively easy to maintain. However, some difficulty may arise in reasonably anticipating the total number of entries that will be made.

A frequent use of this kind of ordered file is to facilitate a correspondence between the order of entries and the physical location or memory address. This principle is used in creating hashed files.

Hashed Files

Hashed files are constructed in similar fashion to preordered files. The location of a record within a hashed file is specified by a *hash code.* Lists in memory may be handled in similar fashion through the use of *hash coded addresses.* A hash code is a way of deriving record position from actual data being sought.

For example, a client list may have 1,000 physical entries, but the range of client numbers for those clients may be from 1 to 10,000. A hash code for deriving the record position of a given client from the corresponding client number might be to divide the client number by 1,000 and use the remainder of that division as the record location. However, in the range of client numbers from 1 to 10,000, there are 10 client numbers that yield the same remainders and, hence, have the same hash code. This situation is known as a *collision,* and records with duplicate hashed addresses are called *synonyms.* In such cases, the hash code is used as a starting point, and a linear search is conducted from that point to locate the desired record. A hash code, therefore, must be thought of as an approximation of the desired record location.

A hashed file usually contains more record positions than actual entries. To insert a new item into a hashed file, the hash code is derived from the appropriate data item in the entry and the result put in memory. The value of the hash code then is used as a pointer into the file. The position indicated by that pointer then is accessed. If the position is empty or contains invalid data, the new entry is placed there. If a valid record already exists at that position, a linear search is conducted to find the next available record position and the entry is placed there.

A *hash search* is conducted in a hashed file by first deriving the hash code from the data item desired. In the previous example, if the record for client number 7,989 must be accessed, the hash code is derived by dividing 7,989 by 1,000 and using the remainder, 989. The file is accessed at record position 989, and if the client number field in the record at that position does not equal 7,989, a linear search is begun at record position 990 and continues until the desired record is found or until all records have been searched.

A complication of hashed files is that entries can be "clustered" in a certain series of record locations. Extensive linear searches may be required to access these records, since the hash code is only an approximation of the record location, and new entries that have hash codes that collide with those records must be placed at the end of the group. If the group is large, the actual location of the new entry may be quite different from the location derived from the hash code.

In such cases, some other means of deriving the hash code may be necessary. One solution may be to use a prime number that is less than the number of entries as a divisor, since dividing by prime numbers tends to yield a more random result and, hence, is less likely to generate collisions.

Names, or alphabetic data, also may be used as keys for deriving hash codes. If, for example, the letters of the alphabet were made to correspond with numeric values 1 to 26, a numerical hash code could be derived from alphabetic string data.

Note that, when conducting a linear search from a hash code address, it is possible to encounter the end-of-file without having found the desired record. In such cases, it is necessary to resume the search at the beginning of the file. The search must be continued from the beginning of the file up to the original hash code position. Only in this way is it possible to be sure that a given item is not included in the list.

Linked Files

A *linked file* has one or more relationships disclosed by pointers embedded in each record. A linked search is most appropriate when searching the file in logical order. As previously stated, binary searches cannot be performed in linked files. Searching linked files is made more efficient by the existence of a separate directory file that corresponds with the linked file.

Summary

File processing typically involves creation of transaction files from temporary serial files or input data followed by the posting of transaction data to master files. The structure of transaction files often is chronological. Master files must be maintained in some logical order.

File structures may take the form of lists or trees. Rearrangement of data is accomplished by sorting. Implementing sorts may involve tradeoffs of processing efficiency with the ease of maintaining the list order.

Four sorting methods are: selection in order, bubble sort, sift, and Shell's sort. The efficiency of a sort is determined by the length of the list to be sorted and whether the list is far out of the desired order.

Ordered lists that are combined are said to be merged.

A list is a group of data items. Forms that lists may take include: serial, or unstructured, lists; sequential, or ordered, lists; and linked lists. Lists may be held in memory during processing or maintained permanently as files.

A list may be a sequential arrangement of data items. This kind of list implies some logical order, as in the sequential access file.

Processing done to preserve the logical order of a list is known as list maintenance.

A given data item that may be searched to find a related group of data items is known as a key. Linked lists do not depend on the physical order of data items to determine structure. A link, or pointer, is information added to a data record that discloses its relationship to other data items. The pointer is numeric information that corresponds with the physical location of the next data item in the list in some logical order.

When data items residing in dynamically allocated memory are linked, the pointer contains a value corresponding with a memory address for the next item. When data items are stored as files, the pointer contains a value for the record number within the file of the next data item.

For lists residing in memory, Pascal allows numeric values for links to be stored as pointer variables. The pointer variable holds a value corresponding with memory location of a data item, and not the value of the data item itself.

The programmer may control the use of unallocated, or dynamic, memory through the use of pointers. Allocation of memory for this purpose is accomplished in Pascal by the predefined procedure NEW.

Linked lists that will reside in memory must group data items through use of the RECORD type, rather than by simple types. List maintenance for linked lists is accomplished by updating the values of pointers to indicate additions, deletions, or changes to the list.

Trees enforce a hierarchical structure on a group of data items. Tree structures in which each node has branches leading to, at most, two nodes below it are binary trees.

One of the most important considerations in designing a program is an evaluation of the trade-off between the difficulty of maintaining a list of data versus the difficulty of retrieving information from that list.

The particular technique used for a search within a list will depend on how that list is ordered. Another consideration is what information is needed from the list. Search techniques include: linear search, linked search, and binary search.

File structures include: random files, sorted files, preordered files, hashed files, and linked files.

Review Questions

1. Under what circumstances must data be rearranged?
2. What design considerations are involved in processing groups of data items?
3. What are some sorting methods, and what trade-offs exist with each?
4. What are lists, and what specific structures may lists have?
5. What is meant by list maintenance, and why is this function important with regard to ordered lists?
6. What is the function of pointers in linked lists?
7. How does the access method of linked lists in memory differ from that used for linked lists stored as files?
8. What is the form of the pointer variable declaration in Pascal, and how is this declaration used?

9. What is the form of a tree structure, and what applications may be implemented by trees?
10. What factors determine the structure to be used for storing a group of data items?
11. What factors may be considered in choosing techniques for list maintenance?
12. What important trade-off exists in maintaining an ordered list?
13. What are some techniques for searching a list, and what are the characteristics of each?

Pascal Practice

1. Enter and compile the example procedures BubbleSort, Sift, and ShellSort as separate programs. Remember that program headers and variable declarations must be included. Include in each program an input section that reads in data items to be sorted from an external file and places them in an array. Set up file names and array names so that the same file may be input to either program. Create two test data files of 25 records each. These files should contain, as record keys, individual alphabetic characters that are to be sorted in alphabetic order. The first test file should be almost in order. The second test file should be in almost completely inverted order.
2. Add WRITE statements to the programs that print intermediate results as shown in Figures 11-1, 11-2, and 11-3. These output statements will allow you to inspect what is happening to the list as each sort progresses.
3. Execute the programs you have written by inputting the two test data files to each program. Time each execution and keep a written record of each trial. Write a narrative that compares the results obtained from executing the three sorting techniques.
4. Write a program that implements a tree structure to alphabetize a list of names. Assume that the names are entered one at a time from the keyboard and are placed immediately on the tree. In addition, write a procedure to list the names in alphabetical order and reverse alphabetical order from the tree.

Key Terms

1. transaction file
2. detail file
3. master file
4. posted
5. audit trail
6. extracted
7. batch
8. list
9. tree
10. key
11. selection in order
12. record key
13. bubble sort
14. standard exchange method
15. sift
16. shuttle sort
17. linear insertion with exchange
18. Shell's sort
19. gap
20. merge
21. serial list
22. extract
23. sequential list
24. list maintenance
25. pointer
26. link
27. linked list
28. directory file
29. overhead
30. double link
31. pointer variable
32. dynamic memory
33. branching
34. binary tree
35. root
36. root node
37. node
38. subtree
39. linear search
40. linked search
41. binary search
42. relational database
43. database management
44. random file
45. sorted file
46. preordered file
47. hashed file
48. hash code
49. hash coded address
50. collision
51. synonym
52. hash search
53. linked file

Pascal Library

1. NIL
2. NEW

12 APPLYING LIST MANAGEMENT

OBJECTIVES

On completing the reading and other learning assignments for this chapter, you should be able to:

- ☐ Describe how list maintenance techniques such as sorting and list updating may be applied in program text.
- ☐ Tell how alternative orders for sorting may be implemented.
- ☐ Explain the impact list maintenance may have on physical file structures.
- ☐ Use correctly the Pascal function ORDinal.

PROGRAM DESIGN FOR LIST MANAGEMENT

The core of this chapter is a case study that builds further on the previous example programs. Chapter 10 presents the program *Account-Management,* which provides for the entry of transaction records and the maintenance of separate external files for transaction data and for summaries.

The previous program allowed two entry types—Debit and Credit. With this information, cash balances for each account may be determined. However, this information does not present a complete picture of a company's cash position. To manage cash flow within a business, it is also important to know what amounts have been invoiced but remain unpaid. These outstanding balances, or receivables, provide a basis for decisions on extension of further credit to customers, possible account collection actions, amount and timing of borrowing from banks, the amount of assets to be presented on the balance sheet, and so on.

In the *AccountsReceivable* program, a new entry TYPE, Rcvbl, has been added to accommodate entry of receivables, or outstanding invoices. The user now is able to enter these items along with Debit and Credit entries. A summary list for receivables is added to the records maintained within InfoFile.

The previous program allows records to be built up in serial fashion, chronologically by time of data entry. However, if the lists of entries for each account are to be useful on a long-term basis, some list maintenance features must be added. In particular, the program provides for:

- Deletion of entries
- Sorting of entries.

Deletion of entries. The previous program has no provision for deleting entries that are erroneous or no longer needed. Accordingly, new records may be added, but no real list maintenance can be performed because deletion is not provided. Specifically, deletion of entries would be necessary when an account is dropped or at the year-end to remove entries that are no longer needed or are saved elsewhere. Also, now that items may represent receivables, these entries will have to be deleted and summaries recalculated when the corresponding payments are received.

For the updating of summary totals for receivables, *AccountsReceivable* has a feature for automatically *decrementing* receivables and posting credits. This feature is implemented in a revised version of the procedure MakeAccountEntries. When a Credit is entered that is not categorized as MISCELLANEOUS, the program assumes that the amount is a credit against one of the receivables entered previously. In such cases, the program adds two entries to the master account file: The first entry is the usual credit posting, and the second is the credit amount—with a negative value assigned and its TYPE changed to Rcvbl. Adding this second entry to the outstanding receivable totals has the effect of decrementing, or reducing, the outstanding balance for receivables automatically as credits are entered.

The procedure that implements user selections for deletion of entries is DeleteAccountEntries. File processing begins with the first record in the file and proceeds sequentially. For each record, the user is prompted by calling the function Yes with the argument 'DELETE THIS ENTRY'. If the user's response is N (No), meaning that the record is to be retained, the record is placed at the first available position in the file. Records that are designated to be deleted will have their record positions overwritten by records that are to be saved. Finally, when the file is closed with the CRUNCH option, a new end-of-file is designated, thus *compacting* the file if any deletions were made.

Before each record is saved, its Totals (held in an array by category) are accumulated in a global array Totals, thus updating summary information while excluding items that have been deleted.

Sorting of entries. In this version of the program, the user is given the ability to sort the items in the master account file according to any one of three possible orders: by entry type, by user-defined comments, or by date. The basic reason for sorting is for the convenience of the user in performing file access. No specific processing efficiencies have been sought within the program. Note, however, that the procedures Delete-AccountEntries and ShowAccountEntries begin by seeking the first record in the file, and processing is sequential from that point. Clearly, the physical order of records in the file will determine how quickly a given record may be found.

Sorting by entry type means grouping records by data types Debit, Credit, or Rcvbl. An enumeration type TransType is defined for such entries:

```
TYPE
 TransType = (Debit, Credit, Rcvbl);
```

This enumeration establishes a scalar relationship such that Debit is lower in order than Credit, which is lower in order than Rcvbl. This ordering may be used to perform logical comparisons within a sort.

The entry record definition includes:

```
EntryRec = RECORD
 EntryType : TransType;
 ..
END;
```

Thus, the procedure SortFile, using a form of Shell's sort, is able to compare two records (represented by the local variables A and B) and perform swaps based on entry types by making the following comparison:

```
CASE
 EnType : Swap := (A.EntryType > B.EntryType);
 ..
END;
```

Sorting records by EntryType, then, will cause a list to be created with debits ordered first, followed by credits, then by receivables. Note that no ordering within these groupings is created by SortFile.

Sorting by comment depends upon what kinds of comments the user has entered for each record. The record definition contains a Comment field that may contain up to 20 characters, which is unchanged from the previous program:

```
EntryRec = RECORD
 Comment : STRING[20];
 ..
 END;
```

Using the Comment field as a key in the sort results in records ordered alphabetically by Comment. This order is determined by the following statement in the SortFile procedure:

```
CASE
 Comment : Swap := (A.Comment > B.Comment);
 ..
END;
```

Sorting by date uses the Date field within EntryRec as the key:

```
EntryRec = RECORD
 Date : mmddyy;
 ..
END;
```

Recall from the previous program that the Date field is itself a record:

```
mmddyy = RECORD
 mm,
 dd,
 yy : INTEGER;
END;
```

The SortFile procedure causes records to be ordered chronologically, or from the lowest ordered date to the highest ordered date:

```
CASE
 Date : Swap := (A.Date.yy > B.Date.yy)
            OR ((A.Date.yy = B.Date.yy)
            AND (A.Date.mm > B.Date.mm))
            OR ((A.Date.yy  =  B.Date.yy)
            AND (A.Date.mm  =  B.Date.mm)
            AND (A.Date.dd > B.Date.dd));
 ..
END;
```

Maintaining the master file in chronological order, of course, would facilitate the deletion of old entries, since these records would be encountered in the lower file positions.

THE ORDinal FUNCTION

AccountsReceivable uses the predefined function **ORD**inal, which returns the *ordinal* value of a given scalar variable or constant, or its numeric position in an ordered sequence. In other words, the ordinal value of a scalar data item is its position within the set of all possible values for that scalar type. For example, given the set of months of the year, the ordinal value of the month September is 9. ORD may be used, for example, to return the numeric equivalents of the ASCII charaters '0' through '9':

```
VAR
 CharValue : CHAR;
 IntValue : INTEGER;
BEGIN
 CharValue := '8';
 IntValue := ORD(CharValue) - ORD('0');
END;
```

The INTEGER value returned to IntValue would be 8. The CHAR constant '8' is held in CharValue as a character and must be converted to a numeric value before arithmetic operations can be performed on it. These operations include subtracting the ORD value of ASCII '0' to produce a decimal value. Note that the sequence of operations above is equivalent to:

```
IntValue := ORD('8')  - ORD('0');
```

The ORD functions return integer values of ASCII 56 and ASCII 48, respectively; and subtracting 48 from 56 equals 8.

The ORD function is used in the program within a coined function Val, which converts strings of ASCII numeric characters to a single INTEGER value. The Val function allows the user's numeric responses to be input to and held in a STRING variable, thus avoiding errors caused by entry of nonnumeric values. The practical effect is that a form of input editing is applied:

```
FUNCTION Val(S: STRING): INTEGER;
VAR
 Index,
 Answer: INTEGER;
BEGIN
 Answer := 0;                              (* start with zero in case *)
 IF S <> '' THEN                          (* string must not be empty *)
  FOR Index := 1 TO LENGTH(S) DO               (* loop through string *)
   IF S[Index] IN ['0'..'9'] THEN    (* if character is an ASCII number, *)
    Answer := Answer * 10            (* shift digit to next column left; *)
            + ORD(S[Index])               (* add value of ASCII number; *)
            - ORD('0');                 (* subtract ASCII number offset; *)
  Val := Answer;                      (* set function variable to result *)
END;
```

Note that if the input string is empty or contains nonnumeric values, a value of 0 is returned for Val. Note that no provision is made for a minus sign (–), which would denote negative values.

The Val function is invoked by the revised function AskChoice, which passes the argument AnsString to Val's parameter S:

```
FUNCTION AskChoice(X,Y:INTEGER;Q:STRING;Min,Max:INTEGER):INTEGER;
VAR
 Answer:INTEGER;
 AnsString:STRING;                         (* user input may be a string *)
BEGIN
 REPEAT
  GOTOXY(X,Y);
  WRITE(Q,' (',Min,'..',Max,') ');          (* ask question; show range *)
  READLN(AnsString);
  Answer := Val(AnsString);           (* convert user's string to integer *)
                                   (* using previously defined Val function *)
 UNTIL (Answer >= Min) AND (Answer <= Max);      (* repeat until in range *)
 AskChoice := Answer;
END;
```

AskChoice displays the question Q and prompts a range of responses (Min . . Max). The user's response is stored as a STRING value in AnsString, which is passed to Val and converted to an INTEGER value.

For example, within the procedure GetAcctEntry, the function AskChoice is invoked to get an entry number (0 . . 9999) and the date:

```
Number := AskChoice(0,4,'ENTRY NUMBER',0,9999);            (* ask number *)
   WITH Date DO
    BEGIN
     mm := AskChoice(9,11,'MONTH',1,12);              (* pass parameters *)
     dd := AskChoice(11,12,'DAY',1,31);            (* note restrictions on *)
     yy := AskChoice(9,13,'YEAR',80,99);               (* possible values *)
    END;
```

PROGRAM *AccountsReceivable*

Program text for *AccountsReceivable* is presented in Figure 12-1. Shaded areas represent portions of the program that have been carried over from *AccountManagement*.

Figure 12-1. Program *AccountsReceivable*.

```
                            ( * NOTE:  Program text areas carried over
                                   from AccountManagement are shaded. *)

PROGRAM AccountsReceivable;
CONST
 MaximumCateg = 10;          (* maximum number of debit/credit categories *)

TYPE
 CategArray = ARRAY[0..MaximumCateg] OF STRING;          (* category names *)
 ReportChoices = (Sum,Percent,BarGraph);          (* report format choices *)

(*  establish a RECORD type for dates *)

mmddyy = RECORD
 mm,                                                             (* month *)
 dd,                                                               (* day *)
 yy:INTEGER;                                                      (* year *)
END;

(* establish enumeration type that defines DEBIT and CREDIT as data values *)
(* also a new type Rcvbl for receivables *)
TransType = (Debit, Credit, Rcvbl);
OrderType = (EnType, Comment, Date);      (* types for defining sort order *)

(* define a subrange value to hold category code values *)

CodeType = 0..MaximumCateg;

(* define a RECORD type to hold the data for each entry in the master file *)

EntryRec = RECORD
 EntryType: TransType;               (* type includes Debit, Credit, Rcvbl *)
 EntryCode:CodeType;                                 (* credit/debit codes *)
 Number:INTEGER;                                        (* number of entry *)
 Date:mmddyy;                                             (* date of entry *)
 Amount:REAL;                                           (* amount of entry *)
 Comment:STRING[20];                   (* description may be 20 chars long *)
END;

(*define a RECORD type to hold common information for all transaction types*)

TransInfo = RECORD
 Name:STRING[6];                                (* holds transaction name *)
 HowManyCategories:INTEGER;    (* category counter for both debits/credits *)
 CategoryList:CategArray;                         (* list of category names *)
 Totals:ARRAY[0..MaximumCateg] OF REAL;                (* category totals *)
 Sum:REAL;                                                          (* sum *)
END;
      (* define a RECORD type to hold debit and credit summaries; note use
                 of enumeration type TransType to specify the array bounds *)
```

```
InfoType = ARRAY[ TransType ] OF TransInfo;

VAR
 ReportSet: SET OF ReportChoices;                    (* users choices *)

 AccountNet,                         (* new variable for net amount due *)
 StartBalance,
 CurrentBalance:REAL;                   (* variables from BalancePlus *)

(* record formats require declarations to set up files *)

 Info:InfoType;
 AcctFile:FILE OF EntryRec;                    (* file for account data *)
 InfoFile:FILE OF InfoType;  (* file for categories, totals--summary data  *)
 ItemCount:INTEGER;                       (* count of entries on file *)
 AccountOpen:BOOLEAN;          (* flag to indicate when account file is open *)
 PageWidth,                            (* variable to hold screen width *)
 LinesPerPage,
 LineNumber:INTEGER;        (* page control variables for report formatting *)

 OutDevice:TEXT;                     (* declare output file for reports *)

 Underline:STRING;                    (* will hold underline characters *)

 Printing,
 FileOpen:BOOLEAN;        (* used to test if an output file is already open *)
(**************************************************************************)
(*                                                                        *)
(*    FUNCTION TO CONVERT A STRING OF NUMERIC CHARACTERS TO AN INTEGER    *)
(*                                                                        *)
(**************************************************************************)
FUNCTION Val(S: STRING): INTEGER;
VAR
 Index,
 Answer: INTEGER;
BEGIN
 Answer := 0;                                  (* start with zero in case *)
 IF S <> '' THEN                              (* string must not be empty *)
  FOR Index := 1 TO LENGTH(S) DO                    (* loop through string *)
   IF S[Index] IN ['0'..'9'] THEN      (* if character is an ASCII number, *)
    Answer := Answer * 10              (* shift digit to next column left; *)
            + ORD(S[Index])                   (* add value of ASCII number; *)
            - ORD('0');                    (* subtract ASCII number offset; *)
    Val := Answer;                      (* set function variable to result *)
END;

(**************************************************************************)
(*                                                                        *)
(*   PROCEDURE TO ERASE SCREEN AND DISPLAY A CENTERED TITLE AT THE TOP    *)
(*                                                                        *)
(**************************************************************************)
PROCEDURE PutTitle(Title:STRING);
VAR
 EndPosition:INTEGER;          (* declare variable to hold the calculation *)
BEGIN
 PAGE(OUTPUT);                         (* clear the screen or start new page *)
 EndPosition := (PageWidth DIV 2) + (LENGTH(Title) DIV 2);
 WRITELN(Title:EndPosition);                              (* display title *)
 WRITELN(Underline:PageWidth);                                (* underline *)
 WRITELN;                                                   (* skip a line *)
END;
(**************************************************************************)
(*                                                                        *)
(*           PROCEDURE TO CENTER A MESSAGE ON THE OUTPUT DEVICE           *)
(*                                                                        *)
(**************************************************************************)
PROCEDURE PageCenter(Title:STRING);
VAR
 EndPosition:INTEGER;        (* declare a variable to hold the calculation *)
BEGIN
 EndPosition := (PageWidth DIV 2) + (LENGTH(Title) DIV 2);
 WRITELN(OutDevice,Title:EndPosition);
END;
```

```
(***********************************************************************)
(*                                                                     *)
(*      PROCEDURE TO DRAW AN UNDERLINE ACROSS THE OUTPUT DEVICE PAGE   *)
(*                                                                     *)
(***********************************************************************)
PROCEDURE PageUnderline;
BEGIN
 WRITELN(OutDevice,Underline:PageWidth);
END;
(***********************************************************************)
(*                                                                     *)
(*   PROCEDURE TO START A NEW PAGE; DISPLAY A CENTERED TITLE AT THE TOP *)
(*                                                                     *)
(***********************************************************************)
PROCEDURE NewPage(Title:STRING);
BEGIN
 PAGE(OutDevice);                  (* clear the screen or start new page *)
 PageCenter(Title);
 PageUnderline;                                          (* underline *)
 WRITELN(OutDevice);                                    (* skip a line *)
END;
(***********************************************************************)
(*                                                                     *)
(*      FUNCTION TO ALLOW THE USER TO CHANGE ANSWER, OR TO CONTINUE    *)
(*                                                                     *)
(***********************************************************************)
FUNCTION OK:BOOLEAN;
VAR
 Character:CHAR;
 Message:STRING;
BEGIN
  Message := '<RETURN> IF OK; <SPACE> TO CHANGE ANSWER';
 REPEAT
  GOTOXY(0,22);
  WRITE(Message);
  READ(KEYBOARD,Character);
 UNTIL (Character = ' ') OR EOLN(KEYBOARD);
  IF EOLN(KEYBOARD) THEN OK := TRUE
  ELSE OK := FALSE;
  GOTOXY(0,22);
  WRITE('':LENGTH(Message));                          (* erase message *)
END;
(***********************************************************************)
(*                                                                     *)
(*                     WAIT FOR USER TO PRESS A KEY                    *)
(*                                                                     *)
(***********************************************************************)
PROCEDURE AwaitAnyKey;
VAR
 AnyChar:CHAR;
BEGIN
 IF NOT Printing THEN
 BEGIN
  WRITELN;
  WRITE('PRESS ANY KEY TO CONTINUE');
  READ(AnyChar);
 END;
END;
(***********************************************************************)
(*                                                                     *)
(*          ASK THE USER FOR A REAL NUMBER AT COORDINATES X , Y        *)
(*                                                                     *)
(***********************************************************************)
PROCEDURE AskValue(X,Y:INTEGER;Question:STRING;VAR Answer:REAL);
BEGIN
 REPEAT
  GOTOXY(X,Y);
  WRITE(Question,' ');
  READLN(Answer);
 UNTIL OK;
GOTOXY(X, Y + 1);
END;
```

```
(**********************************************************************)
(*                                                                    *)
(*   GET THE NAMES OF THE CATEGORIES AND PUT THEM INTO AN ARRAY IN Info;  *)
(*  (THIS PROCEDURE REPLACES BOTH GetCreditCategory AND GetDebitCategory  *)
(*   BY USING THE VARIABLE Kind TO BE EITHER Credit OR Debit)         *)
(*                                                                    *)
(**********************************************************************)
PROCEDURE GetCategories(Kind:TransType);
VAR
 Temp:STRING;
 Counter:INTEGER;
BEGIN
 WITH Info[Kind] DO                 (* WITH...DO shortcut for field reference *)
  BEGIN
   PutTitle(CONCAT('ENTRY OF ',Name,' CATEGORY NAMES'));
(* show all categories currently saved *)
FOR Counter := 0 TO HowManyCategories DO
 WRITELN(Name, ' CATEGORY ',Counter,' : ', CategoryList[Counter]);
(* if list is already full, tell user and don't allow any more entries *)
 IF HowManyCategories = MaximumCateg THEN
 BEGIN
  WRITELN;
  WRITELN('NO MORE ROOM IN LIST');
  AwaitAnyKey;
 END
 ELSE
  REPEAT
(* increment number of categories with SUCC procedure *)
   WRITE(Name,' CATEGORY ',SUCC(HowManyCategories),' ? ');
   READLN(Temp);
   IF Temp <> '' THEN
    BEGIN
     WHILE(LENGTH(Temp) < 20) DO Temp := CONCAT(Temp, ' ');
(* increment number of categories with SUCC procedure *)
     HowManyCategories := SUCC(HowManyCategories);
     CategoryList[HowManyCategories] := Temp;
    END;
  UNTIL (Temp = '') OR (HowManyCategories = MaximumCateg);
 WRITELN;
 END;
END;
(**********************************************************************)
(*                                                                    *)
(*  ASK THE USER FOR A NUMBER FROM Min TO Max, AND REPEAT UNTIL OBTAINED  *)
(*                                                                    *)
(**********************************************************************)
FUNCTION AskChoice(X,Y:INTEGER;Q:STRING;Min,Max:INTEGER):INTEGER;
VAR
 Answer:INTEGER;
 AnsString:STRING;                            (* user input may be a string *)
BEGIN
 REPEAT
  GOTOXY(X,Y);
  WRITE(Q,' (',Min,'..',Max,') ');                (* ask question; show range *)
  READLN(AnsString);
  Answer := Val(AnsString);                 (* convert user's string to integer *)
                                          (* using previously defined Val function *)
 UNTIL (Answer >= Min) AND (Answer <= Max);          (* repeat until in range *)
 AskChoice := Answer;
END;
(**********************************************************************)
(*                                                                    *)
(*     SHOW A "MENU" OF THE AVAILABLE CATEGORY NAMES FOR TRANSACTIONS   *)
(*     AND ASK FOR THE DESIRED CATEGORY NUMBER                        *)
(*                                                                    *)
(**********************************************************************)
FUNCTION AskCategory (Kind:TransType) :INTEGER;
VAR
 Counter,
 Answer:INTEGER;

BEGIN
 WITH Info[Kind] DO
```

```
  BEGIN
  WRITELN;
   FOR Counter := 0 TO HowManyCategories DO        (* display all categories *)
    WRITELN(Counter:8,'. ', CategoryList[Counter]);          (* menu format *)
   AskCategory := AskChoice(10,22,'ENTER CATEGORY',0, HowManyCategories);
  END;
END;
(*************************************************************************)
(*                                                                       *)
(*     THIS PROCEDURE WILL DRAW A BAR GRAPH, USING STARS **** TO SHOW    *)
(*     DATA, AND FINISHING THE LINE WITH DOTS .......................    *)
(*                                                                       *)
(*************************************************************************)
PROCEDURE DrawBar(NStars,GraphWidth:INTEGER);
VAR
 Position:INTEGER;
BEGIN
FOR POSITION := 1 TO GraphWidth DO
 IF POSITION <= NStars THEN
  WRITE(OutDevice,'*')                                     (* show bar graph *)
 ELSE
  WRITE(OutDevice,'.');                                 (* fill out with dots *)
END;
(*************************************************************************)
(*                                                                       *)
(*       THIS PROCEDURE WILL DISPLAY AMOUNTS AS EITHER 1. RAW DATA,      *)
(*       2. PERCENTAGE OF TOTAL, OR 3. A BAR GRAPH 40 CHARACTERS LONG    *)
(*                                                                       *)
(*************************************************************************)
PROCEDURE ShowData(Amount,Total:REAL);
VAR
 I,
 NumberOfStars:INTEGER;
 Ratio,
 Pct:REAL;
BEGIN
 IF Total <> 0 THEN
 BEGIN
  Ratio := Amount / Total;                 (* calculate ratio of item to total *)
  Pct := Ratio * 100;                             (* calculate percentage *)
  NumberOfStars := ROUND(Ratio * 40);              (* length of bar graph *)
  WRITE(OutDevice,Amount:10:2);                            (* show amount *)
  IF Percent IN ReportSet THEN
  BEGIN
   WRITE(OutDevice,Pct:8:2,'% ');              (* show percentage to total *)
   IF BarGraph IN ReportSet THEN
    DrawBar(NumberOfStars,40);                    (* bar graph, show scale *)
  END;
 END;
 WRITELN(OutDevice);                                       (* finish line *)
END;
(*************************************************************************)
(*                                                                       *)
(*    THIS PROCEDURE WILL DISPLAY THE TOTALS FOR THE DEBITS AND CREDITS  *)
(*    THAT HAVE BEEN ENTERED UNDER EACH CATEG, AS WELL AS GRAND TOTALS   *)
(*                                                                       *)
(*************************************************************************)
PROCEDURE ShowDetailTotals;
VAR
 Cat:INTEGER;                                           (* category index *)
 Kind:TransType;
BEGIN
(* list the summaries for each category of transaction *)
 FOR Kind := Debit TO Rcvbl DO
  WITH Info[Kind] DO
   BEGIN
    WRITELN(OutDevice);                                      (* skip a line *)
    WRITELN(OutDevice,'--',Name,'S--');                   (* write heading *)
    FOR Cat := 0 TO HowManyCategories DO              (* for each category...*)
     BEGIN
      WRITE(OutDevice,CategoryList[Cat]);          (* display category name *)
```

```
       ShowData(Totals[Cat],Sum);                                   (* format data *)
      END;
     PageUnderline;                                                     (* underline *)
   (* show total *)
     WRITE(OutDevice,'Name, ' TOTAL          ',Sum:10:2);
     IF Percent IN ReportSet THEN                                 (* if user wants pct *)
     WRITE(OutDevice,'100% ':10);                                      (* show 100% *)
     WRITELN(OutDevice);                                             (* finish line *)
    END;
  WRITELN(OutDevice);                                                 (* skip a line *)
 END;
(**********************************************************************)
(*                                                                    *)
(*      ASK USER WHAT FORM REPORT IS TO TAKE, SET VARIABLE ReportSet  *)
(*                                                                    *)
(**********************************************************************)
PROCEDURE AskReportType;
VAR
 Choice:INTEGER;
BEGIN
(* show user a menu of choices for report format *)
PutTitle('SELECTION OF DATA FORMAT');
WRITELN;
WRITELN('1. DATA SUM');
WRITELN('2. DATA SUM AND PERCENTAGES');
WRITELN('3. DATA SUM, PERCENTAGES, AND BAR GRAPH');
(* get user's choice; if not 1,2, OR 3, ask again; then convert answer
(1, 2, 3) to ReportSet values *)
 CASE AskChoice(0,10,'ENTER CHOICE',1,3) OF              (* pass parameters *)
  1:ReportSet := [Sum];
  2:ReportSet := [Sum,Percent];
  3:ReportSet := [Sum,Percent,BarGraph];
 END;
END;
(**********************************************************************)
(*                                                                    *)
(*     THE FOLLOWING REVISES THE PROCEDURE AskOutputDevice SO THAT IT *)
(*     CALLS TWO NEW PROCEDURES--OpenConsole AND OpenPrinter          *)
(*                                                                    *)
(**********************************************************************)
PROCEDURE OpenConsole;
BEGIN
 IF FileOpen THEN CLOSE(OutDevice);           (* must close if already open *)
 REWRITE(OutDevice,'CONSOLE:');
 FileOpen := TRUE;
 Printing := FALSE;
 PageWidth := 40;                                (* set width of print line *)
 LinesPerPage := 20;
END;
PROCEDURE OpenPrinter;
BEGIN
 IF FileOpen THEN CLOSE(OutDevice);           (* must close if already open *)
 REWRITE(OutDevice,'PRINTER:');
 FileOpen := TRUE;
 Printing := TRUE;
 PageWidth := 80;                                (* set width of print line *)
 LinesPerPage := 60;
END;

(* ask name of output file (PRINTER, CONSOLE) *)

PROCEDURE AskOutputDevice;
BEGIN
 PutTitle('OUTPUT FILE SELECTION');
 WRITELN;
 WRITELN('1. DISPLAY ON CONSOLE');
 WRITELN('2. DISPLAY ON PRINTER');
  CASE AskChoice(0,8,'CHOICE',1,2) OF
   1:OpenConsole;                                (* call above procedure *)
   2:OpenPrinter;                                (* call above procedure *)
  END;
END;
```

```
(***********************************************************************)
(*                                                                     *)
(*     FUNCTION TO ASK A YES/NO QUESTION, WAIT FOR Y OR N AND <RETURN>     *)
(*                                                                     *)
(***********************************************************************)
FUNCTION Yes(Question:STRING):BOOLEAN;
VAR
 Answer:CHAR;
BEGIN
 REPEAT
  WRITE(Question,' ? (Y/N) ');      (* show the question with ? and options *)
  READLN(Answer);                        (* get Answer, await <RETURN> *)
 UNTIL Answer IN ['Y','N'];          (* test if answer is in subrange (set) *)
 Yes := (Answer = 'Y');       (* if answer is Y, then Yes function is TRUE *)
END;

PROCEDURE AskEntryType(VAR Answer:TransType);
VAR
 TempChar:CHAR;
 Kind:TransType;
BEGIN
(* show a menu of transaction entry types, with first letter of each name *)
 WRITELN;
  REPEAT
   FOR Kind := Debit TO Rcvbl DO
    BEGIN
     WRITE(Info[Kind].Name[1],' ');       (* show first letter of each name *)
     WRITELN(Info[Kind].Name);                 (* show full entry type name *)
    END;
   WRITE('ENTER LETTER CHOICE ');
   READ(TempChar);
  UNTIL TempChar IN ['D','C','P','R'];            (* if answer no good, redo *)
 FOR Kind := Debit TO Rcvbl DO                      (* look through the types *)
  IF TempChar = Info[Kind].Name[1] THEN    (* match first letter of answer *)
   Answer := Kind;
END;
(***********************************************************************)
(*                                                                     *)
(*    PROCEDURE TO ADD AN ENTRY TO THE TOTALS IN Info (SUMMARY) RECORD     *)
(*                                                                     *)
(***********************************************************************)
PROCEDURE AddToSums(EntryType:TransType;EntryCode:CodeType;Amount:REAL);
BEGIN
 WITH Info[EntryType] DO
  BEGIN
   Totals[EntryCode] := Totals[EntryCode] + Amount;        (* sum category *)
   Sum := Sum + Amount;                                    (* add to total *)
  END;
END;
(***********************************************************************)
(*                                                                     *)
(*       PROCEDURE TO ASK ALL THE DATA FOR A SINGLE TRANSACTION, OR        *)
(*       ACCOUNT ENTRY; THE FILE IS AcctFile --SO THE FILE POINTER         *)
(*       VARIABLE IS AcctFile^                                             *)
(*                                                                     *)
(***********************************************************************)
PROCEDURE GetAcctEntry;
VAR
 TempString:STRING;
 TempChar:CHAR;
 Index:TransType;
BEGIN
 WITH AcctFile^ DO
  BEGIN
   STR(SUCC(ItemCount),TempString);       (* convert ItemCount+1 to STRING *)
   PutTitle(CONCAT('ENTER ITEM NUMBER ',TempString));          (* put title *)
   AskEntryType(EntryType);                   (* get entry type from user *)
(* get amount and category for item *)
   WITH Info[EntryType] DO
(* get Amount *)
     AskValue(0, 9 ,CONCAT(Name,' AMOUNT $ '),Amount);
```

```
    Number := AskChoice(0,4,'ENTRY NUMBER',0,9999);              (* ask number *)
    WITH Date DO
     BEGIN
      mm := AskChoice(9,11,'MONTH',1,12);                    (* pass parameters *)
      dd := AskChoice(11,12,'DAY',1,31);                   (* note restrictions on *)
      yy := AskChoice(9,13,'YEAR',80,99);                    (* possible values *)
     END;
    GOTOXY(0,8);                          (* advance writing position on display *)
    WRITE('COMMENT ');                          (* ask for description of entry *)
    READLN(Comment);                                        (* get description *)
    GOTOXY(0,15);                      (* advance to next writing line on display *)
    EntryCode := AskCategory(EntryType);                       (* get category *)
   END;
  END;

 PROCEDURE SeekEndOfFile;
 BEGIN
  RESET(AcctFile);                                   (* go to beginning of file *)
  ItemCount := 0;                                (* initialize the record count *)
  WHILE NOT EOF(AcctFile) DO                   (* read all records temporarily *)
   BEGIN                                           (* to get a record count *)
    ItemCount := SUCC(ItemCount);
    GET(AcctFile);
   END;
 END;

 (**************************************************************************)
 (*                                                                        *)
 (*      PROCEDURE TO OPEN THE Acct AND Info FILES FOR READ AND WRITE      *)
 (*                                                                        *)
 (**************************************************************************)
 PROCEDURE OpenFilesForIO;
 BEGIN
  IF NOT AcctOpen THEN
   BEGIN
    RESET(InfoFile,'ACCOUNT.INFO')             (* open Info file and load entry *)
    Info := InfoFile^;                      (* move data into another variable *)
    WRITELN('SUMMARY FILE LOADED');
    RESET(AcctFile,'ACCOUNT.DATA');            (* open Acct file and load entry *)
    WRITE('ACCOUNT FILE OPENED');
    AccountOpen := TRUE;                                            (* set flag *)
    SeekEndOfFile;                              (* go to end and count entries *)
    WRITELN(', ',ItemCount,' ENTRIES FOUND ');                    (* show count *)
   END;
  RESET(AcctFile);        (* reset without name means back to the beginning *)
  RESET(InfoFile);                      (* go to beginning of Info file, too *)
 END;

 (**************************************************************************)
 (*                                                                        *)
 (*                   PROCEDURE TO OPEN THE ACCOUNT FILE                   *)
 (*                                                                        *)
 (**************************************************************************)
 PROCEDURE OpenAccountFile;
 BEGIN
  IF NOT AccountOpen THEN                             (* test: Is file open? *)
   BEGIN
    IF Yes('HAS AN ACCOUNT FILE BEEN CREATED') THEN
     BEGIN
      RESET(InfoFile,'ACCOUNT.INFO');          (* open file and read in entry *)
      RESET(AcctFile,'ACCOUNT.DATA');          (* open file and read in entry *)
      Info := InfoFile^;
      WRITELN('ACCOUNT FILE OPENED');
     END
    ELSE                                (* file not created yet, so do it now *)
     BEGIN
      REWRITE(AcctFile,'ACCOUNT.DATA');          (* create account detail file *)
      REWRITE(InfoFile,'ACCOUNT.INFO');                (* create summary file *)
      WRITELN('ACCOUNT FILE CREATED');          (* tell user what's happening *)
     END;
    AccountOpen := TRUE;                                          (* set a flag *)
   END;
 END;
```

```
(****************************************************************************)
(*                                                                          *)
(*          PROCEDURE TO SORT Acct DATA FILE IN VARIOUS ORDERS             *)
(*                      (THIS IS A SHELL'S SORT)                            *)
(*                                                                          *)
(****************************************************************************)
PROCEDURE SortFile(Order:OrderType);
VAR
 A, B:EntryRec;          (* temporary place to hold records from the file *)
 I, J, Gap:INTEGER;
 Swap:BOOLEAN;
BEGIN
 Gap := ItemCount DIV 2;                       (* initial gap is half list *)
 WHILE Gap > 0 DO                                   (* loop until gap is 0 *)
   BEGIN
    FOR I := 1 TO ItemCount - Gap DO                  (* scan through list *)
     BEGIN
      J := I;                                (* hold index in temporary *)
      WHILE J > 0 DO                              (* J is index for scan *)
       BEGIN
        SEEK(AcctFile,PRED(J));
        GET(AcctFile);                           (* get low entry of two *)
        A := AcctFile^;                               (* put entry in A *)
        SEEK(AcctFile,PRED(J + Gap));
        GET(AcctFile);                          (* get high entry of two *)
        B := AcctFile^;                               (* put entry in B *)
        Swap := FALSE;                     (* set comparison flag FALSE *)
         CASE Order OF                    (* depending upon sort key... *)
          EnType:  Swap := (A.EntryType > B.EntryType);     (*set swap flag*)
          Comment: Swap := (A.Comment > B.Comment);        (* set swap flag*)
          Date:    Swap := (A.Date.yy > B.Date.yy)         (* set swap flag*)
                     OR ((A.Date.yy = B.Date.yy)
                     AND (A.Date.mm > B.Date.mm))
                     OR ((A.Date.yy = B.Date.yy)
                     AND (A.Date.mm = B.Date.mm)
                     AND (A.Date.dd > B.Date.dd));
        END;
       IF Swap THEN                                  (* exchange needed? *)
        BEGIN                                (* exchange entries of file *)
         SEEK(AcctFile,PRED(J + Gap));
         AcctFile^ := A;                 (* put temp A in file variable *)
         PUT(AcctFile);                                (* store file item *)
         SEEK(AcctFile,PRED(J));                (* position file pointer *)
         AcctFile^ := B;                 (* put temp B in file variable *)
         PUT(AcctFile);                                (* store file item *)
         J := J - Gap;                   (* scan backwards -- secondary *)
        END
       ELSE J := 0;                            (* no swap; set flag to 0 *)
      END;                                                 (* END WHILE *)
    END;                                                     (* END FOR *)
   Gap := Gap DIV 2;                                (* divide Gap in half *)
 END;                                                      (* END WHILE *)
END;                                                   (* END PROCEDURE *)
(****************************************************************************)
(*                                                                          *)
(*          PROCEDURE TO ASK HOW TO SORT ENTRIES AND CALL SORT              *)
(*                                                                          *)
(****************************************************************************)
PROCEDURE SortAccountEntries;
BEGIN
 OpenFilesForIO;                    (* call procedure to open file for data *)
 SeekEndOfFile;
 PutTitle('SORT ACCOUNT ENTRIES');                 (* display a menu for user *)
 WRITELN('1. SORT BY TYPE');
 WRITELN('2. SORT BY COMMENT');
 WRITELN('3. SORT BY DATE');
 CASE AskChoice (0,7,'CHOICE',1,3) OF
  1:SortFile(EnType);
  2:SortFile(Comment);
  3:SortFile(Date);
 END;
END;
```

```
(***********************************************************************)
(*                                                                     *)
(*      PROCEDURE TO GET NEW ENTRIES FOR ACCOUNT FILE AND KEEP TOTALS  *)
(*                                                                     *)
(***********************************************************************)
PROCEDURE MakeAccountEntries;
BEGIN
 OpenFilesForIO;                                    (* open file for data *)
 SeekEndOfFile;                                     (* go to end of file *)
 WHILE Yes('DO YOU WANT TO ADD AN ACCOUNT ENTRY') DO
  BEGIN
   WITH AcctFile^ DO
    BEGIN
     GetAcctEntry;                                  (* ask for entry data *)
     AddToSums(EntryType,EntryCode,Amount);         (* put into summary *)
     PUT(AcctFile);                       (* save entry to master account file *)
     ItemCount := SUCC(ItemCount);                 (* increment item count *)
(* if entry is a credit of category other than miscellaneous,
 subtract the amount of the credit from the receivables *)
     IF EntryType = Credit THEN                    (* if entry is a credit... *)
      IF EntryCode <> 0 THEN                    (* and if not misc. category *)
       BEGIN
        EntryType := Rcvbl;                       (* change TYPE to Rcvbl *)
        Amount := - Amount;                       (* make amount negative *)
        AddToSums(EntryType,EntryCode,Amount);           (* add to summary *)
        PUT(AcctFile);                           (* save summaries to file *)
        ItemCount := SUCC(ItemCount);            (* increment entry count *)
       END;
    END;
  END;
 SortFile(Date);                                     (* sort data by date *)
 CLOSE(AcctFile,LOCK);                (* close master file and make permanent *)
 SEEK(InfoFile,0);                         (* point to beginning of Info file *)
 InfoFile^ := Info;                (* move variable contents into file variable *)
 PUT(InfoFile);                        (* put contents of file variable on disk *)
 CLOSE(InfoFile,LOCK);                 (* close summary file and make permanent *)
 AcctOpen := FALSE;                      (* set flag to indicate closed file *)
END;
(***********************************************************************)
(*                                                                     *)
(*     SHOW THE CONTENTS OF THE CURRENT AcctFile RECORD ON CONSOLE OR  *)
(*     ON PRINTER (AS DETERMINED BY OutDevice)                         *)
(*                                                                     *)
(***********************************************************************)
PROCEDURE ShowEntry;
BEGIN
 WITH AcctFile^ DO
  BEGIN
   WITH Info[EntryType] DO
    BEGIN
     WRITE(OutDevice,Name:6,' ');                          (* display Name *)
     WITH Date DO
      WRITE(OutDevice,mm:2,'/',dd:2,'/',yy,' ');           (* display Date *)
      WRITE(OutDevice,Number:3,' ');                     (* display Number *)
      IF Printing THEN
       BEGIN
        WRITE(OutDevice,CategoryList[EntryCode],' ');
(* left justify description string and fill to 20 character field *)
        WRITE(OutDevice,Comment,'':(20 - LENGTH(Comment));
       END
      ELSE
       WRITE(OutDevice,CategoryList[EntryCode]:6,' ');
      IF EntryType = Debit THEN
      WRITE(OutDevice,'(')        (* use brackets () to show Debit amounts *)
     ELSE
      WRITE(OutDevice,' ');        (* no () for Credits, but space needed *)
     WRITE(OutDevice,Amount:8:2);             (* specify output and length *)
      IF EntryType = Debit THEN
       WRITE(OutDevice,')');                (* add right bracket for Debits *)
       WRITELN(OutDevice);                                   (* skip a line *)
      END;
     END;
END;
```

```
PROCEDURE ClearSums;          (* procedure to initialize variables to zero *)
VAR
 X:INTEGER;
 Kind: TransType;
BEGIN
 FOR Kind := Debit TO Rcvbl DO
  WITH Info[Kind] DO
   BEGIN
    Sum := 0;                                              (* clear totals *)
    FOR X := 0 TO MaximumCateg DO                      (* clear categories *)
     Totals[X] := 0;
    END;
END;
(**************************************************************************)
(*                                                                        *)
(*           PROCEDURE TO DELETE ENTRIES FROM THE ACCOUNT FILE            *)
(*                                                                        *)
(**************************************************************************)
PROCEDURE DeleteAccountEntries;
VAR
 Source,
 Destination,
 ThisEntry:INTEGER;
 TempSum:REAL;
BEGIN
 PutTitle('DELETE ACCOUNT ENTRIES');
 OpenFilesForIO;                                     (* open file for data *)
 ThisEntry := 0;                         (* count file entries, zero first *)
 Source := 0;
 Destination := 0;
 OpenConsole;                                   (* open console for display *)
 ClearSums;                                        (* clear summary totals *)
 REPEAT
  ShowEntry;                                     (* show entry on console *)
   IF NOT Yes('DELETE THIS ENTRY') THEN            (* if record to be kept *)
    BEGIN
     SEEK(AcctFile,Destination);           (* point to available position *)
     PUT(AcctFile);                                  (* put record there *)
     Destination := SUCC(Destination);               (* increment position *)
     WITH AcctFile^ DO                        (* shorthand for field names *)
      BEGIN
       WITH Info[EntryType] DO                (* shorthand for field names *)
        BEGIN
         Totals[EntryCode] := Totals[EntryCode]
                            + Amount;          (* recalculate categ totals *)
         Sum := Sum + Amount;                    (* recalculate TYPE sums *)
        END;
      END;
    END;
    Source := SUCC(Source);               (* increment position variable *)
    SEEK(AcctFile,Source);
    GET(AcctFile);                          (* read next entry from file *)
   UNTIL EOF (AcctFile);
   SEEK(AcctFile,PRED(Destination));               (* point to final record *)
   GET(AcctFile);                       (* access the file to set pointer *)
   CLOSE(AcctFile,CRUNCH);             (* close file with new end-of-file *)
   RESET(AcctFile,'ACCOUNT.DATA');                          (* reopen file *)
   SEEK(InfoFile,0);                   (* point to first summary record *)
   InfoFile^ := Info;                     (* put new values in sum file *)
   PUT(InfoFile);                              (* save sums to the file *)
 END;
(**************************************************************************)
(*                                                                        *)
(*        PROCEDURE TO SHOW ENTRIES THAT ARE ON MASTER ACCOUNT FILE       *)
(*                                                                        *)
(**************************************************************************)
PROCEDURE ShowAccountEntries;
BEGIN
 LineNumber := 0;
 AskOutputDevice;             (* see if printer or console desired display *)
 IF NOT AccountOpen THEN                           (* test file open flag *)
```

```
   BEGIN
    RESET(AcctFile,'ACCOUNT.DATA');                    (* open file if not already *)
    RESET(InfoFile,'ACCOUNT.INFO');                     (* open summary file, too *)
    Info := InfoFile^;                          (* move file var into other variable *)
    AccountOpen := TRUE;                                               (* set flag *)
   END;
  RESET(AcctFile);                        (* reposition to beginning and get record *)
  PAGE(OutDevice);                                       (* start new display page *)
  WHILE NOT EOF(AcctFile) DO                    (* GET sets EOF if no more records *)
   BEGIN
    (* if the remainder of LineNumber divided by LinesPerPage is zero, then
          a new page must be started--following text starts new page, also *)
    IF(LineNumber MOD LinesPerPage) = 0 THEN              (* test: Is page full? *)
     BEGIN
      IF NOT Printing THEN                                    (* if on console...*)
       IF LineNumber > 0 THEN                            (* and if not first line *)
        AwaitAnyKey;                                     (* pause before new page *)
      IF Printing THEN                                        (* if on printer...*)
       BEGIN
 (* show heading: *)
        WRITELN(OutDevice,'    -TYPE- --DATE-- NBR ------CATEGORY------',
                         ' ------COMMENT------- --AMOUNT--');
        WRITELN(OutDevice);                                        (* skip a line *)
        END
      ELSE                                           (* display format for console *)
       PutTitle('    -TYPE- --DATE-- NBR -CAT.- --AMOUNT--');
      END;
      LineNumber := SUCC(LineNumber);                    (* increment line number *)
      WRITE(OutDevice,LineNumber:2,' ');                   (* number display line *)
      ShowEntry;                                   (* call procedure to display entry *)
      GET(AcctFile);                             (* get next record from master file *)
     END;
    IF NOT Printing THEN
     AwaitAnyKey;
    CLOSE(AcctFile);                       (* no LOCK needed since nothing changed *)
    CLOSE(InfoFile);                       (* no LOCK needed since nothing changed *)
    AccountOpen := FALSE;                                              (* set flag *)
 END;
(****************************************************************************)
(*                                                                          *)
(*        SHOW TOTALS FOR TRANSACTION CATEGS AND SHOW ACCT BALANCE          *)
(*                                                                          *)
(****************************************************************************)
PROCEDURE CalculateCurrentBalance;
VAR
 Temp:STRING;
BEGIN
 AskReportType;                                          (* get format for output *)
 AskOutputDevice;
 NewPage('TOTAL ACCOUNT ACTIVITY');                            (* new page, heading *)
 WRITE(OutDevice,'CATEGORY                  AMOUNT');              (* write heading *)
 IF Percent IN ReportSet THEN
  WRITE(OutDevice,'PERCENT ':10);                                  (* write heading *)
 IF BarGraph IN ReportSet THEN
  WRITE(OutDevice,'CHARTED');                                      (* write heading *)
 WRITELN(OutDevice);                                                 (* finish line *)
 PageUnderline;                                                        (* underline *)

 WRITELN(OutDevice,'BEGINNING BALANCE  $',StartBalance:10:2);
 ShowDetailTotals;
 CurrentBalance := Info[Debit].Sum + Info[Credit].Sum;
 AccountNet := Info[Credit].Sum
             + Info[Rcvbl].Sum
             - Info[Debit].Sum;
 WRITELN(OutDevice,' CASH BALANCE IS $',CurrentBalance:10:2);
 WRITELN(OutDevice,'==========':30);                 (* = for double underscore *)
 WRITELN(OutDevice,'NET ACCOUNT IS $',AccountNet:13:2);
 WRITELN(OutDevice,'==========':30);                 (* = for double underscore *)
(* give user time to look at data before main menu appears again *)
 AwaitAnyKey;
END;
```

```
(**************************************************************************)
(*                                                                        *)
(*                 INITIALIZE SOME PROGRAM VARIABLES                      *)
(*                                                                        *)
(**************************************************************************)
PROCEDURE Initialize;
VAR
 X :INTEGER;
 Kind:TransType;
BEGIN
 ClearSums;
 FOR Kind := Debit TO Rcvbl DO
  WITH Info[Kind] DO
   BEGIN
    HowManyCategories := 0;
    CASE Kind OF                                       (* establish names *)
     Credit:Name := 'CREDIT';
     Debit :Name := 'DEBIT';
     Rcvbl:Name := 'RCVBL';                   (* add receivables to names *)
    END;
    FOR X := 0 TO MaximumCateg DO                     (* clear categories *)
     BEGIN
      Totals[X] := 0;
      CategoryList[X] := '';
     END;
    CategoryList[0] := CONCAT('MISC. ',Name,'S');          (* init categ 0 *)
    WHILE LENGTH(CategoryList[0]) < 20 DO               (* 20 chars long *)
     CategoryList[0] := CONCAT(CategoryList[0],' ');
    END;
 AccountOpen := FALSE;                            (* set file status flag *)
 StartBalance := 0;                                       (* clear totals *)
 PageWidth := 40;                               (* set default page width *)
 FileOpen := FALSE;           (* default condition of display file: CLOSED *)
 Underline := '';
 FOR X := 1 TO 80 DO Underline := CONCAT(Underline,'-');
 OpenAccountFile;
END;
(**************************************************************************)
(*                                                                        *)
(*             PROCEDURE TO ALLOW USER TO ENTER CATEGORIES                *)
(*                                                                        *)
(**************************************************************************)
PROCEDURE GetAllCategories;
VAR
 Kind:TransType;
BEGIN
 OpenFilesForIO;
 AskEntryType(Kind);
 GetCategories(Kind);
 SEEK(InfoFile,0);
 InfoFile^ := Info;
 PUT(InfoFile);
 CLOSE(InfoFile,LOCK);
 RESET(InfoFile,'ACCOUNT.INFO');
END;
(**************************************************************************)
(*                                                                        *)
(*                         MAIN PROGRAM BLOCK                             *)
(*                                                                        *)
(**************************************************************************)
BEGIN                   (* this BEGIN is for the main program instructions *)
 Initialize;
  REPEAT                  (* main menu repeats until user wants it to stop *)
   PutTitle('MAIN MENU - PROCESSING CHOICES');
   WRITELN;
   WRITELN('1. ENTER TRANSACTION CATEGORIES');
   WRITELN('2. MAKE ACCOUNT ENTRIES');
   WRITELN('3. DELETE ACCOUNT ENTRIES');
   WRITELN('4. SORT ACCOUNT ENTRIES');
   WRITELN('5. SHOW ACCOUNT ENTRIES');
```

```
    WRITELN('6. DISPLAY SUMMARY');
    WRITELN('7. STOP');
    CASE AskChoice(0,15,'ENTER CHOICE',1,7) OF
     1:GetAllCategories;
     2:MakeAccountEntries;
     3:DeleteAccountEntries;
     4:SortAccountEntries;
     5:ShowAccountEntries;
     6:CalculateCurrentBalance;
     7:EXIT(PROGRAM);              (* predefined function for program halt *)
    END;
   UNTIL FALSE;                               (* creates infinite loop *)
 END.                                          (* end of program text *)
```

Figure 12-1. (Conclusion)

Summary

The *AccountsReceivable* program extends the capabilities of *AccountManagement* by adding a new entry TYPE, Rcvbl, for outstanding invoices. A summary list for receivables is maintained as a new record within InfoFile.

List maintenance features are added for deletion and sorting of entries.

Credits received that are not categorized as MISCELLANEOUS cause a credit to be posted and the receivables balance to be decremented. The user is given the ability to delete records in the master account file, which may have the effect of compacting the file.

The user may sort the items in the master account file according to any one of three possible orders: by entry type, by user-defined comments, or by date. Although this feature is provided primarily for convenience, the physical order of records in the file will determine how quickly a given record may be found.

Specifically, the procedure SortFile, using a form of Shell's sort, is able to compare two records and perform swaps based on EntryType (Debit, Credit, or Rcvbl), Comment (a 20-character alphanumeric field), or Date (a record containing fields mm, dd, and yy).

AccountsReceivable uses the predefined function ORDinal, which returns the ordinal value of a given scalar variable or constant. The ordinal value of a scalar data item is its position within the set of all possible values for that scalar type.

The ORD function is used in the program within a coined function Val, which converts a STRING of ASCII numbers to a single INTEGER value, thus applying a form of input editing.

Review Questions

1. What is the effect of introducing an entry type for receivables into the calculation of a company's account balances?
2. How is the management of cash flow related to tracking receivables?
3. What changes to the program text of *AccountManagement* are necessary to accommodate the calculation of summaries for receivables?
4. What is the purpose of the CASE statement in procedure SortFile in *AccountsReceivable*?
5. How might the procedure DeleteAccountEntries cause the master account file to be compacted?
6. What specific file operations are performed in DeleteAccountEntries?
7. How is it possible to sort records by Comment?
8. What would happen in executing the procedure SortFile if the record keys of two records being compared were identical?
9. How might sorting account records by Date affect the processing efficiency of *AccountsReceivable*?
10. What is the syntax of the ORD function, and how is it used?
11. What is the purpose of the coined function Val in the example program?
12. How is a form of input editing implemented by the function AskChoice?

Pascal Practice

1. Develop test data for a fictional company for input to *AccountsReceivable.* Include at least 50 transactions involving debits, credits, and receivables.
2. Once you have entered and compiled *AccountsReceivable,* enter the test data you gathered in the first exercise. Enter the data over several sessions to cause the files to be opened and closed several times, thus exercising the procedures for file operations and calculation of summaries.
3. Write a narrative evaluating the program from the standpoint of the needs of your fictional company. Pay particular attention to program features that might be inconvenient if applied routinely by that company.
4. Modify the program to suit the needs you identified in the previous exercise. You might include procedures for calculating summaries based on the aging of receivables, adding an entry type for payables, verifying the order of entry dates, and so on.
5. Replace Shell's algorithm in the procedure SortFile with the procedure Sift presented in Chapter 11. Modify the procedure as necessary to produce a program that compiles and executes successfully. Apply test data specifically designed to exercise the sorts in both versions of the program. Write a narrative describing the impact on execution time of applying a sift instead of Shell's sort in this case.

Key Terms

1. decrement
2. compact
3. ordinal

Pascal Library

1. ORD

13
TRICKS OF THE TRADE: COMPILER OPTIONS

OBJECTIVES

On completing the reading and other learning assignments for this chapter, you should be able to:

- ☐ Explain how compiler options differ from Pascal program statements.
- ☐ Explain how compiler options are used in program text to enable or disable certain compiler features.
- ☐ Demonstrate how GOTO statements may be allowed by using a compiler option in conjunction with a LABEL declaration.
- ☐ Describe the function of automatic I/O error checking and demonstrate how and why it may be disabled.
- ☐ Tell how a single code file may be compiled from multiple source code files.
- ☐ Describe the function of range checking and demonstrate how and why it may be disabled.
- ☐ Tell the form and uses of compilation listings.
- ☐ Describe how swapping may be employed to implement large programs.

BUILDING PROFICIENCY IN PASCAL

The overall objectives of this book are twofold: to explain the basic principles of program design, which are independent of programming languages, and to describe the specific features of Pascal that allow implementation of program design. It is pointed out several times that one of the significant advantages of the Pascal language is the structure that it imposes, reinforcing top-down design principles.

However, one of the measures of proficiency is knowing when to break the rules. Once you have developed an understanding of the structures provided by Pascal and acquired skill in using these structures in actual programming problems, you may encounter situations that call for more advanced techniques. Many of the advanced techniques in Pascal, including some of the UCSD extensions, amount to methods for temporarily overriding the structures imposed by the language.

The purpose of this chapter and the one that follows is to survey programming options, some of which have the effect of either suspending or modifying Pascal data typing and structures. It is possible to achieve satisfactory program performance without ever employing these techniques. However, certain circumstances may require that the programmer be able to write very large programs, make a program execute faster, or use memory more efficiently. In particular, the programmer should be aware of ways to control critical trade-offs, such as the trade-off between execution speed and allocation of memory space. Techniques that employ compiler options are covered in this chapter. The next chapter deals with memory management.

COMPILER OPTIONS

Compiler options may be thought of as software switches that enable or disable certain features of the UCSD Pascal language. As such, compiler options are not program statements. In general, these options do not affect the processing described in program text. Rather, their effect is on the manner in which the code file is generated.

Compiler options take the form of single-letter codes preceded by a dollar sign ($). This code is enclosed within the comment syntax (*   *) or { }. Many compiler options are enabled by following the option with a plus sign (+) or disabled by using the minus sign (−). Some compiler options exist in an enabled state as default conditions within the compiler, and the appearance of the option syntax in program text serves to turn off the feature. Other options must be enabled explicitly.

The exact syntax for each option is given with the explanations below. Compiler options may appear anywhere within a text file, with the exception of the $S option. The $S option must be placed at the beginning of a program.

Allowing GOTO

The syntax **(*$G + *)** enables use of program statements that employ the reserved word **GOTO**. Use of GOTO statements, or *unconditional branching,* is a commonly encountered feature of languages like BASIC and FORTRAN. In Pascal, however, the appearance of a GOTO statement within a program will generate a compiler error unless this option has been enabled. GOTO transfers processing control to a program statement that is prefixed with a **LABEL**.

LABEL declarations. Labels are unsigned integers that are attached to program statements to allow control to be passed directly to these statements by the GOTO statement. All labels used in a block (procedure, function, or program) must be declared before they are used, and each may be used only once in the block. The GOTO statement cannot transfer control between procedures or functions and is strictly local.

Labels provide a means of identifying portions of the program to which control may be assigned, or transferred, during processing. LABEL declarations, in effect, provide a "handle" on sections of the program for the compiler. A LABEL declaration allows the programmer to use this technique later in the program. A label is always a number, one to four digits long (0000 to 9999). A label is used within the program as the number followed by a colon and preceding the line of the program that will be referred to by a GOTO statement.

The section for LABEL declarations follows the block header and precedes CONST declarations. For example:

```
LABEL
  100;
```

Given the above declaration, the following statements may appear anywhere within the same program block:

```
100: BEGIN
       program statement;
       ..
       program statement;
     END;
```

The following example shows transfer of control to the program statement labeled 200 whenever the value of A is nonzero:

```
(*$G+*)                                     (* enable GOTO statements *)
    IF A <> 0 THEN GOTO 200;
     WRITELN('THIS LINE PRINTS WHEN A = 0.');
     200:WRITELN('THIS LINE PRINTS FOR ALL VALUES OF A.');
(*$G-*)                                                (* disable GOTO *)
```

The corresponding LABEL declaration must have been made within the current program block (procedure, function, or main program). In this case, the declaration would be:

```
LABEL
  200;
```

Thus, program control is caused to *jump* arbitrarily, altering the sequence of processing. Pascal's block structure is intended to discourage the use of GOTO by requiring that a given program block have one point of entry and one point of exit. Within a program block (procedure, function, or main program), GOTO may be used to jump from one statement to another. However, GOTO in UCSD Pascal cannot be used to jump out of or into a procedure or function.

Remember that Pascal's structure primarily exists to enhance program clarity. There may be circumstances in which such a jump is the most straightforward way of implementing an algorithm, even though the same processing could be accomplished by writing a larger number of structured statements. Be aware, however, that use of GOTO statements is dangerous because it can invite logical errors that are difficult to diagnose. Also, the resulting program text will be more difficult to understand because some of the clarity provided by block structure has been removed.

In particular, care must be taken to avoid passing control to an inappropriate program statement. For example, it is poor practice to transfer control to a statement in the middle of a loop from somewhere outside the loop. Transferring control out of a loop is permissable, and may be the most straightforward way of terminating the loop.

To illustrate, here is an example of a program block that employs GOTO properly:

```
(*$G+*)
PROCEDURE Read500Records;
LABEL
 100,200;

VAR
 I:INTEGER;
BEGIN
 FOR I := 1 TO 500 DO
  BEGIN
   GET(SomeFile);
   IF EOF(SomeFile) THEN GOTO 100;                     (* jump out of loop *)
   program statements;
  END;
 WRITELN('AT LEAST 500 RECORDS ON FILE');
 GOTO 200;                                     (* skip the next statement *)
 100:WRITELN('END OF FILE');                    (* GOTO 100 jumps to here *)
 200:next statement;                            (* GOTO 200 jumps to here *)
END;
```

The following example contains an improper use of GOTO, which causes a jump to the middle of a loop. Note that this example also contains an infinite loop, in that program control is caused to jump from 200 to 100 and back again endlessly.

```
PROCEDURE HangTheMachine;
LABEL
 100,200;

VAR
 I:INTEGER;

BEGIN
 IF PoorProgram THEN GOTO 100;
 FOR I := 1 TO 10000 DO   (* this statement skipped if PoorProgram is TRUE *)
  BEGIN
   100:GOTO 200;                                           (* infinite loop *)
   200:GOTO 100;
  END;
END;
```

Trapping I/O Errors

The Pascal compiler normally produces code for *I/O error checking,* or verifying that data transfers have occurred without error. Normally, error checking is transparent to the programmer and to the user. The result is that an I/O error during a program execution causes a program halt and display of an error message. Often, it is desirable to "crash-proof" a program by including routines that provide for automatic recovery if an I/O error is encountered. In other instances, it may be necessary for the programmer to be able to check explicitly the result of a given I/O operation.

For example, the *AccountManagement* and *AccountsReceivable* programs do not provide ways of knowing whether the account files exist already. In these programs, it is necessary to ask the user if a file has been created previously. It is possible, instead, for the programmer to disable automatic I/O error checking by using the $I– compiler option and to use program statements to test the status of the last I/O operation performed.

The compiler option **(*$I – *)** turns off production of automatic I/O error-checking code by the compiler. With $I– in effect, an I/O error will not cause a program execution to be aborted. The status of the last I/O operation may be inspected by invoking the predefined function **IORESULT**.

Every time an I/O operation is performed, regardless of whether automatic error checking is enabled, the value of IORESULT is set with an integer code to show what happened. A value of 0 indicates that the I/O operation was performed normally, without error. Nonzero values indicate error conditions. One feature of automatic I/O error checking is that nonzero values for IORESULT cause abnormal program termination.

In normal circumstances, with automatic I/O error checking enabled, there is no reason to inspect IORESULT, since its value must be 0 if no I/O error messages have been displayed.

However, when automatic error checking has been disabled with $I–, IORESULT should be inspected after each I/O operation. You need not turn automatic error checking back on to inspect IORESULT, but it is poor practice to leave it off unless you check every I/O operation immediately after it has been performed. Otherwise, an I/O error would go undetected. The option **(*$I + *)** turns automatic checking back on.

Good programming practice would be to inspect IORESULT immediately after $I+ has been enabled. The value returned will indicate the status of any I/O operation performed while $I− was in effect.

The following code may be used to open a file, either a new one or an existing one that must be reopened:

```
(*$I-*)                                          (* turn I/O checking off *)
RESET(SomeFile,'SOME.FILE.NAME');            (* try to open existing file *)
(*$I+*)                                          (* turn checking back on *)
IF IORESULT <> 0 THEN                        (* if status is not normal...*)
 BEGIN
  WRITELN('FILE DOESN'T EXIST');                      (* display a message *)
  (*$I-*)
  REWRITE(SomeFile,'SOME.FILE.NAME');                 (* create a new file *)
  (*$I+*)
  IF IORESULT <> 0 THEN                     (* file operation successful? *)
   BEGIN
    WRITELN('CANNOT OPEN FILE');             (* if not, display message *)
    EXIT(PROGRAM);                            (* and terminate program *)
   END;
  WRITELN('FILE CREATED');         (* otherwise, display success message *)
 END
ELSE WRITELN('FILE EXISTS AND HAS BEEN OPENED');
```

It is good practice to save the value returned by IORESULT into a temporary variable if you wish to reuse that value. Remember that any subsequent READ or WRITE operation may change the value of IORESULT. Also, some versions of UCSD Pascal cause the value of IORESULT to be reset to zero after each reference.

The following example acquires all possible disk space for a file. Note that the value returned by IORESULT is saved into the temporary variable TempStat.

```
REWRITE(SomeFile,'SOME.FILE.NAME');                    (* create the file *)
 REPEAT
  (*$I-*)                                        (* turn off I/O checking *)
  PUT(SomeFile);                              (* put file record to file *)
  (*$I+*)                                        (* turn checking back on *)
  TempStat := IORESULT;                            (* save IORESULT value *)
  IF TempStat = 0 THEN                      (* if normal file operation...*)
   RecordCount := SUCC(RecordCount);                (* count the records *)
  UNTIL TempStat <> 0;                          (* until not able to PUT *)
CLOSE(SomeFile,LOCK);                              (* close file; set EOF *)
```

For your reference, Figure 13-1 is a listing of numeric values that may be returned by IORESULT and the status represented by each code. These values may be used in condition tests for I/O failures within program statements. Before using these codes, however, consult the user's guide for the system you are using. Some systems may not use all the values listed, and some may have added values to the list.

To turn off I/O checking, you may place the compiler option (*$I-*) at the beginning of the program, which will have the effect of turning

I/O ERROR CODES

VALUE	STATUS
0	NORMAL
1	BAD BLOCK ON DISKETTE
2	BAD DEVICE OR VOLUME NUMBER
3	ILLEGAL OPERATION
4	HARDWARE ERROR
5	LOST DEVICE—NO LONGER ON-LINE
6	LOST FILE—NO LONGER IN DIRECTORY
7	BAD TITLE—ILLEGAL FILE NAME
8	NO ROOM ON DISKETTE (VOLUME)
9	NO DEVICE—VOLUME NOT FOUND
10	FILE NOT FOUND ON VOLUME
11	DUPLICATE FILE NAME
12	ATTEMPT TO OPEN AN ALREADY OPEN FILE
13	ATTEMPT TO ACCESS A CLOSED FILE
14	BAD INPUT FORMAT—ERROR IN READING *REAL* OR *INTEGER*
15	RING BUFFER OVERFLOW—DATA INPUT TOO FAST
16	WRITE-PROTECT ERROR—DISKETTE IS WRITE-PROTECTED
64	DEVICE ERROR—BAD ADDRESS OR DATA ON DISKETTE

Figure 13-1. I/O error codes notify the system user of the failure of an input/output operation.

off checking throughout the entire program if there is no corresponding (*$I+*) option later in the program. However, if you take this approach, your program should test the value of IORESULT after each I/O operation. Many I/O errors are unexpected by nature, and with error checking turned off, the system will not take action on these errors. To preserve the integrity of valuable data files, be aware of the status of I/O checking and IORESULT throughout the program.

The Include Option

Another use of the $I syntax—unrelated to I/O checking—is to specify other Pascal source files to be included in the current compilation. The format of this option is:

```
(*$I FileName*)
```

The FileName referred to is the external file name containing Pascal program text. This syntax is known as the Include option and requires that the file name be followed immediately by the end-of-comment delimiter, *) or }.

The Include option is useful for building programs from different sources. For example, if you have text files containing routines that are used in many different programs, those routines may be included in any program at the time of its compilation. (Remember, of course, that file and variable names must be consistent, where appropriate.) Also, there may be situations in which a program has grown so large that the UCSD editor cannot load the entire program into memory at one time. In such situations, you may move sections of the text file to other files and include those files by reference in compiling a main text file. Of course, the files to be included must be available to the system while the compilation is in progress. A good practice is to keep all sections of the text for a given program on the same diskette.

When the Include option is used within the declarations section of a program, the included text may contain declarations—such as LABEL,

CONST, TYPE, and VAR. These may be included even if the declarations in the included file are out of formal order in relation to the declarations in the main text file. The compiler will sort the declarations of all included files into the proper order. This feature is useful especially if identical data definitions must be used by different programs.

For large text files, the Pascal editor may be used to extract text portions and write them to separate files. A common practice is to move the text for several procedures in the program into a text file of another name. For example, all procedures that perform report generation may be maintained in a single file for the sake of clarity. In doing so, however, it is important to coin external file names that are descriptive.

To move portions of the text file to a new file, the file utility program may be used to make a duplicate copy of the source file. Perhaps more convenient is the use of the editor to copy the current source file. This copying is done by using the W option to write the file to a new file name. Then, portions of each file may be deleted with the editor to result in the desired text in each file. Caution should be used when selecting the W option, however. If, after saving with the W option to a new file name, you then key S (for Save) when finished editing the file, changes will be made to the new name given in the W option rather than under the original file name. It is important to make sure to rewrite (W) the current file to the original name.

The editor also allows you to set delimiters, or *markers,* in the file to define the bounds of portions to be saved, moved, or deleted. The C command then is used to copy text portions contained within markers or may be used to copy entire files.

Range Checking

An option that must be used with caution is **(*$R – *)**, which disables the production of range checking code by the compiler. Under normal circumstances, the compiler is set to generate special instructions in the code file to verify that variable references and data values fall into allowable ranges. Range checking is a valuable feature of UCSD Pascal because it gives the programmer a margin of safety. If range checking is turned off, the programmer can write references to variables that are outside valid ranges. These references can destroy sections of the data or the program itself.

For example, in indexing an array, the compiler will verify that the index variable is within the range that has been declared previously. Consider the following:

```
VAR
 BigArray:ARRAY[200..500] OF STRING;
 X:INTEGER;
BEGIN
 READLN(X);
 BigArray[X] := 'AN ARRAY ELEMENT';
END;
```

In generating code from the above text, the compiler would insert range checking code to verify that X is within the range 200 to 500 before a value is assigned to BigArray[X]. In effect, the inserted code performs the following processing:

```
IF X < 200 OR X > 500 THEN ValueRangeError;
```

Range checking is crucial to reliable program performance. However, specific circumstances may justify disabling this feature. These circumstances include:

- If a program has been debugged thoroughly, turning off range checking can reduce the size of the resulting code file and cause faster execution. This approach implies that debugging has been done with a prior version of the compilation that includes range checking. Only when several successful executions have been done with representative test data should the program be recompiled with range checking turned off.
- When initializing a large number of array elements that have constant subscripts, range checking may be turned off to reduce the amount of code generated. For example:

```
(*$R-*)                                          (* turn off range checking *)
DAYS[1] := 'MONDAY';                         (* initialize array elements *)
DAYS[2] := 'TUESDAY';
DAYS[3] := 'WEDNESDAY';
     (* continue assignments until entire list is initialized *)
(*$R+*)                                           (* turn checking back on *)
```

- In UCSD Pascal, turning off range checking can provide a shortcut for setting LENGTH for a STRING variable. Recall that the first byte in a given string contains a numeric value for the length, in characters, of the string. So, to truncate a string TempString at 10 characters, the programmer may write:

```
(*$R-*)                                          (* turn off range checking *)
TempString[0] := 10;       (* sets first, or string length, byte to 10 *)
(*$R+*)                                           (* turn checking back on *)
```

To achieve the same objective without turning off range checking, you would have to code:

```
DELETE(TempString, 11, LENGTH(TempString) - 10);
```

Compilation Listings

A *compilation listing* is a line-by-line listing of the program text and is a report from the compiler giving information about the code file that has been generated.

A sample compilation listing is shown in Figure 13-2. The first column of the listing shows line numbers that have been assigned to lines of text in your source file.

The second column gives a *segment* number. Segments are separate files of executable code that may reside outside of memory at program execution time. Use of segments may be required for large programs.

The third column of the listing gives a *procedure number* (P#) and a *lexical level.* The lexical level of a program statement refers to the

```
  1   1:D     1 (*$L #6:PRINTER*)
  1   1:D     1 PROGRAM COLUMNS;
  1   1:D     3
  1   1:D     3 VAR
  1   1:D     3
  1   1:D     3        X,ROW_POSN,INDEX,LEFTOVER,PERCOLUMN:   INTEGER;
  1   1:D     8        COLS,ITEMS,LINES:                INTEGER;
  1   1:D    11        MORE:                            BOOLEAN;
  1   1:D    12
  1   2:D     1  PROCEDURE PRINT_COLUMNS;
  1   2:0     0  BEGIN
  1   2:1     0   IF ITEMS > 0 THEN
  1   2:2     5    BEGIN
  1   2:3     5     INDEX :=1;                        (* INIT COLUMN INDEX *)
  1   2:3     8     LINES :=1;                        (* INIT LINE COUNT *)
  1   2:3    11     PERCOLUMN := ITEMS DIV COLS;      (* CALC # PER COLUMN *)
  1   2:3    16     LEFTOVER  := ITEMS MOD COLS;      (* CALC # TO BE DISTRIBUTED
  1   2:3    21                                          AMONG LONGER COLUMNS *)
  1   2:3    21     FOR X := 1 TO ITEMS DO
  1   2:4    32      BEGIN
  1   2:5    32       WRITE(INDEX:4);                 (* DISPLAY INDEX *)
  1   2:5    42       ROW_POSN := X MOD COLS;
  1   2:5    47       IF ROW_POSN > 0 THEN            (* ROW_POSN=0 MEANS LINE (ROW) DONE *)
  1   2:6    52        BEGIN
  1   2:7    52         INDEX := INDEX + PERCOLUMN;   (* SKIP TO NEXT COLUMN VALUE *)
  1   2:7    57         IF (ROW_POSN <= LEFTOVER) THEN  (* IF THIS COLUMN WILL HAVE EXTRA, *)
  1   2:8    62          INDEX := INDEX + 1;          (* ..MUST INCREMENT NEXT VALUE *)
  1   2:6    67        END                            (* END IF *)
  1   2:5    67       ELSE                            (* ROW_POSN IS ZERO, END OF ROW *)
  1   2:6    69        BEGIN
  1   2:7    69         WRITELN;                      (* END OF ROW, START NEW LINE *)
  1   2:7    77         LINES := LINES + 1;           (* COUNT LINES *)
  1   2:7    82         INDEX := LINES;               (* SET INDEX TO START OVER HIGHER *)
  1   2:6    85        END                            (* END ELSE *)
  1   2:4    85      END                              (* END FOR *)
  1   2:2    85    END                                (* END IF *)
  1   2:1    92   ELSE MORE := FALSE                  (* STOP LOOP *)
  1   2:0    94 END;                                  (* END PROCEDURE *)
  1   2:0   112
  1   1:0     0 BEGIN                                 (* M A I N   PROGRAM *)
  1   1:1     0  MORE:=TRUE;                          (* INITIALIZE FLAG *)
  1   1:1     5  WHILE MORE DO
  1   1:2     8   BEGIN
  1   1:3     8    WRITELN;                           (* SPACE BETWEEN PRINTOUTS *)
  1   1:3    16    WRITELN;                           (* SPACE BETWEEN PRINTOUTS *)
  1   1:3    24    WRITE('ENTER NUMBER OF ITEMS AND COLUMNS - ');
  1   1:3    72    READLN(ITEMS,COLS);                (* ASK FOR 2 VALUES, SEP BY SPACE *)
  1   1:3   100    PRINT_COLUMNS;                     (* CALL PROCEDURE TO PRINT LIST *)
  1   1:2   102   END                                 (* END WHILE *)
  1   1:0   102 END.
```

Figure 13-2. Sample compilation listing for program *Columns*.

nesting relationship of the statement to other statements in the program. Note that the procedure number and lexical level are derived by the compiler; each time a beginning block identifier (for a program, procedure, or function) is encountered, the procedure number is incremented one step and the lexical level is derived from the content of the program statement. A lexical level of D corresponds with data statements, declarations, and definitions. A lexical level of 0 corresponds with beginning block identifiers, and subsequent integral values identify nesting levels of statements. If you have taken care to write your text file with appropriate indentations, the lexical levels reported by the compiler will correspond with those indentations. However, bear in mind that the compiler derives the lexical level from the logical relationships among program blocks—not from the indentations you have included in the program text.

The fourth column gives a *relative byte number,* or *byte address,* for each line of the code file. This number is a count of code byte positions. This relative byte number indicates how far, in bytes, the beginning of a given line of code is from the beginning of the program block (procedure or function). The last column of the listing gives the program text from the source file.

Following the appearance of the compiler option **(*$L + *)** in the text file, a compilation listing will be produced. For a listing of the entire program to be produced, this syntax must appear at the beginning of the text file. If the syntax appears within the body of the text file, the listing will begin with the program statement following the $L+ option. Accordingly, the listing feature may be turned off with **(*$L – *)**. Listings enabled by this option are written to a default file named SYSTEM.LST.TEXT.

It also is possible to send a compilation listing to any designated file. The syntax for this option is:

```
(*$L #DeviceNumber:FileName.TEXT*)
```

The file designated in this option may be any file with a legal name. Instead of the device number, the device names CONSOLE: or PRINTER: may be used to indicate those devices as destinations. The suffix of this file is TEXT, since it is a standard text file. The listing file may be inspected using the editor and later transferred to the printer using the filer or the editor.

For example, the following syntax will send a compilation listing to the file LISTING.TEXT, which resides on device number 5 (disk drive 2):

```
(*$L #5:LISTING.TEXT*)
```

A compilation listing is a valuable tool that may be referred to for debugging execution errors. Error messages generated during execution and displayed on the console give information in the form of segment number (S#), procedure number (P#), and relative byte number (I#). A sample error message is shown in Figure 13-3. The information in the

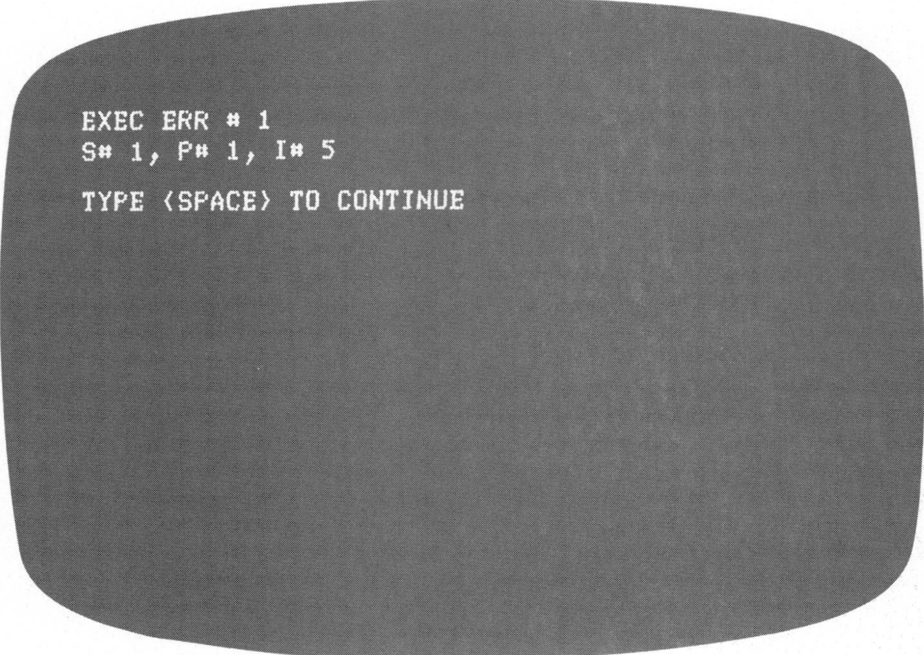

EXEC ERR # 1
S# 1, P# 1, I# 5
TYPE <SPACE> TO CONTINUE

Figure 13-3. Console display of sample run-time error message.

compilation listing will allow you to interpret the error message to find the program statement in which the error was encountered.

For the programmer's convenience in creating compilation listings, a page break, or form-feed, may be caused within a text file by the syntax **(*$P*)**. A new page will begin following the point at which this **Page** option appears in the text file.

Quiet Compile

The option **(*$Q+*)** suppresses, or prevents, the display of a compilation progress report at the console. This option is useful primarily when a printer is being used as the console device and a large compilation would result in a lot of printing. Besides the noise generated, the printer typically is much slower than the console. Enabling the Quiet option would, therefore, have the effect of speeding up the compilation if a printer were used as the console device. This option may be disabled with the syntax **(*$Q–*)**.

Swapping Mode

Normally, the entire compiler resides in memory during compilation. Accordingly, it may be difficult to compile large programs because there is insufficient memory left to hold the program text file.

The option **(*$S+*)** enables a *swapping* mode under which portions of the compiler program that are not being used do not reside in memory. These portions are swapped, or read into memory from the system disk, as required to complete the compilation. This mode frees up memory space for a larger text file.

Although the swapping mode makes the most efficient use of memory space during the compilation, swapping slows compilation. The (*$S+*) syntax must appear at the head of the program text file. The option **(*$S–*)** turns off the swapping mode.

Additionally, the **(*$S++*)** option is provided for further swapping capability. Other compiler options may be offered on your system. Consult the user's guide for options not explained here. In particular, an in-depth discussion of segments is beyond the scope of this book but may be required for the building of large programs.

Summary

Compiler options may be thought of as software switches that enable or disable certain features of the UCSD Pascal language. These options include: allowing GOTO, trapping I/O errors, including other source files in a compilation, disabling range checking, causing compilation listings, causing listings to be saved to files, causing a quiet compilation, and enabling swapping mode.

Review Questions

1. What is the general syntax of all compiler options?
2. What processing action is caused by a GOTO statement?
3. Why is the ability to use GOTO normally disabled in the Pascal compiler?
4. In what part of a block are LABEL declarations made?
5. How is the function IORESULT used in conjunction with disabling automatic I/O error checking?
6. What precautions must be taken in turning off automatic I/O error checking?
7. Under what circumstances is the Include option used?
8. What is range checking, and why is this capability normally enabled in the compiler?
9. What precautions must be taken in turning range checking off?
10. What information does a compilation listing contain, and how is it useful?
11. How is the Page option employed with compilation listings?
12. What is meant by swapping, and how may it be employed during a compilation?

Pascal Practice

1. The program text for *AccountsReceivable* is presented in Chapter 12. Within that program, the procedure OpenAccountFile prompts the user 'HAS AN ACCOUNT FILE BEEN CREATED?' Modify this procedure with the code portion presented in this chapter for automatically testing whether a file exists before creating a new one. Compile this module and execute it with test data.
2. Assuming that you have a version of *AccountsReceivable* that compiled successfully and has been run with test data, recompile the program using a compiler option to turn off the generation of range checking code. Note the size of the resulting code file and compare it to the original version. Execute both versions of the program with the same set of test data. Record execution times for processing modules, such as the sort. Write a narrative describing the effect of turning off range checking on execution time and code file size.
3. Add compiler options for printing of compilation listings and page control for the listings to *AccountsReceivable.* Recompile the program and print out the text file. Making your notations directly on the printout, identify examples of line numbers, segment numbers, procedure numbers, lexical levels, and relative byte numbers. Then, write a narrative describing how this information might assist the programmer.
4. Respond to the following essay question: How is the use of GOTO statements in Pascal inconsistent with the principles of structured programming? Conduct library research to support your answer.

Key Terms

1. unconditional branching
2. jump
3. I/O error checking
4. marker
5. compilation listing
6. segment
7. procedure number
8. lexical level
9. relative byte number
10. byte address
11. swapping

Pascal Library

1. $G
2. LABEL
3. GOTO
4. $I
5. IORESULT
6. Include
7. $R
8. $L
9. $P
10. Page
11. $Q
12. $S

14 TRICKS OF THE TRADE: MEMORY MANAGEMENT

OBJECTIVES

On completing the reading and other learning assignments for this chapter, you should be able to:

- ☐ Use the predefined functions ORD, CHR, and ODD to allow data to be represented as different types.
- ☐ Describe the use of PACKED structures in applying principles of memory allocation and efficiency.
- ☐ Explain the trade-off between execution speed and memory size and under what circumstances efficiencies should be sought.
- ☐ Use properly several techniques for accomplishing I/O operations on blocks of data.
- ☐ Tell how dynamic memory allocation may be used with block I/O operations.
- ☐ Describe how variant records are used to save memory space and enhance program efficiency.
- ☐ Show how multi-dimensional arrays may be declared and how the elements of multi-dimensional arrays may be referenced.
- ☐ Describe why recursion may be useful and tell what cautions must be exercised in implementing recursive procedures or functions.

DATA REPRESENTATION

Some of the programming techniques described in this chapter require an understanding of how certain data types within the Pascal language are represented in binary codes used in machine processing. The table shown in Figure 14-1 demonstrates the relationships among the number of bits associated with a given value, the number of possible values contained, and the numeric range that may be represented.

In Pascal, a word, or 16 bits of binary data, is the default unit of storage for most variables. Accordingly, an INTEGER has a range of ±32,767 because 15 bits hold a numeric value and the last, or sixteenth, bit holds a sign, 0 representing a positive value (+) and 1 representing a negative value (−). REAL numbers have a default size of two words, or four bytes, and are stored in exponential form.

The representation of CHAR and STRING values is somewhat more involved. Recall that a character is represented by one byte of information. Referring again to the table in Figure 14-1, it can be seen that a byte, or eight bits, can hold up to 256 values, or 0 . . 255. Recall also that characters may be interpreted as ASCII character codes that correspond

BINARY DATA REPRESENTATION

Number of Bits (n)	Number of Values (2^n)	Numeric Range	Information Unit
1	2	0 . . 1	one bit
2	4	0 . . 3	
3	8	0 . . 7	
4	16	0 . . 15	
5	32	0 . . 31	
6	64	0 . . 63	
7	128	0 . . 127	
8	256	0 . . 255	one byte
9	512	0 . . 511	
10	1,024	0 . . 1023	
11	2,048	0 . . 2047	
12	4,096	0 . . 4095	
13	8,192	0 . . 8191	
14	16,384	0 . . 16383	
15	32,768	0 . . 32767	
16	65,536	0 . . 65535	one word

Figure 14-1. Binary data representation.

to a decimal number code for each character. Figure 14-2 is a table of these ASCII character codes.

Figure 14-2. ASCII character codes. Control characters are used for machine-specific operations.

ASCII CHARACTER CODES

CONTROL CODES

DECIMAL	CONTROL CHARACTERS*	DESCRIPTION
000	NUL	Null
001	SOH	Start of Heading
002	STX	Start of Text
003	ETX	End of Text
004	EOT	End of Transmission
005	ENQ	Enquiry
006	ACK	Acknowledge
007	BEL	Bell (audible or attention signal)
008	BS	Backspace
009	HT	Horizontal Tabulation
010	LF	Line Feed
011	VT	Vertical Tabulation
012	FF	Form Feed
013	CR	Carriage Return
014	SO	Shift Out
015	SI	Shift In
016	DLE	Data Link Escape
017	DC1	Device Control 1
018	DC2	Device Control 2
019	DC3	Device Control 3
020	DC4	Device Control 4
021	NAK	Negative Acknowledge
022	SYN	Synchronous Idle
023	ETB	End of Transmission Block
024	CAN	Cancel
025	EM	End of Medium
026	SUB	Substitute
027	ESC	Escape
028	FS	File Separator
029	GS	Group Separator
030	RS	Record Separator
031	US	Unit Separator
127	DEL	Delete

PRINTABLE CHARACTERS

Code	Character
032	<SPACE>
033	!
034	“
035	#
036	$
037	%
038	&
039	’ (right single quotation mark, or apostrophe)
040	(
041	)
042	*
043	+
044	, (comma)
045	– (hyphen or minus)
046	. (period or decimal point)
047	/
048	0
049	1
050	2
051	3
052	4
053	5
054	6
055	7
056	8
057	9
058	:
059	;
060	< (“less than” symbol)
061	=
062	> (“greater than” symbol)
063	?
064	@
065	A
066	B
067	C
068	D
069	E
070	F
071	G
072	H
073	I
074	J
075	K
076	L
077	M
078	N
079	O
080	P
081	Q
082	R
083	S
084	T
085	U
086	V
087	W
088	X
089	Y
090	Z
091	[
092	\ (backslash)
093	]
094	^ (or ↑)
095	_ (underscore)
096	‘ (left single quotation mark)
097	a
098	b
099	c
100	d
101	e
102	f
103	g
104	h
105	i
106	j
107	k
108	l
109	m
110	n
111	o
112	p
113	q
114	r
115	s
116	t
117	u
118	v
119	w
120	x
121	y
122	z
123	{
124	|
125	}
126	~

Values from 32 to 127 in the ASCII character set are referred to as *printable characters.* Values from 0 to 31 are *control characters.* These control characters are a standardized set of codes used for system control and many are used only in data communications. Character values may exist, of course, in the range 128 . . 255. These values are not assigned in the ASCII set and generally are used as specialized control codes unique to specific machines.

A STRING is a specialized array of characters, or a series of bytes. The first byte in a string is interpreted as a numeric value indicating the length, in characters, of the string.

CONVERSION OF DATA TYPES

The above data representation schemes relate directly to typing constraints enforced by the Pascal compiler. Some methods of suspending these constraints temporarily are presented in previous programs. For example, the predefined function LENGTH converts STRING length information to an INTEGER value by returning the value of the first byte in the string.

ORD

Similarly, the ORDinal function, which is used in the example in Chapter 12, converts scalar data to INTEGER values. This example presents the ORD function as it relates to any scalar value:

```
PROCEDURE ScalarToInt;
VAR
 Letter:(A,B,C,D,E,F);
BEGIN
 Letter := A;
 WRITELN('THE ORDINAL VALUE OF ',Letter,' IS ',ORD(Letter),'.');
END;
```

The above example will display the following:

```
THE ORDINAL VALUE OF A IS 0.
```

The first value in an enumeration always has an ordinal value of 0, the next is 1, and so on. Thus, the function ORD returns a value of 0 because A is the first scalar value in the defined enumeration. Integers and subranges beginning from zero are already in ordinal form, so ORD(123) equals 123.

The type CHAR is predefined as containing all 255 character values. When used with character constants (such as 'A'), the ORD function returns numeric values corresponding to ASCII character codes. This relationship is illustrated in the next example. Unlike the procedure ScalarToInt above, this example has no defined enumeration:

```
PROCEDURE AsciiToInt;
VAR
 Letter:CHAR;
BEGIN
 Letter := 'A';
 WRITELN('THE ORDINAL VALUE OF ',Letter,' IS ',ORD(Letter),'.');
END;
```

Now the ORD function will return the numeric ASCII equivalent of 'A'. (Refer to Figure 14-2.)

```
THE ORDINAL VALUE OF A IS 65.
```

CHR

When dealing with ASCII equivalents, the **CHR** function works just like ORD—in reverse. Given a numeric value between 0 and 127 (255 on some systems), the CHR function returns the corresponding ASCII character. For example, CHR(65) will return a value of 'A'.

This function is useful when your program must generate ASCII control codes. Since these codes cannot be written as printable characters, it is not possible to code such characters directly in program text. For example, the control character that produces an audible tone, or bell, is ASCII 007. If your system has the bell feature, you may wish your program to generate this character each time an incorrect key is struck. To achieve this, the ASCII numeric equivalent may be passed as a parameter to the CHR function:

```
IF WrongKey THEN WRITE(CHR(7));
```

You will have to consult the user's guide for your system to find out what codes are returned when passing parameters to the CHR function that are in the range 128 . . 255. It is possible to pass an integral value to the function that is greater than 255, but the system will truncate the value to the first eight bits, or 0 . . 255.

ODD

One other predefined function that allows the conversion of data types is **ODD**. An INTEGER parameter passed to the ODD function causes return of a BOOLEAN result. If the integer value is an odd number (1, 3, 5, 7, 9, etc.), the function returns a value of TRUE. If the integer value is even (0, 2, 4, 6, 8, etc.), a value of FALSE is returned.

An interesting application of this function is to sort a list into two columns:

```
FOR I := 0 TO 9 DO
BEGIN
 WRITE(I:20);
 IF ODD(I) THEN
 WRITELN;
END;
```

This program block causes the following list to be printed:

```
0          1
2          3
4          5
6          7
8          9
```

The functions ORD, CHR, and ODD do not perform any transformations on the binary data held in storage. These functions simply cause the compiler to interpret those data in different ways. Thus, certain typing constraints may be suspended for specific purposes.

PACKED STRUCTURES

As discussed above, the default memory space assigned to most types of variables in Pascal is 16 bits, or one word. Exceptions are REAL, which requires four bytes, and STRING, which may occupy many bytes. BOOLEAN variables, even though they may be represented as a single bit (0 or 1, representing FALSE or TRUE) have a default size of one word. The default storage unit for user-defined scalar values is also 16-bit words, regardless of the actual number of bits required to represent the values that will be stored.

Looking again at the table in Figure 14-2, it becomes apparent that assigning 16 bits for each data value to be stored is likely to waste memory space. To enable the programmer to use memory space more efficiently, Pascal provides the reserved word **PACKED** to be applied to data types. Structures of type ARRAY or RECORD may be declared as PACKED. To illustrate, consider the following two declarations:

```
VAR
 BigArray : ARRAY[1..1024] OF BOOLEAN;
 SmallArray : PACKED ARRAY[1..1024] OF BOOLEAN;
```

Both arrays hold the same amount of data. However, BigArray will use 1024 words of memory because one word is assigned to each array element. But, as just stated, a BOOLEAN value may be represented in one bit. The PACKED structure created by the declaration of SmallArray as PACKED causes one bit, rather than one word, to be assigned to each array element. Accordingly, SmallArray occupies 1024 bits, or 64 words, of memory and holds just as much information as BigArray. The effect of the PACKED declaration is to store the values without any wasted space. In this case, there is a space reduction of 16 to 1.

Defining a RECORD as PACKED can result in substantial memory savings. To use a familiar example, consider a record that holds dates:

```
DateType = PACKED RECORD
 Year: 0..99;
 Month: 0..12;
 Day: 0..31;
END;
```

Were DateType not defined as PACKED, each field would be stored using 16 bits, for a total record size of 48 bits (three words). Referring to the table in Figure 14-2, it can be seen that, in the PACKED RECORD DateType, the field Year will occupy seven bits, Month will occupy four bits, and Day will occupy five bits. Thus, the entire record will occupy 16 bits, or one-third the space that would have been used if it had not been defined as PACKED. These specific subranges, of course, were chosen because it seems reasonable to allow ranges of 100 years, 12 months, and 31 days. Of course, Year could have been defined as 0 . . 127 with the same impact upon storage, since that is the maximum range of values that can be stored in seven bits. Similarly, but less usefully, Month could have been defined as 0 . . 15.

If a packed structure is embedded in another packed structure, the reserved word PACKED must be used to define both structures. For example:

```
VAR
 MyArray : PACKED ARRAY[1..10] OF
           PACKED ARRAY[1..15] OF
           CHAR;
(* or *)
```

```
TYPE
 XRec = PACKED RECORD
  (* field definitions *)
  YField : PACKED ARRAY[1..10] OF CHAR;
  (* field definitions *)
 END;
```

MEMORY EFFICIENCY

A savings in memory allocation usually is accompanied by an adverse trade-off in execution speed. For example, in comparing BigArray to SmallArray above, program execution speed will be faster for BigArray. Accessing data in either word or byte units generally results in fast execution times because the beginning of each element or field in memory can be found quickly. With PACKED structures, additional processing must be done each time a value is accessed to determine the exact memory location of the value. In other words, processing must be performed to extract the data from a packed structure.

The trade-off between memory space and speed is encountered often in programming. The correct decision depends on the original design specifications for a particular application.

Besides the use of PACKED structures, other alternate ways of writing program text can result in memory savings. Two specific approaches, one for STRING and SET constants and one for CASE statements, are discussed here as examples of what to watch for in making coding decisions that affect memory allocation and processing speed.

STRING and SET Constants

STRING constants may take the following forms:

```
CONST
 PhraseCon = 'THIS IS A STRING CONSTANT';

(* or *)

WRITE('THIS IS A STRING CONSTANT');
```

If the same STRING constant is referenced several times within a program, it is more memory efficient to declare a variable to hold the STRING and then assign the STRING value to the variable, as in:

```
VAR
 PhraseVar:STRING;
BEGIN
 PhraseVar := 'THIS IS A STRING CONSTANT';
 WRITE(PhraseVar);
END;
```

If this approach is not taken, the compiler will insert the 25-byte constant 'THIS IS A STRING CONSTANT' into the program code each time PhraseCon is referenced—even if the reference is only LENGTH (PhraseCon). Therefore, it is preferable to declare a global variable to hold the STRING and then assign a value to the variable.

SET constants are of the form:

```
CONST
 VowelCon = ['A','E','I','O','U'];

(* or *)

IF Letter IN ['A','E','I','O','U'] THEN
```

As with STRING constants, SET constants that are referenced frequently should be coded as global variables and then assigned explicit values:

```
VAR
 VowelSet:SET OF CHAR;
 Letter:CHAR;
BEGIN
 VowelSet := ['A','E','I','O','U'];
 READLN(Letter);
 IF Letter IN VowelSet THEN
 program statement;
END;
```

CASE Statements with Wide Ranges

The amount of code the compiler generates upon encountering a CASE statement depends upon how wide the range of selectors is and upon the number of selectors. If the values of the CASE selectors cover a wide range, an alternate method may be used to reduce the amount of code produced. For example, the following CASE statement has selectors that are distributed widely throughout the range 'A' . . 'Z':

```
CASE Choice OF
 'A':DoAProcess;
 'M':DoMProcess;
 'Z':DoZProcess;
END;
```

In this case, it would be more memory efficient to code:

```
IF Choice = 'A' THEN DoAProcess
 ELSE IF Choice = 'M' THEN DoMProcess
  ELSE IF Choice = 'Z' THEN DoZProcess;
```

This alternative is both faster and more memory efficient than the CASE statement and represents an exception to the commonly encountered trade-off between these two factors. The disadvantage, of course, is losing the program clarity offered by the CASE statement.

Applying Efficiency

The question of where to apply efficiencies of execution speed and memory allocation is, of course, a matter of judgment. There are, however, some general guidelines that may be helpful.

Processing speed is traded off most easily in the initialization and user-interaction portions of a program. Many preliminary calculations and file references may be performed in the time between user keystrokes. In many cases, fairly comprehensive error checking can be done during user interaction without adversely affecting system reaction time. Remember that the initialization section of a program is executed only once. It is probably a wise trade-off to sacrifice a few seconds in the initialization section to gain speed in the processing sections.

A program's main processing functions often involve repetitive or complex calculations, or "number crunching." These kinds of operations generally require the closest attention to efficient execution. Even a small delay within a loop may accumulate to the limits of tolerance if the loop is executed a thousand times. Specifically, efficiencies that may be sought in processing sections include:

- Where possible, calculations should be moved outside of a loop. This avoids redundant calculations.
- Temporary variables should be used to hold partial results. Otherwise, the value of the main variable may have to be recalculated needlessly.
- Major I/O operations, such as opening and closing files, usually take a few seconds, especially when accessing diskettes. These operations should be minimized through an awareness of the status of files at all points in the program.
- When a procedure or function is called and then returns processing control, a significant amount of "behind-the-scenes" processing occurs that is beyond the control of the programmer. Although good top-down programming practice implies the liberal use of procedures and functions, time-critical repetitive portions of a program may execute faster written as *in-line* code, or programming statements that do not contain procedure or function calls.
- None of these considerations should be allowed to interfere with good programming form unless absolutely necessary. Modest efficiency gains can result in large sacrifices in program clarity and can make debugging difficult. In general, the time to seek efficiencies is when a program is too big or too slow for implementation by more conventional structures.

BLOCK I/O AND DYNAMIC MEMORY

Because of the way I/O operations are performed in computer hardware, accessing data is made more efficient if larger amounts of data are read or written by a single statement. In other words, accessing an entire block of data with a single statement is more efficient than accessing individual bytes or groups of bytes in several statements. This process is referred to as *block I/O.* Fast data management routines, such as copying files, may be achieved with these UCSD Pascal features:

- Untyped FILE
- BLOCKREAD
- BLOCKWRITE
- Dynamic memory allocation.

Untyped FILE

An *untyped file* is declared as a file variable that has no data type associated with it. As such, the file contains data that are interpreted only as blocks of binary code. In other words, no structure is assumed for the file except that each block contains 512 bytes. This does not imply that the file has no structure, however. For example, an untyped file variable may be declared for an external file of unknown structure or having a structure that is not meaningful within the program. Accordingly, the program treats the file as groups of 512-byte blocks, stored adjacent to one another on the diskette. The programmer may make no assumptions about the structure of the file other than the fact that binary data are contained in it.

Unlike formatted, or typed, files, which are declared as FILE OF SomeType, untyped files are declared:

```
VAR
 FileName : FILE;
```

One difference between untyped files and formatted files is that an untyped file has no file pointer variable associated with it. Because no record structure is related to the file, it would be meaningless to make reference to record positions. Also because of the lack of record format and file pointer variable, the action of the RESET procedure is different for untyped files. Recall that RESET not only opens a file but also reads the first record into memory. Since an untyped file is presumed to have no structures that can be accessed as records, a RESET performed on an untyped file opens the file but does not perform any data access.

In moving data from untyped files into variables within a program, it must be remembered that the portion of memory allocated to that variable must be declared large enough to contain at least 512 bytes (one block), or multiple blocks. For example, an array declared to contain one block of data might be declared:

```
VAR
 BlockSize : PACKED ARRAY[1..512] OF CHAR;

(* or *)

VAR
 BlockSpace : ARRAY[1..256] OF INTEGER;
```

If the variable is not large enough to hold all the data to be read in, the incoming data will overflow into adjacent data areas in memory, causing the destruction of the adjacent variables, and other potentially disastrous results.

Data are read into variables from an untyped file in binary form without regard for the type declared for the variable. In the above examples, CHAR only indicates that each array element is to hold one byte of binary data. In turn, INTEGER indicates that each array element is to hold one word. In other words, no checking or typing constraints are applied to the data read into the variable. A variable that receives data from an untyped file may be of any type except FILE; that is, the file variable itself may not be named as the destination of a block input operation.

BLOCKREAD and BLOCKWRITE

Since untyped file access does not use the buffer area of the file variable (FileVar^), access statements GET and PUT cannot be used with untyped files. For this purpose, there are two predefined functions for performing I/O operations on entire blocks of data: **BLOCKREAD** and **BLOCKWRITE**. The value returned by each of these functions is an integer representing the number of blocks transferred successfully. These functions must be used to perform any I/O operations on untyped files but may not be used with typed file variables.

The syntax for passing parameters to either of these functions is identical:

```
n := BLOCKREAD(FileVariableName, VariableName, nBlocks, StartBlock);
(* same syntax for BLOCKWRITE *)
```

In the above syntax, FileVariableName is the program's name for the file to be accessed. In the case of BLOCKREAD, VariableName is another variable declared in the program that is to receive the contents of the accessed file.

When performing BLOCKWRITE, VariableName is a variable containing the data that are to be written into the file. The third parameter, nBlocks, is an integer that indicates how many blocks are to be read or written. The fourth parameter, StartBlock, is optional and is also an integer. The parameter StartBlock indicates a block number in the file at which the read or write is to begin. This block number is a sequential block count relative to the beginning of the file. If no fourth parameter is given, the operation begins at the first block in the file, or block 0 (zero), with subsequent accesses referring to following blocks.

Thus, the following statement causes one block from the file Myfile to be read into the memory area named Buffer, starting at the third block in the file:

```
n := BLOCKREAD(MyFile, Buffer, 1, 2);
```

To read the next two blocks of the same file, the programmer could omit the fourth parameter and write:

```
n := BLOCKREAD(MyFile, Buffer, 2);
```

Note that the third parameter indicates the number of blocks that the operation attempts to access. The integer value returned by the function gives the actual number of blocks accessed. For example, if a BLOCKWRITE attempted to write five blocks near the end of a diskette, the function might return a value of 1, indicating that only one block was written before the device became full. Similarly, attempting a BLOCKREAD of five blocks at a point one block from the end-of-file would return a value of 1, indicating that only one block could be read before the end-of-file was encountered.

If the fourth parameter is omitted, the system keeps a count of blocks accessed on the file so that successive BLOCKREAD or BLOCKWRITE operations will step through the file properly.

The IORESULT function may be used in conjunction with BLOCKREAD and BLOCKWRITE. Of course, to accomplish this it is necessary to turn off I/O error checking by including the (*$I – *) compiler option syntax prior to doing the I/O operation. Then, you may check the operation by invoking IORESULT. IORESULT is useful for verifying whether errors were encountered in performing block I/O. Also, the EOF function may be used to test whether the end-of-file has been reached.

Dynamic Memory Allocation

Dynamic memory allocation is touched upon briefly in the discussion of the NEW procedure in Chapter 11. Pascal is one of the few languages that give the programmer a high degree of control over memory allocation. Dynamic memory is allocated explicitly by the NEW procedure. UCSD Pascal provides additional capabilities through the use of **MARK** and **RELEASE**.

To understand how Pascal provides control over memory use, you must be able to visualize how the Pascal operating system partitions memory. Figure 14-3 is a conceptual diagram of how memory is allocated.

The total UCSD Pascal program environment, typically 64K bytes (or 32K words), ranges from low memory addresses to high memory addresses. Low memory may be thought of as being at the bottom of the memory space with high memory at the top. Your program instructions and any global data occupy a portion of high memory. The remainder of the memory space is dynamic memory, which will be allocated in constantly changing fashion during program execution. This dynamic allocation is one of the reasons Pascal is said to be memory efficient.

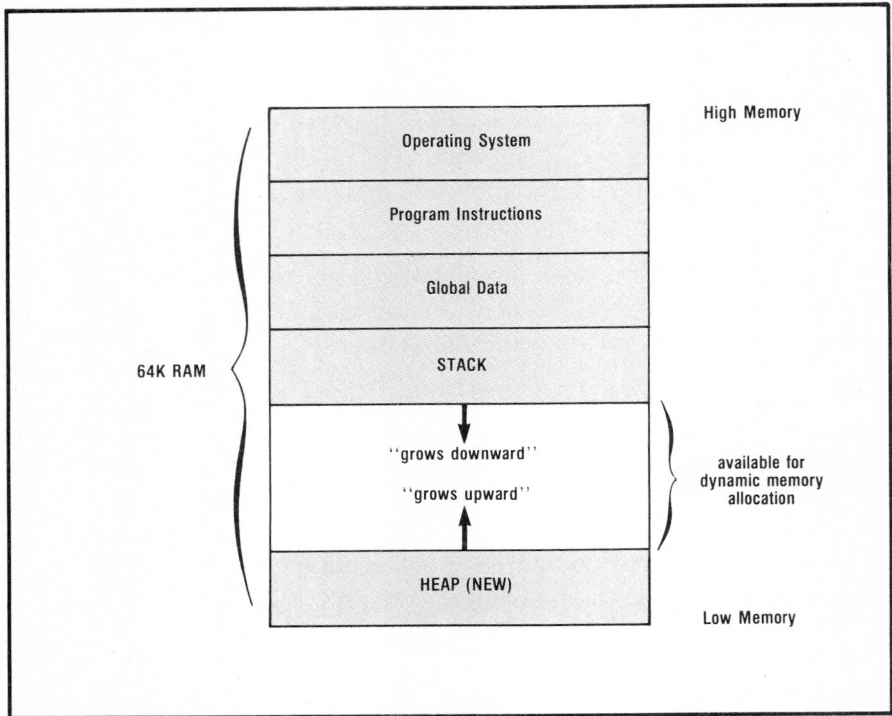

Figure 14-3. Pascal memory allocation.

Pascal divides dynamic memory into two areas—the *stack* and the *heap.* As shown in Figure 14-3, the stack "grows downward" from high memory and the heap "grows upward" from low memory as dynamic memory is allocated. The stack contains the local variables for the procedures and functions in your program. The size of the stack is dynamic because as each procedure or function is called, space is allocated in the stack to hold its local variables. As the procedure or function terminates, its local variables are discarded from the stack and memory space is released.

The remaining memory may be allocated explicitly by the NEW procedure during program execution. Space allocated by this procedure forms the heap.

Thus, the stack and the heap "grow" toward each other as space is allocated. If the programmer does not keep track of the respective sizes of the stack and the heap at each point in the program, the limit of the available space may be reached, at which point a *stack overflow* error will occur. Usually, the only way to recover from stack overflow is to reboot the system, at which point valuable data may be lost.

MEMAVAIL and SIZEOF

UCSD Pascal provides the predefined functions **MEMAVAIL** and **SIZEOF** to help keep track of the amount of unallocated dynamic memory. MEMAVAIL may be called without a parameter and returns an integral value for the number of unallocated 16-bit *words*, or the amount of free space between the bottom of the stack and the top of the heap. A parameter is passed to SIZEOF representing a data type or a variable, and the function returns an integral value for the number of *bytes* occupied by the value contained in the parameter. For example, to determine if there is enough memory available to acquire another record of the type LinkBlk from the file LinkFile, you could write:

```
IF MEMAVAIL > (SIZEOF(LinkBlk) DIV 2) THEN NEW(LinkPoint);
```

Note that the operation DIV 2 is necessary because SIZEOF returns a value in bytes and MEMAVAIL is in words.

NEW, MARK, and RELEASE

To review, when you declare a variable, you are causing the compiler to allocate memory space for the data to be contained in the variable. The variable name is a way of referring to the data within program text. The actual amount of memory allocated is determined by the TYPE declared for the variable. A variable of type INTEGER is allocated space of one word, for example.

Similarly, the TYPE of data to be stored in dynamic memory determines the size of memory allocated by the NEW procedure. Unlike variables, however, these portions of dynamic memory have no names. Instead, reference is made by using the pointer variable, which contains the address or memory position of a data item. Used properly, the pointer variable provides the same capabilities that a variable name does.

When the NEW(PointerVariableName) procedure is executed, the system sets aside a memory space large enough to hold the type of data associated with the pointer. Also, the location of that memory space is stored in the pointer. The memory space allocated is a portion of the heap.

The value placed in the pointer is the current *top-of-heap,* or the lowest available allocated address in dynamic memory. Each time NEW is called, the value of the pointer is changed to correspond with the current top-of-heap. Remember, however, that if the same pointer variable name is used in a subsequent NEW procedure, the previous value of the pointer will be replaced with the current value of the top-of-heap. Even though the data item in the first reference still exists, there would be no way to access it, since the value of the original pointer has been lost. Accordingly, it is good practice to move the value of the pointer into another variable if the same pointer variable name must be passed to a subsequent NEW procedure.

The procedures MARK and RELEASE are both used with the pointer variable:

```
MARK(PointerVariableName);

(* and *)

RELEASE(PointerVariableName);
```

MARK gets the current value of the top-of-heap and places it in the pointer variable given. It has no effect on the amount of memory in the heap. This procedure is used to keep track of the current position on the heap. The reason for keeping track of this position is that once the area created by the NEW procedure is no longer needed it can be returned to available dynamic memory. This is done by the procedure RELEASE, which restores the top-of-heap pointer to the position indicated by the pointer variable passed to it as a parameter. In other words, once the value of a pointer has been set by NEW or MARK, RELEASE gives back all dynamic memory in the heap "above" the pointer.

Thus, MARK may be used to return only a portion of the heap while retaining allocated memory below the mark, or pointer. Both of these procedures are used in the following block I/O example.

Block I/O Example

The procedure presented in Figure 14-4 implements a block file transfer to copy an entire file quickly into another file. All of the block I/O techniques so far described are used.

Dynamic Memory Allocation Examples

The following procedures exemplify different memory allocation problems. The first example creates a linked list of names entered by the user. This procedure illustrates the exception provided in Pascal for the order of declaration where pointers are concerned: The type of dynamic memory must be known so that a size can be established. On the other

```
PROCEDURE CopyFiles;
TYPE
 Blk = PACKED ARRAY[1..512] OF CHAR;    (* define space equal to one block *)
VAR
 Base,
 ScratchPad:^Blk;                             (* declare pointer variables *)

 MemBlocks,
 BlocksIn,
 BlockCount,
 BlocksOut:INTEGER;                          (* declare counters for blocks *)

 InFile,
 OutFile:FILE;                                    (* declare untyped files *)

BEGIN
 MARK(Base);                (* get lowest address in heap as pointer to buffer *)
 BlockCount := 0;                                    (* initialize counter *)
 MemBlocks := 0;                                     (* initialize counter *)
 WHILE MEMAVAIL > 2048 DO         (* leave some memory space as a "cushion" *)
  BEGIN
   NEW(ScratchPad);                                (* acquire memory space *)
   MemBlocks := SUCC(MemBlocks);                  (* increment block count *)
  END;
 RESET(InFile,'SOMEFILE.IN');                          (* open for reading *)
 REWRITE(OutFile,'SOMEFILE.OUT');               (* create/open for writing *)
 WHILE NOT EOF(InFile) DO
  BEGIN
   BlocksIn := BLOCKREAD(InFile,Base^,MemBlocks); (* read blocks into heap *)
   BlocksOut := BLOCKWRITE(OutFile,Base^,BlocksIn);    (* write to OutFile *)
   BlockCount := BlockCount + BlocksOut;
  END;
 CLOSE(OutFile,LOCK);               (* close output file and make permanent *)
 RELEASE(Base);                                 (* give back memory space *)
 WRITELN(BlockCount, ' BLOCKS WERE TRANSFERRED.');
END;
```

Figure 14-4. Procedure CopyFiles.

hand, if the structure itself is to contain a pointer to a similar structure, as is the case in linked lists, there seems to be a conflict over which declaration should come first. For this reason, Pascal allows pointer types to be defined before the definition of the structure to which they will point. Global definitions and declarations are made as follows:

```
TYPE
 LinkBlkPtr = ^LinkBlk;                  (* define pointer to LinkBlk *)

 LinkBlk = RECORD                                (* define record type *)
  Name:STRING;                                   (* field to hold name *)
  NextLinkBlk:LinkBlkPtr;                        (* field to hold link *)
 END;

 VAR
  FirstPtr,
  PrevPoint,                   (* to hold pointer values temporarily *)
  LinkPoint:LinkBlkPtr;                   (* to hold current pointer *)
```

Given the above, the procedure SaveNames presented in Figure 14-5 creates a series of linked records through the use of dynamic memory allocation. (Recall that NIL is a reserved word used to set a value for the pointer to the end-of-list.)

```
PROCEDURE SaveNames;
BEGIN
 MARK(FirstPtr);                                  (* get pointer top-of-heap *)
 PrevPoint := NIL;      (* assign end-of-list indicator to previous pointer *)
 WHILE MEMAVAIL > (SIZEOF(LinkBlk) DIV 2) DO               (* enough memory? *)
  BEGIN
   NEW(LinkPoint);                           (* acquire record space in heap *)
   WRITE('ENTER NAME ');                          (* tell user to enter name *)
   READLN(LinkPoint^.Name);                (* store in name field of record *)
   LinkPoint^.NextLinkBlk := PrevPoint;           (* link to previous or NIL *)
   PrevPoint := LinkPoint;             (* point previous record to this one *)
  END;
 WRITELN('NO MORE MEMORY AVAILABLE');
END;
```

Figure 14-5. Procedure SaveNames.

Given the procedure SaveNames, the next example searches the name list for a particular name. Two parameters must be passed to this procedure: FirstPoint, which indicates a starting position in the list to be searched, and Target, the desired name. The procedure FindName is presented in Figure 14-6.

After the procedure FindName has been executed, NextPtr^ will be either NIL or will point to the record containing the target name.

The next example may be used to acquire all available memory in 1K, or 1024 byte, groups. This procedure assumes that the global variable Base is an indicator for the top-of-heap. A parameter passed to the procedure that will return a different value to the calling block is KCount, a count of the number of 1K groups acquired. The procedure MakeBigBuffer is presented in Figure 14-7.

The memory thus acquired represents the largest number of 1K groups currently available. This space might be used, for example, to hold large blocks of data that must be operated upon by the program.

These examples are illustrative. In practice, it might not be possible to allocate all available memory space, since any procedure following would require stack space in which to operate, causing a stack overflow if the programmer had allocated all the space.

Block I/O operations may be used in conjunction with dynamic memory allocation. This is illustrated by the procedure CopyFiles presented earlier in this chapter. The programmer may create a large

```
PROCEDURE FindName(FirstPoint:LinkBlkPtr; Target:STRING);
VAR
 NextPtr:LinkBlkPtr;                              (* pointer to next record *)
 Found:BOOLEAN;                               (* flag to indicate success *)
BEGIN
 NextPtr := FirstPoint;                          (* start with first record *)
 Found := FALSE;                                        (* initialize flag *)
 WHILE (NextPtr <> NIL) AND (NOT Found) DO
  BEGIN
   IF NextPtr^.Name = Target THEN               (* if desired name is found, *)
    Found := TRUE                                           (* stop search *)
   ELSE
    NextPtr := NextPtr^.NextLinkBlk;         (* get pointer from next record *)
  END;
END;
```

Figure 14-6. Procedure FindName.

```
PROCEDURE MakeBigBuffer(VAR KCount:INTEGER);
TYPE
 OneK = PACKED ARRAY[1..1024] OF 0..255;
 OneKPtr = ^OneK;
VAR
 Temp:OneKPtr;                    (* pointer variable to point to 1K buffer *)
BEGIN
 MARK(Base);                               (* save beginning of big buffer *)
 KCount := 0;                                       (* initialize counter *)
 WHILE MEMAVAIL > (SIZEOF(OneK) DIV 2) DO
  BEGIN
   NEW(Temp);                    (* acquire memory--address is not important *)
   KCount := SUCC(KCount);             (* count number of 1K groups acquired *)
  END;
 WRITELN(KCount,' 1K BLOCKS ACQUIRED IN MEMORY');
END;
```

Figure 14-7. Procedure MakeBigBuffer.

memory area in the heap, and the resulting *buffer* may be filled with data by using the pointer variable associated with that buffer as the variable address into which to copy the data. In the CopyFile example, this data transfer is accomplished by:

```
BlocksIn := BLOCKREAD(InFile, Base^, MemBlocks);
```

This statement will cause a number of blocks to be read from InFile into the buffer. The number of blocks read is determined by the integer MemBlocks. Once read in, the data may be sorted or written to another file, and so on. The buffer provides a convenient means of storage for the data while these operations are being carried out.

ADDITIONAL UCSD EXTENSIONS FOR MEMORY MANAGEMENT

UCSD Pascal provides some other extensions that are useful in manipulating memory content. These extensions include:

- MOVELEFT and MOVERIGHT
- FILLCHAR.

MOVELEFT and MOVERIGHT

The predefined procedures **MOVELEFT** and **MOVERIGHT** perform high-speed transfer of data from one memory location to another. These

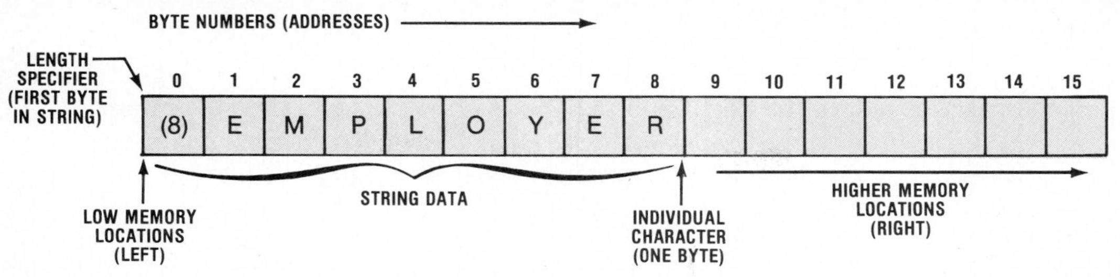

Figure 14-8. Low to high memory locations represented from left to right.

procedures are useful in transferring portions of strings or packed arrays as an alternative to writing a loop to transfer each character. Large blocks of data may also be moved rapidly from one area of memory to another.

Use of these procedures requires visualizing memory in a different way from that just presented for stack and heap. In doing data transfers, it is useful to think of lower memory addresses on the left and higher addresses on the right. Figure 14-8 illustrates this relationship. The first variable declared in the program is assigned the lowest memory address and subsequently declared variables occupy successively higher addresses. The alphanumeric characters that represent a given value, then, may be thought of as reading from left to right, just as these values would appear in program text.

Figure 14-9 illustrates how these procedures would operate on a string 'EMPLOYER'. MOVERIGHT causes the string to be moved from the

Figure 14-9. Results of MOVELEFT and MOVERIGHT on STRING data.

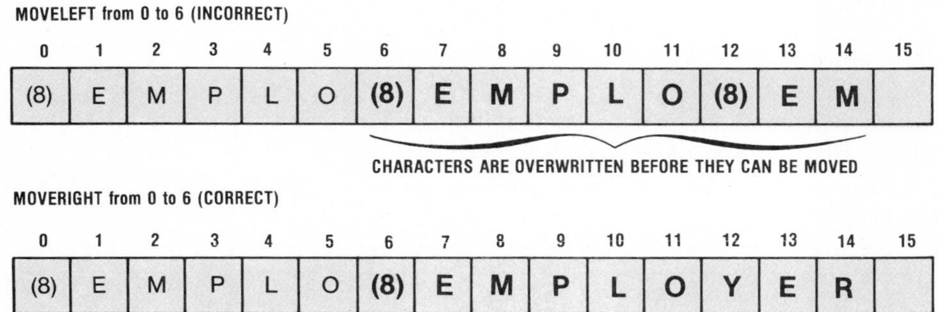

source area into the destination area one character at a time beginning at the right of the source string (with the letter R). The moved character is placed at the right end of the destination area. The syntax used is:

```
MOVERIGHT(Variable1, Variable2, X); (* same syntax for MOVELEFT *)
```

The parameters passed are: Variable1, which corresponds with the name of the source location of the data; Variable2, which is the destination location name; and X, which is an integral value for the number of bytes to be moved.

Care must be taken when moving data within the same variable. If the two memory locations are in close proximity, it is possible that a portion of the source data may reside within the destination location. If this occurs, the source data may be overwritten before being read. Notice in Figure 14-9 that if MOVELEFT is used, a portion of the original string is overwritten before it can be moved.

Figure 14-10 illustrates what happens when the data to be moved is in a higher memory location than the destination. Notice that, for illustrative purposes, EMPLOYER is treated as an ARRAY OF CHAR rather than as a STRING value. (No length identifier is associated with it.) In this

Figure 14-10. Results of MOVELEFT and MOVERIGHT on an ARRAY of CHAR.

ORIGINAL ARRAY

0	1	2	3	4	5	6	7	8	9	10	11	12	13	14	15
							E	M	P	L	O	Y	E	R	

MOVELEFT from 7 to 0 (CORRECT)

0	1	2	3	4	5	6	7	8	9	10	11	12	13	14	15
E	M	P	L	O	Y	E	R	M	P	L	O	Y	E	R	

MOVERIGHT from 7 to 0 (INCORRECT)

0	1	2	3	4	5	6	7	8	9	10	11	12	13	14	15
R	M	P	L	O	Y	E	R	M	P	L	O	Y	E	R	

case, MOVELEFT is correct. MOVERIGHT causes some of the original array elements to be overwritten before they can be moved.

Note that the terms MOVELEFT and MOVERIGHT refer, not to the direction of movement between memory locations, but to the order in which the movement is to take place, beginning at the left or at the right of the source data.

There is a correspondence, though, between the terms and this general rule: Use MOVERIGHT when moving parts of a variable to higher memory locations (to the right) in the same variable, and use MOVELEFT when moving parts of a variable to lower memory locations (to the left) in the same variable.

When moving string data, remember that the first character in a string is actually a length identifier. This identifier will be moved just like any other character. When moving strings, it is best to specify the string variable in the form STRING[Y], where Y is the character position to be moved.

You may not be certain that the given character position is valid. For example, the string might not be long enough. Or, if the string is empty, STRING[1] will cause a range error. In such cases, turn range checking off temporarily with (*$R – *).

FILLCHAR

The predefined procedure **FILLCHAR** offers a fast way to initialize large areas of memory. The syntax is:

```
FILLCHAR(VariableName, ByteCount, Value);
```

In the above, VariableName is the name of the destination location to be filled, ByteCount is an integral value for the number of characters to be placed in the destination location, and Value is any scalar value to be placed in the destination. Bear in mind, however, that only the first eight bits of this value will be used, the equivalent of a character. For example:

```
FILLCHAR(BigArray[20], 200, ' ');
```

This statement will fill 200 bytes with space characters (blanks), beginning with the twentieth element of BigArray. Care must be taken to fill only the number of bytes desired, since no checking is performed to protect the adjacent data.

VARIANT RECORDS

Recall that Pascal's strong typing enforces strict rules governing the validity of certain operations on defined data types. There are occasions, however, when the programmer may need to use a particular data element in more than one way or to define a record as having more than one structure. Suspension of normal typing constraints for these purposes is accomplished in Pascal by *variant record* definitions. A variant record is a formatted record in which a portion of the record, or perhaps all of it, may be defined as having more than one possible structure, even though a fixed amount of memory is allocated to that record.

For example, consider a situation in which a business has a master file containing records for employees as well as for clients. One way to implement the file would be to define a single record that has separate fields for all data items to be stored:

```
TYPE
 BothTypes = RECORD
  Name:STRING;                          (* either employee name or client name
  SocialSecurityNumber:STRING[9];                          (* employee data
  ClientNumber:INTEGER;                                      (* client data
 END;
```

Note, however, that this form of data storage is very inefficient. Individual records are to hold either a Social Security number or a client number, but never both. Thus, one field in each record is always empty—a waste of valuable storage space.

Alternatively, a variant record may be defined for the above example. The definition of the variant record assigns alternate meanings to a single area within the record by giving an alternate *field list.* The syntax for this definition uses the reserved word CASE, which has a similar structure to the uses of this term already encountered. So, the above example may be implemented instead as follows:

```
TYPE
 RecType = (Employee,Client);              (* establish two values for RecType *)
 ClEmpRecord = RECORD
  Name:STRING;                           (* this field is shared, but not variant *)
  Typ:RecType;                                 (* this field hold the record type *)
   CASE RecType OF                                            (* announce a variant *)
    Employee:(SocialSecurityNumber:STRING[9]);                      (* field list *)
    Client:(ClientNumber:INTEGER);
   END;
 END;
```

In this case, the memory used for SocialSecurityNumber begins in the same place as the memory used for ClientNumber. The compiler makes the space allocated for the record big enough to hold the largest of the variants, which in this case is SocialSecurityNumber. The programmer must check the value of the variable Typ to determine which field definition is used for a given record.

An alternate syntax may be used by defining Typ as a *tag field.* This syntax requires that definition be placed after CASE and before the case selectors, or field list:

```
CASE Typ : RecType OF
```

This syntax creates a record identical to the one in the first example but requires one less line of code to define.

To illustrate the use of variant records in the processing section of a program, assume the file ClEmpFile contains records of type ClEmpRec.

The following program block controls processing of fields for both employees and clients:

```
IF ClEmpFile^.Typ = Employee THEN
 BEGIN
  ClEmpFile^.SocialSecurityNumber := '999999999';
  (* perform processing with employee definitions *)
 END
ELSE
 BEGIN
  ClEmpFile^.ClientNumber := 9999;
  (* perform processing with client definitions *)
 END;
```

A CASE . . OF control structure might be used to perform the same processing:

```
CASE ClEmpFile^.Typ OF
 Employee:(*program statements*);
 Client:(*program statements*);
END;
```

Bear in mind also that variant records themselves may contain variant records, but the variant part always must be at the end of each record definition.

Another use of variant records is to be able to treat the contents of a variable as any one of many different types of data. In performing data conversion, for example, it may be necessary to treat an INTEGER as a CHARacter or as a STRING of bits. Consider the following declaration:

```
VAR
 AllType:PACKED RECORD
  CASE INTEGER OF
   1:(Int:INTEGER);
   2:(Ch:CHAR);
   3:(Bits:PACKED ARRAY[0..7] OF 0..1);
  END;
```

Note the use of INTEGER for the CASE variant. This is allowed because INTEGER is a scalar type, having a fixed range and a finite number of members. In this example, it does not matter what the case selectors are, since the fields within each record may be accessed by name. Since AllType is a PACKED RECORD, the three variants declared take up the least possible amount of space: The variant Int occupies 16 bits and the other two variants each occupy eight. The record size is determined by the size of the largest variant; therefore, the entire record occupies 16 bits. Given the above, the following displays a character in three different formats:

```
AllType.Ch := 'A';                                    (* put 'A' into variant *)
WRITELN('VALUE OF ',AllType.Ch,' IS ',AllType.Int);          (* show integer *)
WRITE('IN BINARY, THAT IS ');                          (* prepare to show binary *)
FOR I := 0 TO 7 DO WRITE(AllType.Bits[I]);               (* show binary form *)
WRITELN;                                                      (* finish line *)
```

MULTI-DIMENSIONAL ARRAYS

Recall that arrays may be thought of as lists of elements. The number of elements in the list is defined when the array is declared in the variable declarations section of the program.

Arrays so far encountered in this text are one-dimensional. An example declaration for such an array would be:

```
VAR
 DailyIncome : ARRAY[1..31] OF REAL;
```

The array thus declared may be used to hold income data for a period of one month, or 31 days.

Each element of an array may be, in turn, a list. As mentioned in Chapter 6, arrays of this form are known as multi-dimensional arrays. In fact, Pascal sets no specific limit on how many arrays may be contained within other arrays. There is, of course, the practical limitation of memory size.

There are two ways of declaring multi-dimensional arrays. For example, to index daily income by the months of the year as well as by the days of the month, the declaration might look like this:

```
VAR
 DailyIncome : ARRAY[1..12] OF ARRAY[1..31] OF REAL;
```

This multi-dimensional array can contain 372 elements. (Only 365 elements will be used by the programmer, since not all months have 31 days.) Rather than being a linear list of 372 elements, however, the array may be thought of as a table, as illustrated in Figure 14-11. The months may be thought of as columns and the days as rows. The array is, in essence, a list of lists.

The same structure may be created, alternatively, with the following declaration:

```
VAR
 DailyIncome : ARRAY[1..12,1..31] OF REAL;
```

Alternative references also exist for individual elements within this array. For example, the income entry for September 6, or the ninth month and the sixth day, could be referenced by:

```
DailyIncome[9,6]
```

The same element may be referenced by:

```
DailyIncome[9][6]
```

TWO DIMENSIONAL ARRAY

```
VAR
  DailyIncome: ARRAY [1 . . 12, 1 . . 31] OF REAL;
```

Table of Array Indexes
Reference by DailyIncome[Month,Day]

DAYS \ MONTHS	1	2	3	4	5	6	. .	12
1	[1,1]	[2,1]	[3,1]	[4,1]	[5,1]	[6,1]		[12,1]
2	[1,2]	[2,2]	[3,2]	[4,2]	[5,2]	[6,2]		[12,2]
3	[1,3]	[2,3]	[3,3]	[4,3]	[5,3]	[6,3]		[12,3]
4	[1,4]	[2,4]	[3,4]	[4,4]	[5,4]	[6,4]		[12,4]
5	[1,5]	[2,5]	[3,5]	[4,5]	[5,5]	[6,5]		[12,5]
. .	. .	. .	. .	. .	. .	. .		. .
31	[1,31]	[2,31]	[3,31]	[4,31]	[5,31]	[6,31]	. .	[12,31]

(Note that some array locations, such as [2,31], will have no entry.)

Figure 14-11. A two-dimensional array.

The effect in either case is identical, and the use of either syntax may be determined by whatever is convenient for the programmer.

By extension, a three-dimensional array to hold income data for the years 1980 through 1985 can be declared:

```
VAR
 DailyIncome : ARRAY[1980..1985] OF
               ARRAY[1..12] OF
               ARRAY[1..31] OF REAL;
```

The same structure is created by:

```
VAR
 DailyIncome : ARRAY[1980..1985,1..12,1..31] OF REAL;
```

This structure is diagrammed in Figure 14-12. Multi-dimensional arrays are useful for the representation of hierarchical structures. Note that the income data in the above example could be held in a linear, or one-dimensional, array of 2,232 elements. However, the three-dimensional structure more clearly represents the hierarchy of years, months, and days. For such a list, a multi-dimensional array provides program clarity; it is much easier for the programmer to access data for the date 9-6-84

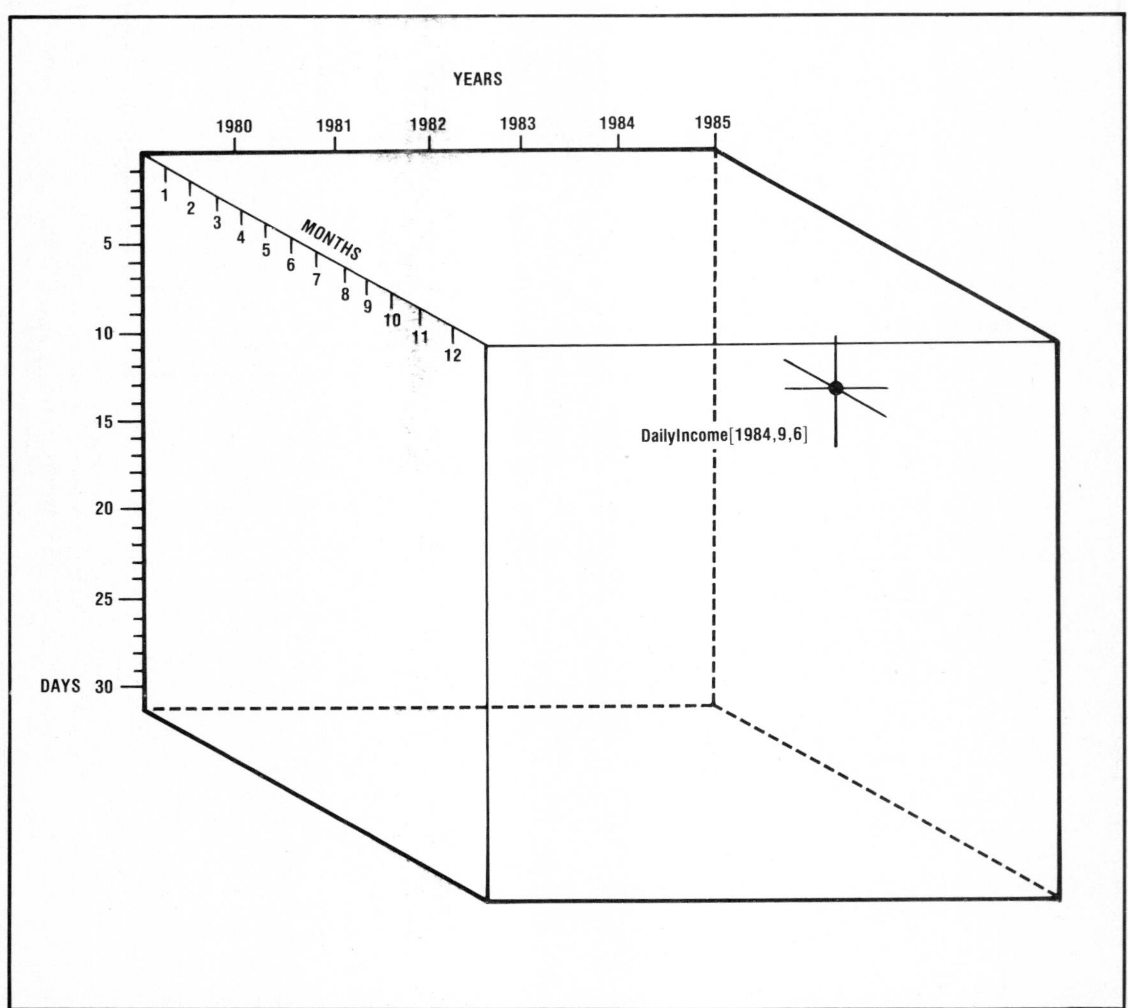

Figure 14-12. A three-dimensional array.

in the multi-dimensional structure than to calculate that the desired item would be entry number 1,742 in a corresponding one-dimensional list!

RECURSION

As discussed in Chapter 4, a procedure or function is said to be recursive when it calls itself. This feature is useful, for example, in implementing binary searches, in that successive partitioning of the list may be done by calling the partitioning procedure recursively and passing parameters to it that represent data gained from the preceding pass.

Caution must be exercised, however, when introducing recursion into a program. The number of recursive procedure calls must be limited—otherwise, all memory in the system may be consumed quickly. This can happen because each time a procedure is called new space for the variables used in the procedure is acquired from the stack and is not released until execution of the procedure terminates.

The important thing to remember is that recursion may cause stack overflow unless the programmer keeps close track of the number of recursive procedure calls that are likely to occur within a given program block. The situation is made more difficult when the number of recursive calls is controlled by program variables.

The example presented in Figure 14-13 implements a binary search using recursive techniques. The desired data item is a string represented by the variable Target, which is a user selection passed to the function BinSrch. Item positions are given by the integral values Low and Hi, representing the boundaries of the current partition, and Middle, representing the mid-point of the partition.

The function BinSrch is called recursively and passed parameters based on the preceding pass. The end-points of the new partition are determined by a condition test that determines whether the desired Target is above or below the mid-point of the preceding pass.

Note in this example that the number of recursions is determined by the size of the list. The binary search is highly efficient; as mentioned previously, an average of only 19 trials need to be made to find an element in a list of a million entries. Other search techniques might not have such limited recursiveness; and for large lists, it would be possible for all available memory to be used before a value can be found for BinSrch.

```
FUNCTION BinSrch(Low,Hi:INTEGER;
                 VAR Middle:INTEGER;
                 Target:STRING):BOOLEAN;
BEGIN
 IF Low > Hi THEN BinSrch := FALSE
 ELSE
  BEGIN
   Middle := (Low + Hi) DIV 2;
   IF Target = List[Middle] THEN BinSrch := TRUE
   ELSE
    BEGIN
     IF Target < List[Middle] THEN
      BinSrch := BinSrch(Low,Middle-1,Middle,Target)
     ELSE
      BinSrch := BinSrch(Middle+1,Hi,Middle,Target);
    END;
  END;
END;
```

Figure 14-13. Function BinSrch.

This is not a reason to avoid recursion; however, the programmer must be aware of the potential for abnormal program termination.

As stated previously, the techniques presented here do not represent the limits of UCSD Pascal. Almost certainly, you will encounter other language extensions and facilities as you continue your study. Also, your ability to coin terms in Pascal—in effect, to create your own language—offers even further flexibility. The ability to use any language and the richness of the language itself grow with frequent use. The tools presented in this book are offered in the hope that your work will contribute to the richness and utility of Pascal.

Summary

Conversion of data types under certain circumstances is provided by predefined functions: ORD, CHR, and ODD.

To enable the programmer to use memory space more efficiently, Pascal provides the reserved word PACKED. Structures of type ARRAY and RECORD may be declared as PACKED. The effect of a PACKED structure is to store data values without wasted space.

A savings in memory allocation usually is accompanied by an adverse trade-off in execution speed. With PACKED structures, additional processing must be done each time a value is accessed to determine the exact memory location of the value.

Memory savings also may be realized by paying careful attention to the way STRING and SET constants are coded. Also, efficiencies may be achieved, in some instances, by substituting IF . . THEN . . ELSE statements for a CASE . . OF structure.

Processing speed is traded off most easily in the initialization and user-interaction portions of a program. A program's main processing functions generally require the closest attention to efficient execution.

A single block I/O statement is more efficient than accessing individual bytes or groups of bytes in several statements. Block I/O operations may be done through the use of untyped file variables and the BLOCKREAD and BLOCKWRITE functions. Block I/O also may be used in conjunction with dynamic memory allocation.

Programs and data reside in the stack, or high memory addresses. Dynamic memory allocation makes use of the NEW, MARK, and RELEASE procedures to control the size of the heap, or dynamic memory area that exists below the stack in low memory.

UCSD Pascal provides the predeclared functions MEMAVAIL and SIZEOF to help in the management of unallocated dynamic memory. Other UCSD extensions allowing the manipulation of memory contents include MOVELEFT, MOVERIGHT, and FILLCHAR.

A variant record is a formatted record in which the latter portion of the record, or perhaps all of it, may be defined as having more than one possible structure, even though a fixed amount of memory is allocated to that record.

Each element of an array may be, in turn, an array, forming a multi-dimensional array. Multi-dimensional arrays are useful for the representation of hierarchical structures.

A procedure or function is said to be recursive when it calls itself. Caution must be exercised when introducing recursion into a program. The number of recursive procedure calls must be limited—otherwise, all memory in the system may be consumed quickly. Recursion may cause logical errors unless the programmer keeps close track of the number of recursive procedure calls that occur within a given program block.

Review Questions

1. How are printable characters and control characters represented in ASCII code, and how is this coding scheme involved in the conversion of data types?
2. What structures may be declared as PACKED, and what does this declaration achieve?
3. What trade-off exists between memory space and execution speed?
4. At what points in a program is the trade-off between memory space and execution speed most critical?
5. How is the use of STRING and SET constants related to processing efficiency?
6. When might it be preferable to substitute IF . . THEN . . ELSE statements for a CASE . . OF structure?
7. How are block I/O operations accomplished in Pascal?
8. How may dynamic memory allocation be controlled?
9. How are the UCSD extensions MOVELEFT, MOVERIGHT, and FILLCHAR used?
10. What is a variant record, and how are such records defined in program text?

Pascal Practice

1. Figure 14-14 presents a structure chart for *Grades,* a grading program that accepts inputs for homework, quizzes, and examinations, applies weighting factors, computes numeric averages, and assigns letter grades. Referring to the structure chart, write pseudocode for the program.

2. From the pseudocode you developed in the first exercise, code a Pascal program for *Grades.*

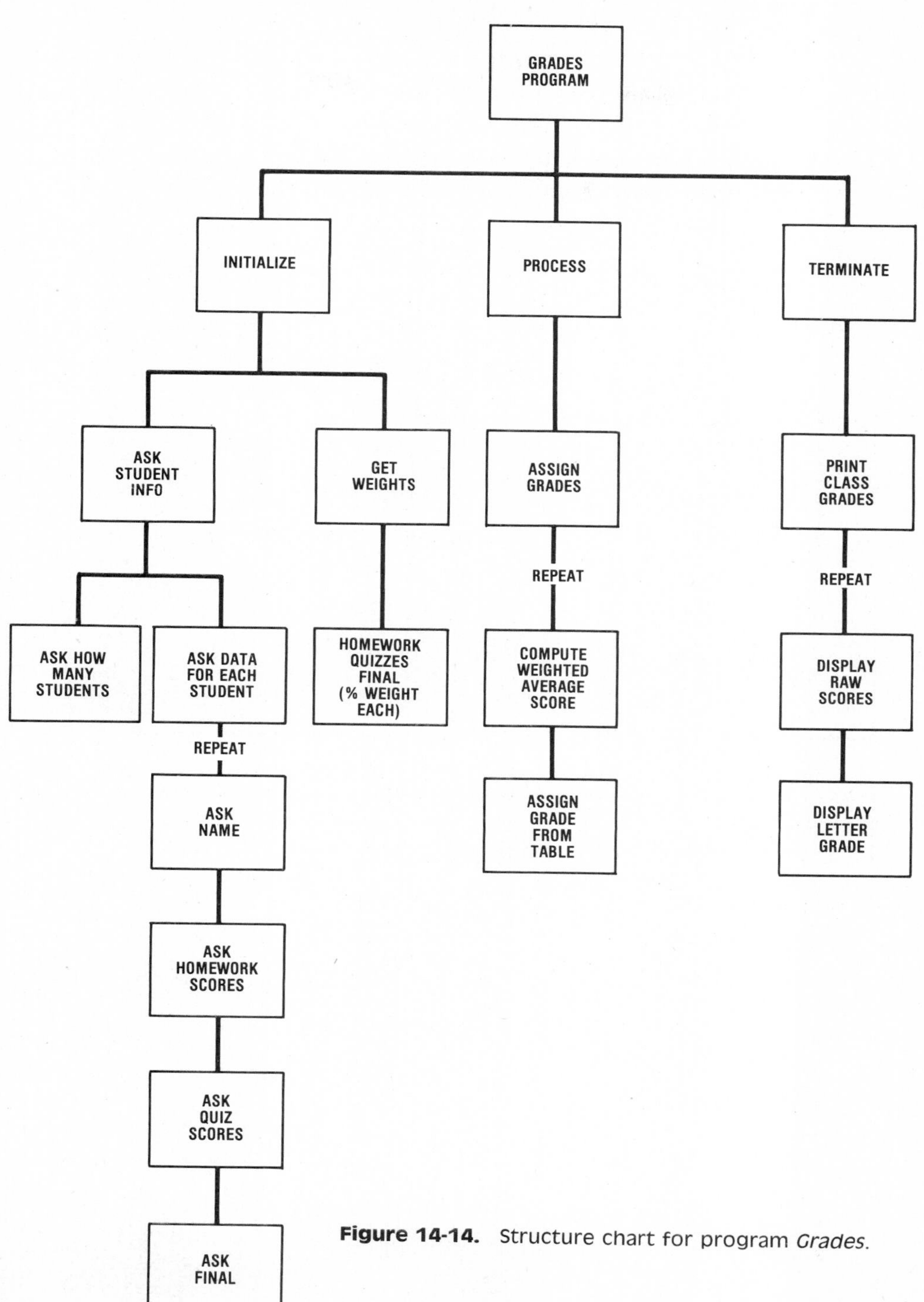

Figure 14-14. Structure chart for program *Grades*.

3. Develop test data for *Grades*. Enter and compile the program incrementally using top-down integration as presented in Chapter 10. Apply appropriate test data each time a module is added to the program.
4. Write a narrative reviewing the performance of *Grades* from a user's viewpoint. Identify program features that you feel should be added.
5. Develop new program specifications based on your performance analysis and revise or rewrite the program accordingly.

Key Terms

1. printable character
2. control character
3. in-line
4. block I/O
5. untyped file
6. stack
7. heap
8. stack overflow
9. top-of-heap
10. buffer
11. variant record
12. field list
13. tag field

Pascal Library

1. CHR
2. ODD
3. PACKED
4. BLOCKREAD
5. BLOCKWRITE
6. MEMAVAIL
7. SIZEOF
8. MARK
9. RELEASE
10. MOVELEFT
11. MOVERIGHT
12. FILLCHAR

A
PASCAL LIBRARY

INTRODUCTION

The Pascal terms, symbols, and codes that have appeared in the text fall into the following categories:

Reserved Words These terms have a predefined, specific meaning that may not be redefined by the programmer.

Standard Procedures and Functions These terms predefine Pascal functions and procedures in a standard and consistent way. The programmer may redefine these terms, but doing so renders the predefined functions and procedures unavailable.

UCSD Pascal Intrinsic Procedures and Functions These terms predefine specific procedures and functions within the UCSD Pascal compiler. Like standard procedures and functions, intrinsic procedures and functions may be redefined by the programmer if the predefined functions and procedures are not desired.

Predefined Data Types These terms indicate data types already known to the compiler. The programmer may redefine these terms if the original data types are not desired.

Predeclared Identifiers These terms include predefined file variable names, constants, and other identifiers.

Standard Symbols These are standard Pascal symbols for arithmetic, logical, and set operations.

Compiler Options These one-letter codes are used by the programmer to alter standard compiler operation.

UCSD Pascal Operating System Terms These terms are used to refer to specific elements of the operating system.

PASCAL LIBRARY

AND *Reserved Word.* Logical operator.

ARRAY *Reserved Word.* Type definition term.

BEGIN *Reserved Word.* Block and compound statement delimiter.

BLOCKREAD *UCSD Pascal Intrinsic Function.* File operation.

BLOCKWRITE *UCSD Pascal Intrinsic Function.* File operation.

BOOLEAN *Predefined Data Type.*

CASE *Reserved Word.* Key word in CASE . . OF statement.

CHAR *Predefined Type.* CHARacter.

CHR *Standard Function.* Data translation.

CLOSE *UCSD Pascal Intrinsic Procedure.* File operation.

.CODE *UCSD Pascal Operating System.* File name suffix.

CONCAT *UCSD Pascal Intrinsic Function.* String operation.

CONSOLE *UCSD Pascal Operating System.* File name.

CONST *Reserved Word.* Key word in CONSTant declaration section.

COPY *UCSD Pascal Intrinsic Function.* String operation.

CRUNCH *UCSD Pascal Predeclared Identifier.* File operation.

DATA *UCSD Pascal Operating System.* File type.

DELETE *UCSD Pascal Intrinsic Procedure.* String operation.

DIV *Reserved Word.* DIVide, arithmetic operator.

DO *Reserved Word.* Clause delimiter in FOR, WHILE, and WITH statements.

DOWNTO *Reserved Word.* Key word used in decrementing a FOR . . DO loop.

ELSE *Reserved Word.* Clause delimiter in IF statement.

END *Reserved Word.* Block and compound statement delimiter.

EOF *Standard Function.* End-Of-File, file operation.

EOLN *Standard Function.* End-Of-Line, file operation.

EXIT *UCSD Pascal Intrinsic Procedure.* Control operation.

FALSE *Predefined Identifier.* Boolean constant.

FILE *Reserved Word.* Type definition term.

FILLCHAR *UCSD Pascal Intrinsic Procedure.* FILLCHARacter, assignment operation.

FOR *Reserved Word.* Key word in FOR . . DO construction.

FORWARD *Reserved Word.* Key word in procedure and function header.

FUNCTION *Reserved Word.* Key word in function header.

$G *UCSD Pascal Compiler Option.* GOTO control.

GET *Standard Procedure.* File operation.

GOTO *Reserved Word.* Control operation.

GOTOXY *UCSD Pascal Intrinsic Procedure.* Screen control operation.

$I *UCSD Pascal Compiler Option.* Text file inclusion and I/O checking.

IF *Reserved Word.* Key word in IF . . THEN statement.

IN *Reserved Word.* Set operator.

INPUT *UCSD Pascal Predefined Identifier.* File variable.

INSERT *UCSD Pascal Intrinsic Procedure.* String operation.

INTEGER *Predefined Data Type.*

INTERACTIVE *UCSD Pascal Predefined Data Type.*

IORESULT *UCSD Pascal Intrinsic Function.* File operation.

KEYBOARD *UCSD Pascal Predefined Identifier.* File variable.

$L *UCSD Pascal Compiler Option.* Listing control.

LABEL *Reserved Word.* Key word in LABEL declaration section, used in conjunction with GOTO.

LENGTH *UCSD Pascal Intrinsic Function.* String operation.

LOCK *UCSD Pascal Predefined Identifier.* File operation.

long INTEGER *UCSD Pascal Predefined Data Type.*

MARK *UCSD Pascal Intrinsic Procedure.* Memory management operation.

MEMAVAIL *UCSD Pascal Intrinsic Function.* Memory management operation.

MOD *Reserved Word.* Arithmetic operator.

MOVELEFT *UCSD Pascal Intrinsic Procedure.* Assignment transfer operation.

MOVERIGHT *UCSD Pascal Intrinsic Procedure.* Memory transfer operation.

NEW *Standard Procedure.* Memory management operation.

NIL *Reserved Word.* Predefined pointer constant.

NOT *Reserved Word.* Logical operator.

ODD *Standard Function.* Type translation.

OF *Reserved Word.* Key word in ARRAY, SET, FILE, and CASE definitions.

OR *Reserved Word.* Logical operator.

ORD *Standard Function.* ORDinal, type translation.

OUTPUT *UCSD Pascal Predefined Indentifier.* File variable.

$P *UCSD Pascal Compiler Option.* Listing control.

PACKED *Reserved Word.* Type definition.

PAGE *Standard Procedure.* File operation.

POS *UCSD Pascal Intrinsic Function.* POSition, string operation.

PRED *Standard Function.* PREDecessor, operation used to decrement scalar values.

PRINTER *UCSD Pascal Operating System.* File name.

PROCEDURE *Reserved Word.* Key word in procedure header.

PROGRAM *Reserved Word.* Key word in program header.

PURGE *UCSD Pascal Predefined Identifier.* File operation.

$Q *UCSD Pascal Compiler Option.* Quiet compile, listing control.

$R *UCSD Pascal Compiler Option.* Range checking control.

READ *Standard Procedure.* File operation.

READLN *Standard Procedure.* File operation.

REAL *Predefined Data Type.*

RECORD *Reserved Word.* Type definition.

RELEASE *UCSD Pascal Intrinsic Procedure.* Memory management operation.

REPEAT *Reserved Word.* Key word in REPEAT . . UNTIL loop.

RESET *Standard Procedure/UCSD Pascal Intrinsic Procedure.* File operation.

REWRITE *Standard Procedure/UCSD Pascal Intrinsic Procedure.* File operation.

ROUND *Standard Function.* Data translation operation.

$S *UCSD Pascal Compiler Option.* Swapping mode, compiler control.

SEEK *UCSD Pascal Intrinsic Procedure.* File operation.

SET *Reserved Word.* Type definition.

SIZEOF *UCSD Pascal Intrinsic Function.* Memory management operation.

STR *UCSD Pascal Intrinsic Procedure.* STRing operation.

STRING *UCSD Pascal Predefined Data Type.*

SUCC *Standard Function.* SUCCessor operation, used to increment scalar values.

.TEXT *UCSD Pascal Operating System.* File name suffix.

TEXT *UCSD Pascal Operating System.* File type.

TEXT *Predefined Data Type.*

THEN *Reserved Word.* Key word in IF statement.

TO *Reserved Word.* Key word used in incrementing a FOR . . DO loop.

TRUE *Predefined Identifier.* Boolean constant.

TRUNC *Standard Function.* TRUNCate, data translation operation.

TYPE *Reserved Word.* Key word in data type definition section.

UNTIL *Reserved Word.* Key word in REPEAT statement.

VAR *Reserved Word.* Key word in VARiable declaration section.

WHILE *Reserved Word.* Key word in WHILE . . DO statement.

WITH *Reserved Word.* Key word in WITH . . DO statement.

WRITE *Standard Procedure.* File operation.

WRITELN *Standard Procedure.* File operation.

:= *Standard Symbol.* Assignment operation.

+ *Standard Symbol.* Addition, arithmetic and set operation.

– *Standard Symbol.* Subtraction, arithmetic and set operation.

* *Standard Symbol.* Multiplication, arithmetic and set operation.

/ *Standard Symbol.* Division, arithmetic operation.

= *Standard Symbol.* Boolean operation, test of equality.

< > *Standard Symbol.* Boolean operation, test of inequality.

< *Standard Symbol.* Boolean operation, "less than."

> *Standard Symbol.* Boolean operation, "greater than."

< = *Standard Symbol.* Boolean and set operation, "less than or equal to."

> = *Standard Symbol.* Boolean and set operation, "greater than or equal to."

B
SYNTAX DIAGRAMS

READING SYNTAX DIAGRAMS

The syntax of the Pascal programming language is well-defined. Syntax diagrams included with this appendix indicate the correct syntax for Pascal statements, identifiers, declarations, etc., covered in the text.

To read a syntax diagram, find the single line that enters the diagram on the left. Follow the line to the first branching. Choose any of the branches to continue through the diagram. A valid Pascal syntax description is obtained by tracing any of the several paths from the left side of the syntax diagram through to the right side.

Symbol Conventions

The diagram symbols are either square-cornered or round-cornered. The square-cornered symbols may appear either as squares or rectangles. The round-cornered symbols may appear either as circles or ovals.

Items enclosed in a square-cornered symbol refer to another diagram, except references to **letter**, **digit**, and **underscore**. The item **letter** means the letters from 'A' to 'Z' and from 'a' to 'z'. The item **digit** means the numbers from 0 (zero) to 9. The item **underscore**, which may not be available on your computer keyboard, is the underline character.

Items enclosed in a round-cornered symbol indicate the actual value that will appear in a Pascal statement. For example, the first word to appear in a round-cornered FUNCTION declaration is the word FUNCTION.

USE OF SYNTAX DIAGRAMS

The diagrams included with this appendix are intended as a reference guide to help in reviewing the syntax of a statement when the programmer is in doubt. However, keep in mind that the diagrams define only the *syntax* of Pascal statements. The constraints that apply to any particular statement relating to the overall *meaning,* or semantic value of the statement are not necessarily indicated in the syntax diagram. It is possible to have syntactically correct statements that do not produce valid results.

Identifier syntax.

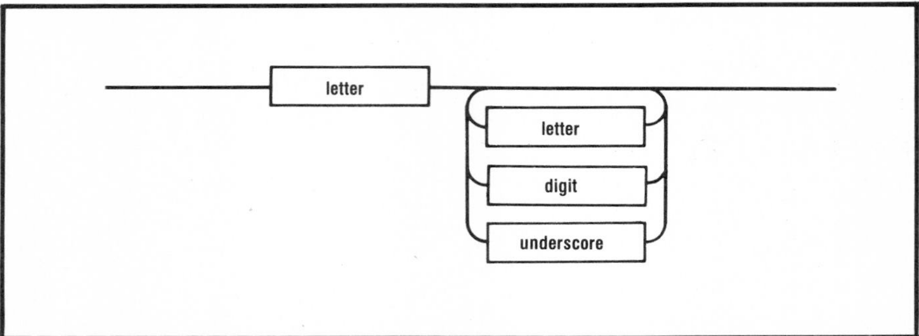

Unsigned Integer syntax.

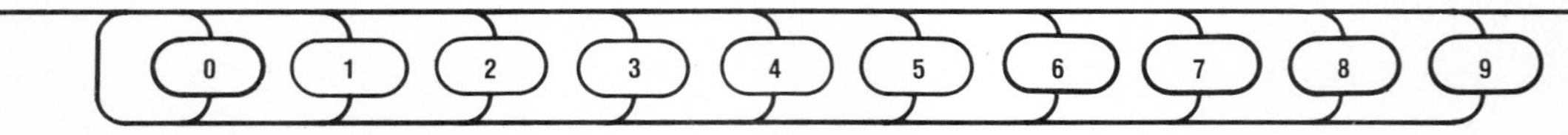

Unsigned Number syntax.

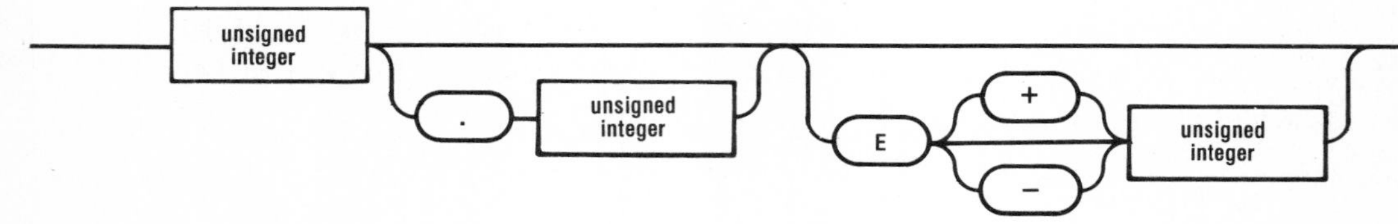

Unsigned Constant syntax.

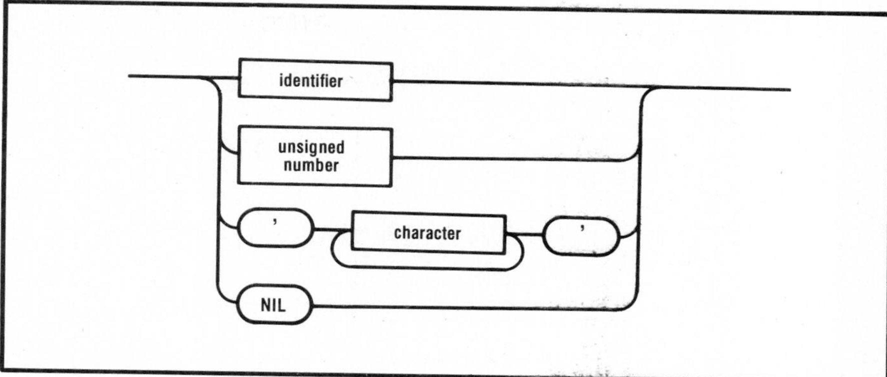

Constant syntax.

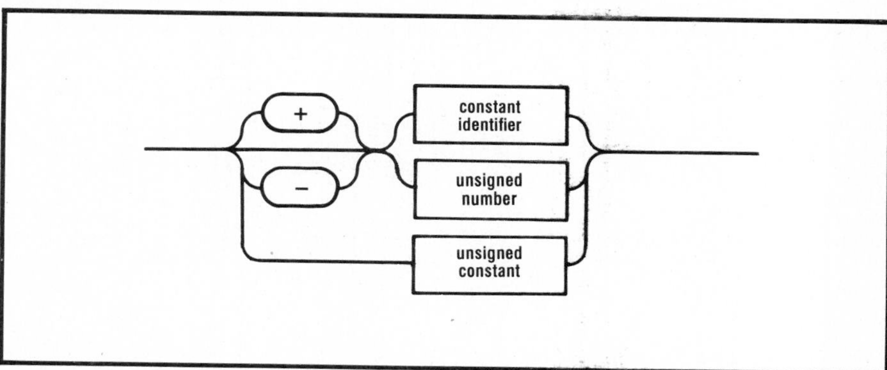

Simple Type syntax.

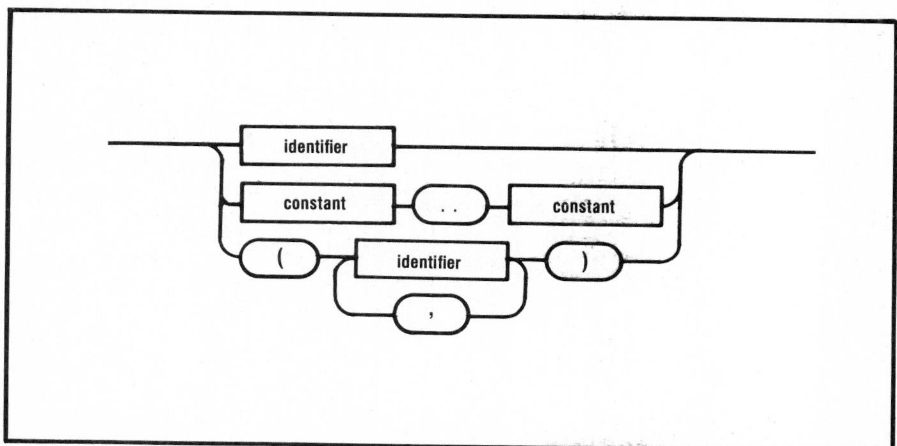

Type syntax.

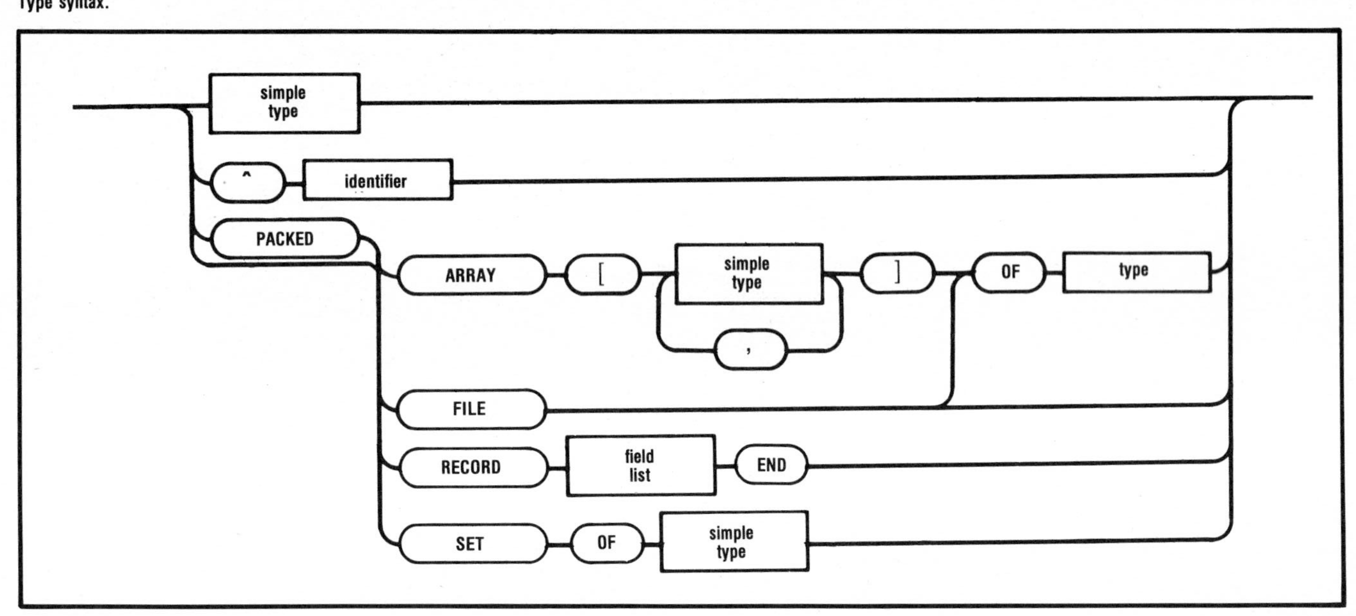

simple type
^
identifier
PACKED
ARRAY
[
simple type
,
]
OF
type
FILE
RECORD
field list
END
SET
OF
simple type

Field List syntax.

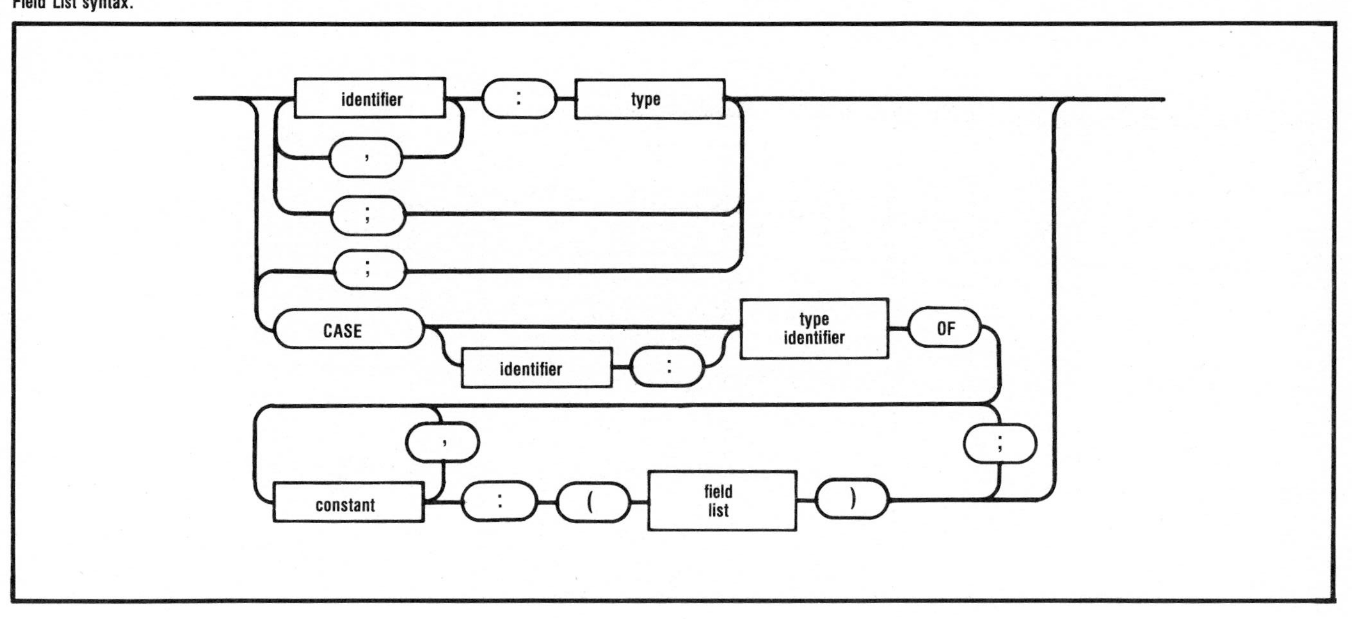

Expression syntax.

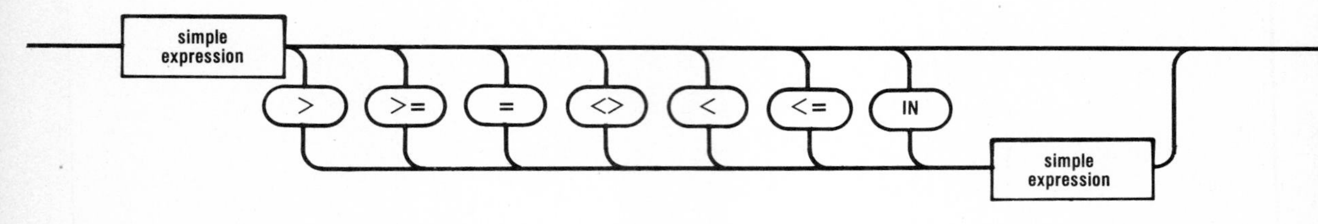

Simple Expression syntax.

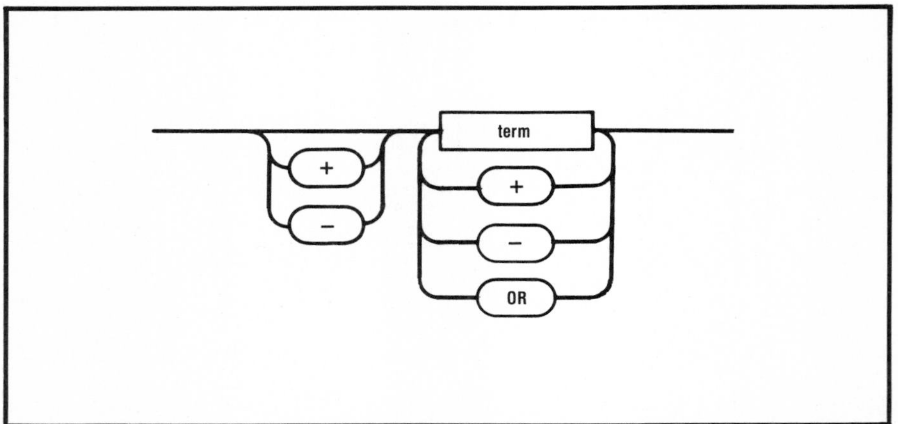

Term syntax.

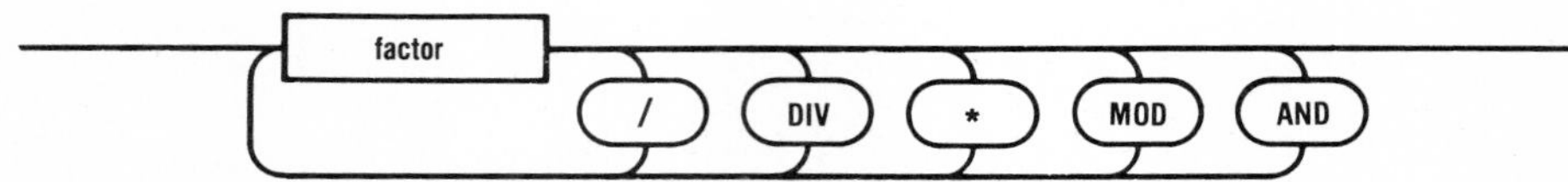

Factor syntax.

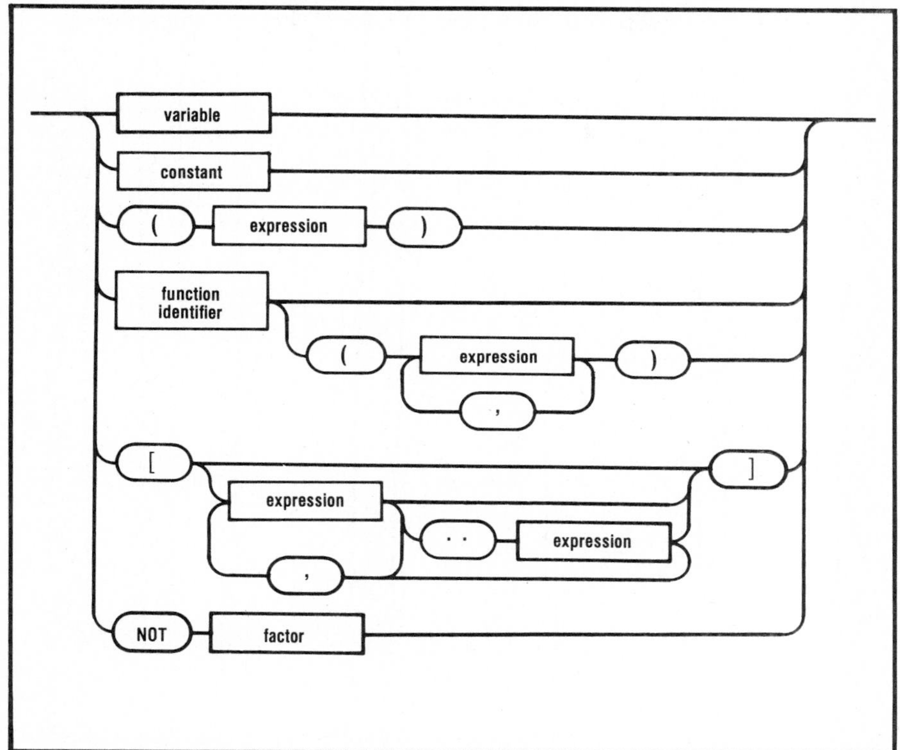

Variable syntax.

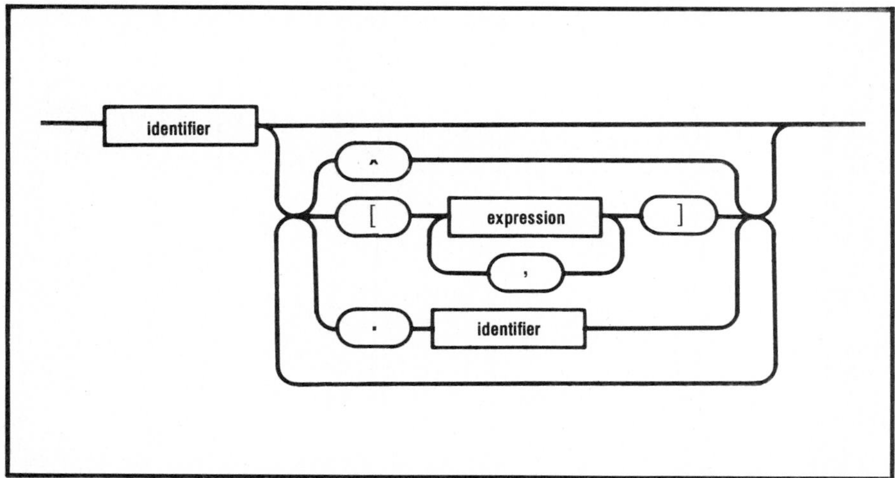

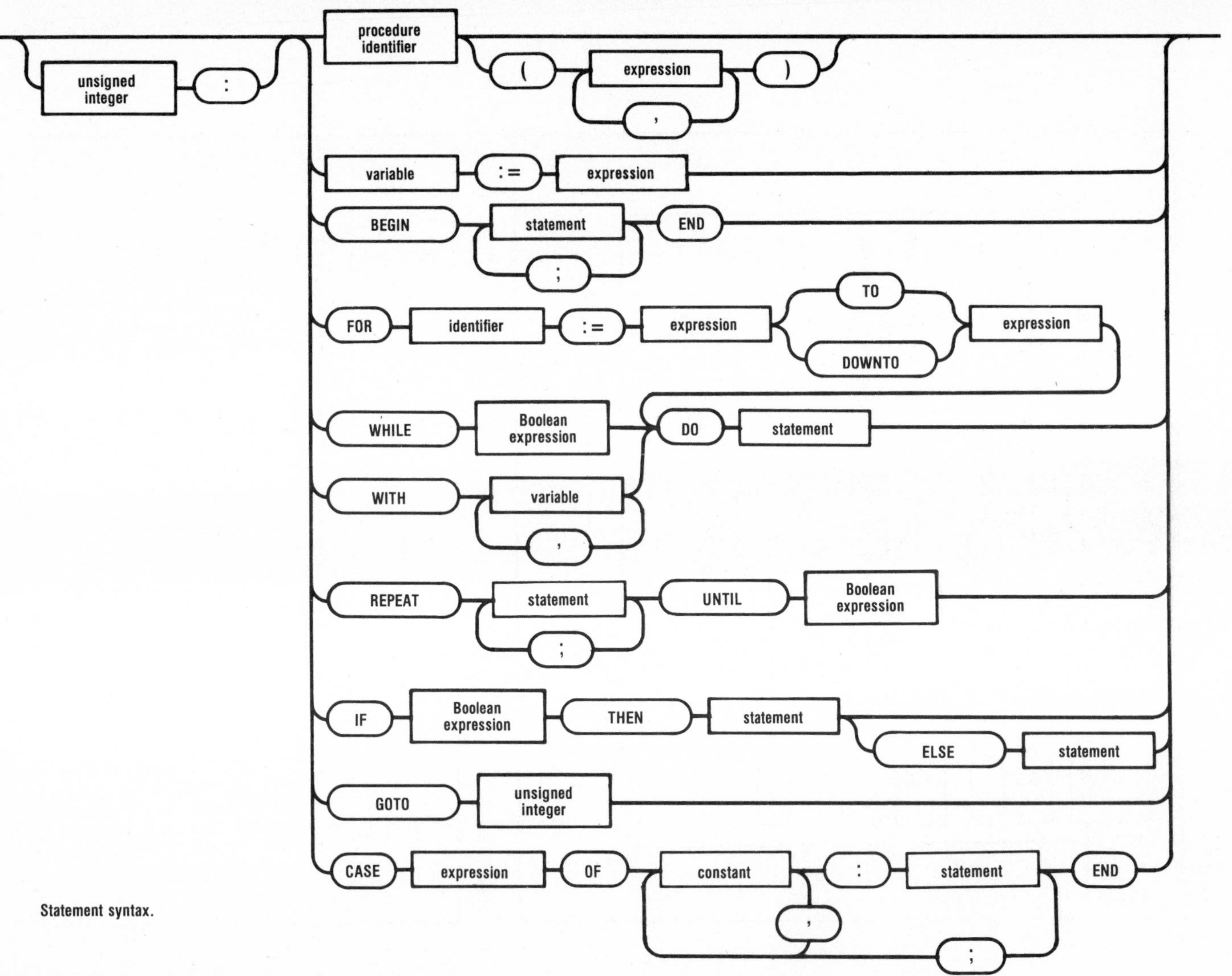

Statement syntax.

Parameter List syntax.

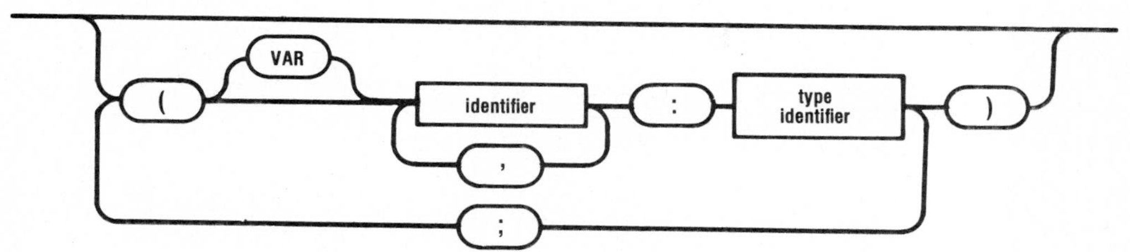

Function Declaration syntax.

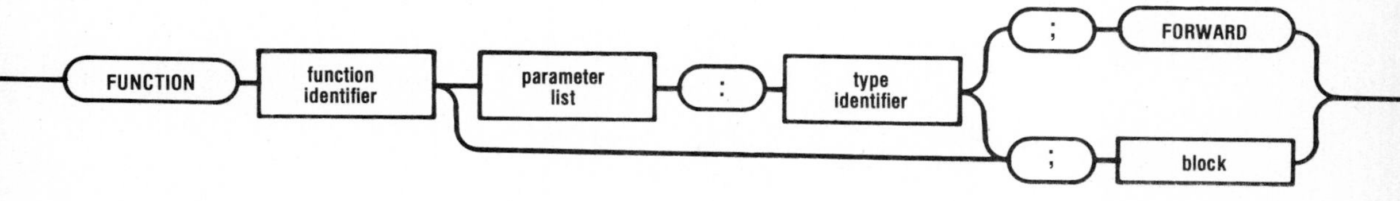

Procedure Declaration syntax.

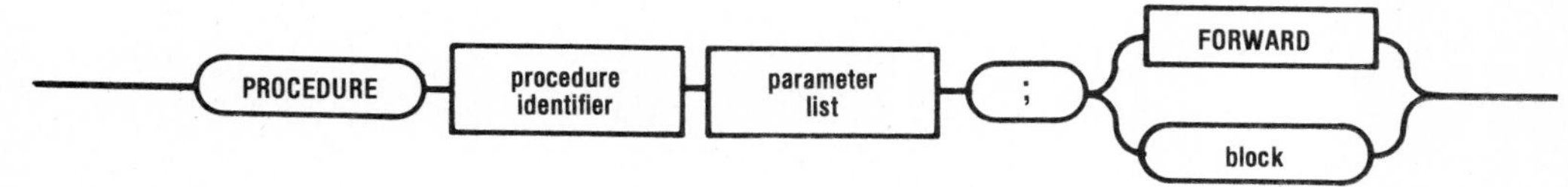

Block syntax.

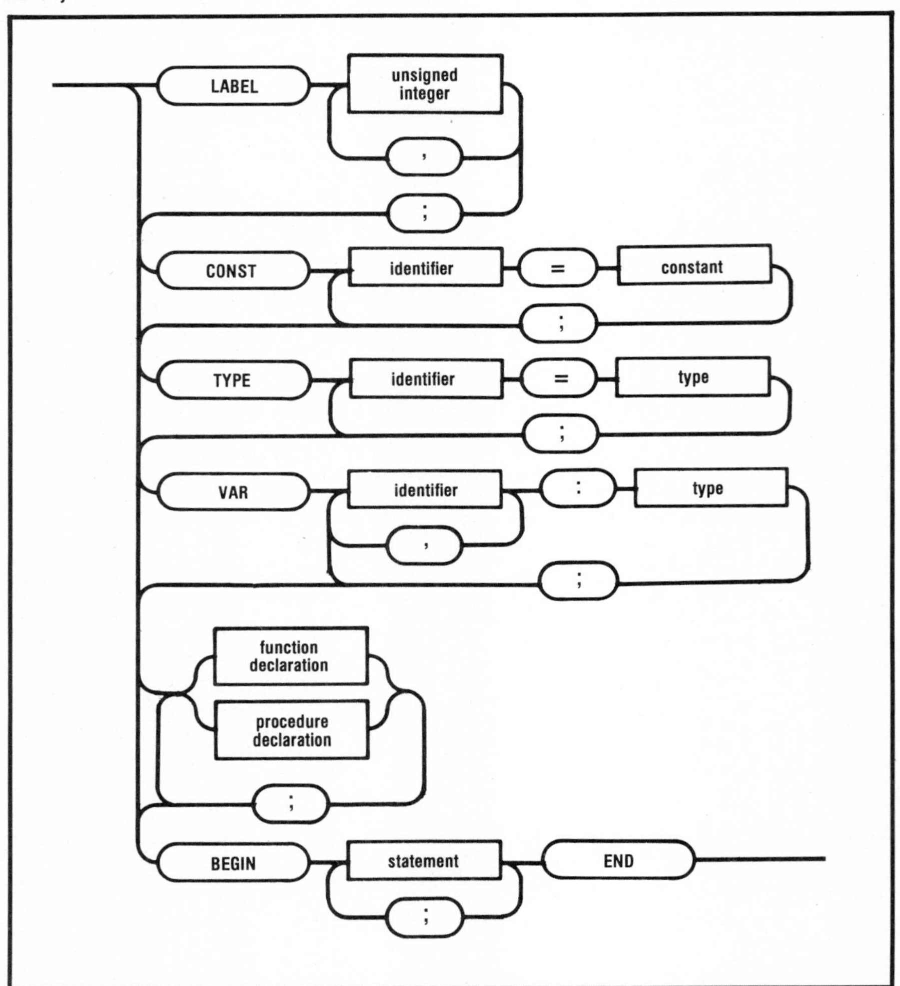

Compilation syntax.

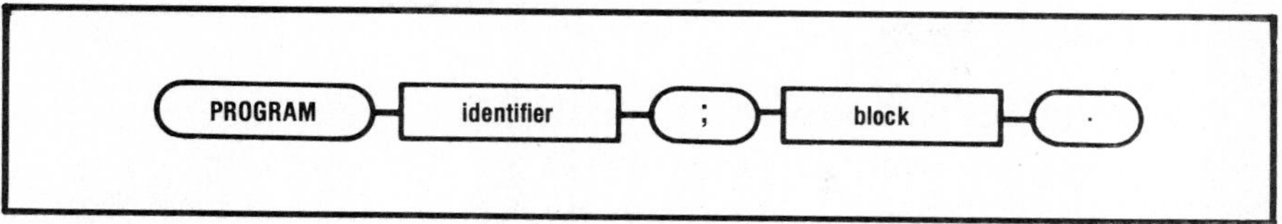

C
RECORD REPRESENTATIONS IN MEMORY

THE IMPORTANCE OF CONSISTENT DATA DEFINITION

This appendix is presented to assist the programmer in understanding how the Pascal compiler organizes memory. For most programming tasks, it is not necessary to know the actual layout of data in memory. However, in certain instances, the memory allocation scheme is critical to program results. For example, program errors that seem impossible to track down can be caused by inconsistency in data definition.

The programmer must take care to define records to be used on external files identically within each program that will access these records. That is, the definitions and syntax must be identical in all instances. Consider the definition:

```
XYZRec = RECORD
 NumberA : INTEGER;
 NumberB : INTEGER;
END;
```

The above definition does not result in the same data structure as the definition:

```
ABCRec = RECORD
 NumberA,
 NumberB : INTEGER;
END;
```

During a compilation, the Pascal compiler scans all field definitions in the order encountered. If a comma follows a field name, that name is put aside in a stack. This stack is a form of list accessed on a first-in, last-out basis. Each name is read in order until the type clause (:TYPE) is found. At that time, the field names are removed from the stack in reverse order (last item first) and allocated memory space in the record. In the first example above, NumberA would occur first in memory, and NumberB would occur second. However, in the second example the order is reversed. NumberB would occur first, and NumberA second.

If a file record were to be defined within one program as the ABCrec record type and within a second program as the XYZrec record type, the second program could not associate the field names with the desired areas of the record. The record would appear to contain nonsense.

Figure C-1 illustrates the importance of identical definition and syntax:

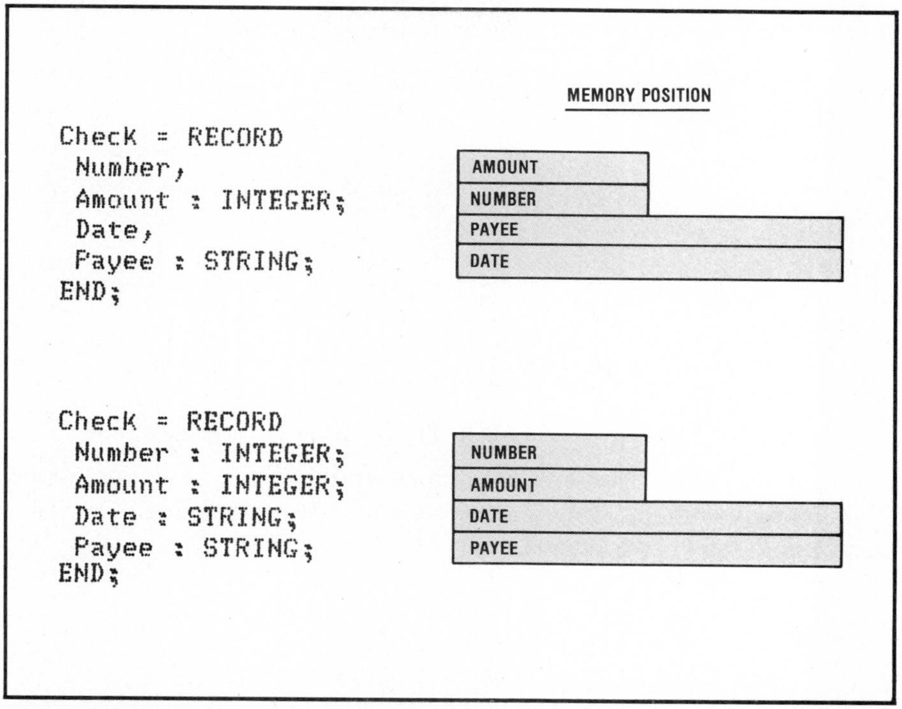

MEMORY POSITION

```
Check = RECORD
 Number,
 Amount : INTEGER;
 Date,
 Payee : STRING;
END;
```

AMOUNT
NUMBER
PAYEE
DATE

```
Check = RECORD
 Number : INTEGER;
 Amount : INTEGER;
 Date : STRING;
 Payee : STRING;
END;
```

NUMBER
AMOUNT
DATE
PAYEE

Figure C-1. Data definitions and resulting memory positions.

PACKED DATA STRUCTURES

The PACKED attribute can be applied to records and arrays to direct the compiler to store data in the least possible amount of memory. A trade-off for this efficient use of memory may be slightly slower execution times, as mentioned in the text.

The purpose of PACKED is to allow as many variables as possible to reside in a single word, without splitting any variable between words. (UCSD defines a word as two 8-bit bytes; other implementations vary.) Areas within words are allotted from the lowest-ordered portion of the word upward to the highest-ordered portion (from low memory addresses to higher addresses).

The PACKED attribute will affect only the scalar elements of the structure—the predefined types BOOLEAN and CHAR, and user-defined types, enumerations, and subranges. Because the INTEGER type always occupies a full word, PACKED has no effect on integers.

In the chart shown in Figure C-2, the number of bits required to represent certain magnitudes of numbers is illustrated.

Referring to Figure C-2, the following record definition will define a record one word long:

```
OneWord = PACKED RECORD
 Flag : BOOLEAN;
 Century : 0 .. 99;
 Letter : CHAR;
END;
```

The memory allocation is shown in Figure C-3.

However, the following definition would result in a two-word memory requirement, shown in Figure C-4. Note that a single data element cannot span two words.

```
TwoWords = PACKED RECORD
 Flag : BOOLEAN;
 Century : 0 .. 150;
 Letter : CHAR;
END;
```

Number of bits	Maximum number in word	Values of each data item: Subrange	Values of each data item: Predefine types of this size
1	16	0 . . 1	BOOLEAN
2	8	0 . . 3	none
3	5	0 . . 7	none
4	4	0 . . 15	none
5	3	0 . . 31	none
6	2	0 . . 63	none
7	2	0 . . 127	none
8	2	0 . . 255	CHAR
9	1		
.			
.	1	see Chart	none
.			
15			
16	1	– 32768 . . 32767	(signed) INTEGER

Figure C-2. Number of data items that will fit into words.

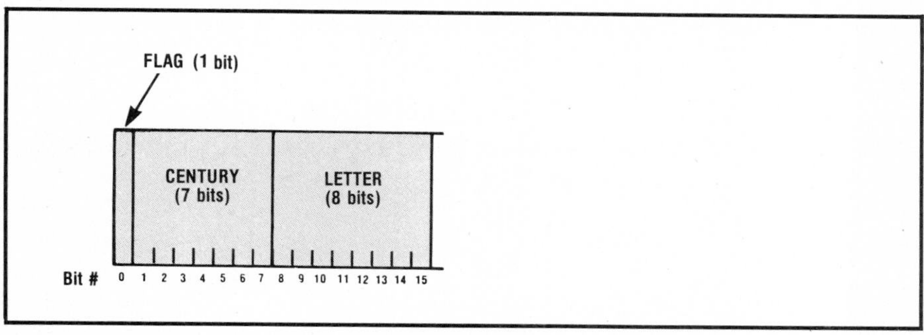

Figure C-3. Memory allocation for PACKED RECORD OneWord.

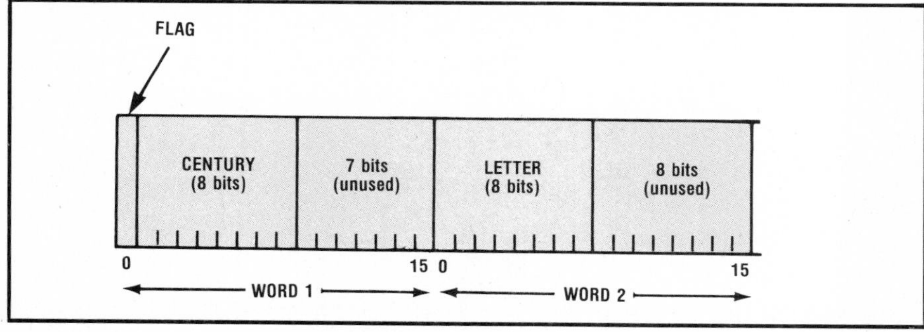

Figure C-4. Memory allocation for PACKED RECORD TwoWords.

If the first example were not PACKED, the record would be laid out as shown in Figure C-5. The second example would be laid out as shown in Figure C-6.

Enumeration types are packed in the same way. The number of elements in the enumeration will determine its minimum space requirement. The following enumeration will require two bits, since it depicts three values:

```
Utensils = (Knife, Fork, Spoon);
```

As explained in the text, the ORD function will return a value of 0 for the first element in an enumeration and 1 for the second, and so on. Thus, the following enumeration will require *three* bits, since there are seven elements whose ordinal values would be 0 . . 6 in subrange forms:

```
Days = (Monday, Tuesday, Wednesday, Thursday, Friday, Saturday, Sunday);
```

Knowing the order and means of data layout can be very useful when using variant records. For example, to determine if a given integer is ODD (without invoking the predeclared function ODD), the variant record could be defined as:

```
VAR
 IsOdd : RECORD
 CASE INTEGER OF
  1 : (Yes : BOOLEAN);
  2 : (Int : INTEGER);
 END;
```

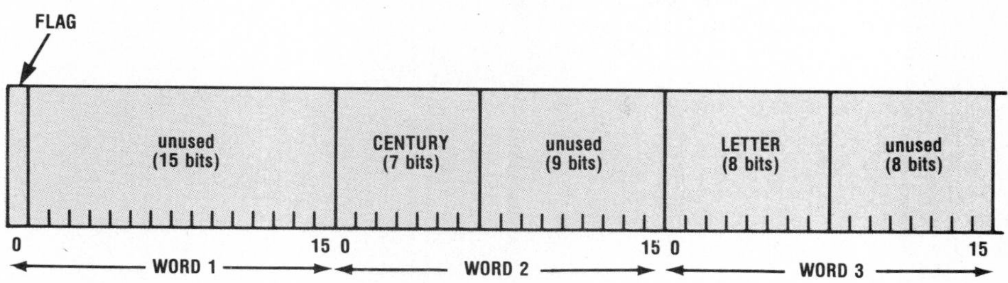

Figure C-5. Memory allocation for RECORD OneWord, not PACKED.

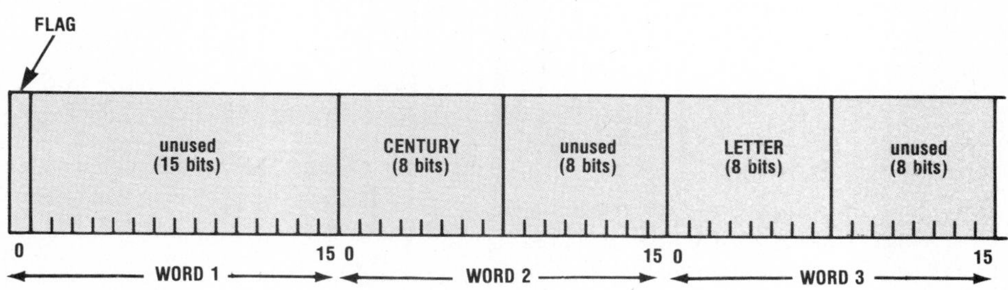

Figure C-6. Memory allocation for RECORD TwoWords, not PACKED.

Then, to test an integer, the following could be coded:

```
IsOdd.Int := SomeInteger;              (* put in as INTEGER *)
IF IsOdd.Yes THEN (* statement *); (* take out as BOOLEAN *)
```

GLOSSARY

A

absolute value A mathematical function that returns a positive value for a given positive or negative number.

accuracy Criterion for mathematical and computational correctness of processing results.

address Label for a location in memory associated with a data item.

algorithm Description of the method for solving a defined problem.

American Standard Code for Information Interchange (ASCII) An accepted scheme of binary codes, having the numeric values 0 through 127, that stands for the alphanumeric character set, standard punctuation marks, and certain other special characters.

answer to a question An output format that consists of a single result in response to a straightforward problem.

application area The user activity that generates the need for a program.

archival Relating to records or documents preserved for a long time.

argument A value, or reference to a value, supplied to the parameters in a called procedure or invoked function.

argument list Arguments present in the call syntax of a procedure or function.

arithmetic logic unit (ALU) Physical device within a computer's processor that performs arithmetic and logical operations on data.

arithmetic operation Any one of the mathematical functions that include addition, subtraction, multiplication, and division.

array A collection of data items, or elements, that are all of the same data type.

array name The variable name assigned to a collection of data items that share the same data type.

ask-and-answer A data entry technique that displays a specific prompt for each entry required.

assembler Low-level programming language that facilitates the writing of machine code.

assembly language Another term for an assembler.

assignment of value Clearing the contents from a given memory location and substituting another value.

audit trail Combination of source documents, files, and electronic logs that facilitate tracing a transaction from its source through all processing done with, or caused by, the transaction.

B

backtab Movement of the cursor from right to left by fixed spacing increments.

batch Group of data records processed together at the same time.

binary Referring to two-state systems that may be in one of two conditions: on or off. Also, referring to the mathematical counting scheme that employs only zeroes and ones.

binary choice Tree structure in which each node has branches leading to a maximum of two nodes below it.

binary search List access by successive partitioning of the range of possible record locations for the desired data item.

binary tree Data tree structure in which each data item is connected to a maximum of two other data items.

bit Term derived from *b*inary dig*it*, meaning the smallest unit of information used by a computer.

blink Display capability that causes characters to appear and disappear repeatedly.

block In Pascal, a program procedure, or function. Also, a unit of data storage consisting of 512 characters.

block delimiter Reserved word immediately preceding or immediately following a block of processing instructions.

block I/O The process of transferring large groups of data in groups of 512 bytes in binary format.

block structure The characteristic of a language such as Pascal that requires the grouping of program statements in blocks, or subprograms.

Boolean logic A system of mathematical rules for comparisons developed by the English mathematician George Boole.

boot Procedure for starting a computer system.

bottom-up Proceeding from the specific to the general. When dealing with integration testing, a procedure that begins by individually testing low-level, detailed modules, then integrates them with higher-level modules for further testing.

bounds error *See* range error.

branch Selection, or processing alternative, presented during program execution.

branching The relationship among data items in a tree structure.

bubble Graphic symbol used in data flow diagrams to represent a processing step, or transformation of data.

bubble sort Rearrangement of data items resulting from scanning an entire list and causing items of higher order to "rise to the top."

buffer A memory area set aside to hold a large amount of data temporarily, often to compensate for a speed discrepancy between input and output functions.

bug An error encountered either in compiling or executing a program.

byte A set of bits, usually eight, that forms a symbolic unit in binary code.

byte address The location in the code file of a given program byte.

C

call To cause the execution of previously declared program instructions by including the identifier for those instructions in a program statement, or call.

calling block A program block in which a procedure name reappears to call a procedure, or subprogram, from another program block.

caret The (^) symbol.

case selector Option indication within a CASE .. OF structure.

cathode ray tube (CRT) A television-like electronic vacuum tube used as a display device for computer terminals.

central processing unit (CPU) Physical device within a computer system that comprises the processor and the main memory.

character position The horizontal location, or column number, of a given character, or letter, on a display.

character printer Output device that prints documents one character at a time.

character string constant Character string or sequence, written within single quotation marks, whose value remains unchanged throughout program execution.

close To cause a file status such that the file may not be written to until it is reopened explicitly by a subsequent program statement.

COBOL Acronym for *CO*mmon *B*usiness-*O*riented *L*anguage, a computer language designed to allow input of English-like statements for processing in business applications.

code Electrical signals that comprise machine language. Also, another term for an object file. More generally, a term encompassing any instructions that may be processed by a computer.

cold start Another term for booting a computer system.

collision Result of a search of hash coded files in which a record cannot be located because two or more records have the same hash code.

command-driven User interface characterized by entry of coded phrases with little or no prompting.

command line Displayed list of command functions, from which a choice can be made to call up separate program modules within the operating system.

compact To reduce in size or extent.

comparison Logical test made to determine if a Boolean operation correctly expresses the relationship of two items, resulting in a value of TRUE or FALSE.

compilation listing Display of the results of the compilation of a text file to produce a code file and showing program text and information on content of the text file.

compiler Program that translates a text file into a code file. Also referred to as translating source code into object code.

completeness Criterion for the thoroughness of processing results.

complex data structure Information storage and access method that includes files.

compound statement A group of program statements that may be treated as a single program statement.

computer output microforms (COM) Output that includes recording information on microfilm or fiche.

concatenate To link together in series.

condition Basis of a comparison made at a program branch.

console Hardware device that allows interaction between the user and the program. Usually refers to the video display and keyboard, when speaking of microcomputer systems.

constant A value that does not change under any circumstances.

constant declaration A declaration that identifies a value that will not be changed by program processing.

control character A byte of information that does not correspond to any in the alphanumeric character set, used to direct system functions. Control characters have ASCII numeric equivalents of 000 through 031.

control structure A form and syntax for program statements that determines the order of processing.

control unit Physical device within a computer's processor that orders the sequence of processing as directed by the program.

coordinate One of a pair of numbers that specifies a unique position in a matrix.

counter variable A value that determines the number of iterations executed for a loop.

counting loop A series of program statements repeated a certain number of times, as defined by a counter variable.

cursor Indicator for the position of the next character to be entered on the display.

D

data Values presented to a system for processing.

data flow diagram Graphic representation of the flow and transformation of data caused by a processing system.

data structure The logical relationships among data items.

data type Restriction on a data item defined in a type definition and associated with a variable in its declaration.

database management File management techniques that allow the user to specify relationships among items in a database and to access those items accordingly.

decision Choice of alternate processing steps based on a condition.

declaration Definition and data typing of an identifier in program text before use of that identifier in program statements.

declaration section Section of a Pascal program or program block that precedes program statements and that defines and declares identifiers to be used in the program statements.

decrement To reduce by discrete steps or intervals. Also, a negative increment.

default condition A value that is preassigned in the program text but may be overridden by user input.

definition The initial presentation of a unique name, or identifier, in program text.

delimiter A symbol, such as a comma, a slash, or a semicolon, used to separate data items or data fields on input. Also, a reserved word used to indicate the logical boundaries of program blocks.

desk checking Visual inspection of program text or compilation listings to spot errors.

detail file Another term for a transaction file.

device number Identifier for a physical device, such as a disk drive, within a computer hardware configuration.

digitize To convert to numeric values.

direct access I/O operations on records or fields within files without regard to the order of those fields or records. Another term for random access.

directory file A file containing physical locations or pointers to records in a linked file used as a means of accessing the linked file.

displayed output Results shown on the console.

document Permanent record produced on an output medium such as paper.

documentation Instructions on program use maintained for user training or reference.

documented output Results displayed on a printing device that creates a permanent copy.

dot matrix Output printing device that forms individual characters by striking groups of small impact devices within a matrix of such devices on a print head.

double linking The practice of maintaining two pointers in each record, one pointing to the following item and one pointing to the preceding item.

driver Test module developed to generate data for lower-level modules during bottom-up integration testing.

dynamic memory Unallocated storage that may be allocated in changing fashion during a program run.

E

echo To repeat or display input data.

editor Portion of Pascal operating system that allows the creation and modification of program text.

electrostatic Referring to a high-speed printing process using electrically charged ink particles.

element An individual data item within an array.

end-of-file Identifier appearing after the last record in a file.

enumeration A method of typing data in which allowable scalar values are listed and an ordered relationship among those values is created.

enumeration type Statement that lists permissible values of coined types.

equal to Referring to a data item that has the same value as a given item, as determined by logical comparison.

error checking System software and/or program features that assure appropriate user inputs and reliable system operation.

error message Displays intended for the user that indicate incorrect or inappropriate inputs or disruptions to program execution.

evaluate To reduce an expression by performing all operations given within that expression.

execute To run a program and carry out its instructions.

execution trace Tracing information included in the first statement in a program module to facilitate the location of errors that cause a program halt.

exponent A superscript indicating that a given number is to be raised to a power, or multiplied by itself the number of times given in the superscript.

external documentation Program usage instructions not contained within the program itself, usually taking the form of manuals.

external file Group of records that resides outside of main memory.

extract To select from a list as the result of a search.

F

false Boolean logic term, also a value in Pascal, indicating an unmet condition test.

fatal error Error that causes a program halt.

feedback Prompts that occur as a result of an input action and allow verification or alternative action, often before processing continues.

fiche Photographic output medium of a larger format than microfilm.

field A particular writing space on a display. Also, a data item within a record.

field list Portion of a record definition that specifies types for fields within the record.

file In Pascal, an array of records declared as a FILE, usually residing in secondary storage and accessible as individual records. In general computer terms, a group of records relevant to a given application.

file buffer Portion of the file variable that holds individual records during I/O operations.

file buffer pointer Caret syntax used to refer to data associated with a file variable.

file directory A lookup table contained in a storage device that allows the operating system to access stored files.

file variable A predefined record that allows creation of and access to records on external storage devices.

fill-in-a-form A data entry technique analogous to filling in the blanks on a manual form.

film recorder Output device that records information on photographic film.

flowchart A graphic diagram of physical processing steps.

form feed Advance of an output printing device to the beginning of the next page caused by a control character.

formal declaration List of parameters in a procedure declaration header that contains names local to the procedure.

formatted record Data items that have been defined explicitly as type RECORD in program text.

FORTRAN Acronym for *FOR*mula *TRAN*slator, a computer language originally designed for translating mathematical and scientific equations.

free-form A data entry format that requires the user to input all data on a single line.

function header The first line of a function declaration that supplies the function identifier and a list of its parameters.

function testing Testing a program as a whole with data derived from anticipated application conditions.

G

gap Referring to Shell's sort algorithm, the partition between segments of a list. Referring to files, the physical interval between records or blocks.

gate Electronic switch in computer circuitry that may be either on or off.

general report An output format allowing the selection of displayed results and the form of display.

global Encompassing an entire program.

graphic character Graphic symbol, such as an arrow, that may be assigned to an individual key on the keyboard.

graphics Information in pictorial form.

greater than Referring to a data item that has a higher value or order than a given data item, as determined by logical comparison.

greater than or equal to Referring to a data item having a value or order that is higher than or the same as a given data item, as determined by logical comparison.

H

hard copy Output in some permanent form, such as printed on paper; a documented output.

hard disk High speed storage device that incorporates rigid, magnetic disks. Disks can be fixed (permanent) or removable.

hardware Physical devices that comprise a computer system.

hash code Indicator for the location of a record within a hashed file disclosed by an operation performed on a data item within the record.

hash coded address A hash code for a record held in memory that discloses the record's location.

hash search Access to a hashed file by means of a hash code.

hashed file File in which there is a correspondence between the order of entries and their physical locations or memory addresses.

header First line of a program or a procedure or function declaration that presents an identifier and, for procedures and functions, may include a parameter list.

heap The portion of dynamic memory outside the stack that is under control of the programmer.

hierarchical design Another name for top-down design.

hierarchy A multi-level structure that embodies a logical order and relationship among its elements as a series of levels, each subordinate to the level above it.

high-level language A programming scheme whose instructions are readily understandable by humans.

highlighting Use of graphic techniques to make some item in a data display stand out from other items.

hypothesis testing Using a hypothesis, or working theory, to describe and check for suspected programming errors.

I

identifier Unique name within Pascal program text.

increment To advance to the next higher value in a given order, as in incrementing a counter variable each time the program statements in a loop are executed.

incremental testing The entering, compiling, and test execution of a program in stages, one module at a time.

index The identifier that appears in brackets after an array name to specify the location of an element in the array.

infinite loop A series of program statements that repeats endlessly, having no termination condition.

information Data that have been transformed for added meaning.

initialization The first phase of an algorithm. Also, the processing required to bring the first record into memory for processing.

initialize To clear variables prior to processing. Also, to format a blank diskette.

initializing the variable Clearing a variable, or register, of any unwanted values prior to processing, usually accomplished by assigning a value of zero.

ink-jet Printing device that sprays magnetic ink particles to form characters.

in-line Referring to program statements that describe processing in a linear fashion, rather than conforming to top-down structure.

input The entry of data into a system for processing. Also, the first phase of physical processing.

input editing The action of subprograms designed to validate data items presented to a program.

input/output (I/O) The physical processing functions of moving data in and out of main memory to be acted upon by the program.

integer A member of the set of whole, or counting, numbers.

integrated circuit Electronic device that incorporates many electrical circuits on a single silicon chip.

integration testing The process of combining modules, first the most general and then progressively lower-level modules, for the purpose of testing the interfaces between those modules.

interpreter Program that translates source code directly into machine actions.

invoke To cause a function to be executed by the appearance of its identifier in a program statement.

I/O Abbreviation for input/output, or data transfer.

I/O error checking Function of the operating system that monitors I/O, or data transfer, and generates error codes when incorrect or incomplete transfers occur.

iteration Repetition of program steps. A single iteration refers to one cycle through a program loop.

J

jump The result of a GOTO statement, causing program control to be transferred to a labeled program statement.

justify To position, or line up, characters according to a spacing rule.

K

key A given data item that may be searched to find a related group of data items.

L

laser printer High-speed document printing device that uses a laser to create the image to be printed.

leg One of the three main branches of a structure chart.

length specifier Program syntax that controls the number of characters output for a data value.

less than Referring to a data item that has a lower value or order than a given data item, as determined by logical comparison.

less than or equal to Referring to a data item having a value or order less than or the same as a given data item, as determined by logical comparison.

level Horizontal relationship of program modules in a structure chart or of elements within a hierarchy.

lexical level Information generated by the compiler that indicates the nesting relationship among program blocks.

limits error *See* range error.

line number The vertical position of a character on a display.

line printer Output printing device that prints documents a complete line at a time.

linear insertion with exchange *See* sift.

linear search Search technique in which each data item in a list is accessed and examined individually, proceeding serially from the first physical location to the last physical item.

line-feed Advance of a printing device to the next writing line caused by a control character.

link Pointer used to relate data items in a linked list.

linked file A file having one or more logical relationships disclosed by pointers embedded in its records.

linked list A group of data items whose logical order is disclosed by pointers contained within the list.

linked search List access conducted in the order of the pointers in a linked list.

list An output format that consists of a series of data items. Also, a collection of stored data items.

list maintenance Processing done to preserve the logical order of a list.

literal data Data item written between single quotation marks to be printed out exactly as it appears.

local Available to a restricted portion of a program.

location The physical storage point for a given data item, as in an address in memory, record or field position in a file, or position of an element within an array.

logarithm A mathematical function that, given a number, finds an exponent of 10 equivalent to that number.

logical boundary The beginning or end of a program block.

logical design Program specifications that describe processing in a manner independent of physical processing.

logical error Program bug that appears as inappropriate program results.

logical function Processing step that describes the flow and transformation of data within a system.

logical operation Processing that involves a comparison, or test of equality, on data items.

logical processing Transformations to data that exist apart from physical considerations of how that processing will be implemented.

logical test Condition test. *See* comparison.

lookup table A group of values used as an index to another group of values.

loop A series of program statements that are repeated based on a condition test.

M

machine language Coded electrical signals that cause computing operations to occur.

main block Program statements that define main processing tasks.

main memory Physical device associated with a computer's processor that holds data and programs involved in active processing.

main processing The program module that carries out the actual computation and logic functions applied to input data.

main program *See* main block.

mainframe A class of large, fast, computer systems.

manipulation operation A function of input, output, and/or storage that moves data within a computer from one location to another.

manual stepthrough Without using a computer, performing processing steps to verify a logical design.

marker A delimiter in a file used to indicate the bounds of portions to be saved, moved, or deleted.

master file File containing permanent or semipermanent information to be maintained over an extended life span.

mathematical function A series of mathematical operations that results in a single value.

matrix A grid system that has an x (horizontal) axis and a y (vertical) axis, allowing spatial location of points by reference to coordinates.

member Constituent of a set.

memory Electronic device for retention of data within a computer system.

memory dump Output statement included at a key point in the program to track the changing values of variables.

memory location Specific address for a data item within a computer's electronic data retention area.

menu Processing alternatives presented to the user simultaneously, from which one response must be selected.

merge The process of combining two ordered lists, or files, into a single ordered list or file.

microfilm Small-format photographic output medium on which information is recorded in miniature form.

microprocessor chip Integrated circuit that implements processing operations.

model A logical representation or diagram of an existing processing system.

module Representation of a program block in a structure chart. Also, a portion of an algorithm or program that defines or solves a particular task.

module testing The entry and testing of individual program modules.

multi-dimensional array An array, or group of elements of the same data type, whose elements are also arrays.

multiple-choice processing A user interface technique that allows a predetermined number of responses.

N

nested Referring to a unit that is identical in form to the larger unit in which it is contained.

nested menu A group of user options within a menu that is itself a menu, or group of options.

nested record Within a record, a field that is itself a record.

node Point in a tree structure where branching occurs.

nondocument Term referring to nonpermanent output, such as CRT display information.

nonincremental testing The entering, compiling, and test execution of a program in its entirety, rather than in stages.

not equal to Referring to a data item that does not have the same value as (is either greater than or less than) a given data item, as determined by logical comparison.

not greater than Referring to a data item that has a value or order either lower than or the same as the value or order of a given data item, as determined by logical comparison.

not less than Referring to a data item that has a value or order either higher than or the same as the value or order of a given data item, as determined by logical comparison.

O

object code Machine code resulting from compiling source code.

off Condition of a gate caused by a binary signal that is low.

on Condition of a gate caused by a binary signal that is high.

one-dimensional array An array having elements identified by a single subscript.

open Characterizing a file that may be written to.

operating system A collection of programs residing in the computer that directs the use of computing equipment and serves to support programming languages.

operation Transformation done on data items according to specific rules.

ordinal Relating to values that imply counting (first, second, third, etc.).

output Information that results from processing. Also, the last phase of physical processing.

overhead The amount of program text, or processing time, required to assure quality rather than produce direct results.

overwrite To output a display line over an existing line. Also, to output a record that replaces an existing record at a given record location within a file.

P

package An application program, or a set of programs, designed for widespread use with a minimum of modification.

pad To add spaces to an output line to fill a given display field.

page break Command or control character that causes a printer to stop printing and move the paper to the beginning of the next page.

parameter A placeholder within a procedure or function into which values can be passed, or from which values may be returned.

parameter list A declaration in a procedure or function header that specifies the data to be used within that block.

parse The process of analyzing a given command to determine whether its syntax is correct.

partition Subdivision of a problem into tasks.

pass by reference Form of syntax that provides to a procedure a memory location with an accessible value, rather than a specific value.

pass by value An alternative syntax to passing by reference that causes a copy of a value held in memory to be provided to a procedure.

p-code Pseudo machine code produced by the UCSD Pascal compiler.

permanent Referring to files that are closed with a LOCK option and may not be written to.

physical device Computer equipment, as distinct from programs or the logical names of devices as referred to in programs.

physical function Processing step that describes the actions of physical devices.

physical processing Specific physical actions required to transform data within a specific system.

plotter Computer-driven graphic output device that can produce images using vertical and horizontal inputs to position a stylus.

pointer Data key that contains the location of a data item.

pointer variable Pascal variable used to reference data items in dynamic memory.

portability The degree to which a computer program can be moved from one computer system to another and used without modification.

post In data processing terms, to update a master file from a transaction file.

predefined Having a meaning that is known to the compiler without having been defined in the program.

predefined data structure A data type that is inherent in the programming language.

preordered file A variation of the sorted file that is set up with an anticipated number of total entries. As each new entry is made, it is placed in its correct physical location in the file, maintaining the desired order.

primary storage device Main memory of a computer system used to retain data needed during processing.

printable character Any one of the symbols in the ASCII character set corresponding to numeric codes of 032 through 127, including all of the conventional alphanumeric characters and punctuation marks.

procedure Sequence of processing steps carried out in a prescribed order. In Pascal, a specific kind of subprogram.

procedure declaration The appearance of a procedure header and its program statements in the declaration section of a Pascal program.

procedure number Sequential numbers assigned to program blocks by the compiler.

processing The series of computer operations that causes the transformation of data. Also, the second phase of an algorithm.

processor Physical device in a computer system that carries out operations on data, consisting of a control unit and an arithmetic logic unit.

program A series of instructions that causes a computer to perform a specific task.

program specification Definition of desired results, prepared prior to beginning of program design.

program statement A line of program text; an instruction.

program structure The underlying logic of the arrangement and relationships among modules within a program.

programming language A vocabulary and a set of rules that govern the form and use of instructions in the coding of computer programs.

programming style The characteristic manner in which a program is written to produce overall quality, including clearly-written program text and user-friendly design considerations.

prompt A message displayed to indicate what further user actions are required for processing to continue.

prompt-driven A user interface that allows the user to select from a small number of predefined responses.

pseudocoding Description of an algorithm in English-like statements that follow the general structure of program text.

R

random access Retrieval of data, usually in the form of records within files, in any order.

random files Records contained within a file in unpredictable order.

randomly addressable Accessible in any order.

range The values defined by setting lower and upper limits, or bounds, for possible, or allowed, values.

range checking The validation of input by verifying that the value of a given data item falls within allowed limits.

range error Error caused by a value outside possible or allowed limits.

reasonableness test The validation of input by comparison with anticipated values.

record A structure applied to data items that allows them to be grouped, typically by transaction, and stored within files.

record key A field that may be used to order records and that may be searched to find those records.

recursive Referring to a procedure or function that calls or invokes itself.

relational database A system of linked files or data entities that have both internal links and external links, producing multiple relationships.

relative byte number A count of byte positions in the code file relative to the beginning of the file.

reliability Criterion for the dependability of processing results.

repetition Performance of a program loop, or iteration.

reserved word Term with a specific predefined meaning, to be used in program text.

reverse character Capability of some displays that causes characters to be displayed in the background color, surrounded by a bright box.

rigid disk Another term for a hard disk.

root The base of a tree structure.

root node The highest ordered, or first, branch occurring in a tree structure.

round To shorten a decimal value to a fixed number of digits, arriving at the closest approximation of the given number.

S

scalar A series of values having a fixed number and range and that implies counting.

scan The process of examining a series of items individually, in sequential fashion.

scientific notation A way of expressing a number as a factor of some power of 10.

scroll To move the display window vertically up or down.

search File access according to specific criteria, usually by record key.

secondary storage device Physical device that retains data for long-term storage.

segment A separate code file that resides outside of memory at program execution time and is read in, as necessary, to complete execution.

selection The choice among alternate processing steps based on a condition.

selection in order Extraction of data items from a list in the order needed for processing.

selector Identifier in a CASE . . OF construction that specifies a processing option.

self-documenting Referring to programs that require little or no external documentation, or reference manuals.

sequence A series of processing steps that are followed from beginning to end without interruption.

sequential access Serial access of records stored in order required for processing.

sequential list Group of data items stored as a serial list that also has some logical order.

serial access Storage and retrieval of records one after the other in the order in which they were written.

serial list A collection of data items whose physical order corresponds to the order of input.

set A grouping of values, or members, according to some common property or rule.

set constant A set whose members do not change.

Shell's sort Named after Donald L. Shell, a variation of the sift sort that first partitions the list into segments, leaving gaps in between, then applies a bubble sort to each segment.

shuttle sort *See* sift.

sift A variation of a bubble sort in which a swapped item to be moved to a lower position is compared to each item lower than its previous position and inserted above the first lower ordered item found.

sort To rearrange data items into a more meaningful or convenient order.

sorted file Sequential access file.

source code Computer instructions in the form written by, or readable by, humans.

specific report An output that has a preexisting format.

square The mathematical operation of multiplying a number by itself; also, the product of such an operation.

square root A mathematical function that returns a number that, when multiplied by itself, results in the given number.

stack A portion of memory that expands or contracts to provide temporary data storage.

stack overflow An error condition, caused by a memory capacity insufficient to continue processing, that results in abnormal program termination.

standard exchange method *See* bubble sort.

storage The retention of data until needed for processing.

string constant *See* character string constant.

structure The underlying logic of a problem or a solution to a problem.

structure chart Graphic representation of the relationship among program modules.

structured programming language A language that reinforces program logic by the form and syntax it imposes on program statements.

structured walkthrough A variation of the manual stepthrough that uses two programmers to verify a logical design.

stub In program module testing, an incomplete or "dummy" procedure or function header included to satisfy the compiler's requirement for declarations.

stylus Pen-like device used to produce graphic images on a plotter.

sublist A group of items extracted from a list. Specifically, a group of data items extracted from a source list as an intermediate processing step when the source list may not be accessed in the desired order.

subprogram Program block that implements a given task.

subrange A typing syntax that defines a range of scalar values using the (..) syntax.

subroutine *See* subprogram.

subscript An identifier appearing within brackets after a variable name.

subtree Group of nodes below, and connected to, a given node in a tree structure.

swapping The process by which portions of a text file are read into memory selectively to complete a compilation.

synonym Records having duplicate hashed addresses.

syntactical error Program bug resulting from the incorrect entry of program text.

syntax Rules governing the formation of program statements.

T

tab Movement of the cursor from left to right by fixed spacing increments.

tag field A syntax used to define the case selector variable in variant records.

target computer system The specific computer hardware for which a given program is written.

termination The processing steps required to close down a processing cycle. Also, the third phase of an algorithm.

termination condition A test performed that, if true, causes the program to exit a loop.

top-down design Hierarchical partitioning of a problem into individually solvable tasks.

top-down testing Integration testing method that enters and checks the most general program modules first, then integrates lower-level modules.

top-of-heap The highest address in allocated dynamic memory.

trade-off Consideration that involves a gain in one area of operation with a corresponding loss in another area.

transaction A single act of doing business. A record is typically a transaction document.

transaction file Collection of records containing data pertaining to current business activity.

tree A form of list that implements hierarchical relationships among data items.

true Boolean logic term indicating that a condition test is met.

truncate To shorten a numerical value to a fixed number of digits, without regard to the meaning of the result.

two-state device Hardware component that may be either on or off, high or low, polarized North or South, positive or negative, etc.

type *See* data type.

type validation Input editing based on verification that a given data item is of a specific data type defined by the program.

typed file Referring to a file for which the file variable is associated with a data type.

U

UCSD Pascal A version of the Pascal programming language developed at the University of California at San Diego.

unconditional branching Program statements that cause a jump to another part of the program as a result of an explicit instruction rather than a condition test.

undefined Referring to a value that cannot be determined and, hence, may not be used in a program statement.

unit testing *See* module testing.

untyped file Referring to a file for which no structure is assumed other than binary data.

user The operator of a computer system. Also, the person for whom a program is written.

user interface The boundary between the actions of a computer and the actions of its human operators.

user-friendly Easy to use, or people-oriented.

user's guide A concise form of documentation that gives step-by-step instructions on program use, intended primarily as a learning aid for first-time users.

user's manual A comprehensive document that includes program usage instructions, intended primarily for reference purposes.

V

validate To check a data item on input to assure that it is acceptable to the program.

value Explicit meaning for a given data item.

variable A name or symbol for a memory location that can hold one of a wide range of values.

variant record A formatted record in which a portion of the record, or perhaps all of it, may be defined as having more than one possible structure, even though a fixed amount of memory is allocated to that record.

video display terminal (VDT) A device that displays alphanumeric characters upon a television-like screen. Often refers to the combination of a CRT and a keyboard, used as the console device.

W

walkthrough *See* manual stepthrough.

word Grouping of binary code consisting of two bytes.

wrap around On a display, to continue a writing line on the next line after an end-of-line has been encountered.

X

x axis Horizontal scale on a two-dimensional matrix.

Y

y axis Vertical scale on a two-dimensional matrix.

yes/no prompting A series of user alternatives that have only yes or no responses

INDEX

Page numbers in *italics* refer to figures in text.

Absolute value, 95
Accessing files. *See* Random access; Sequential access; Serial access
Accumulators, *27*
Accuracy, 53, 70
Address in main memory, 4
Algorithm, 23, 24, 28–29, 46, 54, 58
  for *Adder* program, *28*, 28–29
American Standard Code for Information Interchange (ASCII), 12, *12*
  character code, *383–384*
  control codes, 176, 387
AND operator, 147, 422
Answer to question, 171, 178
  procedure *AskReportType*, 210, *211*
Application area, and user interface, 122
Application program, purpose of, 290
Archival, defined, 178
Argument, 92, 95, 97
Argument list, 92, 115
Arithmetic logic unit (ALU), 8
Arithmetic operations, 6, 426
Array, 153–158, 166, 226
  versus files, 237–238
  multi-dimensional, 154, 158, 411–415
  one-dimensional, 154
  subscripts, 155, 157, 158
ARRAY data type, 422
  PACKED, 388–389
Array index, 154–156, 166
  and range checking, 372
Ask-and-answer data entry format, 130
Assembler, defined, 13, 17
Assembly language program. *See* Assembler
Assignment of value, 3, 78
  for mathematical equations, 104–106, 116–117
  symbol, 33, 46
Asterisks and parentheses, use of, 32
Audit trail, 290, 305

Backtabbing, 174, 177, 182
Batch processing, 144, 291
BEGIN block and statement delimiter, 29–30, *30*, 31, 84–85, 88, 96, 115, 422
Binary, defined, 11
Binary code, 11–13
Binary data representation, 381–382, *382*
Binary devices, 11–12
Binary digit. *See* Bit
Binary search, 306, 329–330, 334, 336
  recursive techniques for, 415, *416*
Binary tree, 318, *323*, 324, 336
Bit, defined, 12
Blink, 176
Block, defined, 29, 31, 240. *See also* Modules; PROCEDURE block; Program block
Block delimiters, 29, 84
  semicolon not used with, 31–32
Block I/O, 393–394, *401*, 417
Block structured code, 87–88, 115
Block-structured language, Pascal as, 31, 46
BLOCKREAD operation, 395–397, 417, 422
BLOCKWRITE operation, 395–397, 417, 422
Boole, George, 6
BOOLEAN data types, 144–146, 150, 166, 205, 388–389, 422
  PACKED attribute and, 440
  set of, 208
Boolean expressions
  set operations and, 6, 208, 212
  standard symbols, 426
Boolean logic, 6, 144–146, 166
Booting, 37–38, *38*

Bottom-up testing, 262, 263
Bounds error, 265–266
Braces, use of, 32, *321–322*
Brackets, 104
Branch, defined, 62
Branching, 318
  unconditional, 364
Bubble, in data flow diagrams, 57, *57*
Bubble sort, 294–298, *296–297*, 335
Buffer, 404
Bug, defined, 44
Byte address, 375
Byte, defined, 12

C (Compile) command, 38–39, 43
Call, 86, 88, 91, 92
  scope of variables in, 98–99, *100*
Calling block, 88, 115
  values returned to, 94–95
Capitalization, 99, 108
  in coding style, *321–322*
Caret syntax, 242–243, 248
  with pointer variables, 313
Case selector, 148
CASE . . OF statement, 143, 147–149, 391–392, 422
  assignment of set variable values by, 210, *211*
  form, 148
  versus IF . . THEN . . ELSE statement, 148–149
  and variant records, 409–411
Cathode ray tube (CRT) display, 9, 174–177, 189
  sample layout form for, *175*
  microcomputers, 176
Central processing unit (CPU), *8*, 9
Character codes, ASCII, *383–384*
CHARacter data type, 36, 46, 150, 193, 194–195, 205, 422
  initializing, 265
  PACKED attribute and, 440
  representation in memory, 382–383
  set of, 208
Character position, 134–136, 174
  printers, 177
  programming, 182
Character printer, 178, *179*
Character string constant, 33
CHR function, 386–387, 388, 422
Chronological order, sorting by, 343
Clearing screen, 193
CLOSE procedure, 239, 246–247, 251, 254, 422
Closed file, 239
COBOL, 15
Code
  ASCII. *See* American Standard Code for Information Interchange
  binary, 11–13
  error, 44
CODE file, 15, 37
  object code in, 15
.CODE file name suffix, 44, 247, 422
Coding sheet, 261
Coding techniques for formatting outputs, 192–224
Cold start, 38
Collision, defined, 333
Colon, use of, 76, 79, 96, 364
Colon and equal sign, use of, 78, 104
Comma, use of, 76, 79
Command line, display of, 38, *39*
Command-driven program, 124–126
  trade-offs, 124–126, 140
Commands, 39–40
Comment, 32, 159
  parameter list repeated in, 102
  sorting by, 342–343
Comment syntax, 32
  braces, *321–322*
  of compiler options, 363–373
Compact, defined, 341
Comparison, logical, 144–145
  equal symbol for, 33, 46
  sorting by, 292–293
Compilation
  data definition and, 439
  steps in, 42–44
Compilation listing, 373, 375–377
  program *Columns*, *374*
Compile module, 32, 38–39, 42–43, *43*, 46
Compiler, 14–15, 17, 37
  errors caught by, 159
Compiler options, 362–378, 421
  compilation listing, 373–377
  GOTO statement, 364–366
  include option, 370
  I/O error checking, 367–370
  Quiet compile, 377
  range checking, 371–373
  swapping mode, 377
Completeness 53, 70, 78
Compound statements, 31, 84, 248
  functions as, 94
Computer languages, 2–5
Computer output microform (COM) devices, 178, 179, *181*
CONCATenate function, 165, 202–203, 205, 222, 422

Condition, identification of, 62
Condition test, 62–63, 144
Consistency in definition, 438–439
Console, defined, 9
Console display, 133–136, 140–141
CONSOLE file name, 212–213, 375, 422
Constant, defined, 33, 96
CONSTant declaration, 96, 106, 422
Content of, symbol, 242–243
Control characters, 177
  ASCII character codes, *383*
  defined, 174
Control code, ASCII, 387
Control key, 40
Control procedure for users, 132–133
Control structures, 143–144, 166
  loop as, 72
  in main processing module, 62–63, 78
Control unit, 8
Conversion of data types, 385–388
Coordinates, 134–136, *135*, 174
COPY function, 203, 205, 222, 422
Copying files, 371, *401*
Counter variable, 150
  incrementing with SUCC function, 270–271
  local declaration of, 264
  range error, 265
Counting loop, 150
Crash-proofing, 367
CRUNCH operation, 247, 254
Cursor, 39–40
  deletions with, 39–40
  in fill-in-a-form data entry, 130
Cursor control, 134–136, 141, 182, 193
  and WRITE and WRITELN procedures, 175

D (Delete) command, 41
Data, 3, 6
Data conversion, 410
Data definition, consistency of, 438–439
Data entry
  formats, 128, 130, 140
  in list management, 340–343
  random sequence of, 183
  second-chance, 132, 136
  sorting, 341–343
.DATA file name suffix, 240
DATA file type, 247–248, 254
Data flow analysis, 58, 78
Data flow diagram, *57*, 57–58
Data structure, defined, 226
  design trade-offs, 324–326
Data type, 30, 226. *See also* DATA file type; Predefined data types
  binary representation of, 381–382, *382*
  conversion of, 385–386
  counting loops and, 150
  declaration of, 35–36
  defining in TYPE definition section, 36
  errors in, 266
  non-structured, 94
  predefined, 421
  REAL, 94, 96
  scalar, 94
Database management software, 331
Debugging, 44–45, 158–159, 258–285. *See also* Testing program or module; Error(s)
  of block-structured code, 87–88, 115
  deductive, 260
  limited capacity of Pascal for, 260, 286
  by modules, 159
  switch, 260
  techniques, 266–269, 286
  test methods, 260–261
Decision, defined, 62
Declaration, defined, 30
Declaration of variable, 234
  data type, 35–36
  and memory allocation, 399–400
  in PROCEDURE block, 85, 86
Decrement, and deletion of entries, 340–341
Default condition for prompt-driven programs, 127–128
Definition, in program text, 30
Definition and declaration statement of PROCEDURE block, 85, 86
DELETE procedure, 203–205, 422
Delimiter, 371
  CASE as, 148
  in free-form data entry, 128
Description, level of, 65, 67
Desk checking, 269, 286
Detail file, 290
Device number, 240
Digitized, defined, 178
Direct access, 245–246
Directory file, 310, 330–331, 334
Diskette, 240–241
Diskette files, 240–241
Displayed output, 9, 25, 174–177
  error messages, 376
  formatting, 133–136, 140–141
  program *BasicAccounting*, 185–187
  tabular reporting, 137
  WRITE statements and, 33, 46
  WRITELN statements and, 46
DIVide arithmetic operator, 105, 422

DO, 422
Document output, 171. *See also* Output headings
Documentation, 124, 126, 127
Documented output, defined, 9
Dollar sign, in compiler options syntax, 363
Dot matrix printer, 178
Double link, 312
DOWNTO, 150–151, 422
Driver, defined, 263
Dynamic memory
  allocation, 315–316, 397–404, 417
  areas of, 398–399
  defined, 315
  linked lists in, 312–314
  pointer variables and, 399–400

E. *See* Exponent
E (Edit) command, 38–39, 43
Edit module, 38–39, 43, 46
  menu, 39, *40*
Editor, 37
Efficiency, guidelines for applying, 392–393
Electrostatic printer, 178
ELSE. *See* IF . .THEN . . ELSE statement
END block and statement delimiter, 29–30, *30*, 31, 84–85, 88, 97, 422
  final in program, 86
  of PROCEDURE block, 85, 115
End-of-file
  indicator, 63, 242, 422
  WHILE NOT test for, 250
End-of-list, pointer to, 402
END OF PROGRAM message, 44
Entering program, 37–42, 158–159
Enumeration, 206–207
Enumeration type, 107
  packing, 442
  in program *AccountManagement*, 275
EOF, 422. *See also* End-of-file
EOLN function, 422
  KEYBOARD variable, 165
Equal sign, 33, 46, 78, 95, 96, 144
Equality, 6
  test of, 144
Error(s), 438
  anticipating, 259
  flagged by compiler, 32. *See also* Error messages
  introduced in rounding, 197–198
  isolating, 259
  logical, 45, 259
  syntactical, 37, 43, 44, 105, 259, 263
  typographical, 259, 263
  variable references misplaced, 264
Error checking, 125, 392
  I/O, automatic, 367–370
Error codes, 44
Error messages, 37, 43, 44–45, 126, 260
  console display of, 376
Escape key, 40, 44
ETX command, 40, 46
Evaluation of expressions, 104, 144
Execute, defined, 4
EXecute module, 38–39
Execution of program
  consol display result, *45*
  defined, 29
  speed of, 326, 390–392, 393, 417
  steps in, 44
Execution trace, 268, 286
EXIT procedure, 213, 222, 422
Exponent, 198
External documentation, 124
Extraction of
  specific information, 327
  summary information, 290, 305, 327
  text, 371

FALSE condition, 144–146, 147, 423
Fatal error, 265, 271
Feedback, in data input, 128
Fiche, 178
Field(s)
  data content of, 242
  defined, 200, 229, 253
  within fields, 230–231
  within records, 229, 253
  in VAR declaration, 228
Field list, 409
File(s), 233–234, 237–238, 253–254
  versus arrays, 237–238
  closing, 239
  compacting, 341
  copying, 371
  diskette, 240–241
  formatted, 394
  moving, 370–371
  opening, 239, 241, 243–244, 245
  processing, 234, 253, 290–291, 335
  random access, 245–246
  reading into memory, 241
  serial access, 244, 245
  storage of, 234, *236*
  untyped, 237, 394–395
File buffer, 234, 242
File buffer pointer, 248, 252
FILE data type, 227, 233–234, 237–238, 423
File directory, 240–241, 254
File management techniques, 308

File organization, 291–292
File structure, 291–292, 332–334
FILE type definition, 247
File variable, 234, 242–243, 254
  declaration of, 234, 237, 253
Fill-in-a-form data entry format, 130
FILLCHARacter, 407–408, 417, 423
Film recorders, 178, 180, *181*
Flowchart, 59–60, *61*
  symbols, 60, *61*
FOR . . DO control structure, 143, 149–151, 153, 166, 423
Form layout, 182, 183
Format/formatting
  coding techniques for, 192–224
  data input, 128, 130, 140
  of general reports, 172
  of output, 182
  report options, 183
  of reports, example, 198–201
  of specific reports, 172
  VARiable declaration section, 76–77, 79
Formatted file, 394
Formatted record, file declarations, 237
FORTRAN, 15
FORWARD declaration, 101–103, 116, 423
Free-form data entry format, 128, 140
Frequency of use, user interface and, 123–124, 140
Function(s), 94–97, 115
  naming rules, 94, 108–109, 117
FUNCTION block, 94–97, 116, 423
Function header, 95
Function parameter, argument passed to, 97–98
Function testing, 262

Gap, 300
Gates, defined, 11
General report, 172–173
GET procedure, 243, 245, 254, 423
  following SEEK procedure, 246
Global variable, 90, 93, 116
GOTO procedure, 364–366, 423
GOTOXY procedure, 135–136, 141, 174, 193, 364–366, 423
Graphic characters, 176
Graphic display techniques, 130, 178, 180
Greater than, 6
Greater than or equal to, 6
Grid system. *See* Matrix of coordinates

Halting processing, 132
Hard copy. *See* Documented output
Hard copy devices, 177–180, *180–181*
Hard disks, 250
Hardware, 7–9
Hash search, 334
Hashed file, 333–334, 336
Header, 29–30
Header section, of PROCEDURE block, 85
Heap, 398–399
  top-of-, 400
Hierarchical structure, 65, 79
  of data items, 318
  multi-dimensional arrays and, 414, 417
  trees and, 324, 336
Hierarchy chart, 65, *65*, 79
Highlighting, 130
Hypothesis testing, for error detection, 269, 286

Identifier, 90
  predeclared, 421
  of procedures, 86
IF . . THEN statement, 146–149, 423
IF . . THEN . . ELSE statement, *103*, 104, 143, 146–149, 166, 422
  versus CASE . . OF statement, 148–149
IN operator, 165, 210, 222, 423
In-line code, 393
Include option, 370–371
Incremental testing, 259, 262–263, 285
Incrementation of counter variable, 150
Indentation, 99
Infinite loop, 74–75
Information, defined, 6
Initialization
  of algorithm step, 24, 28, 46
  of variables, 77, 264–265
Initialization module, 60, 62, 78
  processing speed, 392
  program *BalancePlus*, 139–140
Initializing diskette, 240
Ink-jet printer, 178
Input, 7–8, 27
  and READ AND READLN statements, 34
  specification of, 53, 54
  validation of, 130–132, 140
Input editing, 130–132, 140, 344
  program *BalanceCheckbook*, 137
  second-chance, 132, 136
INPUT file variable, 239, 253, 423
Input layout form, *56*
Input/output (I/O) devices, file names assigned to, 238–239
Input/output error checking, 367–370
  error codes, *369*
  turning off, 369–370

Input/output operations, 238–239, 253–254
  and dynamic memory allocation, 403–404
  fast management routines, 393–399, 417
Input segment, testing of, 262
Insert mode, 39–40, 46
INSERT procedure, 203–204, 205, 423
INTEGER data type, 36, 145, 150, 193, 194–195, 205, 208, 423
  conversion of scalar data to, 385–386
  initializing, 265
  pointers and, 313–314
  range, 382
Integrated circuit, 9
Integration testing, 261–262
INTERACTIVE data type, 238, 243, 254, 423
Interactive processing, 182, 291
  CRT displays and, 177
Interactive program, logical tests in, 144
Interpreter, function of, 14
Intrinsic functions, 421
Invoking, defined, 94
I/O. *See* Input/output *headings*
IORESULT operation, 367, 397, 423
Iteration. *See* Repetition

Jumping, 365
Justification of text, 200

Key, 292, 334, 335
KEYBOARD file variable, 165, 423

Label, defined, 364
LABEL declaration, 364–366, 423
Laser printer, 178, *180*
LENGTH function, 160, 165, 205, 221–222, 272, 274, 373, 385, 423
Length specifier, 165, 194–195
Less than, 6
Less than or equal to, 6
Levels of structure chart, 63, 65
Lexical level, 373, 375
Limits error, 265–266
Line-feed, 177
Line number, 134–136
Line printer, 178, *179*
Linear insertion with exchange. *See* Sift
Linear relationships, tree storage of, 324, *325*
Linear search, 328, 336
Link. *See* Pointer
Linked list, 308–318, 330, 334, 335, 336
  and dynamic memory allocation, 402
  pointer variables and, 312–314
  relationships between data items in, 311, *311*
Linked search, 328, 331, 334, 336
List, 172, 291, 304–318, 335
  linked, 308–318, 334, 335, 336
  merging, 303
  and set variables, 208, *209*
  sorting (*see* Sorting *headings*)
  unstructured, 290, 294, 304–306
List maintenance, 335, 339–361
  for linked lists, 317–318, *319*, *320*
  in relation to program design, 326
  for sequential files, 308
Literal data, 193
Local data, 96
Local variable, 90, 93, 94, 116
LOCK operation, 247, 251, 254, 423
Logarithm, 95
Logical boundary, 84
Logical comparison, 144–146, 166
Logical design, 10–11, 58, 78
  pseudocoding of, 67, 79
  verification of, 70
Logical error, 45, 47, 259
  detection of, 45
  failure to initialize variables, 77
  GOTO statements and, 365–366
  infinite loop as, 75
Logical function, 10–11
Logical operations, defined, 6, 17
Logical test, 6, 144, 146
  compound, 147
  in debugging, 268–269
  in program *BalancePlus*, *146*
Long INTEGER data type, 36, 46, 193–195, 423
Lookup table, file directory as, 240
Loop
  calculations moved outside of, 393
  control structures, 149–153, 166
  function of, 62–63
  implementation of, 143
  infinite, 74–75
  REPEAT . . UNTIL, 71–72, 78, 79, 143, 145, 151, 153, 423
  termination condition, 72, 74

Machine language, 13, 17
Magnetic tape, 250
Main memory, 8–9. *See also* Dynamic memory *headings*; Memory
Main processing module, 62–63, 78
Mainframes, defined, 9
Manipulation operations, defined, 7
Manual stepthrough, 70
MARK procedure, 397, 400, 417, 424
Marker, 371

Master file, 290
Mathematical equations, 104–106, 116–117
Mathematical functions, 95
Matrix of coordinates, 134–136, 174
  printer versus CRT, 182
MEMAVAIL function, 399, 417, 424
Members, defined, 207–208
Memory. *See also* Dynamic memory
  array resident in, 234, *235*, 237
  defined, 4
  dynamic allocation of, 397–410, 417
  efficient use of, 390, 392–393, 440
  function of, 26
  high and low, 397–398
  management of, 381–420
  organization of, 438
  reading files into, 234, 253
Memory dump, 267–269, 286
Memory locations, 4, 26
  and data definitions, *439*
Menus, 38, 126–127
  nested, 132
Merge, 303–304
Messages, 132–133, 140
Microcomputer
  INTEGER data type range, 193
  program development on, 261
  screen display features, 176
  typical installation, *103*
Microfiche, 178
Microfilm, 178
Microprocessor chip, 9
Model, defined, 58
Modules
  defined, 63
  entering, 159
  hierarchical arrangement of, 65, 79
  in relation to procedures, 86–89, 115
  separate entry and testing of, 261
MODulus operation, 27, 194, 424
MOVELEFT operation, 404–407, 417, 424
MOVERIGHT operation, 404–407, 417, 424
Moving text files, include option in, 370–371
Multi-dimensional array, 411–415, *413*, *414*
Multiple-choice, 129, 137

Name. *See* Identifier
Needs, identification of, 10–11, 21–22, 46, 51, 78
Negative value, and errors, 266
Nested
  blocks, 88–89, 99, 115
  menus, 132
  records, 231
NEW procedure, 312, 314–316, 336, 397, 398, 417, 424
  memory allocation and, 400
NIL pointer constant, 318, 402, 424
Node, defined, 318
Nondocument output, 171
Nonincremental testing, 259, 285
Not equal to, 6
NOT operator, 147, 424
Number crunching efficiency, 393
Numeric values
  common errors associated with, 265–266
  converting to string, 271–272
  in output statements, 193–198

Object code, 14, 29
ODD function, 387, 388, 424, 442–443
OF, 424
Open file, 239
Opening file, 241, 243–244, 245, 368
Operating system, defined, 16. *See also* UCSD Pascal operating system
Operations, 2, 3
OR operator, 147, 424
Order of operations, 104–106, 117
Ordered list, 306–308
Ordering. *See* Sorting; Sorting techniques
Ordinal data type, 150
ORDinal function, 344–345, 385–386, 424, 442
Ordinal value, of scalar data item, 344, 358
Output, 7, 11, 27, 170–172, 189
  designing, 170–189
  program *BasicAccounting*, 183, *184–187*
  specification of, 24, 53–54
  verification of, 70
Output device, 174–180, 189
  file names used for, 212–213
  portability of, 180, 182, 189
OUTPUT file variable, 133, 140, 239, 253, 424
Output format, coding techniques for, 192–224
Output layout form, *55*
  for CRTs, *175*
Output operations. *See* Output; Input/output operations
Overhead
  input editing as, 131
  processing, 312
Overwriting, 176

Package, defined, 121
PACKED data structure, 388–390, 416–417, 424, 440–443
Pad/padding, 165, 195, 196

Page break, in compilation listing, 377
Page heading, 137
PAGE procedure, 133–134, *134*, 140, 177, 193, 424
Parameter
  defined, 90, 115
  formal declaration of, 93
  passing by reference, 91, 98, 116
  passing by value, 91–92
  use, with procedures, 90–94, 115
Parameter list
  correspondence with argument list, 92, 115
  defined, 92
  names in, 93
  in procedure declaration, 91–94, 115
  repeated in comments, 102
Parentheses, use of, 193, 206
  in mathematical expressions, 104–105
Parentheses and asterisks, use of, 32
Parsing of commands, 125
Pascal. *See also* UCSD Pascal operating system
  compiler, 14–16, 17
  as structured programming language, 14, 29
Pascal, Blaise, 15
Passing, 91–92, 98
Period, use of, 86
  with END statement, 31
Peripheral devices, as files, 212–213, 237, 238
Permanent file, 247
Physical devices, 7–9
  binary, 11–12
Physical functions, 7–9, 10
  flowcharts of, 60
Physical processing, 10–11
Plotter, 178, *181*
Plus sign, meaning of, 33
Pointer, 308, 309, 335
  end-of-list value, 318
  relationship to data, 314, *315*
  start-of-list, 310
  updating value in list maintenance, 317–318, *319*, *320*, 336
Pointer variable, 335
  data types accessed by, 313
  declaration, 313–314
  and dynamic memory allocation, 399–400
  and linked lists, 312–314
Portability of program, designing for, 180, 182, 183, 189
POSition function, 201–202, 205, 222, 424
Posting, defined, 290
PREDecessor function, 270–271, 286, 424
Predefined data types, 36, 46, 153, 421
Predefined meanings, 29
Preordered file, 332, 336
Primary storage device, 8–9
Printable characters, 385
  ASCII character codes, *384*
Printer, 9, *10*, 177–178, 189
  output design considerations, 177–178
PRINTER file name, 212–213, 424
Problem analysis, 10–11, 51, 53–60, 78
Problem definition, 10–11, 21–24, 46
Procedure(s)
  argument of, 92
  function of, 84, 115
  modular nature of, 88
  names, 86, 93, *93*, 112
  in relation to top-down design, 86–87, 115
  naming rules, 108–109, 117
PROCEDURE block, 84–88, 115
  keyword, 424
  structure of, *85*, 85–86
Procedure call. *See* Call
Procedure declaration, 85, 86, 115
  parameter list, 91–94, 115
  use of VAR syntax in, 90–91, 92, 115
Procedure number, 373, 375
Processing, 4, 27
  of algorithm, 24, 28, 46
  determining, 54, 57–60
Processing operations, 6–9, 7, *7*
Processing segment, testing of, 262
Processing sequence, anticipating errors in, 266
Processing speed, 326, 390–392, 393, 417
Processor, parts of, 8, *8*
Program, 2
  structure of, 60–69, 78
PROGRAM, 29–30, *30*, 46
  EXIT from, 213
Program *AccountManagement*, 269–275, *276–285*
Program *AccountsReceivable*, 344–345, *346–359*
Program *Adder*, 28–29, *25*, 31–36, *35*, *43*, 71, *71*
Program *AddingMachine*, 71–78, *72*, *73*, *74*
Program *BalanceCheckbook*, 109–114, *110–111*, 117, 138
Program *BalancePlus*, 136–140, *146*, 158, *161–165*, 165, 176
Program *BasicAccounting*, 182–183, *184*, *185*, 207, 209, 213, *214–221*, 275
Program block, 84–86, 115
  delimiters, 84
  nested, 88–89, 115
Program *Columns*, 272, *273*
  compilation listing, 374
Program design, 60–65, 78
  anticipating errors in, 259
  for list management, 339–345

tools for, 54–60
trade-offs in list maintenance, 324–326, 336
Program development, elements of, 27, *27*
Program entry techniques, 261
PROGRAM header, 88
PROGRAM key word, 424
Program *Linkit*, 318, *321–322*
Program loop. *See* Loop
Program objectives, defining, 52, 78
Program *Report, 102*
FORWARD declaration in, 102, *103*
Program *SayHi, 5*, 84–85
Program *Scope, 100*
Program specification, steps in, 51–52, 78
Program statement, 3, 31, 85
Program structure, 63–69. *See also* Structure *headings*
Program *TestBalancePlus, 160*
Programming languages, 2–5, 13–16, 17, 67
Programming style, 99, 122, 140
Prompt-driven program, 124
example display, *129*
trade-offs, 126–128, 140
Prompting/prompts, 33, 124
multiple-choice, *129*, 137
value of, 77
for verification of input, 131–132
yes/no, 127–128
Pseudocode/pseudocoding, 29, 46, 54, 67, *68–69*, 79, *110–111*
program *AddingMachine*, 74
program *BalanceCheckbook*, 109, 112
PURGE operation, 247, 254, 424
PUT procedure, 244, 250, 254
following SEEK procedure, 246
P-code. *See* Pseudocode/pseudocoding

Q (Quit) command, 41, 42
Quality, 52–53, 78, 79
Quiet compile, 377, 424
Quotation marks, single, 33, 193, 239

Random access, 245
example, 251–252
with SEEK procedure, 249, 252
Random file, 332, 336
Randomly addressable, defined, 174
Range checking, 131, 371–373, 425
Range error, 265–266
READ operation, 34, 46, 425
KEYBOARD variable, 165
READLN operation, 34, 46, 77, 425
REAL data type, 36, 46, 94, 96, 113, 150, 193, 194–195, 197–198, 205–206, 221, 425
default size, 382
initializing, 265
length specifier, 197
scientific notation default, 198, 221
Reasonableness tests, 131
Record(s), 227–229, 253
in program *AccountManagement*, 274–275
representations in memory, 438–443
RECORD data type, 227–230, 253, 425
items in linked lists grouped by, 316, 336
PACKED, 388–390
pointers and, 313
in program *AccountManagement*, 274–275
in VAR declaration, 228
Record key, 291
Recursion, 99, 415–416, 417
Relational databases, 331
Relative byte number, 375
RELEASE procedure, 397, 400, 417, 425
Reliability, 53, 70, 78
range checking for, 371–372
REPEAT . . UNTIL statement, 71–72, 77–78, 79, 143, 145, 151, 153, 425
Repetition, 62–63, 78
and batch processing, 144
control structures, 149–153, 166
implementation of, 143
Report, 172–173, 178
Report format
example, 198–201, *200*
module in program testing, 262
options, 183
Reserved words, 29, 421
RESET procedure, 239, 241, 243, 245, 254, 394, 425
Resuming processing, 132
Return key, 39, 44, 77, 177
Reverse character, 176
REWRITE procedure, 239–240, 254, 425
Rigid disks, 250
Root node, 318, 324
Root of tree structure, defined, 318
ROUND function, 213, 222, 425
Rounding, 197–198

S (Save) command, 42
Saving record, PUT procedure for, 244, 246, 250, 254
Scalar constant or variable, ordinal value of, 344, 359
Scalar data type, 94, 150, 205–207, 222

Scalar values
  conversion of, 385–386
  of set variables, 208
Scanning of commands, 125
Scientific notation, 195, 198, 221
Scope of variable, 98–99, *100*
Scrolling, 174–175, 182
Search techniques/searching, 248–249, 327–334, 336
  within linked files, 311–312
  recursiveness in, 415–416
  sequential files, 306, 327
  trees, 327
Second chance input, program *BalanceCheckbook*, 137
Secondary storage devices, 9, *10*
SEEK procedure, 245–246, 254, 425
  and random access, 245, 249, 252
Segment number, 373
Selection
  implementation of, 143
  in order, 291, 294, 335
  series of, 144
Self-documenting programs, defined, 124
Semicolon, use of, 4, 31
  with END statement, 31, 78, 86, 97, 147, 148
  between program statements, 32
Sequences, 62, 143
Sequential access, 249
Sequential file, 244, 306–308, *307*
  search techniques, 327
Serial access, 244, 245, 249, 250–251
Serial file, 304–306, *305*
  chronological structure of, 290
Set, defined, 207, 222
SET constant, 210, 390–391, 417
SET data type, 222, 425
Set operations, 210, *211*, 222
  standard symbols, 426
  symbols, *211*
Set syntax, 210
Shell, Donald L., 300
Shell's sort, 300–304, *302*, 335, 342, 359
Shuttle sort. *See* Sift
Sift, 299–300, 335
SIZEOF function, 399, 417, 425
Slash symbol, 105
Sorted file, 332–333, 336
Sorting, 291–292. *See also* Sorting techniques
  basic actions, 292–293
  Boolean logic used for, 6
  by comment, 341, 342–343
  by date, 341, 343
  by entry type, 341
  in list management, 341–343
  processing time, 326
  of serial access list, 305–306
  into two columns, 387–388
  unstructured list, 305–306
Sorting techniques, 249, 291–303, 335
  bubble sort, 294–298, *296–297*, 335
  selection in order, 291, 294, 335
  Shell's sort, 300–304, *302*, 335, 342, 359
  sift, 299–300, 335
  trade-offs, 291, 292, 294, 297–298, 301
Source code, defined, 14
Source program, entering, 37–42
Space bar, 43
Space on disk, 368
Specific report, 172
Speed of execution, 326, 390, 392–393, 417, 440
Square root, 95
Stack, 398, *398*, 439
Stack overflow, 399, 403
Standards for program design, 52–53, 78
Status report, 132
Storage, 7. *See also* Main memory; Storage devices
Storage devices, 9, *10*, 174
  as file, 237
  file directory on, 240
  files contained on, 234, 237
STRING constant, 390–391, 417
STRING data type, 36, 46, 150, 193, 194–195, 205, 239, 425
  first byte in string, 385
  functions operating on variable, 203–205
  LENGTH function and, 373, 385
  length of, 195
  pointers and, 314
STRing procedure, 270, 271–272, 425
Structure chart, 60, 63, *64*
  index numbers of modules in, 65, 79
  program *BalancePlus*, *139*
  and pseudocode, 67, 68–69, 79
  and sequence of module execution, 63, 65
Structured programming, 29–31, *30*, 60–69, 78, 106, *107*
  in relation to top-down design, 67, 79
Structured walkthrough, defined, 70
Stubs, 262
Style of programming, 99, 122, 140
Stylus, 178
Sublist, 327–328
Subprogram, 31
  names, 99–100
  recursive, 99
Subrange syntax, 206
Subroutine. *See* Subprogram

Subtree, 324
SUCCessor function, 270, 286, 425
Summary, 172
Summary information
  extraction of, 290, 327
  from serial access list, 305
Swapping, 425
Swapping mode, 377
Symbols
  flowchart, 60, *61*
  standard, 421, 426
  syntax diagrams, 427
Synonym in hashed file, 333
Syntactical errors, 37, 43, 44, 159, 259, 263
  unpaired parentheses as, 105
Syntax, 14, 428
Syntax diagram, 427–437

Tabbing, 174, 177
Tabular format, 137, 183, 195
  aligning values in 196–197
Target computer system, 123
Temporary variables, 177, 393
Termination module, function of, 63
Termination of program, 213
  abnormal, 416
Termination steps of algorithm, 24, 28, 46
Test data, 45, 70, 79, 265
Test of equality, 144
  equal symbol for, 33, 46
  standard symbol, 426
Test of inequality, standard symbol, 426
Testing program or module, 258–285. *See also* Debugging
  program *AccountManagement*, 269–270
Text data type, 238, 254, 425
  WRITE and WRITELN statements and, 213
Text editor, for program coding and entry, 261
TEXT file, 15, 37
  name, 41–42
  source code in, 15
.TEXT file name suffix, 42, 247, 376, 425
THEN, 425
TO, 425
Top-down design, 63–64, 65, 67, 79, 87
  and menu format, 127
  in relation to program procedures, 86–87, 115
Top-down testing, 262
Top-of-heap, defined, 400
Trade-offs
  execution speed, 390–393
  sorting, 291, 292, 294, 297–298, 301
  user-interface, 124, 126–127

Training expense, 125
Transaction file, 290, 335
Transaction journal, 305
Transferring control, with GOTO statement, 364–366
Transient data, 171
Tree structure, 291, 318, *323*, 324, 335, 336
  search techniques, 327
  storage of linear relationships in, 324, *325*
TRUE condition, 144–146, 147, 425
TRUNCate function, 194, 213, 425
Truncation, 195–196
Two-state device, defined, 11
TYPE definition, 36, 102, 107–108, 117, 425
  long INTEGER size, 194
  pointer variables in, 313
  records and fields in, 227–229
  testing for errors, 266
Type validation, 131
Typed file, defined, 237
Typographical error, 259, 263

UCSD Pascal operating system, 17
  booting, 37–38
  compiler, 37
  development of, 15–16
  editor, 37
  loading, 37
  parts, 16
Unconditional branching, 364
Underscore character, 108–109, 172
Unit testing, 261
Unstructured list, 304–306
  sorting of, 305–306
UNTIL clause of REPEAT statement, 71–72, 77–78, 79, 426
Untyped file, 237, 394–395
User, 25
User interface, 121–142
  program *BalanceCheckbook*, 137
  prompt-driven program, *129*
User messages, 132–133, 140
User-friendly, defined, 121
User's guide, 124
User's manual, 124

Validation of input, 130–132, 140
Value, 34
Variables(s), 26, 34–35
  assigning initial values to, 60
  global, 90, 93
  initializing, 77
  local, 90, 93, 94
  misplaced references, 264

names, 33–34, 35, 84, 94, 95, 108–109, 112
of same data type, 76, 79
scope of, 89–90, 115
uninitialized, 264–265
value of, 34

VARiable declaration, 34, 75–77, 426
ARRAY in, 154
of array elements, 228
format, 76–77, 79
integer values in, 193–194
parameters preceded by, 90–91, 116
pointer declarations in, 313–314
in procedure declaration, 90–92
of record types, 228–229

Variant record, 408–411, 417, 442

Venn diagram, *208*

Verification
of input, 131–132
of output, 70, 79

Video display terminal (VDT), 9

W (Write) command, 41

Walkthrough, 70

WHILE . . DO statement, 149, 151–152, 166, 426

WHILE NOT construction, 250

Wirth, Niklaus, 15

WITH . . DO construction, 231–233, 248, 253, 426

Word, 12, 382, 440

Wrap around, 175

WRITE statement, 33–34, 46, 193–197, 426
cursor position and, 175
device declaration and, 212–213
prompt in, 77
TEXT data type and, 213
translated as OUTPUT, 238

WRITELN statement, 33, 46, 165, 193–197, 199, 426
cursor position and, 175
device declaration and, 212–213
TEXT data type and, 213

X (eXecute command), 38–39

X axis, 134

Y axis, 134

ISBN 0-538-10400-7